Writing Under the Influence

Writing Under the Influence

Alcoholism and the Alcoholic Perception from Hemingway to Berryman

Matts G. Djos

First published in 2010 by
PALGRAVE MACMILLAN®
in the United States—a division of St. Martin's Press LLC,
175 Fifth Avenue, New York, NY 10010.

Where this book is distributed in the UK, Europe and the rest of the world, this is by Palgrave Macmillan, a division of Macmillan Publishers Limited, registered in England, company number 785998, of Houndmills, Basingstoke, Hampshire RG21 6XS.

Palgrave Macmillan is the global academic imprint of the above companies and has companies and representatives throughout the world.

Palgrave® and Macmillan® are registered trademarks in the United States, the United Kingdom, Europe and other countries.

ISBN: 978–0–230–10260–6

Library of Congress Cataloging-in-Publication Data

Djos, Matts G.
    Writing under the influence : alcoholism and the alcoholic perception from Hemingway to Berryman / Matts G. Djos.
        p. cm.
    ISBN 978–0–230–10260–6 (alk. paper)
        1. American literature—20th century—History and criticism.
    2. Alcoholics in literature. 3. Alcoholism in literature. 4. Alcoholism—Psychological aspects. 5. Authors, American—20th century—Alcohol use. 6. Authors, American–20th century—Psychology. I. Title.

PS228.A58D56 2010
810.9′92074—dc22   2009041074

A catalogue record of the book is available from the British Library.

Design by Newgen Imaging Systems (P) Ltd., Chennai, India.

First edition: May 2010

10 9 8 7 6 5 4 3 2 1

Printed in the United States of America.

For Jeanine

Contents

A Note on the Author

Matts G. Djos, Ph.D. has been in public education for more than forty-five years. He graduated from the University of Washington and was awarded a Bachelor of Arts and a Standard Secondary Teaching Certificate in English in 1961. He was awarded a Master of Arts in English from the University of Idaho in 1969; and, in 1975, he was awarded a Ph.D. in English from Texas A&M University, where he specialized in American literature and seventeenth-century British literature.

Dr. Djos taught high school and community college from 1961 to 1975; and, in 1976, he accepted a professorship at Mesa State College in western Colorado where he taught modern American literature and seventeenth-century British literature for the next thirty years. He retired as a Professor Emeritus of English in 2007. Dr. and Mrs. Jeanine Djos now live in the mountains of western Colorado where they built a high country chalet to celebrate their fiftieth anniversary.

Dr. Djos has published on a variety of subjects, including the literature of addiction and American alcoholic writers. He has also free-lanced for a variety of major national publications, and his sailing book, *Fixing Positions: Trailer Sailing the West* (Sheridan House, 2008) has been well received and is available at most major retail outlets.

The Djoses have three daughters, who live in Grand Junction, Colorado, with their families.

Acknowledgments

I would like to thank Susan F. Beegel, Editor of the *Hemingway Review*, Jim Harbaugh, S. J., former editor of *Dionysos*, Felicia Campbell, Editor of the *Popular Culture Review*, and Dr. Jane Lilienfeld and Dr. Jeffrey Oxford, editors of *The Languages of Addiction*, for their help and encouragement in publishing many of the essays and analyses which were revised and reprinted here. I would also like to thank Mr. Lee Norton, Ms. Briggette Shull, and Ms. Rachel Tekula of Palgrave Macmillan and Ms. Rohini Krishnan of Newgen Imaging Systems for their assistance, advice, and encouragement in preparing the manuscript for publication.

Finally, I would like to thank my wife, Jeanine, for her keen editorial sense and unerring judgment in helping me to sharpen the focus of this book.

Foreword

In applying a systematic psychological focus to alcoholic literature, it may be possible to explore some of the more puzzling
facets of the addictive mind set as reflected in the poems and
stories of certain modern American writers. When alcoholics
write about themselves, they are concerned with the fantasies
and frustrations that dog them and that seem to defy any sense
of order or common sense. The analyses and selections on the
pages to follow are focused on these concerns, especially as they
relate to control, anxiety, fear, and depression.

I have organized this book according to certain, specific
markers, including the peculiar nature of alcoholic spirituality,
intimacy, depression, anger, negativity, humor, and misanthropy. These discussions are complemented by detailed explications of four well-known works: Ernest Hemingway's *The
Sun Also Rises*, John Berryman's "Phase Four," Edwin Arlington
Robinson's "Mr. Flood's Party," and Hart Crane's "The Wine
Menagerie." I have chosen these four works because they provide an excellent overview of the various shades and complexities of the disease of alcoholism from a single perspective.

Ernest Hemingway's *The Sun Also Rises* reveals his extraordinary perspective on alcoholism and alcohol abuse in far
greater detail than has been generally supposed, most especially
regarding his familiarity with alcohol and the code of drinking
that is common throughout much of his work. The novel is also
an excellent study of differing modes of alcoholism and provides a solid foundation for a general overview of the disease.
Although the obscure symbolism and self-destructive elements
of Crane's "Wine Menagerie" have been quite well interpreted,
the alcoholic texture has been generally overlooked. Yet, that
texture should be a primary consideration in any analysis
because the poem deals with the connection between

drunkenness, creativity, altered states of consciousness, and alcoholic depression and confusion. Robinsons's poem has been explicated and studied from a host of perspectives, but very few critics have moved beyond the theme of aging and loneliness to consider its alcoholic content, most especially the extraordinary images of loneliness, melodrama, antisocial behavior, and denial. Finally, while Berryman's poem is significant because it was probably written shortly before he committed suicide, it also provides us with some understanding of his unique spiritual perspective and his inability to fully grasp the A.A. Twelve Step program of recovery.

My analyses and conclusions are based in part on the A.A. twelve step model of alcoholic recovery as noted in the A.A. text, *Twelve Steps and Twelve Traditions,* and the "Big Book," *Alcoholic's Anonymous.*[1]

Chapter One

The Foundations of Alcoholic Thinking and the Role of Fantasy, Alienation, and Rebellion

> If I wasn't drunk & blowing wine fumes and peanut breath in your
> face,
> Maybe you'd be nice to me
> —Philip Whalen, "Complaint to the Muse"

Alcoholism is extremely difficult to define, especially during the early stages of an individual's drinking history, when it may be impossible to distinguish heavy drinkers, problem drinkers (who are typically involved in the first stage of alcoholism), chronic alcoholics, and individuals who are cross-addicted to other chemicals. Depending on the source, most formal definitions are likely to exclude or minimize certain aspects of the disease (some sources do not even regard it as a disease) while emphasizing certain other characteristics. Even so, there is usually a common thread in the etiology of the disease. Although most members of Alcoholics Anonymous acknowledge the concept of self-diagnosis, they are likely to suggest that anyone who says he or she is an alcoholic probably *is* an alcoholic. However, they are also likely to insist that rigorous self-examination should be an important precursor of such a diagnosis.

A more specific definition may be found in the *American Heritage Dictionary*, which defines *alcoholism* as a "compulsive consumption of and psycho-physiological dependence on alcoholic beverages" and a "chronic pathological condition, chiefly of the nervous and gastro enteric systems, caused by habitual excessive alcoholic consumption." Webster's definition is much the same, and the *Encyclopedia Britannica* defines it as "a repetitive intake of alcoholic beverages to an extent that causes repeated or continued harm to the drinker." Implicit in this definition and the concept of alcoholism as a disease is the "idea that the person experiencing repeated or long-lasting injury from his drinking would alter his behavior if he could" (*Macropedia,* 1:445).

For the purposes of this book, I will refer to the common thread of these five definitions where appropriate, noting that where a subject's drinking behavior has been regarded as extraordinary by a good number of observers and where it has been noted that an individual has had chronic problems with alcohol, then he or she will be included.[1] In that regard, the opinions of friends and associates have been given a good deal of weight in determining whose work shall be included, especially where the addict has demonstrated persistent, self-destructive drinking behavior or has indicated a profound change in personality when under the influence of alcohol.[2] This is especially important in those instances where the addict's physical and mental health and his or her relationships with others have led to personality changes and no small amount of defensive, antisocial behavior.

A close, textual analysis of most alcoholic writing will suggest that it is often fanciful and self-obsessed in the extreme and typically involves a peculiar element of public humiliation and self-exposure in which confession, anger, and misanthropy may serve as a defense from feelings of inferiority and loneliness. Indeed, it is said that alcoholics are probably the loneliest and most hypersensitive (and most talkative) people in the world; and, indeed, for most, the prospect of surviving from day to day, whether drunk or sober, is often painful and untenable.

To the practicing alcoholic, half-truths, compulsive verbosity, and inordinate lying are so commonplace that they are literally taken for granted as reliable indicators of the severity of the disease. The apparent honesty that Theodore Roethke so claims to fear in his confessional poem, "Open House," is presumed to result not just in art and some kind of hubris, but also in the author's overwhelming pain and alienation. He complains that he is "foreknown," his pain is "self-revealed," and he apparently tries to take refuge from the discomfort implicit in self-exposure by assuming the identity of a naked poet-confessor who manifests a confusing patchwork of martyrdom, evasion, and a kind of reluctant veracity (7–12). To the non-addicted, Roethke's "spare spirit" openness may seem baffling and incongruent, especially because of his apparent reluctant self-exposure. In fact, it may be easy to conclude that there must be something congenitally wrong with anyone who chooses to confess his deepest secrets while claiming that his very "nakedness" is also his "shield."

Yet, this confessional impulse, which is a common aspect of just about all alcoholic writing and thinking, provides us with an extraordinary dimension for probing the peculiar nature of the alcoholic mind set, not simply with interviews, personal histories, and surveys, but by looking carefully and analytically at the testimonials and confessional poetry of the alcoholics themselves.

When confronted about their drinking, the majority of alcoholics will insist that their perceptions, though chemically induced, are congruent with reality—if not a higher consciousness. In truth, however, an alcoholic's creative impulse and his need for alcohol are typically a direct consequence of an extraordinary complex of physical addictions, escapist fantasies, and skewed emotions. In "Last Statement for a Last Oracle," the drinker-poet, Alan Dugan, adopts a rather generic mode of alcoholic martyrdom in claiming that his humanity has been sacrificed on a sanctimonious fire of modernity that is so desolate that life is simply not worth living. That sanctimonious fire is reason enough to quit the mundane business of self-preservation, or, at the very least, a desire to withdraw from society and the day-to-day business of survival; and so he addresses his self-destructive inner persona, advising his "other" self that when he gets drunk that night, he will "pee" on life and disappear in an "acid yellow smoke," although the surviving mortal "remnant" will apparently be forced to continue going in some kind of undefined "unspeakable condition" (16–20).

Dugan is certainly a bitter man. But he is not unlike a good many rebels in choosing to withdraw from the complexities of life so he can curse the insults of fate and circumstance and fantasize a mystical disappearance in a self-generated yellow haze—like a genie of sorts. Yet, it is also obvious that Dugan has no intention of skulking away in silence where he can nurse his grievances in private. He announces his intentions with obscene bravado: he will live the lie, suffer unspeakably, and announce his pain to the world in a venal bellow of protest—and, indeed, this is what distinguishes Dugan, the alcoholic, from the usual, everyday cynic.

William Matthew's fascination with alcohol and urine as well as his obscene disgust with the pains and ravages of being human are a great deal more wine-soaked and a good deal more urgent. In "Pissing off the Back of the Boat into the Nivernais Canal," he writes that his imagination cannot "survive time's acid work"—a most remarkable insight, considering the more immediate challenge of hygiene, his stream, and the probability that he might easily "pitch/ [his] wine-dulled body and wary imagination with it into the inky/canal" (31–40). As he tugs at his zipper, Matthews wonders how much damage his body can absorb and confesses, "How drunk I am. / I shake/my shriveled nozzle." (14–15). Poor Matthews has discovered that even the simple prospect of urinating at the portal of middle age is no easy task, especially when teetering over black water with little to hold onto except his penis.

For most alcoholics, the present is not a very comfortable place. In fact, it is likely to be overlooked or even discarded as irrelevant to the lonely business of survival—and the compulsion to write. A writer may thus find himself entangled in a time warp in which past and future overlap with such confounding intensity that he cannot help but distort any sane perception of what it means to survive and live on a day-to-day basis (hence, the 24-hour program in A.A.). For a great many writers, the world of fantasy may provide the only escape from the untenable prospect of sobriety (consider A.A.'s emphasis on "rigorous honesty"). This is because the peculiar "coping" mechanism of his art allows the addict to devise a kind of fantasy world that is entirely of his own making. He can then use it as an escape—literally—from the stern business of living in reality; and he can reconstruct his "inner" world and populate it with perfectly compliant people whose circumstances are subject to all manner of manipulation according to his wishes, a doubtful luxury in the world of fact (hence, the "Serenity Prayer" that opens most A.A. meetings and that starts with the petition "God grant me the serenity to accept the things I cannot change").[3]

* * *

For the alcoholic, reality and sobriety are terribly unnatural, flat, and boring. Excepting the possibility of pain, hateful behavior, and ostracism, nothing much happens in the "real" world; but, in drunkenness, an individual can experience the illusion of a satiated appetite, the pleasures and thrills of risk-taking, and the illusory prospect of changing his identity and manipulating others according to his will. These are the core and substance of the alcoholic perspective. At times, the prospect of self-destruction and self-immolation may even reflect a kind of adolescent obsession with martyrdom and romance. As Edna St. Vincent Millay, wrote in "First Fig,"

> My candle burns at both ends;
> It will not last the night (1–2)

Here, the quick burnout—an unhealthy prospect by any definition—is perceived in the context of an amorphous but "lovely" light involving rebellion, friends (and foes), and idealized self-destruction. Note, as well, how light is commonly regarded as a symbol of truth, not fantasy; but, in this case, it is unendurable for any length of time, just as Blanche Dubois in *A Streetcar Named Desire* tries to cover the exposed light bulb in the Kowalski's apartment with a paper lantern while dreaming of romantic ocean voyages.

For the alcoholic, there is always the passion for the ready-made, the quick fix, and the illusion of some tentative but fulfilling satiation of the appetites so long as liquor is involved. As Ogden Nash writes in his famous limerick "Reflections on Ice Breaking," some enticements like candy may be "dandy," but others—most especially booze—are a good deal more fundamental, a good deal more urgent, and a heck of a lot faster. Although not an alcoholic himself, Nash is all too aware that pandering wickedness affirms the rebel temperament with perverse cunning. Nash softens his advice with humor—perhaps he is teasing; perhaps he is not! He probably knows that most alcoholics have little patience with the slow, incompliant world of reality; in fact, reality and its cumbersome, practical requirements have no relevance in a world of alcoholic expedience.

Thus, in his self-obsessive hunger, the alcoholic may leave a trail of human wreckage (including his own) behind him, if only because he may feel compelled to persist in satisfying his appetites and manipulating others according to his will, no matter how destructive the outcome.

The obsession with control is endemic among alcoholics. It should be no surprise that Eugene O'Neill crowded his plays with arrogant, alcoholic power drivers; the more willful sometimes went to any length to subdue the fragile and broken to satisfy their insatiable egos. Similarly, the romantic, alcoholic materialism of F. Scott Fitzgerald, well stocked as it was with motor cars, liquors, mansions, and blondes, evokes no end of fantasies, including moonlit nights, lavender-scented sheets, booze, and the hope for eternal, young love. In Hemingway, we find the pine needle romances and vivid portraits of hope and hopelessness, courage and human frailty—quite often with alcoholic preconditions and excessive drinking as a backdrop.

Regardless of their addiction, most alcoholic writers are idealists of the highest order, even as their most intimate relationships are likely to become shipwrecked on the hard rock of reality.[4] If continually frustrated, they may eventually withdraw into a pathological hell; and while they are likely to perceive a dim outline of reality in the darkness beyond, there is little they can do to maintain their sanity and sustain their illusions of power so long as they persist in drinking. No matter what the dream or what the hope, most alcoholics are likely to back away from the ultimate consequences of their behavior. Yet, rather than modify their perceptions or change their behavior, they are likely to become more fantasy-driven, more expansive, more self-centered, and—most important—remarkably indifferent to the integrity of others. The book *Twelve Steps and Twelve Traditions,* which is published by Alcoholics Anonymous, provides an excellent description of the alcoholic's passion for orchestrating circumstances in conformity with certain willful desires:

> When we habitually try to manipulate others to our own willful desires, they [family, friends, society at large] revolt and resist us heavily. Then we develop hurt feelings, a sense of persecution, and a desire to retaliate. As we redouble our efforts at control, and continue to fail, our suffering becomes acute and constant. We have not once sought to be one in a family, to be a friend among friends, to be a worker among workers, to be a useful member of society. Always, we tried to struggle to the top of the heap, or to hide underneath it. This self-centered behavior blocked a partnership relation with any one of those about us. Of true brotherhood we had small comprehension. (53)

As he strains to control his relationships with others, the alcoholic's perception of the human condition may become so painfully out of proportion to reality that he can only find refuge in a fictional world of his own making. This allows him to orchestrate a menagerie of fantasies and events that may appear so real and substantive that they seem to bear a profound similarity to reality. The very act of creating that fiction, however, may generate a euphoria of verbal control that is so deceptive and utterly removed from the real world that any prospect of sobriety and normality is impossible.

In the act of creating, then, a writer may transpose his perceptions into a menagerie of improbable self-justifications and fantasies with extraordinary inventiveness. Miniver Cheevy, Edwin Arlington Robinson's drunken misfit, is larded with self-pity. Miniver is convinced that he was born in the wrong age, an unkind fate that denied him wealth, dignity, and fame. For Miniver, there is no remedy to unkind fate and no legitimate excuse for failure. He will not deal with circumstances as they are and confine himself to a realistic appraisal of what is possible (consider, for example, the control junkie in the film *Castaway* and his ultimate resolve to accept his situation as it is and make the most of what is possible). And so he drinks, scratches, and coughs and then relapses into a paralytic retreat of self-indulgence and self-pity.

Like Miniver, a good many alcoholics tend to be over-whelmed by delusions of lost opportunities and an insatiable desire to restructure their emotions and their perceptions according to an aggregate of remarkable self-serving prescriptions, no matter how unrealistic or untenable. Yet, this revisionist perception may well be the very foundation of their creative impulse. In writing, they are able to give dimension and substance to their illusions; and they can fabricate a literary cosmos of remarkable power and stature, no matter how grotesque or unlikely. Thus, in a drunken tirade of cursing and evasion, Theodore Roethke abstracts a new definition of martyrdom when he describes the "Agony of crucifixion on bar stools"—as if there was any similarity between drunken self-mutilation and the Cross ("The Longing," 1.6). His contemporary, Allen Ginsberg, goes even farther and descends from the stool to crawl tenement hallways where he and his compatriots can guzzle, vomit, and howl; but in either case, the invective is much the same.

In fact, stumbling rebellion and self-destruction may well be the primary feature of the alcoholic mentality. In "Sonnets to Chris," the alcoholic writer, John Berryman, writes how he is "locked and crocked" with four drunken acquaintances, none of whom dare take a false step, lest—like the tottering, urinating Matthews on the Nivernais canal—they stumble to perdition (33: 1–4).

For all his misanthropy, the alcoholic is convinced that his circumstance, however unfortunate, is not of his own making; and since he is strangely powerless—even as he seeks power—his situation is hopeless. This is generic alcoholic thinking, a fatalistic obsession with power and powerlessness and claims of injustice and alienation that are a necessary consequence of the alcoholic's self-perceived creative genius and individuality.

In "An Island," for instance, Edwin Arlington Robinson writes of "fever-laden wine" and a distant "ruinous tavern shine." What is it, he wonders, that Time has made of him, and

What lowering outland hostelry is this
For one the stars have disinherited? (24–32)

The poet feels ruined and disinherited. Fate has made him an alien bed, and a terrible feeling of loneliness impinges with a deafening roar. He concludes that he can only find comfort in drunkenness in a "lowering outland hostelry," but the "fever-laden wine" and "ruinous tavern" are confusing, destructive, and strange; and so he agonizes over his fateful solitude and resigns to a prospect of loneliness and misunderstanding that is presumed to have saintly dimensions.

Unrestrained self-satisfaction and pointless satiation are also a concern of Alan Dugan. In "Prayer," he admits that he refuses to limit his appetites or consider the consequences of his behavior, no matter how bad or self-destructive. Nevertheless, he petitions his higher power with an alcoholic wish list of needs and sensual appetizers that he hopes to buoy with some kind of ready employment. "God, I need a job because I need money/Here the world is, enjoyable with whiskey" (1–2), he complains. On the other hand, without money, his wife gets mad, he can't drink, and he's broke. So, he works! He gets paid! And he can drink; and—perhaps, best of all—he feels classy (3–10). With tongue in cheek, Dugan goes on to describe his happy fate until he tires of the work, gets drunk, quits his job, and ends up broke and sober. "I'm caught in a steel cycle," he complains (18). The stupefied lifestyle of Dugan's idiot pilgrim is both funny and strangely incongruent. He wants to breathe free and feel free, and he wants booze. He wants respect and he wants to get drunk. He wants to work and he wants to quit and go on a bender. And because he seems incapable of resolving the insane contradictions of his roller coaster routine, his situation lacks any kind of sanity or meaning. He can only complain about his "steel" cycle and postulate a litany of injustices whose foundations revolve around self-pity, stupidity, and an aversion to responsible living. Impotence and indecision have a more sinister dimension in John Berryman's poem, "Of Suicide." Berryman confesses that he drinks too much; his wife threatens separation; and they just do not mix all that well (2–4). He goes on,

> Rembrandt was sober. There we differ. Sober.
> Terrors came on him. To us they come.
> Of suicide I continually think. (25–27)

The poet is fed up with the insults, the ambiguities of fate and circumstance, and marital alienation. His antisocial instincts entertain suicide, the ultimate rebellion; but he recognizes the futility of this option. Besides, it is too permanent and scary. "I'll teach Luke," he whimpers. That, of course, is the safe option and far more tenable, although it lacks the intensity of high drama and the pleasures of martyrdom and a permanent, vengeful getaway.

An insatiable appetite for self-destructive masquerades and illusions of martyrdom is often manifested in considerable heartache and regret. Indeed, self-reproach, loneliness, and melancholy are the mainspring of a great deal of alcoholic writing. In "Sonnet 56," John Berryman writes that his divorce is plainly a relief, having endured "Sunderings and luxations," interminable exile, dogfights with love "hangover-long," and nothing much left now but more alcohol and the division of wreckage. On a similar note, in "Sonnet 58," Berryman portrays himself as a self-destructive junkie whose brains have been addled by an excess of booze in a "high wind." Here, the poet-narrator feels that the prospect of drowning is a ghoulish possibility and a welcome relief from the insults and tribulations of life.

This hunger for relief from the bludgeon of truth and the compulsion to self-sufficiency is a powerful force in a good deal of alcoholic writing. In "Eleven Addresses to the Lord," Berryman describes his passion to be reconciled to Divine Will, but he is insatiable; and his hunger persists despite his obstinate "grand endeavors." Still he longs for dreams softened in grace, patience, the gift of a shoulder, and

When all hurt nerves whine [sic] shut away the whiskey.
Empty my heart toward Thee. (5–11)

Berryman prays to resolve his compulsions and learn compassion, patience, and tenderness. He prays that the hunger for whiskey be lifted, that his d.t.'s subside, and that he find some means of surrendering unreservedly to God. The prayer is terrifying in the extreme because it is an admission of helplessness without the redeeming features of grace. Yet, his hunger persists despite his "grand endeavors," and it persists because of his lust for fulfillment and his refusal to be reconciled to circumstances over which he has no control. Because of these reservations, he is defeated before the fact; and there is no way that he can emerge from his depression and self-obsession so long as he persists in half-measures in his petition to surrender to God.

In "Opus Dei," Berryman is confronted with a similar inventory of agonies that accrue from an emotional and spiritual imbalance, an absence of humility, and the catastrophic consequences of his aberrant behavior. He tells us that he "falleth into the fire, and oft into the water. / And he did evil, because he prepared not / his heart to seek the Lord" (*Collected*, 225). For Berryman, the dementia inherent in this bleak mood of social hatred and self-pity is oddly gratifying. It justifies his flamboyant posture as a prophet and martyr, thereby elevating him above the common lot of humanity simply because of his suffering.

Thus, in "Henry by Night," Berryman describes how "Henry" (a sort of alter ego for Berryman) is a nervous wreck who has become self-imprisoned by a vicious cycle of intemperate scribbling, drinking, coughing, and compulsive, "death-like" wandering. Poor Henry's "nocturnal habits" drive his women insane. In a fatalistic and hyperactive resignation to circumstance, he drinks, he smokes, he sweats, shakes, thrashes, and snores; but his strategies are thoroughly reductive and incredibly foolish. It's no way to live, he admits, and "something's gotta give/up for good at five" (17–18). Henry is self-destructing, both physically and mentally, and he is driving himself beyond the limits of sanity. His nocturnal meanderings have no probity, and he is spiritually and physically exhausted; but he seems incapable of doing anything about the "sweating & shaking" because he is both self-victimized and vacuously self-sustaining.

*   *   *

Thus, as we will discover in the chapters to follow, a primary characteristic of the alcoholic temperament is a preoccupation with delusions of power, aggressive rebellion and self-pity, and an insatiable hunger to restructure emotions and perceptions according to certain power-driven prescriptions of control and illusion. In writing and in the refuge of his fantasies and confessions, however, the alcoholic is able to give dimension and substance to his compulsions and illusions; he can fabricate a literary cosmos that is almost entirely of his own making; and he can seclude himself in the delusion that he has somehow managed to remain a creative, liberated, and functional human being of no small worth. That illusion will persist with grim determination throughout the greater part of his drinking history, and it is likely to be manifested in an extraordinary menagerie of visions, a crude inventory of self-destructive behaviors, and—most important for our purposes—an extraordinary psychological portrait of the alcoholic perception.

Chapter Two

Alcoholism in Ernest Hemingway's The Sun Also Rises: *A Wine and Roses Perspective of the Lost Generation*

The Sun Also Rises is a remarkable portrait of the pathology of alcoholism. It has none of the high drama and tragic despair of works like *The Days of Wine and Roses* or *Under the Volcano*, but this makes the story all the more realistic and compelling. Indeed, like the disease of alcoholism itself, the novel may be quite deceptive because it presents no images of addictive self-destruction on a grandiose scale.

The novel describes how Jake Barnes and his expatriate friends spend a good deal of time in Paris drinking and talking about their drinking, how they make a hectic trip over the Pyrenees to Pamplona to go fishing and watch the bullfights, and how, after an astonishing series of foul-ups and misunderstandings, they straggle back to Paris to talk some more and do some more drinking. In fact, even the most cursory reading would suggest that most of the novel is *concerned* with liquor, discussions about liquor, hangovers, drunkenness, and, of course, finding more liquor (Gelderman 12):

> *You were quite drunk my dear.* (54)
> *I say, Jake, do we get a drink?* (54)
> *He loves to go for champagne.* (55)
> *Let's have a drink, then. The count will be back.* (56)
> *You know he's extraordinary about buying champagne. It means any amount to him.* (56)
> *I think you'll find that's very good wine,...we don't get much of a chance to judge good wine.* (56)
> *This is a hell of a dull talk,.... How about some of that champagne?* (58)
> *You're always drinking, my dear. Why don't you just talk?* (58)

*I like to drink champagne from magnums. The wine is better but it
would have been too hard to cool.* (59)
*There, my dear. Now you enjoy that slowly, and then you can get
drunk.* (59)
*She is the only lady I have ever known who was as charming when
she was drunk as when she was sober.* (59)
Drink your wine. (59)

It might be assumed that at least three of the characters—
Jake Barnes, Brett Ashley, and Mike Campbell—are only
heavy drinkers; but there is a considerable difference between
heavy drinking and the kind of self-destructive, alcoholic
drinking that we read about in the novel. Indeed, Hemingway
himself may have felt obliged to acknowledge the alcoholic
focus of the story. When asked about its libationary focus, he
appears to have grudgingly conceded that it was "a book about
a few drunks" (qtd. in Dardis 163); but, as Tom Dardis notes
in his excellent discussion of the writer's alcoholism, the drinking behavior described in *The Sun Also Rises* is both pro-
nounced and addictive, regardless of the motives (163).
Hemingway may have thought that imbibing on such a monu-
mental scale simply classified the inebriate as a sort of generic
"rummy," but, as Dardis writes, he was ignorant of the fact
that "alcoholism breeds its own kind of pressure, that of alcoholic depression" (163).

In defining Mike, Brett, and Jake as practicing alcoholics, we
should consider what constitutes a legitimate portrait of the
addictive temperament.[1] That is, we might want to consider
what it is that characterizes someone whose life is dominated by
an obsession with liquor. Most social scientists have concluded
that alcoholics have a higher level of anxiety, dependence, and
defensiveness. This is sometimes reflected in a remarkable
degree of moodiness, impulsivity, hostility, and distrust (see,
e.g., Ward 168 and Weston, 39–41).[2] A good number of studies
have also concluded that alcoholics have low self-esteem, are
more goal oriented, strive more for a superficial feeling of
achievement, and consistently exhibit an intense need for personal power (see, e.g., Ward 169). Such problems may also be
manifested by the development of facades suggesting a great
deal of uncertainty regarding sexual identity (Ward 176).

If we critique *The Sun Also Rises* with these criteria in mind, it should come as no surprise that Jake, Brett, Mike, and even Robert Cohn and Bill Gorton match the alcoholic profile in no small measure. Regardless of the setting or scene, the bars and the bottles are omnipresent and serve as a focal point for the bullfights, the eating, the peregrinating, the flirting and seducing, the fisticuffs, and even the fishing. Between Paris, Pamplona, and Burguete, Jake gets very drunk every time we see him, Bill is rarely sober; and even Cohn spends a good deal of time in his cups—and all of this happens during the two weeks or so that we as readers follow the story. Drinking on this kind of scale cannot even begin to resemble normalcy, and it is most certainly a substantive foundation for addiction and obsessive dependence. Of course, as with most practicing alcoholics, any talk about abuse is usually focused on "other" people in the group, or it is jokingly discounted as the "right" kind of drinking that supports the jolly, good nature of the inner circle.

A key aspect of the alcoholic temperament is the desire for control. There is hardly a single major character in *The Sun Also Rises* who is not a compulsive manipulator, and very few characters of any significance—outside of the Romero group— are not enveloped in self-pity because of their powerlessness to compel others to do their will.

Jake and his companions are terrified that fate and circumstance might shatter their facade of civilized deference. Sometimes, they barely make it from day to day; sometimes, they appear to be trying to just make it through the next hour, a common enough problem among a great many alcoholics. These people lack the skills and the sanity to break their addiction to self-sufficiency and their destructive loop of unmanageability. Instead, they seek refuge in broken relationships, in changes of scene, in drunkenness and the illusion that, however meager, they can find some iota of pleasure in their brief interludes of time and place. There is a great deal of fear here, fear of self-understanding, fear of emotional and physical inadequacy, and—very important—fear of each other.

Jake is the terminal man. Having been emasculated in the war, he has gotten tangled up in a vicious cycle of emotional self-mutilation. Regardless of whether he is alone or in company, he is resigned to the belief that he is powerless to change much of anything; and his situation is hopeless. So he secludes himself in a mantle of self-pity and chooses to withdraw in a Faustian tragedy of self-denial rather than do anything about his problem. More often than not, he gets drunk or ends up alone in a hotel room or in his flat, staring at the ceiling while grousing about the hopelessness of his condition and the impossibility of establishing any kind of enduring connection with Brett. Thus, in his refusal to break out of his self-destructive prison, he persists in remaining self-condemned before the fact:

> My head started to work. The old grievance. Well, it was a rotten way to be wounded and flying on a joke front like the Italian. In the Italian hospital we were going to form a society. It had a funny name in Italian.... There was a statue for Ponte, or maybe it was Zonda. That was where the liaison colonel came to visit me.... I was all bandaged up. But they had told him about it. Then he made a wonderful speech: "You, a foreigner, an Englishman" [any foreigner was an Englishman] [*sic*] "have given more than your life." What a speech! I would like to have it illuminated to hang in the office. He never laughed. He was putting himself in my place, I guess. "Che mala fortuna! Che mala fortuna!"
>
> I never used to realize it, I guess. I try to play it along and just not make trouble for people. Probably I never would have had any trouble if I hadn't run into Brett when they shipped me to England. I suppose she only wanted what she couldn't have. Well, people were that way. To hell with people. The Catholic Church had an awfully good way of handling all that. Good advice, anyway. Not to think about it. Oh, it was swell advice. Try and take it sometime. Try and take it.
>
> I lay awake thinking and my mind jumping around. Then I couldn't keep away from it,... I was thinking about Brett and my mind stopped jumping.... Then all of a sudden I started to cry. (31)

Like many alcoholics, Jake is convinced that his self-imposed martyrdom is terminal. He systematically destroys his potential for any kind of fulfilment because of his ludicrous assumptions about what might have been if he had not been wounded; and he has set down the terms of his life with uncompromising severity because he is convinced that his world is different, his front was a "joke," and he has given "more" than his life for Italy. So he feels hopeless about any kind of meaningful relationship with Brett, tries to resign himself to circumstance without recognizing any reasonable option, and thinks about not thinking.

Like Jake, Brett is self-victimized by her catastrophic thinking and her remarkable penchant for charades, seduction, and booze. She discounts her title—Lady Brett Ashley—but seems to parade it at every opportunity. She is a voluptuary of prodigious dimensions who disguises her fear in the sexual control of men. And through it all, she canonizes herself as noble and self-sacrificing. It is a pretty little game she plays, but her strategies are riddled with drunken fakery. If viewed from a psychological perspective, Brett personifies the generic female alcoholic with a remarkable prejudice for manipulation and orchestration. She seduces; she complains; she plays the kitten; and then she runs. She targets the emotions of any man who will have anything to do with her, hopeful that he will somehow restore the integrity of her womanhood. And she knows no boundaries in her hunt. Just about anything male is fair game; any assertion of power might affirm that she is not a victim of circumstances herself. If seduction can lead to a trophy, she will seduce; if abandonment can lead to an assurance of her skill at breaking hearts, she will abandon; and if sheer, mind-boggling mental torture will do the job, then tempt and attack she will.

For Brett, change as a means of resolving fear is not an inside job; change is something imposed on others for the sake of her own insatiable appetites; and, when she fails, as she invariably must, she founders in self-pity, gets drunk, and crashes Jake's apartment to mourn the cruelty of circumstance and cry on his shoulder. And then she promptly punishes him for penetrating her shell.

Mike is a masochist and village crown. He uses his money and his connections to control others, to martyr himself, and to confirm that, after all, he is little more than a drunk. If he is given a chance and enough liquor, he will attack anyone weaker than himself, a typical enough behavior of any fear-ridden alcoholic. Then, if parried too strongly, he will shake off the bully boy image and be a "good fellow." Mike has failed at just about everything—his prospects for marriage, work, sex—and he knows it and even seems rather proud of it. While he adopts the pose of an idle playboy and jolly intoxicant, he is neither interested in sobering up nor skilled enough to break away from himself or his surroundings. His title and what little money he has left are sufficient to keep him mildly functional despite his drinking, and his self-esteem is meager enough to keep him from even thinking about sobering up and making any real changes. And so he stumbles on without meaning or purpose—a kind of wealthy vagrant without connections or much of a future.

Although Cohn does not at first appear to have some of the drinking problems of his more bibulous companions, it is ironic that he provides a vivid example of the capricious personality flaws that are commonly perceived in the standard profile of a practicing alcoholic. Indeed, because of his insufferable emotionalism, his addiction to self-pity, and his co-dependent proximity to Jake's retinue, he seems to manifest the standard characteristics of a "dry drunk" or "prealcoholic" personality (see, e.g., Ward 181–182). Such individuals are commonly recognized around alcoholic circles because they behave like practicing alcoholics, even though they do not appear to have an obsessive need to drink. Indeed, they provide a striking example of the fundamental distinction between people who are "dry" and people who are "sober."[3]

In any case, when Cohn does get drunk, he behaves like a lap dog; and yet, like so many of his kind, he tries to comfort himself with illusions of masculinity and self-sufficiency. Of course, that euphoria can easily collapse in a stream of apologies and tears of self-pity, as in the drunken fight with Romero.

For Jake and his companions, liquor can fuel the appetites and rebellious instincts, but it cannot defuse fear. Drinking isolates these people and fragments their relationships, culminating in rebellion, antisocial behavior, and an addiction to social fakery and make-believe. Even the conversations are maddeningly incongruent. We sense that each character talks to himself through a muddled backwash of trivia and banality. Connections are short, focused on externals, and filled with nonsequiturs. Most of the talk is centered on bullfights, the food, the quality of the wine, the festival at Pamplona, the various affairs, or banalities of an insufferable texture; but we never know how anyone *really* feels or even if any intelligence or sensitivity supports this masquerade of maturity and self-sufficiency. Consider the following scene when Jake sees Brett in Paris:

> A taxi passed, some one [*sic*] in it waved, then banged for the driver to stop. The taxi backed up to the curb. In it was Brett.
> "Beautiful lady," said Bill. "Going to kidnap us."
> "Hullo!" Brett said, "Hullo!"
> "This is Bill Gorton. Lady Ashley."
> Brett smiled at Bill. "I say I'm just back. Haven't bathed even. Michael comes in to-night."
> "Good. Come on and eat with us, and we'll all go to meet him."
> "Must clean myself."
> "Oh, rot! Come on."
> "Must bathe. He doesn't get in till nine."
> "Come and have a drink, then, before you bathe."
> "Might do that. Now you're not talking rot."
> We got in the taxi. The driver looked around.
> "Stop at the nearest bistro," I said.
> "We might as well go to the Closierie," Brett said. "I can't drink those rotten brandies." (74)

The confabulations between Jake, Bill, and Brett are simple enough and casual enough—seemingly concerned about bathing, napping, bistros, and rotten brandies; but the connections never seem to progress beyond bromides. When these people meet, they are preoccupied with making arrangements to meet again sometime; and if they talk for any length, conversations are cluttered with superficial evaluations of the quality of the booze, the problems of hygiene, and the complications of meeting and/or not meeting again. In one scene, they go to the *Lilas*; they order whiskey; they talk about travel and promise to meet "later." During the "later" at the *Select*, they talk about Brett's hat, Michael's nose, and a few other trivialities. Then they break up, go to a fight, meet again the next day at the *Select,* and start drinking and palavering all over again.

These people are on dangerous ground; communication is restrained and indeterminate; they talk about talking; they talk

about "other" people and "other" circumstances; and they talk
about liquor, about affairs, and travel while zealously avoiding
personal references that might unhinge their charade of emotional stability. Each expects the other to be a mind-reader and
interpret his obscurity. Each expects the other to provide some
understanding of unasked questions and to affirm his integrity
and his self-worth. But words do not match actions; actions do
not match claims; and fantasies and hopes are totally out of
sync with what is possible. None of these people seems to have
any real understanding of the meaning of love or friendship—in
the deepest sense of the word. In the case of Jake and Brett,
both are inclined either to deny that they have any kind of connection or to define the relationship in fanciful or catastrophic
terms. The consequences of such a perception are disastrous
because neither is capable of fulfilling the fantasies or ideals of
the other with the rigorous consistency that is demanded. In
describing the problems of intimacy as they relate to such people, the A.A. publication, *Twelve Steps and Twelve Traditions*,
notes,

> The primary fact that we fail to recognize is our total inability to form
> a true partnership with another human being. Our egomania digs two
> disastrous pitfalls. Either we insist upon dominating the people we
> know, or we depend upon them far too much. If we lean too heavily on
> people, they will sooner or later fail us, for they are human too, and
> cannot possibly meet our incessant demands. In this way our insecu-
> rity grows and festers. (53)

An aggressive, manipulative, and self-centered impulse is
thus a primary aspect of the alcoholic perception and the alcoholic's relationships with others. Perhaps this is why Jake and
Brett articulate fantasies and hopes that exceed the sphere of
normalcy, and perhaps this explains why they have chosen to
draw judgments that are grounded in chemically induced,
self-centered perceptions. Admittedly, there is some talk about
the "problem," but these people seem incapable of sincerity,
except to complain or commiserate with a superficial regard
for any workable solution. Jake drones on about his "old
grievance"; Brett tells him she has been "so miserable" (24);
the two of them discuss "that hell" after a rousing kiss in the

taxi; they agree to "shut up" about Jake's wound; Brett goes on to complain that she has to "pay" for what she has done; and Jake tells her not to be a fool (25–26). It seems that any opportunity for a genuine conversation about the pain, the frustration, and the limits and possibilities imposed by circumstance is frustrated by denials, evasions, unanswered objections, tentative groping, or simply a refusal to consider the matter any further.

As far as Jake and Brett are concerned, it is assumed that genital affection is the only option in a male-female relationship. Denied that possibility, there is no other recourse but to whine about unkind fate, refuse compromise, and dismiss the possibility that sexuality may involve a great deal more than coitus and penile fascination—as any paraplegic would be happy to explain. In any case, it is blatantly obvious that Jake would rather withdraw into his own misperceived loneliness, absolve himself of any opportunity for a solution, and get drunk.

Jake's congenital preoccupation with evading any substantive consideration of his circumstance is vividly illustrated in his relationship with Bill Gorton. When Jake is with Gorton, his closest friend, he appears to be having a good time—indeed, the experiences and conversations seem a long way from the standard, alcoholically dysfunctional context of so much of the rest of the novel. However, a careful analysis of his behavior might suggest that the friendship is severely limited—indeed, badly strained—by his fear of personal exposure.

Certainly, when the two go fishing in the Pyrenees, the descriptions and the scene are appealing enough. Jake and Bill take a long walk, bait their hooks, discuss where to fish, toss out their lines, get a nice catch, pack it, eat lunch, drink wine, and discuss eggs and drumsticks. Later, having gotten "cock-eyed" on wine, they have a brief conversation about Jake's "problem":

> "Say," Bill said, "what about this Brett business?"
> "What about it?"
> "Were you ever in love with her?"
> "Sure."

"For how long?"
"Off and on for a hell of a long time."
"Oh, hell!" Bill said. "I'm sorry fella."
"It's all right," I said. "I don't give a damn any more."
"Really?"
"Really. Only I'd a hell of a lot rather not talk about it." (123–124)

And that is the end of it. Bill says he is going to sleep—and
he does.

Jake has apparently decided that intimacy must necessarily be
predicated on genital voyaging. As a consequence, his prospects
for any kind of connectedness to Brett—or anybody else for that
matter—fluctuate with maddening irregularity. "I've had plenty
to worry about one time or other. I'm through worrying," he
says early in the novel (11). Even so, it seems that he has a remarkable penchant for continuing to worry, deny, and rationalize
throughout the remainder of the story; indeed, his drunken esca-
pades are an epic study in self-destruction, complaint, and evasion. He tells us at one point that he has gotten a "little drunk,"
not in any "positive sense," as he calls it, but "enough to be care-
less" (21). When he is with Brett in a taxi in Paris, they kiss and
discuss how his wound is "funny." "I never think about it," he
lies. He burbles on to insist that he's "pretty well through with
the subject," having considered it from various "angles" (26–27).
Of course, he feels like "hell" every time he stops being "through";
indeed, the entire novel is full of liberally sprinkled affirmations
that he has quit thinking about his problem.

In trying to deal with circumstances and frustrations, then,
Jake and his circle only seem to know how to run from their
problems. They dash from Paris to the Pyrenees, from the
Pyrenees to Pamplona, and from Pamplona to Madrid. They
dare not stay in any one place too long; and they certainly
dare not find any substantive connection with each other.
Instead, they are continually setting themselves up for the
next drama, the next broken relationship, the next argument
or barroom brawl, or the next shattered romance or fouled
relationship.

Jake is a seasoned runner who feels powerless and he hates
it. We learn that he has fled his family in the States; and, in

Paris, when the emotional and physical connections get uncomfortable and presumed unmanageable, he runs from Brett and goes fishing. Later, he runs from the festival in Pamplona when the bullfighting, the boozing, and the romancing get confused and threaten to pierce his neatly constructed shell of self-sufficiency. He sets up a party, a trip, an evening; he scurries off to a bar, a hotel, or a sporting even of some sort; his friends congregate, dish out the dirt, cry, joke, and confess. And Jake listens and says almost nothing. He has found a hook: silence invites talk; talk invites him in. And he does not have to do a thing in return—except to disappear when someone gets too close. He is in a sense the "father confessor" who has something on everybody and whose own life is a ludicrous mystery. Except for Bill Gorton, whose status and understanding of Jake are somewhat questionable, no one really seems to know very much about Jake, what he is *really* thinking, or what he feels; and, strangely enough, this very quality is his attraction: he represents the possibility of a connection without a commitment, a friendship without the gift of intimacy. For Jake, stupefied drunkenness, whirling ceilings, bathos, loneliness, pain, and self-pity are a gloomy constant in an otherwise unmanageable life.

Jake may feel unique, but his is a terminal kind of uniqueness; for he has set down the terms of his life with uncompromising severity. Like so many alcoholics, he has forged his personal catastrophe to a black-and-white perspective that allows no middle ground. Convinced that he is worthless, he has selfishly mapped out the outcomes of his self-imposed martyrdom before the fact. And, of course, that map excludes any truly intimate connection with any other human being. Given the slightest excuse, then, he returns to his cups, regresses into self-pity, and, as the liquor takes hold, subsides into impenetrable bathos.

Brett is also an accomplished runner. She runs from a defunct marriage; she runs from Jake when he starts getting too close; she runs to Romero; and, having seduced him, she runs away and returns to poor Jake—and always with a drink, or two, or more for support. Early in the novel, when she drags the Count over to Jake's apartment, she comforts the poor sot, tells him she is leaving, takes him out and dances with him, and concludes the evening with a full measure of bittersweet adieus and farewells. "Good night, Jake. Good night darling," she purrs. "I won't see you again" (65). The crescendo ascends a pitch higher. They kiss, she pushes him away, they kiss again, and finally she stumbles away to her hotel.

Brett's oscillations are superficial and insubstantial; half the time, she refuses to consider her options. "Isn't there anything we can do about it?" she wonders (26). Then, having asked the question, she denies the possibility of an answer and chooses to suffer in silence for a while. In one scene, typical of many, she complains, "Let's not talk. Talking's all bilge" (55). Back in Paris at the end of the story, she shows up at Jake's apartment, admits that she has broken up with Romero, and concludes, "'Oh, hell!' . . . . 'let's not talk about it. Let's never talk about it'" (242).

Mike is a runner and escapist of a somewhat more decadent complexion. He runs from his infantile preoccupation with being helpless; he runs from his friends and from "friends" who are not friends. He runs from his anger at being "used"; he runs from his dismal failure as a prospective husband; and he runs from his fear that he may be, after all, little more than a drunk. When we meet this jolly English tippler, he is tight, his nose is bloody; and he wants to get laid by Lady Brett who is "a lovely piece" (80). In Pamplona, he gets drunk, fights with Cohn, and seeks refuge in Brett's room. He is pathetic and decent in a weird sort of way, but there is not much to redeem this bankrupt, overindulgent patrician—except in his role as a victim of circumstance who must "suffer" the peripheral benefits of co-dependence.

Like most alcoholics, Jake and his friends are rebels. They do not seem to recognize boundaries; they are hell-bent on testing and bending the rules; and they are obsessed with denying their connectedness with the order of things. While Jake spends some of his time writing, preparing for his vacation, ordering his tickets, and undertaking a few other mundane, everyday affairs; we can hardly regard such behavior as substantive evidence of normalcy—indeed, he is in truth generally removed from the mainstream of life. We know very little about his family back in the States, his relationship with Brett is a disaster, and his work does not seem to amount to much. At the "office," he reads the papers, smokes, and sits at the typewriter (writing, I assume). Later, he goes out to watch a politico, has lunch, and goes back to the "office later"—to do what, God knows (36–40). Mainly, we are told that he stumbles off to his hotel, to the *Rotonde*, or to his flat; he has some drinks; he hails his friends; he goes to the races; he has a scene; and, in quiet moments, he feels just plain crummy.

This is a world of eating and visiting, of race tracks or of "turning up" someplace after a four-day blackout—Bill rubs his forehead to describe his loss of memory during a binge in Vienna (70). It is a world of boxing matches, horse cabs, stuffed animals, and bars where no one is especially interested in returning to the States (or to England) and where the idea of a family—in some cases, even marriage—seems to be out of the question. Playing, drinking, and seducing are far more important than work; and risk-taking and "running" command a high priority. What is more to the point, however, is the fact that we, as readers, have hopefully seen enough insanity, enough emptiness, and enough self-destruction and self-reproach to discredit the friendships, the values, the drinking, and the lives of these characters.

Those who regard the bullfights, the fishing, or the festival at Pamplona as the central focus of the novel could be missing the point. *The Sun Also Rises* is not simply a novel about sterility or the "code" or about rebellion or running in meaningless circles. Critical as these themes may be, they skirt some important questions about the integrity of the kind of courage, or should we say lack of courage, that Hemingway has apparently tried to portray. Although the ring may be a dramatic proving ground for Romero, its values have little real or workable effect on Jake or any of his friends, except in their role as spectators—and spectatorship automatically excludes involvement. For Romero, the ring may demand grace, self-mastery, and control; his actions may be a pretty thing to watch. However, Jake and his friends need none of this. They have already attempted far too much control of appearances, and they give those appearances far too much power as a means leading to an affirmation of self. As spectators, they have also learned too well how to pretend grace and mastery of circumstances that do not involve them and over which they, in truth, have no control at all.

When Jake and his companions make judgments and translate themselves to the morality of the bullring, they are transferring the wreckage of their lives to a harmless, irrelevant arena—insofar as they do not have much prospect of being employed as bullfighters or demonstrating grace under pressure to a few thousands fans and aficionados. Because they have degraded themselves to spectators without insisting on the kind of courage they need to confront their own problems, they are little more than sterile witnesses to a fabricated tragedy.

Brett, Cohn, Mike, and Jake appear unaware that the true battle-ground of the self, the personal "bullring" of their fears and their wounds and their addictions, lies in how they perceive themselves and how they deal directly with their misfortunes and circumstances. Whatever enjoyments, pleasures, or health they find, whatever balancing of life's risks and rewards they realize, will only be possible with an honest and fearless inventory of their own conduct, not a superficial fabrication of a "code" of courage and sensuality that has little to do with the business of living. That would require a good deal more honesty than they are capable of demonstrating, and it would require too heady a dose of the very courage they claim to admire.

On the surface, then, the Hemingway "code" appears to provide a strict set of rules and values defining how the experiences of life, how courage itself, can be maximized. In this particular case, however, that "code" is degraded by the behavior of Jake, Mike, Brett, and Cohn. It promises order and meaning and resolution, but it cannot deliver. The fishing scenes, the mountain idyll, and the friendships are also red herrings. Jake seeks some kind of serenity and some inner balance and wholeness when he goes fishing with Bill Gorton. But the search does not work—it cannot work. Again, what

Jake seeks has to come first from himself; it cannot be generated from a material setting or escapist impulses. In running from himself—in running to a trout stream or the mountains—he is doomed, for he can find peace only by learning to understand and accept himself for what he is. Fish, drink, and run as he does, Jake has yet to learn to accept the fact there is a great deal that he cannot change; and he has yet to find the courage to change what he can. So the trip is a bust. His nerves are shattered by the arrival of Cohn, by the drinking, by his loneliness and resentment, and by the pain of his wound.

The Sun Also Rises is a portrait of degeneration without solutions. It is a portrait of estrangement and emotional adolescence and "running"; and it is a portrait of a bankrupt value system that depends far too much on appearances and dramatics. It is a novel about spiritual bankruptcy, codependence, and people who enable each other to withdraw and become emotionally impotent because they support each other in erecting a meaningless facade of self-sufficiency and bathos. In the final analysis, it is a novel about people who feel compelled to fabricate a code of conduct that has very little do with living and even less to do with integrity. As such, it is a portrait of what can begin to happen when emotionally damaged people seek refuge from themselves in the desensitizing and addictive effects of liquor where ignorance, insanity, escape, and waste are manifested in abundance.

Chapter Three

Addiction and Spirituality in Contemporary American Poetry: Frustration and Paradox

O Bible chopped and crucified
in hymns we hear but do not read,...
stiff quatrains shovelled [sic] out foursquare—
they sing of peace, and preach despair;
...they gave darkness some control,
and left a loophole for the soul.
　　　　　—Robert Lowell, "Waking Early Sunday Morning,"
　　　　　　　　　　　　　　　　　　49–50, 53–56.

Most alcoholic writers are strangely incongruent; and, while they are capable of extraordinary eloquence, their spiritual focus is typically dark and uncertain. Although the poems of Theodore Roethke, Robert Lowell, Charles Olson, John Berryman, Hart Crane, Edwin Arlington Robinson, Edna St. Vincent Millay, and Alan Dugan have been quite well explicated by such well-known addiction critics such as Thomas Gilmore, Donald Goodwin, and Tom Dardis; they have yet to fully consider the mercurial nature of alcoholic spirituality, most especially its perfectionist equivocations and catastrophic hopelessness.

For most alcoholics, life comprises a mind-dulling regimen of diurnal responsibilities and an extraordinary preoccupation with self-gratification. In "Eleven Addresses to the Lord," John Berryman agonizes over his spiritual double nature and his obsession with self-sufficiency. He reviews the terrors of childhood, his loss of faith after his father's suicide, and his unconscionable life during the years that followed. Is he not living proof of the temporal insufficiency of self-management? He prays for the singular blessing of Divine guidance that he might subvert his self-obsessed priorities and surrender to God's incomparable love. He will place himself "Under new management," "having solo'd mine since childhood" when his father killed himself and "blew out his most bright candle faith." Yet, for all his apparent sincerity, it seems that Berryman is attempting to discount personal responsibility for his lack of faith and his spiritual equivocations. His inventory—his "look at me" perspective—does not seem like an honest prerequisite to reform. In fact, one wonders if it is simply a strategic retreat from the rigorous prospect of self-examination and change.

In the next stanza, Berryman reviews his catastrophic conversion through a series of violent images that focus on the power and immensity of Christ's suffering and how—almost three weeks before—in a sudden conversion, Christ "pierced the roof/twice & twice again" and "fused" his double nature, in Berryman's case, the doubting, rebellious adult and the simple child of faith.

Berryman's perception of the Passion, then, is strangely distant and uncertain, perhaps because his relationship to Christ is expressed in repetitive exclamations and irreconcilable opposites; and, in confessing his "double nature," he has foolishly attempted to replicate the power of the Crucifix with its apparent opposition of the eternal and temporal.

Berryman's obsessive concern with spiritual deterioration and the power of irreconcilable opposites should be no surprise to anyone familiar with the conventional perspective on creativity and addiction. Gifted writers are *supposed* to be manic, confused, and compulsive; they are *supposed* to be self-destructive, alienated, spiritually bankrupt, and misunderstood; and they are *supposed* to have experienced life's dizziest heights and its most grotesque horrors. Suffering and confusion are the price of creativity, and we should not be surprised that a good many of the poets discussed here have tried to fulfill these prescriptions with a vengeance. Thus, Edwin Arlington Robinson writes that this "special" breed of gifted humanity,

Must each await alone at his own height
Another darkness or another light

> If inference and reason shun
> Hell, Heaven, and Oblivion,
> May thwarted will (perforce precarious,
> But for our conservation better thus)
> Have no misgiving left
> Of doing yet what here we leave undone?
>   ("The Man against the Sky," 192–199)

Robinson elevates the wounded and lonely—each man "alone" to a tragic but ingenious plain of titanic proportions. In their lonely self-dominion, they shun the divine prospect of reward and punishment, including the horrible prospect of oblivion, even as they persist in their sacred passion for understanding and reassurance. Confounded and emasculated by the puzzling scheme of the *Eternal*, the forsaken souls he describes are suspended between Heaven and oblivion, which serves to exonerate them from any necessity of self-justification and "self-eloquence." Hence, they are compelled to deal with the prospect of impending doom; but that, he claims, is the price of genius and one's special place in the scheme of things.

Robinson further describes this tension between the insistent demands of Eternal Judgment and the ethical requirements of human endeavor in his remarkable poem "The Laggards." Here, he writes of the opposition between human "groping and the towers of God" (4) where man is both master and slave, human endeavor is sealed with misery, and a select few have endured worse than death, "Only to pay seven fold, and seven times seven/...and for cause not always plain." These unfortunates, we are told, "are the laggards among those who strive/ On earth to raise the golden dust of heaven" (11–14). It is a strange and troubling perspective. Robinson denies the possibility of any reconciliation with God because of the irrefutable and capricious nature of moral payback and Christ's tale of forgiveness seven times seven. In this case, the question of moral "laggards" who hope to reconcile eternity with transience is contravened by the urgency of an earthly heaven with the "golden dust" of a fallen humanity. Thus, while man will not be denied his eternal birthright, he must also accept the curse of mortality where he is condemned to wander the "dusty leagues"—like Cain.

Here, as with so much of his writing, Robinson is concerned
with the gifted perfectionists and equivocators who are
self-exiled to an irredeemable vision of divine grace through a
material divinity—the "golden dust"—that will exceed the
despair of mortality and rebellious scepticism. While these
"enlightened" laggards are disillusioned by human imperfection and disenfranchised by the legacy of Eden, they still have
"one foot shod/with skyward wings, but are not flying yet"
(1–2), for their divinity will be born of hard experience and
time-worn integrity. These martyrs will exceed the toil of those
who have not gathered such an "accumulated debt," since they
exceed the superficiality of people who have not struggled and
doubted.

In "Eleven Addresses to the Lord," Berryman expresses a
more rhapsodic perspective on divine grace and mercy, and
he praises the radiance and measureless perfection of the
Creator who is incomparable, extravagant, omnipotent, and
whole.

Berryman confesses that he does not have the resources to
deny God's mercy and must necessarily capitulate to Divine
Power "according" to His will, but his egoistic hymn of praise
is centered on a highly elective perspective of God in the
Calvinistic tradition that does not fully grasp the meaning and
significance of unqualified forgiveness. He recalls how God res-
cued him again and again during his most "impassable" dysfunctional years while seeming to allow his friends to destroy
themselves. To Berryman, this makes no sense.

Unlike Robinson, we see here a highly personal focus on
an inconstant divinity whose love is mysterious and unex-
plainable. Perhaps these images recall the enigmatic rigidity
of Berryman's early Catholicism, but there are negative
undertones in the image, for it seems impossible for the poet
to fully appreciate the unconditional love of Old and New
Testament Divinity. In addition, despite all his claims of
ecstasy, humility, and submission, it is apparent that he cannot resolve his temporal obsession with himself, even as he
petitions the Creator for understanding. On the one hand, he
states that he is willing to submit and surrender; yet he aspires
to a personal connectedness with God on terms that are very

much of his own making. Granted even that qualification, he is confounded by the prospect of God's appalling justice and divine indifference to the fate of his friends. Hence, we witness his confusion and self-serving equivocations, most especially as they are reflected in his strange preoccupation with manifesting some kind of highly qualified act of personal degradation and payback as a form of penance—as God's "guinea pig."

A similar theme is developed in Berryman's "The Facts & Issues." Here, the possibility of a personal God appears freakish and illogical, and the prospect of any kind of unqualified spiritual connectedness is unthinkable because it requires a transcendent perspective that is both constant and perfect. He cannot accept the possibility that Christ's terrible suffering and the horrors of the Crucifix ransomed his "disgusting vices"; but the payback is too much, because it delivers far more than he has any right to accept. "I am so happy I could scream!" he exclaims. "I can't BEAR ANYMORE." (31–39).

For Berryman, the prospect of unconditional grace is untenable, not only because it defies any reasonable sense of justice or temporal balance, but also because he feels that he cannot bridge the infinite distance from poet to Savior. Indeed, even if he could, Berryman suspects that God would necessarily burden him with spiritual baggage that he could not possibly sustain.

The poem ends on a note of absolute despair and confusion: God's great glory is overwhelmingly incomprehensible, and the poet is so satiated with grace and understanding that he has little choice but to surrender to Divine Will, but his prayer of adoration is untenable because it attempts to resolve the paradoxical bondage of the artistic persona and the infinitely defiled mortal beneath the surface of things.

Although most alcoholics may try to deal with spiritual uncertainty through self-mastery and a remarkable litany of excuses and self-justifications, their sincerity is dubious at best, and their hunger for a "God of rescue"—as John Berryman called it—will be condemned to futility before the fact. Like Berryman, the alcoholic may be fearful of dying, but he is likely to choke on the remedy, since there is damnation in any kind of legitimate connectedness with anything higher than bathos and self-interest. Hence, suffering, anger, and self-immolation are transitory but estimable pleasures that provide an excellent barricade against any insinuation of Divine understanding and love.

In "Skunk Hour," for example, Robert Lowell—a contemporary of Berryman—describes (with no slight debt to John Milton) his demonic self-obsession, his infinite distance from God, and his disenchantment with the prospect of spiritual integrity:

> I hear
> my ill-spirit sob...
> as if my hand were at its throat... [sic]
> I myself am hell;[1]
> nobody's here— (32–36)

Lowell suffocates in a self-centered graveyard of savagery and insanity and has become his own hell, a damned and solitary pilgrim who feels compelled to choke on life and whose sick soul can only grieve at the utter nakedness of melancholy circumstance.

This passion to condemn the workings of unkind fate and consign a suffering humanity to the Divine mercy of oblivion is also expressed in Theodore Roethke's "Judge Not." He writes of howling drunkards, death and suffering, and women, "their eyelids like little rags,/I said: On all these, Death, with gentleness, come down" (7–10). Here, Roethke focuses on human frailty and the price of suffering and imperfection to nullify any prospect of grace or understanding—indeed, it appears that his condemnation of humanity before the fact discounts any affirmative prospect of mortal endeavor that might assuage his purist intentions.

Roethke's perspective is a far cry from Edna St. Vincent Millay's airy spirituality that is divested of the prospect of crushing pain (a favorite image of Millay's) because it is coincidental with mortality. Yet, in her lowly corporal life, she claims that she must forever crawl and kick

> hoping never to see
>   Above my head the limbs of my spirit no longer free
> Kicking in frenzy, a swimmer enmeshed in weeds.
>   ("Above These Cares," 14–16)

Divinity is an exquisite prospect to her earthbound soul, and she tries to escape her mortal limitations in a frenzy of confusion; but, in the final analysis, her spiritual ideal of some kind of self-constructed resurrection is hopeless because she hopes to free herself rather than rely on the divine intervention of a loving God.

Although some writers may try to resolve their fears through reveries of loneliness, incantations of futility, or hopeless depression or impotence, most of them are likely to focus on a select group of negative catalysts involving confusion, pain, inquisition, and despair. In "Ave Maria," Hart Crane writes of the "incognizable Word" and the "enchained Sepulchre" of the spiritual pilgrim who sleeps apart between life and death,

> And all the eddying breath between dost search
> Cruelly with love thy parable of man, —
> Inquisitor! incognizable Word
> Of Eden and the enchained Sepulchre. (59–62)

Crane is convinced that he will never escape the terrors of eternal retribution because Divine Vengeance is an inevitable consequence of human frailty. Such thinking is not unusual among practicing alcoholics, especially when they ponder their despicable behavior while "under the influence." In "Elegy for a Puritan Conscience," Alan Dugan, an alcoholic contemporary of Berryman's, describes his spiritual degradation and his fascination with personal redemption in strangely masochistic terms. In a strange reversal of circumstance, he claims to have fallen in love with sin, pinned his mouth with rusty nails, drunk from garbage pails, and even (rather foolishly—if only symbolically) crushed his scrotum. It is an astonishing image of self-mutilation in which the Dugan persona appears to integrate the idea of rebellion and spiritual redemption with pain, obscenity, sin, and self-mutilation. Of course, the poem is not so much a petition as an angry rejection of Divinity and Divine Retribution—which he hopes to supersede with his own brand of carnal justice. The poem has very little to do with a higher power and everything to do with self-hate, masochism, rage, compulsivity, and an intense disdain for the anguish and justified pain of Eternal Judgment. Indeed, Dugan's rebellious nature is vividly expressed in his fascination with the violence implicit in self-aggrandizement. In the poem "For Masturbation," he writes that he has allowed himself a special corner beneath the stoop where he is "God" and will

> do as I will,
> either as act as act,
> or dream for the sake of dreams. (1–7)

Dugan imagines that he can transcend his mortality by playing god with his penis. In equating self-indulgence with godlike powers and the fabrications of human will, he admits a weird preoccupation with carnality and genital transcendence, but his strategies suggest a perverse obsession with erotic rebellion and simple carnal self-indulgence, no matter how sublime the experience. He is thus obstructed by a peculiar form of Gnosticism that is ultimately based on defiance and obscenity.

Robert Lowell, an alcoholic, bipolar contemporary of Dugan's, also tried to establish a personal, power-centered relationship with God; but, in this case, he was hamstrung with frustration and side-tracked by the prospect of his own cunning rather than any kind of divine, regenerative power. During an especially trying moment, Lowell wonders whether he is hopelessly and inescapably imprisoned; and, thus, he asks,

> [is] there no way to cast my hook
> *Out of this dynamited brook?*
> ("The Drunken Fisherman," 21–22)

Lowell suspects that fishing in the stream of life is a rotten prospect, perhaps because it is impossible to catch anything on his own initiative or through will power. Consequently, he insists that he will mitigate his fate and catch what he will by putting aside his fishing line, with its overtones of the Gospel, so he can dynamite the stream of life and cheat his way to Christ. Thus, fisherman Lowell hopes to countermand Divine Will by taking control and revising life's game to suit his own purposes. He will then be in a position to deal with Christ and Satan on a level playing field of his own making where he "will catch Christ" with the "greased worm"—his bait of sinfulness. If he is successful, Christ will be compelled to transform his soul into a Christly fisher king—despite all that Satan "the Prince of Darkness," may do. In some ways, his strategy is not unlike that of the seventeenth-century poet, John Donne, who turned his back on Christ that he might be chastised into a personal relationship with his redeemer, but Donne's meditation is a good deal more reverential; and, while it contains certain metaphysical elements, there is no attempt to trick anyone. Rather, Donne's poem is essentially a heartfelt plea of desperation and hope.[2] In Lowell's case, since the thought is not addressed to God but to himself; it is hardly redemptive and serves only to confirm the poet's remarkable appetite for control as he tries to find some means of tempering the full power of Divine Justice.

Theodore Roethke adopts a more elevated strategy for dealing with the supposed capriciousness of the God. Instead of trying to level the field of play, he chooses the redemptive power of psychosis by equating madness with divine grace and nobility of the soul. In his poem "In a Dark Time," the correspondences of nature are contrasted with the poet's insatiable hunger for a transforming connectedness with God. He writes of storms, insanity, death, desire, and "natural shapes blazing unnatural light." His soul "like some heat-maddened summer fly,/Keeps buzzing at the still. Which I is I?" he asks. Perhaps it does not matter. He is himself his own salvation; and he will climb out of his "fear" until his

> mind enters itself, and God the mind,
> And one is One, free in the tearing wind. (22–24)

Roethke recognizes the integrity and power of divine perfection, but his images are qualified, oblique, and disjointed—a night flowing with birds, midnight in broad daylight, all "shapes blazing unnatural light." From Roethke's perspective, natural appearances are twisted and uncertain when they are perceived in a spiritual context. Thus, his soul is equated with a "heat maddened" summer fly that is indeterminate, uncertain, hyperactive, and minute as it "keeps buzzing at the sill." Even so, he appears to contradict himself by rejecting these limitations. Rather, he will set aside the image of the poet as an insect so he can be transmuted into his own redeemer. Thus, with typical alcoholic self-indulgence and grandiosity, he will climb out of himself and exceed his mortality until he is sufficiently transformed to be self-sustained and self-contained. Then, as this miraculous act of will is actualized, he claims that his mind will enter itself to become invested with God until he *becomes* God. Thus, Roethke adopts a strikingly Gnostic perspective on man's prospects for divinity, although—in this case—he appears to have exceeded even the highest ambitions of the Gnostics by transmuting *himself* into God.

Rather than aspire upward like Roethke, Robert Lowell moves in the opposite direction. In his earlier poems, we noted his "greased worm" trick and transformation to his own hell; but now he perceives the human condition in terms of a diminished, penultimate low. In his poem "After the Surprising Conversions," he writes of melancholy Christian souls, "Good people of too much or too little wit" (12), who lived in Northampton, Massachusetts. Their bland, religious certitude was extinguished by the suicide of their pastor and,

> At Jehovah's nod
> Satan seemed more let loose amongst us: God
> Abandoned us to Satan. (31–33)

Lowell based his poem on an incident described in Jonathon Edward's narratives.[3] In this case, he is fascinated with a religious perspective that is moribund, devastating, and cataclysmic. "We were undone," Lowell writes. God had withdrawn and the undoubting congregation,

> Once neither callous, curious nor devout,
> Jumped at broad noon, as though some peddler groaned
> At it in its familiar twang: "My friend,
> Cut your own throat. Cut your own throat. Now! Now!" (40–43)

Lowell permits no middle ground. Instead, he insists that unquestioning mediocrity and lukewarm spirituality lead inevitability to a sudden descent into the pit because they are inadequate to the requirements of spiritual fitness and Divine Will.

In "What Can I Tell My Bones?" Theodore Roethke, like Lowell, expresses a good many doubts about the sustaining power of faith and the benefits of taking a personal, spiritual inventory. He complains that his soul is a beginner in perpetuity that "knows not what to believe" (3). As Roethke sees it, man struggles with his own darkness on an elementary plain. He is a beginner in perpetuity, and so there is no redemptive security to be gained by a spiritual pilgrimage because it cannot assuage the conflicting claims of the body and the soul. Yet, rather than resort to the self-destructive denial and violence we see in Lowell, Olson, and Dugan, Roethke is rather wistful and apologetic about his confusing double nature. "Loved heart," he asks, "what can I say?" Once, as a lark, he sang; as a worm he devoured and his heart denied any affirmation of his soul, but still he wondered,

> The pond lapses back into a glassy silence.
> The cause of God in me—has it gone?
> Do these bones live? Can I live with these bones? (50–52)

Roethke puzzles over the material and spiritual foundations of perfection—"the cause of God in me"—while hungering for some kind of intimate connectedness with a First Cause. Do all things material go their own way, do they lapse into "silence," including streams, the pond, his own bones? He ponders his own spiritual essence: did it betray him when his rational mind delivered him into confusion and denied him purity and perfection? From Roethke's point of view, the manifestations of God are somehow implausible, and life itself is something daft, sluggish, and terrifying. Consequently, he is left with only shadows, the circular impression of sense and materiality, the passions of the worm, and the irredeemable wound of love. In this case, the barest expression of any kind of truth is thus inherently flawed and transient.

Another of Roethke's poems "In Evening Air," describes the conflicts inherent in man's carnal-spiritual duality. He asks, "Make me, O Lord, a lasting, simple thing" that exceeds time's irrepressible movement. How can this not be possible, for,

Once, I transcended time:
A bud broke to a rose,
And I rose from a last diminishing. (10–12)

Roethke hungers for the intimate and minute—perhaps even the commonplace. In a line echoing Edward Taylor's "Huswifery"—"Make me, O Lord, thy Spin[n]ing Wheele compleate,"[4] Roethke's petition confesses his need to simplify and to endure, but the dual nature of his invocation reveals its contradictory focus. In his thirst for immortality, he yearns for both simplicity and grandiosity. He would be as God, but he is not God. Thus, he is compelled to deny the impending darkness that must invariably accrue from spiritual doubt, as if it were possible to discover grace only in stolen moments—if even then. Roethke's perspective is not unlike that of Charles Olson, who confessed that he "had to learn the simplest things last" (maximus, to Himself," 1). Indeed having cynically damned himself and damned his mother, he concluded that he could die since he had just "begun to live" "moonset, Gloucester, December 1, 1957, 1:58 AM").

As long as writers such as Alan Dugan, Charles Olson, Theodore Roethke, Edwin Arlington Robinson, Hart Crane, Robert Lowell, Edna St. Vincent Millay, and John Berryman—all of whom were problem drinkers—continue to write about issues of religious belief and the rigors of trying to understand man's relationship to a higher power, they will likely depict a series of catastrophic, crises-driven, emotional, and intellectual conflicts. As a result, their writing is a powerful and enduring record of the alcoholic fascination with appropriating Divine sanctions for some kind of personal agenda or self-indulgent obsession. Most alcoholic writers feel that there is an intimate connection between creativity and spirituality; and, in claiming to apprehend more than the immediate and apparent, they hope to discover some means of re-creation that will provide them with an extraordinary measure of spiritual control—in other words, they aspire to control the will of God. Thus, for all its contradictions, their poetry stands as a paradoxical record of the hesitation, self-obsession, and intensity of the alcoholic's spiritual hunger and his appetite for apprehending some kind of personal meaning that exceeds mere appearances. In that regard, it is a memorable testimony, not only to the human need for some higher meaning and purpose that exceeds that apparent transience of things but also to the unique texture of that need when it is interwoven with the distorted perceptions of the addicted person.

Chapter Four

John Berryman's "Phase Four" and His Precarious Attempt to Find a Compromise between Drunkenness, Sobriety, and the A.A. Twelve Step Program of Recovery

John Berryman's inability to grasp the A.A. program of recovery may appear somewhat baffling, especially when we consider his remarkable intelligence, the horrific consequences of his drinking, and his apparent, ongoing involvement in the A.A. Twelve Step program of recovery. However, a careful analysis of "Phase Four" may help to explain his difficulties in maintaining any semblance of normality, as well as his interest in compromising A.A., his misunderstanding of the Twelve Step focus, and his apparent inability to deal honestly and uncompromisingly with his alcoholism.

The fact that Berryman wrote the poem shortly before his suicide cannot be overlooked in developing any legitimate explication, but this should not exclude other considerations. Indeed, the very presence of this dramatic element may further confuse any analysis of Berryman's perspective because it is tempting to circumscribe an interpretation with a host of biographical issues that may or may not provide some kind of insight into the poet's thinking, most especially as they are reflected in the basic thrust of the piece. Finally, since the poem appears to focus on certain aspects of the A.A. Twelve Step program, I would presume that some understanding of A.A. principles is essential in developing a valid explication.

The poem deals essentially with the process of "bottoming out" and the crucial first three steps of the A.A. Twelve Step program. The program is commonly perceived in three increments: admission of the drinking problem and the decision to seek recovery (steps 1–3); activity focused on reintegration of the candidate into society with particular emphasis on truth-telling, a personal inventory, a relationship with a higher power, and amends (steps 4–9); and the maintenance of sobriety by putting three basic principles into action: the taking of a daily, personal inventory; a conscious effort focused on spiritual fitness and a closer relationship with a Higher Power; and philanthropic community service with regard to other alcoholics (steps 10–12).[1]

The first three steps are commonly regarded as the gateway to recovery and serve as a foundation for the remaining nine steps. Essentially, they involve an admission of helplessness with alcohol, recognition of the insanity of one's behavior, and a decision to seek the benevolent guidance of God as the candidate understands him.[2]

In explicating "Phase Four," it should be understood that the first three steps of A.A. do not include the act of "bottoming out," even though this particular event is a necessary predeterminant of an alcoholic's commitment to recovery. However, in writing "Phase Four," Berryman was very likely concerned with both the "bottoming out" phase and at least the first three steps; and there can be little doubt that he knew that these four stages were critical precursors to sobriety—at least according to the A.A. model. Thus, while Berryman may have ultimately hoped for some kind of amendment to suit his own particular perspective, he also very likely understood the inherent difficulty of adopting such a position, especially since it would have compromised A.A.'s tenets.

Berryman's drinking very likely became problematic some time around 1947, when he first admitted that he was beginning to have difficulties with alcohol. Ten years later, in 1959, he was admitted to Regent Hospital in New York because of alcohol and stress. In 1967, he was admitted to Abbot Hospital for the same problems; but the heavy drinking persisted following his release, and his longest period of sobriety lasted only from September to December of 1968.[3] In November of 1969, he was admitted to Hazeldon, a well-known alcohol treatment center in

Minneapolis, where he was diagnosed with "chronic severe alcoholism" (Haffenden 357). A student who knew Berryman at the University of Minnesota and who was an orderly the night the poet was admitted recalled being surprised that,

> such a man of wit and genius could be so incredibly broken down and so ordinarily intoxicated....I went through the usual admitting procedure. His beard at the time was untrimmed and shaggy, his eyes hollowed out, and there were large blisters on his hands from wayward cigarettes. He trembled a bit, and talked incessantly. He was still quite intoxicated. (Haffenden 365)

It was at this time that Berryman began working with A.A., although he later admitted having "conned" his way through the First Step, which he regarded as "merely circumstantial" (Haffenden 374). Still, he continued with the program and even attempted a Second Step because of an apocalyptic experience with a Reverend Jim Zosel (Haffenden 370). We are also told that he even worked work a Fifth Step with the encouragement of a Reverend William J. Nolan (Haffenden 372). It was at this time that he thought about abandoning his Roman Catholic faith to become Jewish, but nothing came of the idea.

After his release from Hazeldon, Berryman sought weekly counseling for his drinking and marital problems, but his efforts apparently proved ineffective; and he was readmitted to Abbot Hospital in 1969. A year later, in 1970, he was admitted to the alcohol rehabilitation center at St. Mary's Hospital in Minneapolis. He continued with A.A. after his release and proudly earned his sobriety coins, even going so far as to attend weekly A.A. meetings at Stillwater Prison with other members of the St. Mary's group (Haffenden 408). He suffered a series of relapses during the next year and a half; and on Friday, January 6, 1972, he ended his life by jumping from a bridge high above the Mississippi River.

The vocabulary and focus of "Phase Four," which was very likely one of his last poems, tell us a good deal about Berryman's frustration and his concerns about A.A's tenets regarding acceptance, serenity, truth-telling, compliance, and surrender.

Such struggles are commonplace among recovering alcoholics, even though they are integral with the nomenclature of the A.A. program.

In writing "Phase Four," Berryman establishes a set of propositions whose balance is so precarious as to appear almost irreconcilable. As such, the poem appears to serve as a qualified endorsement of the A.A. program, a rejection of certain of its principles, and a petition for understanding. He speaks of his battle with alcohol as being half lost *and* half won (2), as if some kind of partial commitment to A.A. might be sufficient. Berryman was no doubt familiar with the A.A.'s primary text, *Alcoholics Anonymous*, which makes it clear that the candidate must be willing to "go to any length" to attain sobriety and that anything less than total compliance will probably lead to failure. As Bill Wilson, the co-author of the book and cofounder of Alcoholics Anonymous, writes, "Half measures availed...nothing" (59). Wilson's concern about the pointlessness of half measures has served as a cornerstone for many of the values and perspectives of A.A.— indeed, for many recovering alcoholics, it serves as a categorical absolute because it establishes an uncompromising perspective on the maintenance of sobriety and the integrity of A.A.'s Twelve Step method. Thus, in presuming he had "won" in any degree, regardless of whether it was in halves or increments of some sort, Berryman was probably hoping to find some way of compromising A.A.'s program, and—in so doing—he may well have condemned himself to failure before the fact. Certainly, because of his familiarity with the twelve steps and the A.A. text, we should not be surprised at his use of the word, "half," but it is interesting to note his corruption of the term and his attempt to appropriate its meaning to his own purposes. In this particular case, "acceptance," "lost," "half," and "battle" are perceived in contexts that A.A. would doubtless never endorse.

Berryman also appears somewhat confused because he starts the poem at the "end." This is a common tactic among many newly recovering alcoholics who may be tempted to "two-step" the A.A. Twelve Step Program.[4] Such whimsical selectivity cannot, and will not, work. Most alcoholics who have been able to follow an effective program of recovery would agree that anyone who wants to attain sobriety can only begin at the beginning and rigorously follow the program step by step in the order given, regardless of personal prejudices, fears, or selfish inclinations. By "beginning"—to use Berryman's own word—at the "fourth" phase instead of the "first," be it only in his poem, he may well have provided some evidence that he was self-condemned to defeat before the fact. The word, "surrender," the fourth and final phase as Berryman calls it, is predicated on "Acceptance." And this is his sticking point because he assumes that it can only be "known in Heaven" (3–4).

Berryman would also have known that A.A. believes that sobriety can only be founded on an admission of powerlessness over alcohol, the crucial first step in the A.A. program of recovery. He may have felt that he could somehow control his drinking or that he could recover from alcohol dependence in his own way, and this may have been his nemesis. Also, in writing about being "final," he may have anticipated his own death, especially because the word "Heaven" is found only two lines later.

In considering the implications of the poem's vocabulary, the word, "surrender," is not as difficult to understand as Berryman would suggest. As a still suffering alcoholic, he had already been compelled to surrender to his addiction anyway. That "surrender" might well have been extended to a submission to "life" without alcohol, which involves a willingness to defer to the sanity inherent in a positive relationship to a higher power *of his own choosing.* In Berryman's case, however, it appears that he devised a cunning method for circumventing the spiritual tenets of the Twelve Step approach, a common strategy of alcoholics who are terrified by the prospect of living without liquor.

It should be understood that the Second Step, which precedes Berryman's "surrender," is actually not an imperative action that is taken by the alcoholic; rather, it involves a redemptive spiritual relationship that happens *to* him. *Alcoholics Anonymous* makes this very clear in stating that the recovering alcoholic "Came to believe that a power greater than ourselves [*sic*] could restore us to sanity" (59). Thus, the Second Step is not so obviously a "phase" in the alcoholic's history as a moment of grace leading to Step Three. Berryman also misconstrues the Third Step. It stipulates that the alcoholic commit his life and his will over to the care of God *as he understands Him.* This step is necessarily the fourth "phase" in an alcoholic's history as Berryman describes it, but the poem makes it clear that this "phase" or step is his sticking point. Perhaps he was unable to make the critical spiritual decision involved in this step because the God he appears to describe could not be trusted, grasped, or understood by his "finite" perception. In his intellectual rigor, he appears to have felt that surrender to such uncertainty was untenable. The higher power he does describe is a God of laurels, lawns, and lakes, a God whose sacristy was so banal as to be meaningless. This explains the title of the poem and Berryman's four phases: bottoming out, admission, acceptance, and surrender.[5] It should be realized that A.A.'s first three steps do not describe the process of awareness and bottoming out, since they are the necessary but destructive predeterminants of an alcoholic's commitment to a program of recovery; and A.A.'s twelve step program is focused *only* on recovery. In any case, the surrender that comes with the Third Step is articulated by Berryman in catastrophic terms, because it is perceived as a surrender of self; and for Berryman, this apparently meant a living death. He is thus restricted by his inability or, perhaps, his unwillingness to understand the possibilities of spiritual recovery described by A.A.

Berryman has also confounded himself in lexicon. He writes that he cannot understand the "word," "Surrender," which is preceded by "acceptance," and is itself perceived as a "thing"; but his skewed perceptions and skewed vocabulary, like his life, disrupt any possibility of following the A.A. program with any consistency, and this undermines his prospects for recovery. The A.A. First Step, that life had become unmanageable because the candidate was powerless over alcohol, is thus discounted through lexicon, argumentation, and subordination. At the same time, "surrender" is paradoxically inflated to an impossible dimension known only "in Heaven," while "Acceptance" is perceived in the context of a "finite" struggle and "infinite" aid. But, here again, Berryman both understands and limits his perceptions. The "Serenity Prayer," a critical element in any A.A. meeting or program, petitions God to *help* the candidate accept what cannot be changed (see note 6 for the complete prayer). As such, the prayer is a petition that God grant serenity so that one might accept the fact of alcoholic dependence and acknowledge powerlessness in all matters external to the self (including, of course, alcohol) and in most matters involving the self. Such a petition is a hard order, but it is an honest admission of one's personal limitations and addictive compliance.

Berryman is thus entangled in a pointless, finite struggle. He pleads remembrance by those who have attained sobriety, but his petition to these less "defiant" souls appears derisive:

> if after finite struggle, infinite aid,
> ever you come there, friend,
> remember backward me lost in defiance. (5–7)

Berryman seems to equate his defiance with the high-flown dramatics of characters like Faust, who wagered with the devil, or Ahab in *Moby Dick,* who shook his fist in defiance at the Almighty and was struck by lightning for his arrogance. It is, perhaps, the ultimate alcoholic fantasy: to usurp the prerogatives of both God and Satan.

Berryman also insists that his resistance is his "Weapon One" of self-preservation. Yet, that "Weapon," his bottle, his intellect, his defiance, is suicidal, as he oscillates between the pronouns "I" and "we" and tries to generalize about the human condition while admitting his confusion and unmitigated resistance to recovery. When he writes, "We cannot tell the truth, it's not in us" (9), who is the "We"? Is it the unrecovered alcoholic? Berryman's "other" self? Humanity in general? Those who cannot or will not surrender? Berryman is not clear. Certainly, he would have recognized the implicit relationship between truth-telling, acceptance, and surrender, simply because the fearless inventory required in Step Four of the A.A. program requires uncompromising honesty (it is common knowledge among A.A. veterans that a person who does not undertake an honest and fearless Fourth Step is likely to go out and drink again). For the alcoholic, habituated as he is to lying, denial, grandiose fantasies of self, and hypocritical postures, the truth "comes hard," but it is absolutely essential. Although Berryman appears to resist a Twelve Step inventory, which would be his "phase five," he is wrong to suppose that it is not possible to tell the truth because it "is not in us" (unless, of course, he is speaking of himself). Thus, in establishing himself as "half" lost and "half" won, Berryman appears to equivocate between life and death in the same manner that he equivocates between sobriety and drunkenness.

Berryman seems to have presumed that the only acceptable means of dealing with his sickness was an obsessive preoccupation with the limits of his own resources. He apparently was determined to sober up *his* own way (despite his history of failure), to follow the A.A. program selectively (and perhaps hypocritically), and to become himself a weapon "one" against himself. He seems to be saying that he chooses to win his battle with liquor on his terms only, but those terms necessarily require his own death—a kind of "half" victory in which he would be sober but dead. The other half of the equation would denigrate the prospect of sobriety to a form of death-in-life, which he probably considered equally unpalatable.

In the final lines of the poem, Berryman describes the "rest" who have attained sobriety through the A.A. program. His description of "rest" echoes the pun of George Herbert's in his poem, "The Pulley." In Herbert's classic poem, God denies man any "rest" by not pouring the "rest" of the cup of blessings as a portion of his divine inheritance. Like Herbert's "cup" nearly four hundred years earlier, Berryman's cup of "blessing" is void of "rest." This includes the "rest" of the A.A. program of recovery, perceived obligingly as including the serenity that he coveted, but which would probably have only been possible through an uncompromising surrender to God's will.[6] It appears, then, that Berryman feared that sobriety was a resignation to inertia, comatose mildness, and mind-numbing submission. But neither A.A. nor Herbert had such a penal resignation in mind. A program of sobriety cannot be based on a reclusive sacristy that denies involvement in the life process, and it cannot be founded on laurels. Certainly, the two "stands" of laurel that he describes might foreshadow some kind of grace which constitutes a form of "rest" for those who are "blessed" in sobriety.[7] However, Berryman appears to have rejected this "blessed" state in life; indeed, one wonders whether the laurel he coveted had any significance at all—except in his own fantasies, because it was compromised by a refusal to affirm the sobriety promised by A.A. Similarly, his reference to the "sacristy"—that place where the sacred vessels are kept—appears to have a direct connection to the sacramental wines, now reserved for the chosen few and denied those who are perceived as "blessed" and "mild" (and sober?!) in their humble reception of the sacristy.

Despite all that he professed in his earlier poetry, Berryman never seems to have been able to manifest Step Two and believe in a power *truly* greater than himself, so he self-destructed through alcohol and apparently accepted death as his delivery and salvation. Although he gives every indication that he believed otherwise, it appears that Berryman could not acknowledge that he was not surrendering his humanity, but his inhumanity. Surrender was thus perceived as some kind of covert degradation of his intellectual freedom, his integrity as a poet, and his connectedness to life itself. That he accepted and chose to be defeated by alcohol rather than surrender and offer up his own "demons" testifies to the insanity, albeit creative, of alcoholism. Finally, that he defiantly refused to surrender to life and to spiritual wellness is also tragic; for it imprisoned him in the drunkenness and alcoholic dependence that may have presaged his own suicide.

Chapter Five

The Grand Illusion: Evasion, Survival, and Self-Hate

What is better than leaving a bar
In the middle of the afternoon
...You can stare up at the whole sky:
It's blue and white and does not
stare back at you like the bar mirror.
　　　　　　—Alan Dugan, "Swing Shift Blues," 1–5, 8–10.

Alcoholics cannot distinguish fantasy from reality. They are easily frustrated by setbacks and disappointments; and they are, perhaps, the ultimate risk-takers—the speeders, spenders, fighters, voyeurs, adulterers, power-junkies—who minimize the consequences of their dunderheaded recklessness with nonsensical excuses and a puzzling complex of self-hate and evasion. It is a strangely confusing prospect, a patchwork of Jekyll and Hyde behaviors that are predicated on a paradoxical mix of powerlessness, control, and self-punishment.

In "Long Live the Weeds," Theodore Roethke claims that the pleasure of getting drunk in a "vegetable realm" of humanity is sufficient to justify his creative association with the dregs of society because it is "undefiled" and is thus a perfect setting for unrestricted personal growth. But his argument makes no sense. The scurrilous "purity" he seeks is a contradiction in terms; and, while he drinks and matches wits with the rough and rugged edge of humanity, his opportunities for true companionship and honest growth are doubtful at best. In fact, one cannot help but wonder if Roethke is indulging in a certain amount of egalitarian posturing. While he claims that he has been shaped by "toil" and condemned by "All things unholy," his oblique reference to the Fall and his love of "weeds," wickedness, liquor, and "bitter rock" suggests a certain amount of hyperbolic negativity where his opportunities to hope and love and create in uncontaminated freedom are dubious at best.[1]

The problem of survival and freedom involves an entirely different perspective in Roethke's poem "The Waking." Here, the poet describes his daily, cautionary routine in a villanelle that is remarkable as much for its structure as for its exceptional message. With extraordinary genius, Roethke writes of his precarious emotional footing as he tries to reconcile the contradictions of fate and necessity that lie at the very core of his fears. He writes, "I wake to sleep, and take my waking slow," (1) as he goes where he must go, and carefully learns of life and necessity as he plods through the day. He writes, "We think by feeling.../I hear my being dance from ear to ear" (4–5). Here, in a tacit recognition of the alcoholic difficulty of living only twenty-four hours at a time, he realizes that his fears are distorted and indeterminate; that is, he acknowledges that truth is more visceral than intellectual; but, in dealing with his condition and the necessity of recognizing what he cannot change, he is also suggesting that he is exactly where he is supposed to be, which is *in* the moment, even as he is going exactly where he is *supposed* to go. To deal with larger increments of time would be catastrophic because a great deal of what he must learn must be stoically experienced in the course of day-to-day living and will not be disclosed on command or through wishful thinking.

Roethke also says that he "thinks" by feeling. Considering his position, such an assertion would appear to contradict all common sense. What he appears to suggest, however, is that he is overwhelmed and confused by a myriad of unfounded fears, all of which assert themselves in a complicated host of evasions. Emotions contaminated by alcohol have very little legitimacy; but, as Roethke suggests, (in sobriety?) we think by feeling; that is, if we recognize the power of honest and uncontaminated visceral truth as a register of what is actually happening, we are likely to move through our fears which will then "fall away."

The shaking Roethke describes may well be the effects of medication for manic depression or the d.t.'s, or it may have something to do with a relapse. At the same time, the "steady" he describes may mean steady in *resolve*. However, he seems to recognize that it is possible to put the past—with all of its unsteadiness and all of its fears—behind him, even though what is discarded—his prohibitive emotional baggage and his pointless fears—will never be entirely dismantled.

Nonconformity, social ostracism, and anger are the hallmarks of a great deal of alcoholic thinking; and it should come as no surprise that Sherwood Anderson created a population of misanthropic outcasts and oddities in his Winesburg, Ohio, while Edwin Arlington Robinson devised an entire community of misplaced and forgotten souls in his Tilbury Town. And we are reminded again of the menagerie of confused and eccentric oddities in the plays of Tennessee Williams and the alien assortment of conflicted humanity in Faulkner's saga of Yoknapatawpha County. We have also seen how John Berryman elected to rearrange his psychological landscape by creating a three dimensional alter ego by the name of "Henry Pussycat," who was probably a confessional persona that allowed him to deflect attention from his problems with alcohol, while Hart Crane devised a host of nonconformist alter egos and romantic illusions that served to protect him from the discomforts of intolerance and misunderstanding.

In just about every case, these writers created a world of self-destructive neurotics, perhaps because it helped to exonerate them from having to deal with their own pain, and it minimized their responsibility in recognizing the hateful consequences of their behavior. Yet, there were times when their defenses failed, and they were compelled to admit their preoccupation with the degradations of mediocrity and their obsession with self-mortification. In "Sonnets to Chris, number 88," Berryman writes, "—who am I? a scum" (6). Edwin Arlington Robinson's dementia and self-degradation are embellished by his expert use of description and his linguistic perfectionism and poetic genius, but his meaning is much the same. Certainly, his invective is scarcely less degrading. He writes of the persona, Fernando

Nash, in "The Man Who Died Twice," referring to him as a,

> crapulous and overgrown sick lump
> Of failure and premeditated ruin,
> What do you think you are—one of God's jokes?
> You slunk away from him, still adequate
> For his immortal service, and you failed him;
> And you knew all the while what you were doing.
> You damned yourself while you were still alive.
> You bulk of nothing, what do you say to that? (365–372)

Robinson expresses the penultimate damnation of human kind: Nash, a kind of "everyman," is cursed in the extreme. Human endeavor is essentially ruinous, damned, and worthless; and man—in this case, the generic Nash—is "a pitiful, paramount whale of lust and drunkenness,...a thing that was" (373–374). Robinson asks, "what do you say to that?" The question and the allegations are universal; the insinuation demonic. In a similar manner, Allen Ginsberg inventories a host of resentments and missed connections and disconnections in "My Alba." In this particular case, he writes of his artistic renunciation of self and the five fatuous years working in Manhattan "without a dime in the bank" where he had little (27) to show for it and was "damned to Hell" (31). The poem is a cynical rebuttal to the Manhattan of Walt Whitman with no songs of self or patriotic cadences in praise of industry, hard work, or humanity. For Ginsberg, the heavy-handed labors of his commercial sellout have been fruitless and mechanistic; and, like Roethke, Berryman, and Robinson, he curses profit, conformity, social etiquette, and whoever "drank my blood bank/innocent evil now" (21–22).

Hart Crane favored a more romantic perspective in describing self-destruction and the sellout to delusion and alcoholic oblivion. In "To the Cloud Juggler," he wrote of a smuggler, a "rum-giver," who slid ashore by moonlight and provided,

> quarts to faithfuls—surely smuggled home—
> As you raise temples fresh from basking foam. (11–12)

Crane rhapsodizes about the fantastic elements of personal deception; and from his perspective, the business of "smuggling" and deliverance comprises a wondrous panacea. But he unwittingly alludes to the liquor's capacity to assert oblivion by equating it with drowning; and he perceives the "rum-giver" as a peculiar god of sorts and the creator of divine trances, but his imagery is larded with escapist fantasies, questionable "pleasantries," and "smuggled" dreams.

In the realm of fiction, Ernest Hemingway was a good deal more hard-boiled than Ginsberg, Robinson, Berryman, or Crane. He rarely wrote a novel in which he did not kill off the major character and a sizable portion of the supporting cast, perhaps if only to purge himself of the missteps and mistakes of his own life. F. Scott Fitzgerald, whose life was a phantasmagoria of parties, regrets, and tattered memories, was almost addicted to the practice of killing off his protagonists, male and female alike, while Tennessee Williams, Jack London, and Eugene O'Neill had a remarkable sense of the pathetic and hopeless in the all-too-frequent demise of their major characters, who confronted a naturalistic world of such extraordinary fatalism that it could only lead to failure.

Such rigidity, regardless of whether it is sleep or suicide, is well expressed in Edwin Arlington Robinson's "Octave XV." Here, frustration and fear subvert the poet's inability to adapt and change. He clings to old habits where he can rehash old deceits and remember the ruins of old, lost opportunities, and outworn insults. But he refuses to seek outside help. From an alcoholic perspective—and for Robinson—there is considerable profit in martyrdom. But fear lies at the core of his thinking, and the intimate bedfellow of fear is anger. Like Berryman's "Henry," Robinson's persona is resigned to the enumeration of past ills and wrongs and the rehashing of old achievements. Thus, Robinson insists that we "lack courage to live our lives" (1), even as we are too changeable to accept the old and proven ways and the wonders of the past or "consecrate the magic of dead things,/And yieldingly to linger by long walls/Of ruin" (4–6).

A somewhat different perspective on the alcoholic strategy of movement and evasion is presented by Hart Crane. In "Chaplinesque," he describes the precarious balance of those who totter between catastrophe and tenderness; and—like the

infamous little tramp of the actor-comedian, Charlie Chaplin—
sidestep the puckered thumb of doom. Perhaps the more agile
may even pirouette Chaplin-like; and, for an instant, evade
annihilation and "all else but the heart:/What blame to us if
the heart live on" (17–18). Like Robinson, Crane provides a
remarkable description of alcoholic tenderness, but he also
shows how that tenderness can be mated to lies and evasions.
He is not just concerned with man's grotesque absorption in
blithely evading some kind of demonic self-destruction from
above. Rather, he insists that the "Chaplinesque" dance and
nimble sidestepping will accrue in a protective act *and* gesture.
It may even disclose a universal truth. He writes, "And yet
these fine collapses are not lies/More than the pirouettes of any
pliant cane" (13–14). In "Chaplinesque," a promise of tender
and humane survival is imminent. But, like John Berryman's
"Henry," who paces, coughs, and drinks, the "Chaplinesque"
acrobatics cannot defeat the impositions of circumstance, and
fate cannot ultimately be denied. However, Crane does suggest
that, while the intellect is self-serving, the heart persists in telling the truth because memory cannot be thrashed into conformity with desire.[2]

  This perspective is not uncommon from the alcoholic point
of view. In "The Dead Village," Robinson writes,

> And over the forgotten place there clings
> The strange and unrememberable light
> That is in dreams. The music failed, and then
> God frowned, and shut the village from His sight. (11–14)

Here, dream and reality seem irreconcilable; beauty fails; the
light clings—and with the light, desire. But if any hope is generated, it is so vague and indiscernible as to be lost and forgotten
in a macabre setting of failure and darkness.

  In "Idyll," Roethke focuses on the sublimation of that dim
border between light and darkness, sleep and terror, oratory
and weaponry. In this case, the borderline preoccupation with
precarious balances finds its ultimate rejection in an image of
pathetic alienation as "A drunk man stumbles by, absorbed in
self-talk" (2). And yet, like the drunk and like the balance of

light and dark and sleep and horror, the maintenance of any sustenance insists on a perilous equilibrium between God and mortality. In "The Abyss," Roethke wonders about the gravity of human progress and redemption. Do we gradually move closer to God or simply move irrevocably to some other condition. He writes,

> I rock between dark and dark,
> My soul nearly my own,
> My dead selves singing. (78–80)

This attempt to maintain some kind of balance between the immediate and the eternal is equivocated in a metaphor of evasion where the perilous equilibrium of the "idyll" has been compromised by a resignation to morbidity and an alcoholic preoccupation with despair and hopelessness.

For the guilt-ridden alcoholic, then, an incoherent strategy of self-sabotage is perceived as the only relief from the burden of self-hate, control, imperfection, and hopelessness.

The A.A. text, *Twelve Steps and Twelve Traditions*, provides a first-rate description of the consequences of these strategies. It also provides a clear understanding of the role played by the alcoholic preoccupation with self-sufficiency, grandiosity, alienation, and betrayal:

> We are certain that our intelligence, backed by willpower, can rightly control our inner lives and guarantee us success in the world we live in. This brave philosophy, wherein each man plays God, sounds good in the speaking, but it still has to meet the acid test: how well does it actually work? One good look in the mirror ought to be answer enough for any alcoholic.
>
> Should his own image in the mirror be too awful to contemplate (and it usually is), he might first take a look at the results normal people are getting from self-sufficiency. Everywhere he sees people filled with anger and fear, society breaking up into warring fragments. Each fragment says to the other, "We are right and you are wrong." Every such pressure group, if it is strong enough, self-righteously imposes its will upon the rest. And everywhere the same thing is being done on an individual basis. The sum of all this mighty effort is less peace and less brotherhood than before. The philosophy of self-sufficiency is not paying off. Plainly enough, it is a bone-crushing juggernaut whose final achievement is ruin. (37)

Thus, in trying to manipulate the world to conform to his distorted perspective, the alcoholic tries to deny that he has any legitimate responsibility to the human community. Instead, he is self-elevated to the status of a god-head, an evasive moral and ethical force of his own contrivance whose misanthropic strategies have little regard for the sensibilities and integrity of others, but whose very foundation is based on evasion, self-justification, self hate, and denial.

Chapter Six

The Alcoholic Isolation and Fall to Self-Destruction in Edwin Arlington Robinson's "Mr. Flood's Party"

Edwin Arlington Robinson's "Mr. Flood's Party" has enchanted and delighted readers of poetry for decades. Perhaps its appeal lies in its poignant descriptions of the pains and frustrations of getting older; perhaps it has something to do with the poem's remarkable viscerality; perhaps the poem is appreciated simply because it describes a rather sentimental interlude in the life of a lonely old bachelor who gets thoroughly soused while trudging home. I would suggest, however, that, while all these perspectives indicate a commendable appreciation for the piece, they do not take full account of its remarkable capacity to portray the overwhelming confusion that is integral with aging, alcoholism, and depression, most especially as that confusion has a direct relationship to the A.A. model of disease and addiction. In this regard, perhaps a detailed socio-critical explication might help us to appreciate the poem's genius even further. At the same time, such an approach might also provide a more comprehensive perspective on the crippling effects of long-term, abusive drinking among senior citizens.[1]

As the poem begins, it is late and a rather scholarly old hermit named Eben Flood has gone to town to fill his jug and is now making his way home. Eben is a disheveled and somewhat eccentric fellow; and, as we get to know him further, it becomes evident that his intoxication and solitary circumstance are a natural consequence of the painful relationship between alcoholism and aging, abandonment, and loneliness. In fact, it appears that Eben has come to the somewhat hasty conclusion that his chosen mission in life is to despair, to isolate himself, and to contemplate his lonely and rather curious situation—and to drink.

On the particular evening that we meet him, he is in no great hurry to get back to his hermitage; and, indeed, as he trudges up the road, he is delayed even further when he stops unexpectedly and looks warily around. At first, this is something of a mystery; but it quickly becomes evident that the old fellow is planning on taking a private a nip from his jug and carrying on just a bit. We should not be surprised, then, if he is strangely self-conscious, because he has probably been thinking for some time about taking that drink—though, judging by his behavior, he has already had a good many other drinks farther back down the road. In any case, we may assume that the old man is concerned that someone might have seen him take those early drinks and take another before that; and, therefore, he would most certainly be concerned that someone might be watching him now as well.

Perhaps this kind of thinking might seem rather odd and paranoid; but, since he is already quite bibulous and, since (as we are soon to discover) he does indeed have a drinking problem, we should not be surprised that the old fellow would not want anyone to measure his intake—that is simply a very natural part of the alcoholic mind set.

We might also note that when Eben pauses, he is neither in the village nor at home. He is between places, both metaphorically and literally; so that he is really nowhere, rather as if suspended in a kind of limbo between life and death as well as between society and the hermitage. This is suggested obliquely in Eben's ascent to his lonely hermitage away from the village where there might be some kind of balance between the heavens above and mortal life below. In living above the town, then old Eben has figuratively stationed himself above all earthly affairs, both egotistically and physically; and his painful upward trek to his mountain hut suggests a literal determination to distance himself from humanity in a concerted withdrawal from society and the companionship of Tillbury Town where he had gone to fill his jug.[2]

And so Eben begins to talk to himself and proposes a drink to himself and reminisces about himself to himself and insists on another drink to himself. While there is a certain humor underlying all his self-talk, one also wonders if perhaps the old man drinks literally to his addiction and his dual Jekyll and Hyde nature. Except for the other duality implicit in the reflected light of the harvest moon, suggesting perhaps his own harvest of years, he appears caught, both literally and figuratively, in darkness and in confusion. This is particularly evident in his long hike down the road to fill a jug that will likely be nearly exhausted from drink after drink before he gets home. Like Sisyphus and his infamous stone, the old man pushes up the mountain, drinking as he goes, only to find that he must eventually return down the mountain to fill his jug, only to have to return back up the mountain, drinking as he goes, only to return again.

And so old Eben begins his speech, quoting a romantic poem, singing a maudlin song, and toasting himself as he goes along. To get just the right perspective on things, the old man paces away in the reflected light; extends his hand—a nice, dramatic gesture; transforms the roadway into a stage—as an intoxicant, he would love stages and a dramatic sense of things; and begins to talk to himself. The bird of time "is on the wing," the old man says. No doubt, he would know *The Rubaiyat* well. It would be a favorite poem for anyone who feels maudlin, bibacious, and scornful of consequences and the capriciousness of fate. Eben would be all too aware of the *carpe diem* perspective in FitzGerald's masterpiece, and he would be all too aware of its very direct reference to his own condition and his prospects for the future. Indeed, he seems to exhibit very little concern about consequences of all his tomorrows, except that, from his perspective, the only thing that can be held up to any kind of guiding light is his jug; and, as for his future, it leads invariably and unrelentingly to loneliness, emptiness, and death. That is not a pretty picture, and it apparently is reason enough to drink—at least for old Eben. And so, he addresses himself very politely—as if in the company of a special friend who is deserving of good manners and just the right protocol:

"Well, Mr. Flood, we have the harvest moon
Again, and we may not have many more;

The bird is on the wing, the poet says,
And you and I have said it here before,...." (9–12)

And so, having confessed to the pressures of the passage of time and previous occasions with his jug and his impending death—and having then toasted himself politely in the middle of the road, Eben argues with himself rather superficially about having another drink—and another. It is interesting to note that he feels that this urging to intoxication must be premised on a bit of old-fashioned etiquette, if only for the sake of civility. "Only a very little, Mr. Flood," (41) he chirps. Only we know that Flood has had a great deal more than a "very little" already, and, like his name in the *ebb* and flow of life, he is becoming *flooded* in liquor, even as his life *ebbs* away.

As it turns out, Eben has begun to feel rather maudlin about finalities and the harvest of years. Some readers will have no difficulty acknowledging the pains and disappointments of old age; but it is apparent that Robinson is not simply content to present a bathetic portrait of a lonely old man who does not have much longer to live. Rather, he has chosen to heighten our appreciation for the futility of Eben's circumstance by injecting a mock heroic element. With obvious tongue in cheek, the poet tells us that Eben is a shadowy compatriot of Roland's ghost; that like the tragic Roland, he too is a scarred and armored knight; that he too has managed to hold on, "as if enduring to the end" (17). This chivalric costuming of the old man, while sympathetic enough, is also fraught with overstatement and melodrama. In truth, of course, Eben could not possibly be a knightly shadow of Roland: his "end" involves no great "epic"; it embraces no chivalric battle. While he raises his jug to his mouth, it hardly resembles the silent, epic horn that Roland raised to his; nor is the old fellow engaged in princely combat for a sacred cause like his ghostly compatriot. Admittedly, his situation does indeed appear rather hopeless; and perhaps, as with Roland, it may be too late for much hope, but this is in an alcoholic sense, not from the standpoint of chivalric combat. In point of fact, while the old man is something of a gentleman and addresses himself to himself by his last name, he is no liege. He is only a tired and befuddled old intoxicant who has wrapped himself in such a haze of booze and melancholia that his thin "shield" of armor, such as it is, offers very little protection from the pains of a reality check or loneliness or the insults of aging.

And back down the road where he might find an element of sanity and fellowship in the common ground of humanity, we learn that the village has closed its doors and that Eben has become something of a pariah. He can expect no living welcome. Only its dead are perceived as offering a phantom salutation that "Rang thinly till old Eben's eyes were dim" (24). Old Flood might fancy that he is hearing a sentimental ovation. Considering his intoxication and his alcoholic tears, he would probably *love* a sentimental ovation—especially one that is rather morbid, for that is characteristic of the intoxicated perception. In truth, however, the phantom ovation–like the phantom ghost of Roland—is histrionic, a pathetic and rather sentimental hallucination that only confirms the old man's loneliness and the depths of his overcharged sentimentality.

Consider how Eben treats the jug he has gone so far to fill, for it is of no small importance to him. Robinson tells us that he lays it down, "as a mother lays her sleeping child" (25) and cradles it with a perverse tenderness, "knowing that most things break" (28).[3] We are reminded that Eben himself is cradled between life and death, even as he is cradled between the town and the upland hermitage. When Eben drinks, then, he is also setting himself "down." The jug is his "road," his harvest, his alcoholic bottom. For Eben, then, life, his circumstances, and his liquor are all much the same. They are connected irretrievably to his jug. No wonder that he treats it tenderly. It is his ultimate progeny and his final legacy.

And so the old fellow takes another drink, makes another speech, rationalizes a bit about the last time he got drunk in the middle of the road, and welcomes himself home, although he is really only in the middle of the road. And then, following one more drink, he closes his tender little party by singing "*For auld lang syne*"—to himself, although it is a song of fellowship. His choice of music is horrifically sentimental.

Burns' poem, appreciated by some, has more recently degen-
erated to a mawkish New Year's ditty and is perhaps best
endured by midnight celebrants who have three sheets to
the wind.

It is interesting to note that Eben's two moons do not seem
to bother him in the least. We may assume that he is quite
accustomed to double vision—proof positive of his stupendous
intake. In fact, the "lunacy" of the two moons is very likely
enjoyed in much the same way as he enjoys his two selves.[4]
Symbolically, they reflect perhaps the few or so odd remaining
years of Eben's own life; and, in that regard, they tell us a good
deal about the falsehood of the old man's life and fate and his
circumstance as an ambiguous and blurred reflection of opaque
reality, suggested obliquely in the blue light of the two orbs
above him.

The melancholy of the moment and the last notes of the song
provide a good reason—although he does not really need one
(but consistency is not one of Eben's virtues, anyway)—for
raising the jug once again, though regretfully, to the light. By
this time, the old man has become flooded—though he still
proceeds to argue again about how much he should drink as a
matter of propriety. We might remember, of course, that as a
man with a serious drinking problem who is already very
intoxicated, Eben does not really need a reason for drinking or
adding a bit more to his intake. It is likely that he has always
had a reason for drinking; and, it is likely that, were he to run
out of reasons—be it loneliness, old age, injuries, injustices—he
would probably drink anyway, because that is the nature of
alcoholism and that is the nature of abusive drinking.[5] And so
we are told that,

> He raised again the jug regretfully
> And shook his head, and was again alone.
> There was not much that was ahead of him,
> And there was nothing in the town below—... (51–54)

As the poem closes, the old man enters the final depressing
stages of drunkenness. His bleak shaking of the head affirms
his realization that nothing works, that he is entangled in a

hopeless, numbing world that leads nowhere, neither up nor down, and that, perhaps, as Shakespeare noted, his life has deteriorated into "a tale...signifying nothing." The poem's ending, then, stands in vivid opposition to the sentiment presented in the opening scene. This, then, is the old man's actual future–not fellowship or birds or booze or songs, but a fate that is bleak, hopeless, intoxicated, pointless.

In writing "Mr. Flood's Party," Robinson very likely described drunkenness as he has experienced it and as he personally understood it.[6] Whether he *meant* to describe a charming little party with a bleak ending or *meant* to describe a pathetic alcoholic with no future may not be the point. Consciously or not, Robinson has invited us into one of the most critical areas of the alcoholic mind, shown us its twisted perceptions, its self-destructiveness, its isolation, its denial, its insanity. In so doing, he has presented a richly textured, clinically accurate portrait of a man who is fast approaching the most destructive and hopeless stage of his disease.

Eben and people like Eben are frightened. They are frightened of themselves, frightened of lost hopes and dreams, frightened of the onset of time, and frightened of others. Their perceived solution is not to deal directly with their frailties and take a strenuous personal inventory; rather, they choose to define themselves in epic proportions, delude themselves with dreams of what might have been, and wrap themselves in the doubtful comfort of an alcoholic stupor.[7] This is the real Eben Flood. He is not a delightful, tipsy old pilgrim as some critics would have us believe. He is a very sick, old man who is surely dying and who refuses to put a stop to his horrible program of self-destruction.

This, then, is the ultimate tragedy of Eben Flood; and, in that regard, Robinson's poem presents a terrifying and heart-breaking profile of the social and emotional consequences of a lifetime of alcoholic abuse, alcoholic denial, and alcoholic withdrawal. That, if for no other reason, makes the poem remarkable and well worth reading.

Chapter Seven

Sex and Promiscuity: Conjugal Detachment and the Fear of Intimacy

> *Goodnight to the moonlight in brandy,*
> *Adieu to the warmth of the wine.*
> *I think I can finally stand me*
> *Without a glass or a stein.*
>
> —Barton Sutton, "Sober Song," 5–8.

Anyone who is crippled by the disease of alcoholism is not likely to have much sensitivity to the integrity of others. He consistently violates the most sacred boundaries of self-respect and decency; if he is dishonest with his friends, he is the worst of deceivers with his family; if he feels shame and overwhelming guilt, he projects that shame on his family with even greater force; and where he sees himself as worthless and shallow, he suspects those same qualities in those he pretends to love.

To the alcoholic, the most intimate of relationships are perceived as totally "other"; sex amounts to little more than a gymnastic exercise where a certain amount of detachment is perfectly acceptable; and longstanding concerns of a deeper texture are hatefully evaded.

Robert Creeley's "Ballad of the Despairing Husband" is a perfect example of conjugal hypocrisy, choked as it is with acid compliments, denials, adultery, and just plain stubbornness. The wife has fled the marital nest and left her reprobate husband "with hardly a damn thing on the shelf" (6). He tries to lure her back and pleads his case with some shaky oaths of fidelity and a transparent (short-term) commitment to love, civility, and decency. He even embroiders the deception with some shaky compliments on her feminine worth and a promise of fidelity, but she will have none of it. With typical alcoholic cynicism and no small amount of desperation, he goes on to pledge "love" for the poor little woman, "love" for his home, "love" for the children. It is only right that she come home quickly, and he trots out the standard apology—duly enunciated by all such conjugal libertines: he will turn over a new leaf; the other women did not mean a thing; and he loves only her. But she will serve herself, thank you; and she will wear what she chooses and dance with whom she chooses and catch whom she chooses. The shoe is on the other foot; but the narrator does not give up, switches tactics, and tries the penitent-humility game. He will, tolerate anything, swear to anything, and submit to anything; but the marital merry-go-round has come to a dead stop, and no number of pledges can save the day or change her mind. She's done with the charlatan, plain and simple. Besides, our drunken philanderer's hollow pledge is firmly illustrated in the final lines. Having vowed perfect behavior and a marital bond that is utterly devoid of self-interest, he backs down a half inch and concludes with a request for an exception—no doubt the first of innumerable exceptions: "Oh lady, grant me time,/please, to finish my rhyme" (48–49). And that is the substance of the philanderer's pledge: a rhyme, a limerick, a vacuous ditty.

It is common knowledge that continued alcohol abuse will lead invariably to sexual impotence. In an effort to recover their virility, a good many alcoholics—both male and female—will search out new sexual experiences with little regard for the consequences. Their predatory zeal may provide a momentary respite from the loss of virility, but it is incredibly short-lived and self-defeating. Sexual campaigns dominated by personal anxieties, a search for novelty, physical deterioration, paranoia, and drunkenness are condemned to failure before the fact. Indeed, because of their astounding self-obsession and their inability to find any degree of connectedness with others, most alcoholics are simply incapable of transcending the emotional and physical barriers that constitute the very essence of their disease. Thus, no aggregate of codependent lovers, innovative partners, or erotic techniques can possibly assure a renewal of sexual potency; and no amount of liquor can salvage a drunken confabulation, no matter how strange or perverse.

In "Drunks," a poem written when he was married to Kathleen Donahue, John Berryman describes the shenanigans of a tacky New Year's party where, having passed out, the poet-narrator was stowed on the hostess's bed with two other inebriates: his friend "H" and an impassioned blonde who was the wife of a critic and mistress of a local book club.[1] But no one—not the damsel, not "H," certainly not Berryman, is feeling particularly bookish or sexually competent at the moment; and the complications of putting it "in" and being "in" and, indeed, any chance for a cultured meeting *in* this odd assortment of minds and bodies seems to have been pretty much lost *in* the bottom of the last bottle. As might be expected, the sozzled little conclave ends in abysmal failure and embarrassment, which is just about all that can be expected when a couple of drunks end up on the same mattress with a bibulous female.

Most alcoholics have no real understanding of love; and, while they assume that they are capable of genuine tenderness, their passions are usually chemically induced and sexually reductive. In fact, there may be times when their relationships are sustained by little more than liquor and dunderheaded stubbornness. In "Love Song: I and Thou," Alan Dugan provides a hilarious perspective on the alcoholic tendency to equate screw-ups and masochism with true and eternal love and a compliant helpmate. In this piece, he admits that his miscalculations were conceived from an obsession with whisky, a love affair with rage, and a penchant for clumsiness. He tries to build a domestic love nest; but it is a mess; and he has only himself to blame, since he built the roof himself, the walls himself, the floors himself, and even got hung up in it himself.

Bowed but undefeated, our carpenter-poet managed to hammer himself into his domestic hovel and "danced with a purple thumb...drunk/with my prime whisky: rage" (13–15). Poor persona Dugan screams, screws, and pounds his scullery into a carpenter's nightmare; and while it may be "hell," our home builder-wrecker is not about to give up on his project. He has screwed his soul into the framework; and he will "live" in it, even if it kills him. Like so many alcoholics, he is incredibly pig-headed and unrelenting in his determination to complete the job and settle in, regardless of the pain or stupidity. He draws a humorous parallel between himself and The Carpenter, although his is a singular enterprise, requiring only a small amount of outside help. The sticking point in his project of enraged self-sufficiency centers on the fact that he can erect the scaffold on his own, he can get up on the cross and nail part of himself to it, but he cannot finish the job himself. Like so many alcoholics, he needs an *enabler*; and he pleads that his love, his helpmate, his wife, complete the execution and seal his martyr complex; and if she *really* loves him, she ought to grab a hammer, climb up there with him, and nail him *real good*.

Like most alcoholics, the alcohol dependent writer is likely to gauge relationships in terms of paybacks. This can generate a lot of resentment on the part of others, and it will most certainly amplify a writer's dissociation from society and provide fertile territory for the cultivation of distorted and conjugal resentments.

In his poem "Man and Wife," Robert Lowell complains that the marriage is finished; the fighting is over; and the abused and impetuous wife is no longer interested in her husband's salvation. Exhausted and burned out, she has withdrawn to her private sacristy and turned her back to grieve in silence. Lowell recalls the infuriating madness and homicidal drinking that once tore at the very fabric of their relationship and how they "outdrank the Rahvs in the heat/of Greenwich Village" (17–18). Braced by liquor, his emotions playing havoc with his heart, the young, poker-faced Lowell had passed out at the feet of his bride-to-be. The resulting "invective" was so furious that it "scorched the traditional South" (22); but somehow, perhaps miraculously, his pride was salvaged in his gift for words and his infernal capacity for liquor. For all the drinking and cursing, he still managed to marry the woman and gain access to the conjugal bed; but twelve years later, her "invective" has subsided to stony silence, and the relationship has degraded to a simple equation of endurance and private pain. The marriage bed is now a killing field, testifying only

E.E. Cummings describes the indiscriminate, indifferent, exploitation of women in quite another way in "it started when Bill's chip let on to"—and yet the theme of indifference and pain is much the same. Here, the woman is degraded to a lump of procreative plasma, where her orgasmic powers are used and discarded with abusive efficiency and paternity is reductive and biological. Cummings' female victim of fleshly necessity and carnal impulse is crudely shoved around like some kind of inert mass to service Eddie's penile interests. The immovable female is thus perceived as a subhuman hunk of breasts and hips—an indifferent and compliant toy who is prepared to spawn and please, but who has no human identity, except as a receptacle and a sensual propellant. This is the ultimate degradation of woman, for it both shames and dehumanizes.

The alcoholic writer and cynic, Dorothy Parker, provides a final note to these masquerades of commitment and to the cynical treatment, the lies, the pretended passion, and the indifference that separate the sexes. As Parker notes, by the time the lady swears that she is his, and he vows his undying love,

> Lady, make a note of this:
> One of you is lying.
> (Unfortunate Coincidence, 5–6)

With hilarious ingenuity and no small element of truth, Parker suggests that the chasm between the sexes cannot be bridged, simply because the hypocrisy, pretense, and theatrics stifle any real possibility for intimacy. The sexes are simply too far apart and too preoccupied with masquerading, with nailing each other for a trick or two, and with moving on to a new partner and new sexual adventures to find a common ground of tenderness and understanding. This, of course, is all the more likely where liquor fuels the differences, where power-centeredness and self-centeredness are the primary markers of a relationship, and where physicality is a surrogate for intimacy. As Delmore Schwartz insisted in "The Heavy Bear Who Goes with Me," a part of him "Howls in his sleep for a world of sugar" (12). That part—the "caricature" the "stupid clown"—drags him to "The

Scrimmage of appetite everywhere" (34), and he is helpless to
do anything about it.

When we consider the complex of emotions, appetites, and
obsessions underlying the alcoholic perspective, most especially
as they relate to the perverse fantasies and the tendency to escape
personal commitments in drunkenness, it is easy to understand
why the alcoholic is inclined to charge his most intimate relationships with an extraordinary complex of aggressive prejudices. Perhaps this is why so much alcoholic writing is
contaminated with the limited perspective of a misanthrope.
Thus, while an alcoholic may seek comfort by attaching himself
to codependent enablers, such relationships are profoundly
destructive because they erode any possibility for true affection.

For more successful writers, there is a partial validation of the
illusion of objectification and control because of the magic of
publication and through public acclaim which may ensue from a
successful run. Thus, creativity and publication constitute a devilish endorsement of a partial truth relating to the power of
objective sexuality and the illusion of self-sufficiency. What a
published writer may *not* acknowledge is that self-sufficiency for
an alcoholic may well be a preface to self-destruction and the
loss of any genuine opportunity for intimacy.

Yet, because of the power of their delusions and because of
the genius of their writing, the writers we have discussed have
provided us with a memorable glimpse into one of the darker
and more enigmatic facets of the alcoholic mentality. That alone
justifies a careful study of their work; and that alone is reason
enough to consider the tenuous relationship between creativity,
morality, intimacy, and the distorted appetites of the alcoholic
mindset.

Chapter Eight

Alcoholic Guilt and Emotional Paralysis: Bathos, Incongruity, and Frustration

I know the purity of pure despair,
My shadow pinned against a sweating wall,
That place among the rocks—is it a cave,
Or winding path? The edge is what I have.
—Theodore Roethke, "In a Dark Time," 9–12.

Fear is the mainspring of the addictive perception. The alcoholic is terrified that his needs may not be met, although he makes no clear distinction between what he may *truly* require and what he simply wants. This connection between fear and frustration is described quite clearly in the A.A. publication *Twelve Steps and Twelve Traditions*:

> We have seen that we were prodded by unreasonable fears or anxieties into making a life business of winning fame, money, and what we thought was leadership. So false pride became the reverse side of that ruinous coin marked "Fear." We simply had to be number one people to cover up our deep-lying inferiorities. In fitful successes we boasted of greater feats to be done; in defeat we were bitter. If we didn't have much of any worldly success we became depressed and cowed. Then people said we were of the "inferior" type. But now we see ourselves as chips off the old block. At heart we had all been abnormally fearful. It mattered little whether we had sat on the shore of life drinking ourselves into forgetfulness or had plunged recklessly and willfully beyond our depth and ability. The result was the same—all of us had nearly perished in a sea of alcohol. (123–124)

Fear, then, is predicated on the alcoholic's low self-esteem and his insatiable appetite for power and self-gratification. It is born out of a deep sense of insecurity, unfilled needs, and an addiction to certain forms of overachievement. Thus, it is not unusual to read a poem, novel, or play that involves an excessive preoccupation with the satisfaction of personal needs while denigrating fundamental values to the trash heap. Such an obsession may limit an addict's capacity to adapt or accept limits, thus further compounding his fears and exacerbating his frustration. The book *Alcoholics Anonymous* describes the genesis of this response from a first person perspective:

> When I am disturbed, it is because I find some person, place, thing, or situation—some fact of my life—unacceptable to me, and I can find no serenity until I accept that person, place, thing, or situation as being exactly the way it is supposed to be at this moment. Nothing, absolutely nothing happens in God's world by mistake. Until I could accept my alcoholism, I could [*sic*] not stay sober; unless I accept life completely on life's terms, I cannot be happy. I need to concentrate not so much on what needs to be changed in the world as on what needs to be changed in me and in my attitudes. (449)

For the alcoholic, the inability to change and to accept life as it is will invariably lead to drunkenness and the conviction that some kind of unpleasant emotional or physical payback is imminent. In "Eye and Tooth," Robert Lowell is caught in an impossible situation. He smokes all night, worrying through a moral dilemma that is clouded—both figuratively and literally—with unresolved childhood memories and unrelenting pain. The rainfall is like pinpricks; the house is a gallows; the roof rots; and his mind returns again and again to his boyhood confusion as a peeping Tom who was drawn irresistibly to the "triangular blotch" and glimmering white skin of the nude women behind the door. He cannot dislodge the memory; *"an eye for an eye,"* he writes; for there will be no relief for the youthful voyeur at the keyhole "when the women's white bodies flashed/in the bathroom. Young, my eyes began to fail" (31–32).

The narrator's naïveté and prurient fascination is discomfiting and guilt-ridden—a covert fascination with forbidden fruits that is deeply troubling because he does not understand his youthful compulsion, nor can he discount his childhood curiosity—not even as an adult.

For the alcoholic, an insatiable obsession with clandestine sexuality and uninhibited masquerades of a doubtful complexion are often manifested in considerable heartache and regret. Most relationships are likely to be terminated in failure and with no small amount of self-reproach, frustration, and withdrawal. In "Sonnet 56," John Berryman writes that his divorce is plainly a relief, having endured "Sunderings and luxations" and interminable exile; dogfights, with love "hangover-long"; and nothing much left now but the division of wreckage. On a similar note, in "Sonnet 58," Berryman portrays himself as a self-destructive junkie whose brains have been addled by an excess of booze in a "high wind." In this case, Berryman feels that the prospect of escape by drowning might be a ghoulish possibility.

Berryman's addictive perception was frequently manifested in quasi-psychotic illusions of power and in a rather puzzling complex of shame, denial, and depression. In fact, a great deal of his poetry describes the generic alcoholic cycle of drunkenness, insolence, guilt, and more drunkenness. In "Dream Song 373," this self-destructive pattern of behavior and response is made clearly evident in the declared intentions of the Henry persona. Although he is trying to recover from one hangover, Henry is already planning his next drunk, a new query, new demons, and, of course, another thrashing and another hangover. Life without liquor is "odd" because it is neither crisis driven nor catastrophic. Without liquor, there are no girls, no marathon phone calls, and no problems to evade. Life without a drink amounts to little more than death in life—a pointless test of human endurance that is invariably dull, boring, and glum.

Edna St. Vincent Millay was a good deal more sentimental than Berryman—as one might expect. Rather than pursue an unqualified and somewhat masochistic preoccupation with the nuances of getting through the day, she preferred a more temperate approach and wrote of frustration and loneliness in romantic fantasies of self-pity, love lost, and disconsolate lovers—in her particular case, dreams of forgotten faces and forgotten kisses, glimmering firelight, and wistful ferryboat rides. When she writes of the past, she may recall a tortured fairy tale that was hostage to memory and the "tranquil blossom on the tortured stem" ("Sonnet XIX," 10), or she may describe the redemptive beauty of music and passion recalled only vaguely and with regret. For Millay, time and pain may exceed the "unforgivable crowing of the hour" ("Sonnet VIII," 8), surpassed for at least an instant, if only for some kind of relief from the inescapable pain of intimacy. In "Sonnet XV," she writes of firelight, jazz and broken shadows and how she only

> will permit my memory to recall
> The vision of you, by all dreams attended.
> And then adieu, —farewell! —the dream is done. (7–9)

For Millay, essence supersedes substance. The wreckage of a broken relationship may be transposed to precious melancholy; and the dream is remembered not for specific images, but only because it amplifies her emotions. Still, there is a certain pleasure in the bathos of separation and the dramatic posturing of martyrdom and dissolution.

Disorientation, dissolution, and the fear of meaninglessness are also vividly expressed by Randall Jarrell in "90 North," where all his efforts are accidental and meaningless, and—whether living or dying by accident—he is still alone. He confesses that all knowledge "wrung from the darkness—that the darkness flung me—/Is worthless as ignorance: nothing comes from nothing" (28–29).

Like the North Pole itself, the narrator is wretchedly consumed by his own kind of cold—an extreme north of emptiness where he is compelled to resign all effort like a polar explorer without purpose or direction. Here, the narrator is focused on a single, abstract center of cosmic ignorance where the whirlpool of human endeavor is reduced to a meaningless abstraction, and pain has led to nothing beyond itself. He writes, "Pain comes from the darkness/And we call it wisdom. It is pain" (31–32). Jarrell attempts to discount the wisdom gained from hard experience, but he reveals a fundamental tenet of the alcoholic perspective: melancholy may be easily transposed to cynicism, and wisdom may be cynically discounted as pointless intellectual wandering that goes nowhere.

We see here the penultimate alcoholic low, the degradation of human affairs to a hopeless posture and catastrophic denouement. As Roethke says in "The Abyss,"

> Each time ever
> There always is
> Noon of failure. (9–11)

The majority of alcoholics cherish the illusion that their self-inflicted martyrdom may serve to dampen feelings of emptiness and the terror of futility. Yet, the peculiar dementia inherent in their bleak moods of social hatred and self-pity is oddly gratifying. At the heart of it, the alcoholic does not really like himself very much; and he most certainly hates the arbitrary nature of fate and circumstance. At the same time, his acrimony may well be a corollary of low self-esteem and its natural consequence, self-hate and frustration. Thus, he is inclined to discount his own worth and his right to any substantive fulfillment or happiness, perhaps because depression is the inevitable consequence of chronic drinking and his attitude is necessarily grim, dark, and frightful. Such a perspective is clearly modeled after certain fantasies about what *ought* to happen if the world had not been so intransigent and he had been granted a full measure of control. For the alcoholic writer, however, there may be some relief because the prospect of rewriting his life and revising his perspective to suit his fantasies allows him to play at the "God business" and arbitrate reality with unrestricted freedom.

Perhaps this is why Ernest Hemingway made a fictional connection with his boyhood sweetheart, Agnes Kurowsky, who was disguised as the fictional Catherine Barkley in *A Farewell to Arms*. It may also explain why F. Scott Fitzgerald held fabulous, fictional drinking parties in overstocked mansions populated by beautiful people, including the simple-minded Daisy, Zelda's double, in *The Great Gatsby*. In the meantime, Faulkner mythologized the Deep South in such a neatly orchestrated, psychological labyrinth of confusion and violence that any possibility of clarity or resolution was utterly impossible. Similarly, Allen Ginsberg, John Berryman, Theodore Roethke, Hart

Crane, Edna St. Vincent Millay, Robert Lowell, Delmore Schwartz, and a host of other poets have referred to events in their own lives with an extraordinary revisionist perception. Sometimes they rewrote those events or shaded the truth because they hoped for greater clarity and a sense of control, as in the case of Berryman, Ginsberg, and Roethke. Sometimes the revision took the form of a qualified inventory or oblique confession, as was often the situation with Hart Crane and Edna St. Vincent Millay.

Although most alcoholics hope that excessive indulgence may provide some kind of release from their deepest and most intransigent inhibitions, most of their efforts have been so devastating and untenable that one cannot help but wonder at the depression and hopelessness of their work. In such instances, we should not be surprised that they were inclined to back away or discount their conclusions with a certain amount of humor and cynicism. Theodore Roethke's comic response to the unnerving requirements of mortality involves a semi-sensual denial of the insults accumulated from servile pandering to his body's requirements. As he writes in "Prayer," if he must lose his senses, he would like to choose "Which of the Five I shall retain/Before oblivion clouds the brain" (2–4). Roethke's preoccupation with satisfying his body's accursed pleasures can only lead to self-condemnation and inconceivable devilishness. But, like so many alcoholics, he is obsessed with light and death and self-destructive palavering, sensual satiety, and Platonic idealism. Roethke claims—with a devilish bit of humor—that he favors the holy light, something that he would have "attend me to the grave!" But his pilgrimage is lacking in the singular blessedness he so earnestly requires, primarily because he is not really in a position to choose. The question he asks, which sense to retain (?), is pointless, because Roethke as he is, is Roethke in the present, with all his senses intact, no doubt. His discussion of the dilemmas of choice makes about as much sense as insisting that one's casket have a reading light. Drunkenness or self-mutilation may provide a weird opportunity for a fanciful revision, but—as the situation stands—Roethke is firmly placed in the present tense with no easy escape from the troubling present, regardless of what he might prefer!

For Alan Dugan, there is no easy reconciliation either. As he states in "On Leaving Town," living in the present "must be a bad dream" in which he is a "captive animal" to the incivilities of the city. Dugan is uncompromising in his insistence that he is captive to the present, and the present is exactly where he does *not* want to be. Like so many alcoholics, he is not prepared to live from moment to moment or, for that matter, even *in* the moment.

In "The Harbor Dawn," Hart Crane adopts a very different perspective on the alcoholic fascination with frustration and withdrawal. He rhapsodizes about the past and a drunken stevedore whose howl "and thud below/Comes echoing alley-upward through dim snow" (8–9). With typical alcoholic sentimentality, Crane merges dreams, a fog horn, harbor chaos, steam, and pallid air into a surreal muddle of classic imagery and industrial power. He suggests that the harbor, complete with a gaggle of sirens and some other classic props, is a romantic sanctuary of sexuality and hope, pastoral sleep, and unrelenting machinery. It is a fantasy of extraordinary dimensions that spans, as he puts it, "400 years and more"; but, as with so many alcoholic perceptions, it seems only vaguely related to the real world and the mechanistic images of harbor life directly in front of him.

In "Quaker Hill," Crane again tries to elevate the mundane and incongruous, in this particular case, by juxtaposing a series of extraneous images, "the persuasive suburban land agent/In bootleg roadhouses where the gin fizz/Bubbles in time to Hollywood's new love-nest pageant" (34–36) and "volcanoes roar/A welcome to highsteppers that no mouse/Who saw the Friends there ever heard before" (38–40). Here, the prophet-cynic focuses on the boozy world of roadhouses, bubbling gin, Hollywood tinsel, and party high steppers; but his alcoholic posture of superiority parades as romance where self-indulgent sensationalism and romantic airiness is confused with social criticism.

Thus, most alcoholics will devise a weird complex of self-justifications for their fears, their intolerable behavior, and their self-centeredness. The present is not a very comfortable place, so it is likely to be conveniently overlooked or even discarded as irrelevant to the business of getting on with life and the business of writing. A writer may thus find himself entangled in a time warp in which past and future overlap in such a way as to skew any reasonable concept of what it means to live in the present. *Twelve Steps and Twelve Traditions* discusses the alcoholic's difficulties with living in the moment and the consequences that are likely to ensue:

> When a drunk has a terrific hangover because he drank heavily yesterday, he cannot live well today. But there is another kind of hangover which we all experience whether we are drinking or not. That is the emotional hangover, the direct result of yesterday's and sometimes today's excesses of negative emotion—anger, fear, jealousy, and the like. If we would live serenely today and tomorrow, we certainly need to eliminate these hangovers. This doesn't mean we need to wander morbidly around in the past. It requires an admission and correction of errors *now*. (88–89)

Any obsession involving a refusal to live in the present may envelop the alcoholic in a rigid continuum of emotions in which he may try to extort others to act according to his will and his insatiable appetite for power. This may well be a major reason why so many writers have had no small amount of difficulty adjusting to circumstances over which they have no control. For a writer, this revisionist obsession may provide a temporary psychological milieu in which perceptions are congruent with the fictional assortment of prescriptions or idealized situations which are the basis of his art, but which deny the incongruity between reality and the extraordinary menagerie of fabrications that he carries around in his head.

Chapter Nine

The Contaminated Vision:
The Alcoholic Perspective in
Hart Crane's "The Wine Menagerie"

When I first read "The Wine Menagerie," I was both perplexed and fascinated: the imagery was contradictory and unfocused; the language was strangely obscure; and Crane's intent and the primary focus of the piece were somewhat baffling. I surmised that his personal difficulties with alcohol had something to do with its skewed intellectuality and peculiar imagery, most especially as they related to his concerns about the integrity of altered consciousness and the long-term effects of addiction. On the other hand, I also suspected that a close socio-critical explication might just reveal a good deal more about his intent and point of view, especially with regard to his contrived symbolism, organizational tenor, and theme.

It is likely that Crane's alcoholism may have ultimately been his creative nemesis. In that regard, "The Wine Menagerie" may have served as an oblique confessional of sorts, although it hardly stands as a final conclusion regarding Crane's perspective on the tenuous relationship between intoxication and creativity. In fact, we know that he continued to drink heavily right up to the time of his suicide. In any case, he was certainly not unique in his suspicion that alcohol was of no positive benefit to the creative impulse. Even the most cursory study of American literature would suggest that a crippling addiction to alcohol has been relatively common among a great many twentieth-century American writers; and, while it may have been endemic, there is very little evidence to suggest that it enhanced their work. As Thomas Gilmore noted in his landmark study of alcoholism and literature, *Equivocal Spirits,* while "some artists will doubtless always wish to experiment with the heavy use of alcohol or drugs, in my view such experimentation will increasingly come to be regarded as an exercise in futility" (175). Gilmore noted that, so far as the benefits that might accrue from drinking are concerned, he found an increasing contemporary attitude that was

> skeptical of its benefits, cognizant of the high cost of heavy or alcoholic drinking, doubtful that any achievements can ever justify the payment of such a price, and devastatingly inimical to the kind of willful blindness or self-deception that some alcoholic writers only a generation or two ago could use to deny their illness and its effects. (175)

Crane would likely have agreed with Gilmore—albeit reluctantly. In fact, if we distinguish the persona of the intoxicant-observer in "The Wine Menagerie" from that of Crane himself, it would be nearly impossible to conclude that the poem has anything good to say about intoxication as a liberating force; and, indeed, the primary focus of the piece appears to refute any assumption that an excess of liquor could possibly be a positive advantage in the creative milieu.

Even so, I was surprised to learn that a good many scholars have persisted in affirming that Crane articulated the value of intoxication in the creative process—most especially as it related to "The Wine Menagerie." Samuel Hazo, R.P. Blackmur, R.W.N. Lewis, and Herbert Leibowitz have considered the poem extraordinary because it portrayed a kind of elevated quasi-Dionysian perspective of the writing process. In fact, it was assumed that artistic genius was a romantic correlative of addiction and dysfunctionality (Hazo 43, Lewis 193–196). However, it seems to me that any affirmation about some kind of high-toned Bacchanalian creativity would indicate a certain amount of confusion about the poem and a remarkable degree of confusion about the destructive nature of alcoholism; and, indeed, they have all failed to recognize the sinister effect of alcohol, most especially as it relates to the bizarre perceptions of the writer-intoxicant in the poem. This is especially evident in the final lines where we witness his terrified attempt to escape the hallucinogenic visions in which he had become entangled.

The poem begins on an almost fatalistic note coupled with the poet-drinker's dubious affirmation of the regenerative effects of wine and its capacity to sharpen his perceptions:

> Invariably when wine redeems the sight,
> Narrowing the mustard scansion of the eyes,
> A leopard ranging always in the brow
> Asserts a vision in the slumbering gaze. (1–4)

The intoxicant's vision of poetic feet in a line of mustard jars facing the bar is horribly contrived. Except that his fascination with the mustard is strangely transmuted into an incongruous poetic scansion and has little to do with his fantasy of leopard-like transmutation, the drinker's attempt to invoke a predatory liberation to creativity is illusory and makes very little sense. On the one hand, the drinker is humorously self-obsessed as condiments morph into poems, and his brain watches itself watching itself mutate to a leopard, as if the very act of transcending the limitations of his bar stool with or without a predatory interest could be transcribed to feline creativity.

Crane's description of the drinker's mental processes as a leopard in the brow might also be interpreted as an attempt to describe the poet-intoxicant in the context of fraud, a more traditional definition of the symbolic role of a leopard. In this sense, the fraudulent, creative impulse is redefined and asserted in the crapulous stupor and slumbering gaze of the intoxicant, whose perceptions are dulled to somnambulatory incoherence by an excess of liquor.

In the next stanza, the intoxicant fixes his "slumbering gaze" on something more compelling: the wine decanters across the bar, his reflected image in their glittering bellies, and his transposition to the street through a series of bulbous reflections. However, it is likely that the row of decanters is no "glozening" glossary to interpretation, as some critics have suggested.[1] Rather, in examining his reflections, the intoxicant unwittingly confesses his liquored, literary self-inflation during the pouring of a fresh libation as he is conscripted to the grotesque illuminations of his intoxicated brain. Still, he manages to contrive a cynosured fantasy of applause as the wine is poured, but it is apparent that the wine and his illusions of creativity have little to do with his actual prospects, which are necessarily predicated on a moment of unqualified delusion, dribbling wine, and a love of overindulgence (see, e.g., Hazo 43–44 and Lewis 195).

In the next stanza, the intoxicant's misanthropy and isolation are reflected in his description of the putrid emulsion coating the walls of the saloon as it is strangely transposed to a couple of patrons who are involved in a nasty argument. The leopard image of fraud is now transmuted to a musical-surgical image of the fearsome wench whose false "forceps" smile and hammering "mallet" eyes are sufficiently intimidating to unnerve her male companion—perhaps because he too is a fraud and has been found out. He sweats percussively; there can be little doubt that his discomfort is unsettling; the lady is merciless with tong and hammer; and the saloon is now transformed to a psychological battleground of pounding fear, conjugal aggression, and squalor (Lewis 195–196).

It is interesting to note that, while the poet-drinker appears to harbor elaborate fantasies of creative genius, he is increasingly consumed by loneliness and fear, much like the combative pair. Still, he tries to revive his prospects for Dionysian creativity and fantasizes a serpent image with octagon skin and transept eyes, perceiving both its fraud—as in the serpent of Eden—and its transforming guile and poison.

Although our intoxicant may hope to be unskeined and transposed into a new identity, his mind is confused and restricted; his attention span is short; the dramatic arrow of carrilloned speed is doomed to collapse (Leibowitz 211); and his serpent skin—like the serpent of Genesis—admits betrayal and contains only facsimiles that betray his hope for some kind of creative "arrow."

The patchwork of fraud is now extended to the window-pane where "guile drags a face"—a beer-buying "urchin" nudges a "cannister across the bar" (22)—Crane does not tell us the duplicitous boy's intentions, but apparently he is up to some kind of mischief.

As the intoxicant's inebrious flight to creative ecstasy begins to turn back on itself, the caricatures in the saloon mutate into grotesques; and his prospects of creative wonderment are enveloped in paralyzing fear as he suddenly feels circumscribed by the image of two black tusks on a nearby wall:

> Unwitting the stigmas that each turn repeal;
> Between black tusks the roses shine! (27–28)

The drinker tries to evade a sense of terror and imminent destruction by focusing on the opposing, redemptive shine of the roses. They might yet prefigure new and wonderful poems and new heights (Quinn 53); and, if he can evade the tusks and the prospect of imminent destruction; perhaps his intoxication might still be a prelude to a rose embroidered carol where he can escape his mortality, fling his arrow of creative fantasies to a fanciful, feathered heaven, and regenerate his creative "talons" with the power to seize new "purities" (Lewis 198). But, while the drinker may yearn for spiritual and creative power, he provides no material evidence that he has been able to generate anything poetic from the sozzled ruins of his perception; he hopes to transcend his earthly self by shooting to heaven on his creative arrow; but his perceptions suggest no union with a higher truth, much as he would like to imagine otherwise.

It is becoming clear that wine is not the father of insight. Nor can it provide a profound metamorphosis into creative genius or extra-logical truth (Hazo 45). Rather, the wine talons of drunkenness clutch at the intoxicant with all kinds of romantic nonsense about his breadth of genius; and, even though he grandly exalts his creative powers, his unadulterated drunkenness and sentimentality are clearly evident in his rhapsodic yearning to travel alone in a tear and sparkle in the saintly martyrdom of hopelessness. He vows that he will distill the purity of his art and mutate to a bird of prey, but his description is a clear admission that he is over-strained by his bizarre expectations. It is also clear that the insights he claims are hyper-inflated fantasies that are hopelessly blurred by his self-indulgence.

Thus, while he may seek creative redemption in the roses of idealism, the drinker is forced to capitulate to the grotesque and repulsive tooth of reality and all things transient.

The intoxicant (author Crane having now switched from first person "I" to second person "you") is now forced to admit that he is circumscribed by a self-created hell; but his suffering and helplessness are by his own appointment, and his vision of new purities is acknowledged as worthless, an "inheritance of sand" that is as perishable as the snow. This pilgrim of the literary inferno of drunkenness and duplicity is now stuck on the ruddy and very sharp tusk of reality. His altered consciousness, his unfocused depression, and his creative flights of despair are about to destroy any anticipation of artistic mastery; and, indeed, he is finally compelled to admit that his magnanimous profundity is mere puffery. He abandons the bar; but, as he plods through the "crumbs" of dissolution, he stumbles over a terrible hallucination: the severed, whispering heads of Holofernes and John the Baptist. These Old and New Testament curiosities, at once so profound and so incongruous, float through his stupefied mind, mock his pretensions of grandeur, and compel him to flee the speakeasy and its astonishing apparitions. In a final act of capitulation, he pivots into the street like Petrushka's valentine:

> "—And fold your exile on your back again;
> Petrushka's valentine pivots on its pin." (48–49)

The wine menagerie has been transposed into a mechanism of personal obliteration. Religious images have been reduced to a catastrophic litter of corpses and waste, and the drinker's disorientation and his visions of death and absurdity now cast him adrift to spin helplessly in a topsy-turvy world of terror and confusion.

The question remains, however: is this a good poem? If it is viewed as a portrait of the integrity of the creative process powered by alcohol, as some critics would have us believe, it probably is not. However, if the poem is recognized for the alcoholic confusion, narcissistic depression and insanity, and the self-deception that are characteristic of a chronically addicted writer, it is a remarkable portrait of the effects of intoxication, most especially as it concerns overcharged, liquor-induced fantasies and revelations whose decadence reflects an almost fatal obsession with self-aggrandizement and the allure of loneliness.

For Crane, as for so many alcoholic writers, there can be little doubt that a drinking obsession might have provided a temporary psychological milieu in which perceptions might be rendered strangely congruent according to the peculiar assortment of prescriptions he carried around in his head. And, yet, in reading "The Wine Menagerie," it is readily apparent that he was fully cognizant of the potential insanity of chronic drunkenness, most especially as that insanity related to certain alcoholic fantasies about the integrity of liquor-induced revelations. In this regard, "The Wine Menagerie" provides us with an intimate perspective on what it means to be an alcoholic who is paradoxically debilitated by fear and illusions of grandeur. In the final analysis, then, it clearly demonstrates the fallacy inherent in any assumption that the addicted artist-poet is somehow endowed with a more than usual portion of humanity or creativity. That, perhaps, is an excellent reason for studying this remarkable poem, even as it may be the ultimate justification for its extraordinary genius.

Chapter Ten

Clowns and Bedlam: The Dark Side of Alcoholic Humor

At one-thirty a drunk wandered in and passed a remark which was considered insulting to Doc. Mack hit him a clip which is still remembered and discussed. The man rose off his feet, described a small arc, and crashed through the packing case in among the frogs. Someone trying to change a record dropped the tone down and broke the crystal.

No one has studied the psychology of a dying party. It may be raging, howling, boiling, and then a fever sets in and a little silence and then quickly quickly it is gone, the guests go home or go to sleep or wander away to some other affair and they leave a dead body.

The lights blazed in the laboratory. The front door hung sideways by one hinge. The floor was littered with broken glass....Whisky glasses lay sadly on their sides. Someone trying to climb the bookcases had pulled the whole section of books and spilled them in broken-backed confusion on the floor. And it was empty, it was over.

John Steinbeck, *Cannery Row*, 114–115.

Very little has been written about the dark side of contemporary alcoholic humor. The popular press has generally confined itself to advice on drinking and the nuances of recovery, and the few scholarly analyses that have been written have dealt almost exclusively with the strange connection between addiction and creativity. This is especially baffling because the penchant for self-debasement and pathological buffoonery is one of the most remarkable characteristics of the alcoholic mindset.

Alcoholic humor is both evasive and socially disarming and is generally derived from a litany of misanthropic attitudes and a passion for nonconformity. A comic perspective objectifies behavior by discounting the moral implications of an untenable situation and the consequences of addiction. As

John Berryman has noted in his first person narrative of the incorrigible persona, Mr. Bones,

> Nothin very bad happen to me lately.
> How you explain that? —I explain that, Mr. Bones,
> terms o' your bafflin odd sobriety
>   (Henry's Confession, 1–5)

For sad, old mischievous Bones, "Nothin" much happens in sobriety, as if life without a drink is necessarily dull, boring, and glum. The day just drags on—no thrills, no kicks or perversions, and no antisocial antics. It is an unbearable prospect, most especially because "Bones" seems to find a modicum of fascination in sex, marathon phone calls, miscues, and missed connections. His *joie d'vivre* is a correlative of petulance; and, given his love of mischief, sobriety is a mind-numbing prospect with nothing "bad," no comic relief, no dunderheaded opportunities to make trouble, and no masochistic refuge from the tedium of sobriety.

Bones fascination with the nuances of antisocial behavior is typical of the alcoholic perception. Drunkenness is not simply a question of acrimony and mischief—indeed, given enough liquor, it may also involve a stumbling, incoherent train of exclamations and expletives. As E.E. Cummings has noted, such a person might be,

> a he as o
> ld as who stag
> geri
> ng up some streetfu
> l of peopl.... ("a he as o," 1–5)

Cumming's fractured, bumbling pilgrim is disjointed and angry; and the scattered syntax and typographical oddities drop some fifteen more chaotic lines before they stumble to a halt with the simple word, "pencils." And, thus, we (or shall we say, the drunk) are compelled to wonder what could possibly be meant by

> i s
> ell drunk if i
> be pencils.

Here is perhaps the epitome of an intoxicant's unassailable query—a bumbling, incoherent question—something about "pencils"!

In his poem "America," Allen Ginsberg is perhaps similarly unhinged; but, in this case, he is a bit less scattered and just a bit more focused as he nags at circumstance, his daily regimen, and the hard, unbending world of fact. He yearns for salvation through some kind of psychiatric nirvana; but he is enveloped in psycho-political (!) double-talk that is laughable, impotent, and meaningless. He complains,

> When I go to Chinatown I get drunk and never get laid.
> My mind is made up there's going to be trouble.
> You should see me reading Marx.
> My psychoanalyst thinks I'm perfectly right.
> (America, 30–33)

In a somewhat more comic and personal vein, E. E. Cummings wrote a sonnet about his closest (and lifetime) friend, J. Sibley Watson, an extremely talented critic and essayist who was a co-owner of *The Dial* at the time that Cummings was involved in the literary life of the Harvard Yard. This hilarious rhyme was written when Cummings was a good deal less than sober and reveals a remarkable capacity for irony, even when writing "under the influence" and teasing a lifelong friend:

> O Watson, born beneath a generous star[,][1]
> Oft have I seen thee draped upon a bar[;]
> Thou might'st have slain us with a bloody couteau.
> (Softly from Its Still lair on Plympton Street, 9–11)

Here, Cummings presents a set of ludicrous options in a rather silly rhyme on drunkenness, crossed stars, mistaken fates, and morbid salutations. But his good friend, Watson, is blessed in a perverse sort of way, having escaped to liquor where he could dedicate his talents to the honor of Ms. Manners, "thy fair beatitude"—a nice equivocation—instead of something more fortuitous: the terrible prospect of his satiric pen which was withheld because of a sense of propriety and good taste.

Thus, while they would like to assume that they are capable of genuine passion, good humor, and tenderness, most alcoholics are much too wired on liquor to feel much of anything, except a bibacious mix of comic-grotesque perspectives, which—often as not—may be discounted with black humor and a remarkable amount of aggression—an interesting strategy that allows them to distance themselves from the consequences of their actions. As John Berryman writes about poor, overwhelmed Henry in "Dream Song 311,"

> Hunger was constitutional with him,
> Women, cigarettes, liquor, need need need
> Until he went to pieces. (7–10)

Although he is not interested in any priorities, we are told that Henry's passionate craving for women, booze, and cigarettes is "constitutional," suggesting that his weird appetite for sensual self-indulgence and self-destruction is something comically natural and inborn. Of course, while the poem masquerades as a confession, it hints strongly of disjointed pride and a voracious appetite for martyrdom. Indiscriminate insatiability of this sort is the very foundation of alcoholic misanthropy, and it destroys any real opportunity for a respectful and loving relationship with others. Still, this is the very essence of Henry's unappeasable hunger—at least as Berryman presents him.

While their appetites and conduct may be unconscionable, most chronic drinkers are inclined to discount the damage that must invariably accrue from abusive drinking; and, in some cases, this is only possible through the refuge of black humor where a writer's grim, escapist prejudices may be expressed in an excess of sentiment and buffoonery. In some cases, an obsessive tippler may simply want more and more—as with liquor, as with sex, as with power, and as with social excess. But, all may not be lost. As E.E. Cummings, writes—with tongue-in-cheek optimism, "nobody loses all the time." Old Sol, "who was a born failure," apparently never recognized his calling (vaudeville), screwed up at vegetable farming (because the chickens ate the vegetables) and chicken farming (because the skunks ate the chickens) and even skunk farming (because the skunks caught cold and died).

And so old Sol drowned himself in the water tank and had an auspicious funeral where everybody cried "like the Missouri," until someone pushed a button, and

        down went
    my Uncle
    Sol

    and started a worm farm)
            (nobody loses all the time, 35–38)

The long and short lines—giving the long and short of Sol's up's and down's—add a ticklish note to his "sad" little tale; but the ultimate fall of this clown, who cannot seem to recognize his calling, has its compensations and ends in a "splendiferous" funeral and a measure of agricultural success—at least as a "farmer" *of sorts* (however doubtful).

It is easy to get lost in puffery and profundity or simply bad (or late) timing; for, as the knuckleheaded driver/talker, Robert Creely concludes, since the end is near and "the darkness surrounds us," "why not, buy a goddam big car"—a simple enough, self-serving prospect. His temporal friend is a bit more freaked, however, not about darkness or metaphysics or big cars, but about driver-Creely, who seems determined to kill them both forthwith, darkness or no darkness: "for/christ's sake," he burbles, "look/out where yr going" (I Know a Man 11–12).

Sometimes, it is tough staying on target (and on the highway)—especially when grandiose ideas take hold of a "grandiose" brain.

On the other hand, even the happiest and loveliest of times can be wretched, given a strong dose of pessimism and a bad case of the grouchies. As that master cynic of cynics, Dorothy Parker wrote (no doubt with *some* indebtedness to that master of all pessimists, Macbeth): "Life in itself/Is nothing," especially when April comes "like an idiot, babbling and strewing flowers" (Spring 1–2, 6).

*   *   *

In 1944, John Steinbeck was asked by a group of soldiers to "write something funny that isn't about the war"; and, in some measure, he succeeded when he wrote *Cannery Row*. But the darkness and terror of World War II still found their way into the very fabric of the comic-grotesque tale; so, perhaps in one sense, he failed. For all the oversimplifications and the strange gloss of laughter and melodrama, the drifters who populate the story are thinly veiled beneath an alcoholic film of isolation and desperation. Perhaps the core of the novel and its essential meaning lie in the very first paragraph of the novel, which presents Cannery Row in all its simplified prettiness, but which, in truth is a strange mixture of the intolerable, whimsical, and repulsive:

> Cannery Row in Monterey in California is a poem, a stink, a grating noise, a quality of light, a tone, a habit, nostalgia, a dream. Cannery Row is the gathered and scattered, tin and iron and rust and splintered wood, chipped pavement and weedy lots and junk heaps, sardine canneries of corrugated iron, honky-tonks, restaurants and whore houses, and little crowded groceries, and laboratories and flophouses. Its inhabitants are, as the man once said, "whores, pimps, gamblers, and sons of bitches," by which he meant Everybody. Had the man looked through another peephole, he might have said, "Saints and angels and martyrs and holy men," and he would have meant the same thing. (1)

The novel is strangely amusing and ambiguous, a remarkable portrait of boozy misfits and have-nots whose lives are centered around two drunken parties: a surprise party for the central character, Doc, which turns into a drunken brawl; and a birthday party, which turns out far better than expected. Most of the other major characters, Mack and the boys at the "Palace flophouse and grill"; Lee Chong, the grocer; and the madam, Dora, are dispossessed outcasts on the fringe of society. With the exceptions of Doc, they are economic orphans, and while the novel could easily degenerate into a disjointed tale of misfits, drunkards, and simple-minded cast-offs, it is salvaged from the possibility of failure because of its strangely sentimental optimism. Steinbeck's tender portrait is not simply predicated on companionship and kindness, as some critics would have us believe. No matter how appealing the burlesque or how ludicrous the propensity of this little tight knit community to care and do good, there is no way that Steinbeck could possibly make this tragic world beautiful with words and token sentiments.

Cannery Row is a comic, bleak tale of melancholy and failure—but, perhaps, that is the essence of comedy, most especially human comedy, which insists that we distance ourselves from the victims of our laughter that we might enjoy banana peel acrobatics, the pie in the face, and the thunderous fall. The ensuing tension, mixed as it is with awe, is softened by a reassurance that everything is really ok and nobody got hurt. But sometimes, there is an element of sadness in the business of laughter; and, if we look a bit more carefully and perhaps a bit too closely, we are essentially witnesses to failure, frustration, and pain. As Mac says to Doc, "Everything I done turned sour... If I done a good thing, it got poisoned up some way... I don't do nothing but clown no more. Try to make the boys laugh" (119). For Mac, laughter is the final alternative to despair; the answer to sadness and misery, and, when all else fails; as in *Cannery Row*, the outrage of suffering is transposed to humor, perhaps to moderate the true and terrible reality of hopelessness.

William Faulkner knew all too well the power of alcohol and the unrelenting need for a "restorative" from his earliest years as a young man (Dardis 25). It was not long before his morning bracer was hardly sufficient to see him through the day, and a good number of his biographers claim that he eventually drank so much that he began to pass out on a daily basis—a plight much worse than that of his fictional character in "The Golden Land"—his only tale that dealt unapologetically with alcoholism. Yet, strangely enough, and with the exception of "The Golden Land" and "Uncle Willy," he rarely had much to say concerning abusive drinking. On the other hand, his gothic humor, his macabre settings and caricatures, and his two-dimensional clowns and Southern oddities thoroughly betray his alcoholic mindset, most especially his remarkable capacity to discount human foibles and buffoonery. It is easy to be transfixed by the genius and ingenuity of his work—to literally fall off one's chair in laughter—even as we as readers recognize the dark and unyielding mark of alcoholic humor in the greater portion of his literary canon.

For all his melancholy violence and grim humor, Faulkner has created a mythology of sorts, transforming images of meaningless degeneration into significant doom and paradoxical buffoonery; and, yet, beneath his extravagant verbiage and elevated narrative style—mixed as it is with colloquial dialogue, we sense a powerful vein of Quixotic humor and an incongruent mélange that softens the pathos and brutality of most of his stories. The underlying cracker culture that is the foundation of much of his work is expressed in a baffling patchwork of cruelty and anecdote, while ambivalence, perversity, and caustic inversion reduce many of his characters to disembodied, illogical oddities. Some of his finest humorous tales, "Spotted Horses," "Uncle Willy," and "As I Lay Dying," are especially notable, although very few of his stories do not invoke some form of dark humor. There can be little doubt, however, that "Mule in the Yard" is a classic, if for no other reason than its improbable jumble of catastrophic events and the furious pursuit of the mule as it gallops in and out of the fog and in and out of Mrs. Hait's shack while scattering washtubs, chickens, and a jumble of household goods in every imaginable direction:

> With that unhasteful celerity Mrs. Hait turned and set the scuttle down on the brick coping of the cellar entrance and she and old Het turned the corner of the house in time to see the now wraithlike mule at the moment when its course converged with that of a choleric-looking rooster and eight Rhode Island Red hens emerging from beneath the house. Then, for an instant its progress assumed the appearance and trappings of an apotheosis: hell-born and hell-returning, in the act of dissolving completely into the fog, it seemed to rise vanishing into a sunless and dimensionless medium borne upon and enclosed by small winged goblins.
> ("Mule in the Yard," *Collected Stories of William Faulkner*, 251)

The chaos, the violence, the pandemonium, the burnt down home, and old Het's sense of justice are all compacted into a final, literally unbelievable conclusion, which—considering the absurdity of the tale—somehow manages to make sense:

> Old Het was watching Mrs. Hait.
> "Honey," she said. "Whut did you do wid de mule?"....
> "I shot it," she said.

"You which?" old Het said. Mrs. Hait began to eat the biscuit. "Well," old Het said happily, "de mule burnt de house en you shot de mule. Dat's what I calls justice." It was getting dark fast now, and before her was still the three-mile walk to the poorhouse. But the dark would last a long time in January, and the poorhouse too would not move at once. She sighed with weary and happy relaxation. "Gentlemen, hush! Ain't we had a day!" (264)

And so ends the day and the chaos and the final justice—with a house burnt to the ground, a dead mule, and old Het summing it all in, "Ain't we had a day!"

In "Uncle Willy," Faulkner takes a different turn with an oblique comment on the destructive power of alcohol as the "good women" of Jefferson try to break poor, happy Uncle Willy from his heroin habit; but the reformation results in all kinds of pandemonium: an addiction to alcohol instead of heroin, the deterioration of poor Uncle Willy, and a mysterious, new household guest who baffles the busy-body, do-good town with her antisocial behavior and bawdy sexuality—which are made explicitly evident as she goes shopping one day. Faulkner writes,

...and how the young men and boys that didn't work and some of the men that did would drive back and forth past Uncle Willy's house to look at her sitting on the porch and smoking cigarettes and drinking something out of a glass; and how she came down town the next day to shop, in a black hat now and a red-and-white striped dress so that she looked like a great big stick of candy and three times as big as Uncle Willy now, walking along the street with men popping out of the stores when she passed like she was stepping on a line of spring triggers and both sides of her behind kind of pumping up and down inside the dress until somebody hollered, threw back his head and squalled: "YIPPEEE!" like that and she kind of twitched her behind without even stopping.

("Uncle Willy," *Collected Stories*, 237)

In *The Town* and *The Reivers*, we see a more genial humor, but, as with Steinbeck, there is a thin line between comedy and sentimentality. Both require a certain amount of distortion and hyperbole, and both displace the dark side of life with laughter. But in Faulkner even more than in Steinbeck, the comedy precludes any possibility of looking unflinchingly at the truth; and the essence of humor—incongruity and a certain element of surrealism—cloaks the sinister world beyond. As with Steinbeck, humor in Faulkner allows a kind of double focus; but, in Faulkner's case, the incongruity may reduce the unbearable and starkly painful to such a burlesque of perversity and absurdity that we are protected from the horrible reality that lies beyond.

Perhaps this is the essence of the alcoholic perspective: the illusion and vague foreboding of terrifying dependence and degenerative obsession that is somehow dissolved in the comic fumes of laughter. That may well be the essence of the comic, alcoholic perspective; for in laughter lies the hope that the reality of addiction is illusory, moral disintegration can be comfortably discounted and ignored, and the ragged process of recovery to decency can be compromised for another day.

Chapter Eleven

Through a Glass Darkly: Death and Dissolution

Alcoholics can be perversely defiant—perhaps because of a callous disregard for their own welfare and the welfare of others or perhaps because of the chronic morbidity, which is a natural consequence of the "bottoming out" or terminal phase of addiction. In some cases, they may be so devastated that a stoic resignation to death or suicide is a foregone relief.[1] Even suicide can be meaningless. There may be nothing to kill, because they are only a shadow of their former selves with no recollection of who they are or where they are going or even the night before.

In F. Scott Fitzgerald's *Great Gatsby*, the valley of ashes half way between West Egg and New York is a deathscape of waste and desolation where,

> ashes grow like wheat into ridges and hills and grotesque gardens [and where]....a line of grey cars crawls along an invisible track, gives out a ghastly creak and comes to rest, and immediately the ash-grey men swarm up with leaden spades and stir up an impenetrable cloud which screens their obscure operations from your sight. (27)

This foul dumping ground is barely noticeable—except when the drawbridge is raised to let the barges pass through, and it is possible to stare at the dismal scene for a half hour or so. The valley of ashes is not simply a crumbling land of houses and chimneys; it is also the burnt-out repository of human flotsam and of dreams that have come to nothing.[2]

For all its extravagance, Gatsby's West Egg mansion amounts to little more than a repository as well; and, like his star-struck dream of a recapturable past and his illusions of Daisy, it barely disturbs the indifferent East Egg netherworld of wealth and self-indulgent materialism. Gatsby's parties and dreams are inconsequential; and, in the final chapters of his story, his enormous swimming pool is reduced to marble crypt as the dead young millionaire floats here and there among the debris like a dead leaf:

> There was a faint, barely perceptible movement of the water as the fresh flow from one end urged its way toward the drain at the other. With little ripples that were hardly the shadows of waves, the laden mattress moved irregularly down the pool. A small gust of wind that scarcely corrugated the surface was enough to disturb its accidental course with its accidental burden. The touch of a cluster of leaves revolved it slowly, tracing, like the leg of a compass, a thin, red circle in the water. (170)

Gatsby's facade—the despair of betrayal and the musty remnant of a life destroyed—is similar to the slow disintegration of Dick Diver in Fitzgerald's later novel, *Tender Is the Night.* Diver's tormented degeneration (like Gatsby's death), is barely noticed—not even by Diver himself, because it happens so quickly and so subtly:

> He had lost himself—he could not tell the hour when, or the day of the week, the month or the year. Once he had cut through things, solving the most complicated equations as the simplest of problems... [but] the spear had been blunted. (201)

There is no single moment in the break-up; Diver is simply and slowly pushed down a fateful staircase to oblivion one horrible step at a time. What destroys him, as with so many alcoholics, is no single force, but a combination of forces that he can neither control nor understand—but the devastation is final and irreversible.

In some ways, the novel reflects Fitzgerald's own tragic decline, his alcoholism, and his suffering and loneliness, including the incomprehensible, inexorable tenor of his descent to an early death. Diver's story is like Fitzgerald's—including his excesses and those of his beloved Zelda, who, by the time the novel was completed (1934), was spending most of her time in mental hospitals. Tragically, the few occasions she and Scott were together were a disaster; and she burned to death in 1948. Fitzgerald had died of a heart attack eight years earlier on December 21, 1940. He was forty-four.

In Ernest Hemingway's remarkable short story "A Clean, Well-Lighted Place," the older waiter is a step above Dick Diver in recognizing his own, meaningless life and the imminence of death that underpins his of fear of nothingness. As he turns out the lights and closes the cafe, he thinks about an aged, intoxicated client who had only his dignity to sustain him, and he wonders about his strange, disordered fear and the darkness around him. What was it that kept him awake all night and what was it about the fear and emptiness that bewildered him. He asks,

> What did he fear? It was not fear or dread. It was a nothing that he knew too well. It was all a nothing and a man was nothing too. It was only that and light was all it needed and a certain cleanness and order. Some lived in it and never felt it but he knew it all was *nada y pues nada y nada y pues nada.* "Our *nada* who art in *nada nada* by thy name thy kingdom *nada* thy will be *nada* in *nada* as it is in *nada.* Give us this *nada* our daily *nada* and *nada* us our *nada* as we *nada* our *nadas* and *nada* us into *nada* but deliver us from *nada; pues nada.* Hail nothing full of nothings, nothing is with thee." He smiled and stood before a bar with a shining steam pressure coffee machine.
> "What's yours?" asked the barman.
> "*Nada*" (Complete Short Stories, 291).

Like Hemingway, William Faulkner was also a risk-taker, a strenuous physical activist, and a prodigious drinker. He bought his own airplane after he left the Canadian Flying Corps and flew it in air shows; he went sailing in rough weather; he hunted with inordinate relish; and he even trained and rode two wild horses. Faulkner also had a foreboding of violence and oblivion, and almost all of his work contains elements of the macabre that both repel and amaze. In "A Rose for Emily," the jilted bride, Emily, retreats into her old mansion to hide from the town of Jefferson after her disgrace at being left at the altar. Emily's story of love and betrayal by the Yankee interloper, Homer Barron, is a ghoulish tale of timeless revenge and remarkable self-will. Following her death when her family is at last able to enter the old mansion where she lived, they discover how,

> The man [Homer Barron] himself lay in the bed.
> For a long while we just stood there, looking down at the profound and fleshless grin. The body had apparently once lain in the attitude

of an embrace, but now the long sleep that outlasts love, that conquers even the grimace of love, had cuckolded him. What was left of him, rotted beneath what was left of the nightshirt, had become inextricable from the bed in which he lay; and upon him and the pillow beside him lay that even coating of the patient and biding dust.

Then we noticed that in the second pillow was the indentation of a head. One of us lifted something from it, and leaning forward, that faint and invested dusty dry and acrid in the nostril, we saw a long strand of iron-gray hair.

(Collected Stories, 130)

Here is the ultimate fantasy of unmitigated denial—the conviction, however macabre, that one can deny reality and prevail against time and circumstance (in some ways, perhaps like Gatsby). In reading the story, one cannot help but think of the many Al-Anons—the spouses and families of alcoholics—who, like Emily, are blind to reality and, in utter denial, are sleeping with a corpse night after night, even as they cling to the strange delusion that a long dead romance might be resurrected despite all evidence to the contrary.

Denial is an essential element in much of Faulkner's work—as it is, perhaps, the hallmark of much of the South: that the Civil War (that "late unpleasantness") was not lost, that the "old" South is alive and well, that Confederate gallantry is not just a memory, and, regardless of a slip of paper (to Emily, it is nothing more), she has "no taxes in Jefferson"— and the town fathers can do nothing to change the mind of this willful spinster.

A great many alcoholics have suffered terribly—some have lost everything, even their sanity and the will to survive. Yet, for some, guilt-ridden and bewildered as they are, the prospect of death and perhaps some kind of eternal punishment is likely to take on nightmarish proportions because it embraces the prospect of eternal damnation. As Robert Lowell writes of the spider that is so vividly described in Jonathon Edwards's eighteenth-century Puritan sermon, "Sinners in the Hands of an Angry God,"

> On Windsor March, I saw the spider die
> When thrown into the bowels of fierce fire:
>   There's no long struggle, no desire
>   To get up on its feet and fly—

It stretches out its feet
And dies. This is the sinner's last retreat;....
....
How long would it seem burning! Let there pass
A minute, ten, ten trillion; but the blaze
Is infinite, eternal: this is death,
To die and know it. This is the Black Widow, death.
                (Mr. Edwards and the Spider, 28–33, 42–45)

Here we read of the ultimate horror—compounded in the spider's passive surrender to infinite pain. Death is the price of urgency and unrelenting circumstance; and, as both Edwards and Lowell make clear, it is born of the foul smell of humankind and mortal intransigence—for, of course, the poem is not just about spiders. There is no redemption for the tiny predator—nor does it even struggle or hide from the prospect of damnation—it is inevitable and unavoidable. This is the ultimate mark of hopelessness and depression without even the chance to endure but merely to perish eternally and never cease to perish, for there is no end.

That the alcoholic anticipates the darkness born of his addiction and his alcoholic hell and the damnation within damnation should come as no surprise. Given a chronic history of insolence and addiction and a litany of grievous horrors, he is so numbed and defeated that he feels hopelessly lost beyond fear or apprehension. That is a death beyond death. What reason, then, to struggle, to let the heart endure, because it is eternally dissipated in the bowels of hell where—like the burning spider— he must forever "die and know it."

Lowell is all too familiar with the horror of death, the indifference to suffering, and the intolerable blood lust of humanity. A New England poet from an old and venerable family of Brahmins and an admirer of Herman Melville, he knew full well the bloody heritage of Nantucket whaling and the callous indifference to life and suffering that was part and parcel of the hunt. In "The Quaker Graveyard in Nantucket" he writes of the cruelty and indifference that are integral with whaling and the sea where,

The bones cry for the blood of the white whale,
The fat fluke and whack about its ears.

The death-lance churns into the sanctuary, tears
The gun-blue wingle, heaving like a flail,[3]
And hacks the coiling life out: it works and drags
And rips the sperm-whale's midriff into rags,...
Gobbets of blubber spill to wind and weather. (5: 95–101)

Here, we read of death and greed as Lowell describes how Melville's harpooner would have hacked the victim whale, Moby Dick, into gobbets; and the God above, who formed man of the slime of the sea and breathed into his mouth the breath of life, might have looked on and would not have retracted his promise, the "rainbow of His will," disgusted as He might have been. Here, again, we witness Lowell's concern with the anguish of humanity, man's fascination with destruction and death, and his acceptance of the dark side of life.

Lowell's imagery is reminiscent of Randall Jarrell's description of the death of the ball turret gunner who awoke and died in the flak and nightmare of attacking fighter planes and was simply (and efficiently) "washed" out of his turret (6). Here, infantile innocence—indeed, the blood of the lamb in the perverse womb of the airplane—is sacrilegiously (and perilously) rinsed away with a hose.

In contrast with Jarrell, John Berryman' imagery in "Homage to Mistress Bradstreet" is somewhat more esoteric as he wonders about the fate of his soul and God's divine and fatal judgment. Berryman feels suspended between heaven and hell and fears the penalty of mortal wickedness and his lost war with temptation. He knows that eternal judgment (as we see with Edward's spider, Lowell's whale, and Jarrell's gunner) is final and cannot be evaded. He writes,

Crumpling plunge of a pestle, bray:
sin cross & opposite, wherein I survive
Nightmare of Eden. Reaches foul & live.
he for me, this soul
to crunch, a minute tangle of eternal flame.
                ("Homage to Mistress Bradstreet," #36)

Despite the damnation of Eden, the possibility that he is "entirely alone," and the stark horror of God's judgment, Berryman tries to mitigate his fate by perceiving himself as a composite of good and evil, a nightmarish inheritor of God's fallen Eden who pleads that he might be redeemed from the fires of hell and evade the eternal flame through God's mercy; but he admits that he has left a trail of wreckage in his wake; and, indeed, he ponders, as do so many of his compatriots, whether his situation is so bad that his prospects are hopeless.

Berryman is somewhat unlike most chronic alcoholics, for he is not yet fully self-condemned to an untimely death, a meager room in a hotel flophouse, or a cardboard shelter with no one to care about his passing as he dies slowly in ultimate oblivion. Yet, most of these "low bottom" alcoholics understand that such an obscure death is probably their ultimate and unavoidable fate so long as they persist in drunkenness; and they understand that premature death, whether slowly by alcohol or by suicide, is an absolute certainty.

This intensely personal fear of death, loneliness, redemption, and oblivion is richly described by the alcoholic poet, Conrad Aiken, as he writes of "The Room" and the struggle of darkness, crushed and driven downward, contracting so powerfully that,

> it was as if
> It killed itself; slowly: and with much pain.
> Pain. The scene was pain, and nothing but pain. (79)

Aiken's vision of chaos and meaninglessness, darkness, and violence, and, of course, the absolute power of pain is excruciatingly vivid. In the worst of situations, darkness and anguish are compounded; and, indeed, were it to end there, the vision would be horrifying in the extreme; although Aiken goes on to describe the agony of rebirth in the following stanza. However, as a poet and witness, he apparently knows all too well the terror of darkness—a vision much more unpalatable than any dynamic mélange of death or evil, for—as with Hemingway's senior waiter, it is the utter void of nothingness. This is the final horror—absolute oblivion, not darkness, not even a vacuum. Here there is neither struggle, nor rejection, nor anger, nor defiance. It is not, as with Allen Dugan, a curse or denial, for in Dugan's intractable anger, there is at least the dubious comfort of defiance; and, in that defiance, some small element of humanity. For all his confounding rebellion, Dugan manages to affirm an astonishing degree of insolence that allows him to challenge the Divine scheme of things. In his trenchant opposition, he asks,

> What's the balm
> for a dying life,
> dope, drink, or Christ,
> is there one? (Poem 1–4)

Dugan would hope for some element of release, some balm of comfort in death, whether in dope, alcohol, or religion; but—in the end—it seems that nothing works, and he finds no hope and no resurrection or redemption—except to admit stupefied helplessness, get along as best he can, curse the folly of circumstance, and relegate any affirmative prospect as worthless as fertilizer. Death may come to nothing but emptiness—but at least he has the will to curse and assert the power of defiance. Dugan's perspective is much like Ginsberg's rebellious testament in denying the power of life by embracing the madness of self-destruction. In "Howl" he writes of those,

> who created great suicidal dramas on the apartment cliff-banks of the Hudson under the wartime blue floodlight of the moon & their heads shall be crowned with laurel in oblivion,...
> who cut their wrists three times successively unsuccessfully, gave up and were forced to open antique stores where they thought the were growing old and cried,
> who were burned alive in their innocent flannel suits on Madison Avenue amid blasts of leaden verse & the tanked-up clatter of the iron regiments of fashion & the nitroglycerine shrieks of the fairies of advertising & the mustard gas of sinister intelligent editors, or were run down by the drunken taxicabs of Absolute Reality,
> who jumped off the Brooklyn Bridge this actually happened and walked away unknown and forgotten into the ghostly daze of Chinatown soup.
>   (46, 55–57)

Ginsberg's profane death wish is unmitigated and intemperate. Although his manifesto is a hyperbolic indictment of society, it is weakened because of his preoccupation with the darker side of existential pessimism. Obscenity is sacramental and cathartic, and yet the protest is not just a catalyst for spiritual frustration; it is a cannibalistic "howl" against life in which fear and its usual corollary, anger, are propelled into an apocalyptic condemnation that Ginsberg both loathes and embraces.

On the other hand, Delmore Schwartz, an occasional drinking buddy of Robert Lowell's, was a good more reticent and uncertain about the human condition and life's finalities. He wrote of "guarding love with hate" (For One Who Would Not Take Life in His Hands," 27), and—indeed—he wondered what he would do with his own life before "death's knife" provided the "ultimate, appropriate answer" and sucked him helplessly into the "famous unfathomable abyss" ("All Night, All Night," 40–41, 44, 47).

The alcoholic obsession with death and self-destruction reflects a peculiar obsession with masochism and frustration. It is a consequence of exhaustion and depression, of being "sick and tired" of being "sick and tired."—even as the addict himself hungers for release from the addictive demons that are destroying his health and his life and that threaten to destroy his sanity. Alcoholics drink to escape and evade and to deny their responsibilities and prospects of fulfillment, either out of an inherent sense of unworthiness or deep-seated guilt. This obsession with denial and a ghoulish preoccupation with death and dying lies at the very core of the alcoholic mindset; and, indeed, for those at the very last and worst stages of their disease, only death or a rigorous program of rehabilitation offers any kind of release from the ongoing and constant pain of being.

Afterword

Although chronic alcoholism is endemic among modern American writers, only a select number of writers have been included in this book. Some of them have been chosen because their drinking history was legendary, and their obsession with alcohol was clearly evident throughout most of their work. Others are notable because their peculiar mindset is an excellent marker for exploring the fears and fantasies that are generic to the alcoholic perspective.

Although I have been primarily concerned with a comprehensive overview of the most significant characteristics and nuances of the alcoholic perception and mindset as a whole, readers who are interested in a more biographical-critical study may want to consider Tom Dardis's excellent book, *The Thirsty* Muse. It provides a good perspective on William Faulkner, Ernest Hemingway, F. Scott Fitzgerald, and Eugene O'Neill. Thomas Gilmore also provides an additional critical dimension on the foundations and effects of addiction in his book *Equivocal Spirits*, which is concerned with such writers as Malcolm Lowry, Evelyn Waugh, Eugene O'Neill, John Cheever, and Saul Bellow. Finally, Jane Lillienfeld and Jeffrey Oxford have collected a number of first-rate essays in their anthology, *The Languages of Addiction*.

Some readers may think of the alcoholic as a puzzling aberration; however, it is important to realize that alcoholics are really not much different from anyone else—except that they have inordinate difficulty coping with frustration, loneliness, failure, and the complexities of social interaction, most especially when they are "under the influence" and their emotions and judgments are skewed to hyperbolic proportions. It is at such times that the disease is so confounding—even to the alcoholics themselves, and we are compelled to search outside the customary realm of scientific analyses to consider just what makes them so baffling.

Perhaps there is no way to describe the incalculable damage that necessarily accrues from abusive drinking. Although we are fortunate to be able to study the peculiar genius of alcoholic writing firsthand, it should be noted that the writers we have discussed probably succeeded in creating some remarkable poetry and fiction *despite* their addiction, not because of it. It is hard to imagine that a writer—or anyone else for that matter—could do much of anything very well with a muddled brain, and the fact that most of their work is well written and worth reading is notable. Conversely, I hesitate to suggest that their work might have been better without their addiction. Alcohol is integral with the very heart and content of much of their work. It expresses in deeply human terms the issues and frustrations, the difficulties of adjustment, and the overwhelming emotional pain that are common precursors to the kind of creativity that is evident in the poems and stories that we have read.

The need to write and find some means of self-expression—if only to relieve the emotional pressures of an untenable life—is often predicated on painful memories and the difficulty of overcoming years and years of emotional paralysis. This kind of urgency may not only be true for addicted writers and artists; it may also be true for *all* alcoholics and addicts; for there is no reason to suppose that writers and artists are a particularly unique species of humanity, and their drinking obsession is in some way exclusive to the creative temperament. The difference between the alcoholic writer and nonwriter is relatively simple: one of them has a talent for words and has been able to publish his or her work, and the others are compelled to find some other means of self-expression. Whether talented or not, both the writer and the nonwriter are similarly addicted and overwhelmed, both think and feel much the same way, both have suffered and been frustrated and laughed (if not rather grimly) in the same manner, and both have endured much the same despair, alienation, and fear. This book has focused on the alcoholic writer, for they do indeed provide us with a window on the alcoholic mindset, but it is also a portrait of all alcoholics, their mental perspective, the terrible loneliness, and the frustration that are integral with the disease.

Perhaps some readers will think that I have been unduly harsh in my analyses; but I am concerned with a direct and honest appraisal of the peculiar mindset that is part and parcel of the disease of alcoholism, and I see no reason to moderate any analysis of alcoholic writing and the deep-seated fear, insanity, and anger that it discloses.

While it is focused on recovery, not analysis, the book, *Alcoholic Anonymous,* which is the model I have used in my explications, is very clear about the importance of an honest appraisal of the damage that accrues from consistent, uncontrolled drinking. Chapter six of the book describes how the recovering alcoholic is "revolted at certain episodes he vaguely remembers" (73), and how he comes to disdain life itself and the prospect of "oblivion and the awful awaking to face the hideous Four Horsemen—Terror, Bewilderment, Frustration, Despair" (151).

This tells us something about the importance of rigorous honesty, which is a necessary prerequisite to sobriety. It also supports the importance of straightforward thinking in any assessment of the disease.

A.A. is also very clear about half-measures and half-truths. As far as they are concerned, neither pleasantries nor denials are of much worth in understanding the devastation of alcoholism. Although the media and a number of celebrities have discussed and written about their twelve step recoveries, the dark side of addiction has sometimes been minimized or described in somewhat romantic or sentimental contexts—perhaps as a form of public confession and public expatiation, perhaps as a form of vanity, perhaps out of a simple need to write about the disease. However, a careful socio-critical analysis of the work of alcoholic writers—absent the popular images, late night TV interviews, or edited testimonials—will provide a very different picture of the nature of addiction and with none of the softening and with all the confounding guilt and confusion that are a natural consequence of uncontrolled drinking. In that regard, I hope that the preceding analyses will help in some small measure in providing a more comprehensive perspective on the insidious and destructive power of alcohol and the confounding disorder of the addictive temperament.

Appendix 1

A Note on the Author

Conrad Aiken (1889–1973). Aiken was born in Savannah, Georgia. His father killed his mother and then himself when Conrad was eleven, and he moved to New Bedford, Massachusetts, to live with his great aunt. After attending Middlesex School in Concord, Massachusetts, he was admitted to Harvard University, graduated with a B.A. in 1912, and, shortly after, married the first of three wives.

Although relatively obscure and somewhat dated in style, he was awarded practically every literary prize of any significance, including the Pulitzer Prize and National Book award. A respected essayist and critic and editor of the *Dial*, he was twice divorced and once attempted suicide. His work is intensely psychological and at times vitriolic. He died in the city of his birth, Savannah, Georgia, in 1973.

John Berryman (1914–1972). Berryman was born John Smith in McAlester, Oklahoma, but the family moved to Florida when the boy was ten. John's father threatened to drown both himself and his son by swimming far out to sea; and having failed at this, he shot himself beneath the boy's window. His mother moved to New York and remarried, and John took the name of his stepfather. He graduated from Columbia and Clare College, Oxford, returned to the United States, and taught English at Brown, Harvard, Princeton , and the University of Minnesota.

Berryman's major work and most significant publication is the 385 *Dream Songs*—a series of narratives about a character referred to as "Henry Pussycat," but who is very likely a persona for Berryman himself. A series of broken marriages, alcohol addiction, and counseling along with the tensions of his personal life make up the gist of his work. He has often been compared

with Homer, Dante, and Whitman. Berryman waged a lifelong
battle with alcohol and committed suicide on January 7, 1972.

Hart Crane (1899–1932). Although Crane was born in
Garrettsville, Ohio, he spent his boyhood in Cleveland; and,
while his father was determined to prepare him to take over the
family candy business, young Hart was just as determined to be
a writer, although he was not particularly successful and had to
depend on his father for financial support throughout most of
his life. Although he never quite got over his differences with his
father, he had an extremely close if not unhealthy relationship
with his hypochondriacal mother (Crane's parents fought constantly and eventually divorced). He traveled alternately to
Pines, Cuba (to visit his mother) and to Paris and New York,
where he was occasionally employed as a writer in advertising.

Crane suffered from depression and was deeply involved in a
number of intense sexual relationships with other men. He
began to drink heavily during his late twenties and wrote less
and less after concluding that he had squandered much of his
talent on projects of questionable value. The financial support
of Otto Kahn enabled him to complete his major work, *The
Bridge,* which received mixed reviews; and, in 1931, he was
awarded a Guggenheim Fellowship to travel to Mexico where
he planned to write a long poem about Mexican history.
However, nothing much came of the project; and, a year later,
he killed himself by jumping off the stern of the vessel that was
returning him to New York.

Robert Creely (1926–2005). Creely was born in Arlington,
Massachusetts and was educated at Harvard (which he left
because of excessive partying and drinking), Black Mountain
College, and the University of New Mexico. He taught at Black
Mountain College, the University of New Mexico, and the State
University of New York at Buffalo. He edited the *Black
Mountain Review,* a highly influential literary journal and came
to be regarded as a leading proponent of the "Projectivists"
school and the Black Mountain School of poetry, although he is
essentially regarded as having something of a Puritan sensibil-
ity. Thrice married and constantly hounded by mental problems,

he associated for a time with the writers of the "Beat" generation, including Kerouac, Ginsberg, and McClure. It was at this time that he became interested in the creative effects of psychedelic drugs and alcohol.

E. E. Cummings (1894–1962). The son of a Boston clergyman, Cummings earned both his B.A. and M.A. at Harvard. He joined the Ambulance Corps in World War I and later served in the infantry. Following the war, he lived in Paris and New York and divided his time between writing and painting. Known for his unusual versification, spelling, and linguistic experimentation, he was something of a pagan moralist, satirist, and a passionate enthusiast of youth, anarchy, nonconformity, and sensuality. Thrice married and very possibly bisexual, Cummings traveled widely and was both praised and criticized for his unique poetic style and wide range of subjects, including alcohol, physical regeneration, the natural world, and erotic love. He received the *Dial* award, held the Charles Eliot Norton Professor of Poetry chair at Harvard, was elected to the American Academy of Arts and Letters, and was awarded the Bollingen Prize in Poetry.

Alan Dugan (1923–2003). Dugan was born in Jamaka, Queens, attended various Colleges, and graduated with a B.A from Mexico City College in 1949. Trenchant and rebellious in content and style, his poetry is notable for its intense and forthright examination of the disenchantments of daily life. An avowed Marxist with an admitted fondness for alcohol, he was awarded the Pulitzer Prize and the National Book Award as well as numerous other prizes.

William Faulkner (1897–1962). For sheer literary genius and his remarkable descriptive skills and character development, Faulkner has very few peers. His major work consists of a complex reconstruction of Lafayette County in northern Mississippi, which he renamed "Yoknapatawpha County." This is the setting for much of his work and almost all of his novels.

Born of an old southern family in New Albany, Mississippi, in 1897, the family later moved to Oxford, the seat of the University of Mississippi. William joined the Canadian Flying

Corps in 1918 (although he never saw combat), returned to Oxford; and, in 1924, he attended the University of Mississippi for two years. In 1926, he moved to New Orleans where he did a good deal of writing and publishing. After a six month tour of Europe, he returned to Oxford, where he continued to write and publish for the remainder of his life.

Best known for his complex style and experiments with point of view, some of his most notable works (along with many of his remarkable short stories) include *The Sound and the Fury* (1929), *Sartoris* (1929), *As I Lay Dying* (1930), *Light in August* (1932), *Abasalom, Absalom* (1936), and *The Unvanquished* (1938). He was awarded the Nobel Prize for Literature in 1950, the National Book Award, and innumerable other literary prizes.

Faulkner drank excessively on a daily basis during most of his life, usually until he passed out; and the fact that he was able to produce so much great literature is in itself astonishing, although it is generally agreed that much of his later work is not of the same quality as his early material.

F. Scott Fitzgerald (1896–1940). Fitzgerald is commonly regarded as the spokesman and symbol of the Jazz Age, which he named and described with extraordinary brilliance. He was born in St. Paul, Minnesota, and attended Princeton briefly where he did a good deal of partying and very little studying. The memories of his years at Princeton played a major role in much of his later work. Fitzgerald joined the wartime army as a lieutenant at staff headquarters, but the war ended before he could be assigned abroad. In 1919, he married Zelda Fitzgerald, a southern belle, and—with the immense profits from his short stories and his first novel, the two bought an estate in North Carolina, although they were constantly on the move and spent a good deal of time in New York, The Riviera, Paris, and Hollywood.

A chronic alcoholic, he and Zelda partied continuously and carelessly throughout most of their marriage and attained a certain amount of notoriety because of their carefree and nonconformist (though self-destructive) antics and arguments. Zelda had to be confined to a mental institution after a breakdown in

1930; and Scott continued on, working and writing to support her confinement, although, in his own words, he felt that he left his "capacity for hope on the little roads that led to Zelda's sanitarium." His finest novel, *The Great Gatsby* (1925) was not well received at first, and he did not complete his last novel, *Tender Is the Night,* until 1934. He eventually overcame his addiction to alcohol with the help of columnist Sheila Graham (who described her relationship with Scott in her book, *Beloved Infidel*), but he was unable to recover his health and died of a heart attack in 1940. He was writing *The Last Tycoon* at the time (it was never completed). Eight years later, Zelda died in a fire in the hospital where she had been confined because of intermittent episodes of schizophrenia.

Allen Ginsberg (1926–1997). Ginsberg was born in Newark, New Jersey, and graduated from Columbia University in 1948. He was a leader of the "Beat" Movement and the San Francisco Renaissance, suffered a nervous breakdown, did a stint with the Merchant Marine, reviewed for *Newsweek,* and was awarded grants from the Guggenheim Foundation, the National Endowment for the Arts, and the National Institute of Arts and Letters. In 1974, he was a co-winner of the National Book Award with Adrienne Rich.

Ginsberg's first major poem "Howl," a confessional poem of sorts, is a significant milestone in the evolution of American letters. His travels in Europe, Asia, and South America; his interest in hallucinatory drugs, advocacy of Zen Buddhism, civil rights, and war resistance; and his homosexuality and alcoholism have kept him in the public eye, although there can be little doubt that his revolutionary poetic style, profane content, and incantatory verse have had a profound effect on the evolution of American poetry.

Ernest Hemingway (1901–1961). Hemingway is perhaps best known for his sharp, concise prose, his superb management of plot and character, and his semi-autobiographical style. He was born in Oak Park, Illinois, in 1899. After graduating from high school, he worked as a reporter for the *Kansas City Star* and later served as an ambulance driver with the Italian army.

Following the war, he moved to Paris as a foreign correspondent for the *Toronto Star*. He was a war correspondent during the Spanish civil war and World War II. Best known for his dynamic life style and love of adventure, he wrote numerous excellent short stories and sketches and his life seemed to feed his work. His early novels, including *The Sun Also Rises* (1926), *A Farewell to Arms* (1929), and—in some measure—*For Whom the Bell Tolls* (1940) are remarkable for their literary merit, excellent organization and plot, and extraordinary character development. Hemingway was awarded the Nobel Prize for literature in 1954. His short novel, *The Old Man and the Sea* (1952) unquestionably played a part in the award.

Hemingway drank heavily throughout much of his life, and some critics contend that it had a profound influence on his work—his worst and least commendable publications having been submitted in the years just before his death. His father's suicide in 1928 may account in part for the younger Hemingway's fascination with death, self-mastery, and risk-taking. Ernest committed suicide in his home at Ketchum, Idaho, in 1961, very likely due to a combination of factors, including the suicide of his father, ill health, and a series of very painful and critical airplane accidents and a car accident.

Randall Jarrell (1914–1965). One of America's foremost black poets, Jarrell was born in Nashville, Tennessee, and educated at Vanderbilt University, where he was awarded degrees in psychology and English. He served in the U.S. Army Air Corps during World War II; and, following the war, he taught at a number of colleges and universities, including Sarah Lawrence, Kenyon, the University of North Carolina, and Princeton. He was also a literary editor for *The Nation* and a critic for the *Partisan Review* and the *Yale Review*. His numerous awards include an appointment as Consultant in Poetry at the Library of Congress, membership and chancellor of the Academy of American Poets, a grant from the National Institute of Arts and Letters, a National Book Award, and Guggenheim fellowships.

Jack London (1876–1919). While London is mentioned only briefly in this book because he has published somewhat earlier than the standard literary canon known as "modern" American literature, he certainly deserves recognition, most especially because of his Darwinistic determinism and because he was unquestionably alcoholic and wrote *John Barleycorn* (1913), the first "modern" autobiography on the devastation, fear, risk-taking, and bewildering power of alcohol addiction.

Robert Lowell (1917–1977). Lowell was born in Boston and inherited a distinguished family tradition of New England history—something that at first embarrassed him as a youth but which eventually proved to be a literary resource of considerable merit. Lowell gradually developed a psychological interest in family relationships, something that emerges in the tragic and comic themes that are integral with his work.

Lowell attended Harvard and graduated from Kenyon College, where he was encouraged to write by John Crowe Ransom and Randall Jarrell. He converted to Catholicism not long after his graduation, although he continued to be interested in the writings and theology of the original Puritans. When World War II broke out, he tried to enlist twice but was refused. He was later drafted and declared himself a conscientious objector. He taught at various universities, including Harvard and the University of Iowa; and he was strongly influenced by William Carlos Williams, Ezra Pound, and the New England Puritan, Jonathon Edwards. He has received numerous awards for his work, including the Pulitzer Prize, the National Book Award, and the Bollingen Poetry Translation Award. Thrice married, Lowell suffered from manic depression and alcoholism and was hospitalized on numerous occasions. He died of a heart attack in a cab in New York while on his way to visit his second wife, author Elizabeth Hardwick.

William Matthews (1942–1997). Matthews was born in Cincinnati, Ohio, and graduated from Yale University and the University of North Carolina at Chapel Hill. He taught at Wells College, the University of Colorado, the University of Washington, Columbia University, and the City College of New York. Matthews received grants from the National Endowment for the Arts and the Guggenheim and Ingram Merrill foundations.

Ogden Nash (1902–1971). Nash was born in Rye, New York, attended Harvard for a year, taught briefly, and moved to New York to work as a bond salesman, editor, and advertising copywriter. He quit the business world during the depression to dedicate himself entirely to writing. His work is at times autobiographical, although he is best known for his puns and nonsensical puns. Nash was elected to the National Institute of Arts and Letters in 1950.

Charles Olson (1910–1970). Olson was born in Wester, Massachusetts, and educated at Wesleyan, Yale, and Harvard— where he received his doctorate. He taught at Black Mountain College, Harvard, and the State University of New York at Buffalo. While his early work was widely hailed as a breakthrough in American letters, his dependence on alcohol, amphetamines, and marijuana and his self-focused egotism destroyed his common law marriages and may have led to the suicide of his second wife. His early work was commended by William Carlos Williams, and he had a profound influence on a number of contemporaries, including Denise Levertov and Robert Duncan. However, his last works shortly before his death by cancer are generally regarded as defuse.

Eugene O'Neill (1888–1953). O'Neill is ranked among America's foremost, revolutionary playwrights. Deeply concerned with the conscious and subconscious perceptions of reality, he brought new vitality and new depths to the American stage. During his youth, he traveled extensively with his father, who was a romantic actor. Eugene was privately educated and briefly attended Princeton before he was ejected for an undergraduate prank. He traveled widely, eventually returned to the States, and, after recuperating from tuberculosis, he worked in George Baker's famous dramatic workshop at Harvard. In 1915, he joined the Provincetown Players and was successful with a number of one act plays.

In 1920, O'Neill won the Pulitzer Prize for his first long play to be produced, *Beyond the Horizon* (1920). With the writing of *Emperor Jones* (1920), *Anna Christie* (1921), *The Hairy Ape* (1922), and a number of complex psychological dramas, he was soon recognized as a playwright of extraordinary genius and influence—despite his addiction to alcohol and psychological issues relating to his chaotic childhood. O'Neill was awarded the Nobel Prize in 1936 and won the Pulitzer Prize on four separate occasions—the fourth posthumously.

Dorothy Parker (1893–1967). Born in West End village of Long Branch, New Jersey, Dorothy's mother died in 1898 when she was four. Her father remarried in 1900; but she detested both her stepmother and father, and family life was deeply strained. Her brother died in 1912 aboard the *Titanic,* and a year later her father died. These family tragedies had a profound effect on Dorothy throughout the remainder of her life. In 1917, she married Edwin Parker, a stock broker and alcoholic, but the marriage lasted only a short time. In the meantime, she began to write for *Vanity Fair,* but she was fired in 1921 because of her sarcasm. She then moved to *Ainslee's* and later to *The New Yorker,* where she wrote short stories, prose, and poems. Readily acknowledged for her remarkable wit and unshakeable principles (she refused to testify before the House Un-American Activities and pleaded the Fifth Amendment), Parker was dogged by alcoholism and depression throughout her entire life. An avowed socialist, she left her entire estate to the NAACP.

Edwin Arlington Robinson (1869–1935). Robinson spent his youth in Gardiner, Maine, which became the "Tillbury Town" of his later poems. His youth and early poems reflect a series of severe emotional strains, including the sickness and debts of his older brothers, the early death of his mother, and the loss of his inheritance during the depression of the nineties. He spent two years at Harvard, returned to Gardiner, and later moved to New York, where he held a variety of jobs and dedicated himself to his poetry. He was awarded the Pulitzer Prize three times and was elected to the National Academy of Arts and Letters. One of America's foremost poets, who was both a perfectionist and remarkably versatile, Robinson was especially concerned with the various nuances of human psychology and the darkness and "spiritual kindergarten" of humanity. Much of his life was spent trying to deal with depression, chronic pain, alcoholism, and the complications of trying to support himself—for which he was wholly unfit.

Theodore Roethke (1908–1963). Roethke's primary subject has been the power and continuity of life rooted in nature. He was born in Saginaw, Michigan, attended the University of Michigan and was awarded his bachelor's degree in 1929. He took graduate courses at Michigan and Harvard and taught at Lafayette College, Pennsylvania State University, Bennington College, and the University of Washington. Roethke has been awarded just about every major literary award of any significance, including two Guggenheim fellowships, the Pulitzer Prize, the National Book Award (twice), and the Bollingen Prize in Poetry. Roethke was dogged by depression and mental illness all of his life and was often obsessed with death and dying. He died prematurely of a heart attack at age 55.

Edna St. Vincent Millay (1892–1950). Millay was born in Rockland, Maine, earned her B.A. at Vassar College in 1917, and moved to Greenwich Village in New York where she joined the Provincetown Players as an actress and playwright. She was awarded numerous honorary degrees and was elected to the American Academy of Arts and Letters. She is best known for her sonnets, some of which have been favorably compared with the Shakespeare sonnet sequence. An ardent feminist, romantic, and acknowledged bisexual and freethinker, she had numerous affairs with both men and women. In 1923, she married Eugen Jan Bossevain, and the two moved to a farm near Austerlitz, New York, although she continued openly to have affairs, even as Bossevain continued to support her career. The night before she died, she stayed up very late and into the morning reading and writing terrifying notes to herself in very careful handwriting (which was not her usual practice). She had left a glass of wine and a bottle on the staircase and had gone upstairs, but had not gone to bed. As she returned downstairs, she pitched the full length of the steep staircase and was found later that day at the foot of the stairs, her neck broken, her head resting on some magazines and letters and on her notebook. It contained a mark of blood and a draft of a poem with a penciled ring around the last three lines:

> I will control myself, or go inside.
> I will not flaw perfection with my grief.
> Handsome, this day: no matter who has died.

Delmore Schwartz (1913–1966). Much of Schwartz's literary output was hampered by the emotional problems he experienced during the last twenty years of his life and by his battles with psychosis, alcohol, and barbiturates. He gradually severed all relations with friends and institutions; and, when he died (very likely of a heart attack), his body lay unclaimed for three days. He was born in Brooklyn, attended the University of Wisconsin, and graduated from New York University in 1935. He attended graduate school and taught at Harvard University while publishing a series of poems and stories that would provide the basis for his first book, *In Dreams Begin Responsibilities* (1938). He later taught at a considerable variety of colleges and universities, including Princeton, New York University, Kenyon, and Syracuse.

John Steinbeck (1902–1968). Steinbeck's distinctive lyric style, his California regionalism, and his status as a protagonist of social justice have won him universal if not reluctant recognition as a writer of extraordinary power. Born in Salinas, California, he grew up in the hill country around Monterey Bay, the location for many of his stories. In 1919, he entered Stanford University, but the necessity of supporting himself kept him from following the standard curriculum.

During his earliest period, he supported himself at various menial jobs which served as the basis for much of his later work, and he served as a war correspondent in Italy during World War II and later in Russia. Steinbeck is probably best known for *Tortilla Flat* (1935), *In Dubious Battle* (1936), *Of Mice and Men* (1937), *The Grapes of Wrath* (1939), and *Cannery Row* (1945). It is generally agreed that his later work does not equal his earlier achievement.

Although he tended to avoid publicity and was a relatively private person, it is well known that much of his personal and family life was characterized by abuse, estrangement, and chronic alcoholism. He was awarded both the Pulitzer Prize and the Nobel Prize.

Tennessee Williams (1911–1983). Williams was born in Columbus, Mississippi, and lived in various southern towns before his family settled in St. Louis in 1918. His memories of living with his clergyman grandfather had a profound influence on his work.

He attended the University of Missouri for three years without graduating, studied briefly at Washington University, and completed his B.A. at the University of Iowa in 1938. By this time, he had seen a number of his plays performed, although he rose to national prominence with the *The Glass Menagerie* (1944). Although he was a novelist, short story writer, and poet, Williams's best work was as a playwright. Much of his work has been successfully adapted for the screen, which indicates the versatility of his state management and his use of modern stage techniques.

Appendix 2

The Emotional, Spiritual, and Physical Dimensions of Alcoholism: An Overview

Alcoholics drink in the hope of transcending their perception of reality. Although some religions are involved in hallucinogenic ceremonies that are congruent with age-old beliefs, such rituals are concerned only with transcendent spiritual visions and are highly regulated. There can be little doubt that the alcoholic is similarly motivated in his desire to achieve some kind of transcendent consciousness; and, while this may involve certain elements of the spiritual and sublime, his behavior and drinking obsession bear little relationship to the age-old ceremonial rituals that are focused on the pursuit of a higher consciousness through chemical agents. These tribal ceremonies, while bearing a remote similarity to the alcoholic obsession with euphoria and the obliteration of personality, constitute an entirely different approach from that of the confirmed addict.

The practicing alcoholic does not know the meaning of self-lessness and moderation, nor is he interested in the strict discipline and highly controlled settings of priest-centered worship. To the alcoholic, there is little meaning in control and moderation—indeed, the exact opposite is true. If a little is "good," then "more" is better; and, in matters of drunkenness and altered states of consciousness, the same attitude holds true: "more" (in this case, liquor) is invariably better than less, and most chronic alcoholics have a prodigious capacity for alcohol. They can and will drink a great deal more than non-alcoholics, and they will persist in their obsession despite the traumatic consequences to their mental, physical, and spiritual well-being. While some alcoholics drink to excess daily and others drink intermittently or periodically, the ultimate consequences to their physical and mental health are much the same. Indeed, many alcoholics are reluctant to acknowledge their personal responsibility in contaminating their own lives and the lives of others; and they are inclined to discount the conflicted relationships and the terrifying pitfalls that accrue from their addictive perceptions.

The physical craving peculiar to alcoholism is well known and relates directly to the inability to process alcohol normally. Rather than expel alcohol through the breath, through urination, and through like processes of metabolism, the alcoholic's body is likely to convert alcohol into something very much like morphine. This "secondary" narcotic is then retained and is the basis for the craving that is integral with the disease.

The inability to process alcohol is one of the reasons that alcoholism is sometimes referred to as an inherited disease. The victims of alcoholism do not ultimately choose their addiction and suffering any more than they are capable of choosing their parents. Indeed, there is considerable evidence that the children and grandchildren of alcoholics have a very good chance of becoming alcoholics themselves. According to some studies, the odds of becoming an alcoholic are 50 percent greater if a parent or grandparent was an alcoholic. It is also well known that certain ethnic and national groups—most notably Native Americans, Irish, and Scandinavians—have a very high predisposition to become alcoholic—some say as much as 50 percent greater (see e.g., *Encyclopedia Britannica*, vol. 1, "Alcoholism— Prevalence of Alcoholism"). This is not to say that a Swede with an alcoholic father has 100 percent chance of being alcoholic. However, if he does choose to drink, he is dealing with some very serious odds.

There is overwhelming evidence that genetics play a major role in any reasoned definition of alcoholism. The physicality of alcoholism is further reinforced by studies that reveal considerable differences in the brain waves of alcoholics, regardless of whether they drink or not. This is especially true for young males whose fathers were alcoholic.

Regardless of the genetic heritage, it should be realized that, as with so many substances—even salt or sugar for that matter—alcohol is a toxin if ingested in large amounts. Given sufficient abuse, alcohol will poison every part of the body: skin, hair, internal organs, muscles, and skeletal features. It breaks down the nervous system and kills brain cells beyond repair—a condition known as "wet brain." It also damages and will ultimately shut down the liver, kidneys, and pancreas. Circulation is slowed and this, coupled with the damage to the nervous system, can result in delirium tremens (known popularly as the "d.t.'s") and deadening of the extremities—sometimes evident in a condition known as "drop foot." Brain functions are also severely damaged and are typically manifested in alcoholic hallucinations, memory loss and disorientation, difficulty in speaking, and problems with physical coordination.

Finally, the immune system is weakened from prolonged drinking, and the alcoholic is more likely to suffer from a host of diseases and disorders ranging from recurring influenza and the common cold to tuberculosis, heart attacks, strokes, and cancer.

The chronic alcoholic may be easy to recognize because he tends to develop the familiar flushed complexion. Blood vessels are weakened and circulation is slowed. Ultimately, this flushed condition evolves into facial and skin distortions such as the familiar bulbous nose, although generally bad health may also be evidenced by jaundice, in which the eyes, indeed the entire system, is poisoned, and the hair becomes flat and lifeless. Some beauticians claim that they can easily tell if a client has been drinking the night before simply by the texture and behavior of the hair.

The alcoholic is dying from poison. Some studies claim that an alcoholic's life is cut short by an average of twenty-seven years, that is, if he is not killed in an accident or does not commit suicide first.

The health of the abusive drinker is similar to an individual who suffers from influenza. If that suffering is compounded, we have some idea of the painful and debilitating effects of the disease. Anyone who has experienced a hangover after a severe drinking spree can understand the toxic effects of extended, abusive drinking. A hangover, complete with vomiting, listlessness, fatigue, a pounding headache, and a lack of appetite are the commonplace, daily experiences of alcoholics during the advanced stages of the disease.

Despite his suffering, the alcoholic is driven by an intense craving for the very poison that is killing him, and he will do anything to satisfy that craving. When levels of alcohol drop below tolerable limits, the nerves become twisted and agonized; and the search for alcohol intensifies. This is why many heavy drinkers awaken in the middle of the night. The body has metabolized enough alcohol to fall below tolerable limits, and the craving has begun anew; this happens at times even in the case of moderate drinkers. However, it is always a warning sign because it signals some degree of alcohol dependence. Sleep is disturbed, the abuser wakes up, and the search for more liquor commences. This accounts for the so-called "hair of the dog" remedy (a half ounce or so of liquor the morning after a heavy drinking spree) and the Bloody Mary, both of which are well known by abusive drinkers. In such instances, the downward spiral into depression is slowed by replenishing some of the alcohol that has been expelled the night before.

It is difficult to provide some idea of the horrible craving that drives the alcoholic to continue drinking, even when it is so contrary to his best interests. One alcoholic tried to illustrate his hunger by holding his hand over a burning candle. He claimed that his need for alcohol exceeded his need to withdraw his hand. Another confessed that his craving overshadowed his love for his family, his most intimate relationships, his desire even to survive to the next day.

Recovery from alcoholism is not simply a matter of willpower, as so many untrained laymen would like to believe. The disease is far too destructive and far too insidious to lend itself to simplistic solutions or quick-fix, self-help solutions; for it is not a moral-ethical disorder, a minor personality flaw, or something having to do with lack of character. It involves a complicated interaction of innumerable factors that relate to the physical, mental, and spiritual health of the addict.

Perhaps this is why the alcoholic facade—the supports that the addict so painfully and perilously develops to protect his convenient and self-serving fantasies—are fragile at best, because any kind of demolition would destroy his carefully erected illusions of grandiosity, power, denial, self-confidence, and the pains and terrors of withdrawal. As a consequence, the alcoholic can be impossibly trenchant in defense of his addiction; for if he fails, he will be compelled to surrender his refuge and commence a rigorous program of rehabilitation and recovery. That, of course, is the last thing he wants to do. Thus, so long as the prospect of intoxication is perceived as the only effective way of dealing with an unmanageable and indifferent world, he will continue to drink.

For the alcoholic, liquor serves as both a tranquilizer and a stimulant; it quiets his fears and inflates them, even as it diverts his frustrations and nourishes his anger and sadistic impulses. It may be presupposed that it can stifle the terrors and insecurities that plague him; and, in so doing, it may reinforce the illusion that he is empowered to determine his fate. In drunkenness, however, he believes that he can replace those terrors and those insecurities with a facade of vivacity and—paradoxically—a remarkable predisposition to martyrdom, self-destruction, and denial.

Most chronic alcoholics live almost entirely in the present. The past is a muddled cacophony of memories and emotions and the future lacks substance and meaning. The present is a refuge of sorts, comprised of an extraordinary complex of fantasies where consequences can be eluded and relationships are tenuous. So long as this kind of thinking persists and so long as he refuses to get help, the alcoholic is doomed to an endless cycle of self-destruction, insanity, and finally and inevitably, an untimely death.

Appendix 3

Twelve Step Programs and the Literature of Addiction

*He has taught the Universe to realize itself,
and that must have been; very simple....*

*I do grow,...a little confident
that I will never down a whiskey again
or gin or rum or vodka, brandy or ale....*

It is, after all, very simple.

You just never drink again all each damned day.
John Berryman, The Alcoholic in the 3rd Week of
the 3rd Treatment. (1–2, 5–8, 12–13)

Alcoholism has probably been endemic ever since humanity discovered the rhapsodic pleasure of an altered perception or became fixated on certain types of repetitive behaviors. Every child who has visited an amusement park knows the pleasures of a slightly altered mental state, and who among us can forget the merry pleasures of a playground swing, especially if we twisted the strands and spun in dizzy circles while the sky rotated like a ceiling fan. The earliest preliterate societies knew about fermentation; and, later, the empires of the Middle East and Far East developed a prodigious love of beer and wine. Centuries later, in Europe, the nobility indulged liberally in all manor of spirits and were generally "under the influence" throughout most of the day. For some reason, however, drunkenness was hardly regarded as a problem of any significance; and, in most cases it was even the norm. The underclasses were not far behind (consider the paintings of Brueghel, for instance), although most had to settle for cheap gin and watered down beer instead of the more refined liquors of the wealthy.

It is also a wonder that the grand, old sailing ships of the past managed to go anywhere at all, let alone engage in battle with any degree of effectiveness. Spirits and an excess of beer or wine were a daily staple, although the officers were entitled to the more refined liquors, while the crew below deck had to settle for beer and a daily portion of rum (a tradition among the British that apparently holds true to this day). By the early nineteenth century, the fascination with altered mental states had expanded considerably. Laudanum, opium, absinthe, and cocaine were cheap and commonplace and were available to just about everybody; and plain, old fashioned moonshine was a staple of any outland farm, even as it continues to be quite popular in some of the more remote regions in America. By the turn of the century, with the onset of social enlightenment, alcoholism and addiction were beginning to be recognized as a problem, and temperance groups sprang up like dandelions in an untended garden. Most of these groups were generally ineffective in curbing the fascination with alcohol. In fact, they achieved something of a reputation as Puritans and busybodies, despite the fact, that death and clinical insanity were commonplace.

It was not until the early twentieth century—most especially following World War I, that a number of recovery programs and hospitals began to gain credibility (most especially with regard to opium and liquor which were used as pain killers), although a truly effective strategy of recovery had to wait for the genius of a small group of alcoholics who founded a local recovery group that they called "Alcoholics Anonymous," which was based on an older program known as the "Oxford Movement." This was in 1935, although a good twenty years would pass before they were to gain much notoriety and their twelve step approach would be acknowledged as a truly effective strategy for recovery.

The primary reference of A.A. was and is *Alcoholics Anonymous: The Story of How Many Thousands of Men and Women Have Recovered from Alcoholism* (1st edition, 1939), and it has served as a proven guide for addiction recovery ever since. Indeed, the effectiveness of A.A's Twelve Step program appears to have exceeded all other methods of rehabilitation; and, if a candidate can make it through the first year, there is a good chance that he will stay sober the rest of his life.

A.A.'s companion reference to the primary text, *Twelve Steps and Twelve Traditions* (1952), clarifies in considerable detail the rigorous demands of the Twelve Step Program of Recovery, but this smaller book does not contain the testimonials that are found in the larger book.

Although much of the literature of the nineteenth century adopted a more skeptical view of addiction, A.A.'s Twelve Step texts do not regard alcohol dependence as a moral failing or as a defect of character that can be remedied by love, spiritual rebirth, or will power. Rather, A.A. treats alcoholism as a disease that has little to do with morality, strength of character, or integrity. The Twelve Step program is focused on physical and psychological matters, especially the problems emanating from fear, frustration, unresolved personal issues, depression, the physical predisposition to drink, and the alcoholic's spiritual, mental, and physical deterioration.

Candidates for recovery attend meetings and learn how to practice the twelve steps from fellow alcoholics, who are likely to demand rigorous honesty and who quickly recognize the candidate's denials and obfuscations, since they were once practicing alcoholics themselves. However, it has been claimed—perhaps with tongue in cheek—that a castaway with 100 cases of liquor and a soggy copy of *Alcoholics Anonymous* could at some point in the future recover from his passion for alcohol and use the remaining cases as cooking fuel.

A.A.'s theories about alcoholism and addiction are now widely respected, and its methods have been adapted to treat a considerable variety of related addictive-compulsive disorders. Such organizations include Debtors Anonymous, Gamblers Anonymous, Narcotics Anonymous, and Overeaters Anonymous. In fact, there are twelve step recovery groups for just about every addictive disorder imaginable, perhaps because addiction and dysfunctionality are now endemic. Contemporary twelve step groups may include individuals with compulsive eating disorders such as bulimia, anorexia, and excessive weight gain; sex, pornography, and cybersex; computers, discussion and chat groups; the Internet; nicotine; amphetamines, sedatives, and hard narcotics such as heroin, crack, and coke; video games that detach the player from any sense of reality; and even caffeine (just about everyone knows the importance of a morning coffee or tea, the cranky feeling without it, the headaches of withdrawal, and—for some—the pleasures of an afternoon Coke or Pepsi). Indeed, twelve step recovery programs appear to have become something of a fad. We are all familiar with celebrity testimonials and biographies, the fluffy media confessions that promote various twelve step approaches, and the upscale rehab facilities for the rich and famous. Even the television networks have become involved with popular programs of recovery such as *Celebrity Rehab* and *Intervention*. All of these programs are focused on a twelve step approach to rehabilitation, and most of them use a text that is quite similar to the classic 1939 recovery text of Alcoholics Anonymous.

The standard twelve step approach to recovery will usually require that the candidate follow the steps exactly as described in the A.A. publication, *Alcoholics Anonymous* (sometimes called *The Big Book*). It requires that a candidate admit powerlessness over alcohol and believe in the restorative capacity of a higher power of his or her own understanding. At this point, the candidate should be willing to believe that this higher power can restore the candidate to sanity—it being assumed that the irrational nature of the addiction to alcohol is, itself, a form of insanity (steps 1–3). The twelve step method then requires that the candidate undertake a rigorous and thorough moral inventory, admit to a God of his own understanding and to another human being the exact nature of those wrongs, and—having completed these steps—is entirely ready to have God remove those defects of character (steps 4–6). The candidate is then to ask God to remove those defects, and he or she is to make a list of those who had been harmed and make amends, except when to do so would be harmful to the person who was wronged (steps 7–9). Finally, the candidate is to continue to take a personal inventory and promptly admit any wrongs. The candidate also makes a commitment to practice all the previous steps in the course of daily life, pray and meditate on a daily basis , and help others with the same addiction or disorder (steps 10–12). This is a heavy and complicated order, and most members of

A.A. require at least a year to complete the twelve steps with any degree of thoroughness.

It is generally understood that, with the exception of Step One, A.A.'s Twelve Step Program cannot be done to perfection; however, all candidates are encouraged to do the best they can, and most A.A. veterans have gone through a full twelve step program a number of times.

A key aspect of Twelve Step meetings and Twelve Step literature is the testimonial. Such testimonials describe the experiences of recovering alcoholics and note the difficulty and loss of control before recovery and how the addict changed following recovery. These testimonials are meant to encourage others and are often a staple of Twelve Step meetings.

Most Twelve Step meetings follow a relatively similar format: someone usually volunteers to arrive early (most A.A. meetings are held at churches, community centers, or at an A.A. office) to make coffee, lay out the texts, and arrange the chairs, tables, posters, and pamphlets. Meetings may be held throughout the day, but in more populated areas, early morning (just before going to work), noon, and early evenings are the most popular. A "leader" (someone with a solid record of sobriety) is elected to "chair" the meeting, and it opens with the *Serenity Prayer*, which is followed by a reading of the twelve steps, the A.A. Preamble, the serenity prayer, and selected paragraphs from the recovery text, *Alcoholics Anonymous*. These are followed by a discussion or lengthy testimonial from one of the members and a closing prayer (usually the Lord' Prayer) when all attendees stand in a circle and hold hands to confirm the unity of the group and the conviction that principles are more important than personalities.

Twelve step meetings are usually divided among study groups as they relate to the study of A.A. texts, discussion groups, and testimonial meetings. Study groups are highly focused: usually each person in attendance reads a paragraph or two from either the text, *Alcoholics Anonymous*, or *Twelve Steps and Twelve Traditions* (there are separate meetings for each text). The reader may then make a brief comment on the paragraphs, and the readings and comments continue throughout the hour. If it is an especially large meeting, the "leader" will appoint the readers.

Finally, A.A. will specify whether the meetings are "open" to anyone interested in addiction or whether they are restricted by sex or to admitted addicts or individuals who are cross-addicted to other narcotics—an increasingly common phenomenon. There are also special meetings for the spouses, relatives, and children of the addict—in the case of A.A., these individuals are called *Al-Anons*.

Although the general format for A.A. meetings is typically the same, they actually differ considerably because different meetings tend to attract different kinds of individuals. Hence, most newcomers are encouraged to attend a variety of meetings until they find a group where they feel most comfortable. Finally, even the most seasoned A.A. members are encouraged to find a "sponsor"—someone in whom they can confide and turn to in difficult times.

Most A.A. meetings follow the twelve step format described earlier, although it is typically modified according to the special needs of the group. Anonymity and privacy are of the essence. There are usually one or two table signs that read, "Who you see here, what you hear here, let it stay here." In some cases, there may be special, private meetings for individuals in a position of responsibility where anonymity is of great importance, as in the case of physicians, clergymen, professionals, legislators, judges, and the like.

One of the A.A. traditions specifies that A.A.'s relations with the general public should be characterized by personal anonymity and names and pictures "ought not be broadcast, filmed, or publicly printed" (Tradition Eleven). A.A. is also self-supporting. In fact, contributions—even by members of A.A. are limited (to avoid undue influence). Finally, while A.A. may cooperate with related groups, they are not affiliated with anyone and do not publicly solicit funds (Traditions Six and Seven).

A great deal of modern literature and film is generally in accord with the perspective of *Alcoholics Anonymous*. These include Charles Jackson's film, *The Lost Weekend* (1944), William Inge's play and the film, *Come Back, Little Sheba* (1950), Gerald E. Groggins' *The Anonymous Disciple,* and Blake Edward's film, *The Days of Wine and Roses* (1962) with its haunting theme song by Henry Mancini. More recently, films that have adopted the twelve step perspective on alcoholism include *Leaving Las Vegas,* the story of an alcoholic who purposely drinks himself to death. Some individuals have also enjoyed the film, *When a Man Loves a Woman,* although it has been panned for its sentimental portrait of recovery. Other films include *The Drunkard, Shattered Spirits, I'll Cry Tomorrow, Under the Volcano,* and *28 Days.*

Twelve Step programs have also played a major role among writers, as we have noted in this book. In addition to the literature noted, John Berryman's autobiographical novel, *Recovery* (1976) and David Foster Wallace's *Infinite Jest* (1996) are especially notable. Finally, Nelson Algren's novel, *The Man with the Golden Arm* (1949), is a vivid and telling portrait of the effects of heroin addiction.

Almost all twelve step programs are concerned with the maintenance of anonymity, and, other than those noted earlier, very few books with a named author deal with the theme of recovery through the twelve steps (one of the A.A. traditions explicitly requires anonymity at the level of press, radio, and television). However, a great many books contain veiled references to twelve step groups. In some cases, a fictional book may actually serve as a qualified admission of alcoholic dependence and twelve step membership, or it may involve an oblique confession that presents and rearranges the author's addictive landscape as a part of the story. Conversely, a great many writers who have been concerned about the nature of addiction have created fictional demons of the darkest possible complexion to satisfy whatever concerns they wished to nurture or exorcise. Jack London's autobiographical novel, *John Barleycorn,* and the work of Edgar Allen Poe are quite notable, if only because they anticipated certain A.A. principles long before they were ever conceived. Malcolm Lowry's *Under the Volcano* is a vivid portrait of alcoholic self-destruction and is remarkably effective in portraying the despair and the final, horrifying effects of the disease. A good many plays have also dealt with the problems of addiction and alcoholism from a twelve step perspective. Tennessee Williams has described the consequences of addiction and psychosis in a good number of his plays, most notably his portrait of Blanch DuBois in *A Streetcar Named Desire;* Eugene O'Neill's dramas contain a great number of characters who are bent on alcoholic self-destruction, most notably in *Long Day's Journey into Night* (1956) and *The Iceman Cometh* (1946).

The study of alcohol-related publications may help in understanding the nature of the disease, but it should not be confused with recovery, for, as A.A. itself states, "Knowledge availed us nothing." Publications such as *Alcoholics Anonymous* are focused on methods of recovery and the testimonials of recovering alcoholics, not the causes or basis of alcoholism, the nature of the alcoholic mind set, or the foundations of any other addiction. However, readers who are interested in a further study of the nature of the disease and the alcoholic perspective may want to refer to the list of suggested readings in Appendix 5.

Appendix 4

A.A.'s *Primary Texts:* Alcoholics Anonymous *and* Twelve Steps and Twelve Traditions: *A Review*

In some ways, *Alcoholics Anonymous* is not particularly well written. It lacks unity and coherence; it is sometimes rambling and unfocused; it postulates an extraordinary litany of claims and demands; and it can be strangely inflexible and incongruent. Yet, despite its quaint 1930s cultural references and 1940s paragraphing and verbiage, it continues to be cornerstone of the A.A. twelve step program.

Indeed, for all its shortcomings and oversights, *Alcoholics Anonymous* is unquestionably one of the most remarkable and influential books ever written, primarily because of its proven effectiveness as a blueprint for sobriety and addiction recovery and its capacity to offer hope and the possibility that millions of addicts and alcoholics may no longer have to suffer the misery and pain of chemical dependence.

Most of all, the twelve step program that *Alcoholics Anonymous* describes *works*; and, while a select minority of professionals and candidates have insisted that the program is unrelenting and psychologically unsound, thousands of doctors, academics, spiritual leaders, and psychologists have enthusiastically endorsed A.A. and its primary text, *Alcoholics Anonymous*.

Much the same can be said for A.A's companion publication, *Twelve Steps and Twelve Traditions*, which was published in 1953. In this particular text, Bill W. Ebby, who was the author of *Alcoholics Anonymous* and a cofounder of A.A., discusses the Twelve Step Program in much greater detail, while appending a second section on A.A. traditions, something that was not included or even conceived when *Alcoholics Anonymous* was first written. *Twelve Steps and Twelve Traditions* has none of the testimonies of the larger text, is dedicated solely to a discussion of the twelve steps and twelve traditions, and is not necessarily intended for employers, families of alcoholics, or interested parties. It has served as a model for a number of other recovery texts, although none have been endorsed or published by A.A. These related texts have included *A Woman's Way through the 12 Steps, Buddhism and the Twelve Steps, Twelve Steps for Christians* (there are a number of Buddhist and Jesuit elements in A.A.'s twelve step program), and a twelve step text for overeaters, the sexually compulsive, adult children of alcoholics, the chronically ill, and twelve step skeptics, codependents, and young people.

The first edition of *Alcoholics Anonymous* was published in 1938, three years after the official founding of A.A. Author Bill W. Ebby (sometimes affectionately referred to as "Bill W.") had been a stockbroker and golden boy whose promising career as a bond salesman had been ruined by alcoholism. In 1935, while on a business trip in Akron, Ohio, Ebby met a prominent local surgeon and alcoholic, Dr. Robert Seiberling (known as "Dr. Bob" in A.A. circles), and the two hit upon the idea of a twenty-four hour program of sobriety, which seemed much more manageable and a good deal less intimidating than a lifetime of struggle. In the meantime, their sobriety meetings, which were an offshoot of the Oxford Group of the 1920s and 1930s,[1] continued to expand; and, in 1938, Ebby wrote *Alcoholics Anonymous*, with the help of Ruth Hock, who acted as his secretary and editorial consultant. Although the book was originally intended for alcoholics who could not attend meetings (personal contact is an important element in any A.A. program of sobriety), it gradually achieved notoriety among all alcoholics, whether alone or with others. It has continued to serve as a standard reference for A.A., although it has been revised and edited four times to adapt to the changing interests and needs of contemporary A.A. members. However, the first section of the book, including the doctor's opinion and Ebby's 164 page twelve step discussion, has remained unchanged.

In writing the book, Ebby drew on the ideas of a close friend and supporter, Dr. Sam Shoemaker, who placed special emphasis on one-on-one sharing and the Oxford Group's "Four Absolutes" (honesty, purity, unselfishness, and love). Ebby also borrowed from William James's *Varieties of Religious Experience*[2] and the Oxford Group's six step program to sobriety. A discerning reader will also note a great many of Ebby's ideas reflect (and even paraphrase) the poetry and ideas of Walt Whitman and the work of such transcendental writers as Ralph Waldo Emerson, Amos Bronson Alcott, and Henry David Thoreau.

Hock typed, revised, and mimeographed the initial draft and sent it to a considerable number of publishers and financial backers. It eventually attracted the attention of Eugene Exman, the religious editor of Harper Brothers Publishers, who offered to publish the book; but an A.A.colleague, Hank P., convinced Ebby to publish the book himself. Ebby started his own company at $25.00 a share with a first run of 400 books, which were sent to a number of alcoholic and addiction professionals. Dr. William Silkworth and Dr. Henry Fosdick suggested including a doctor's opinion in one of the opening chapters, and, on April, 1939, 5,000 copies of the revised version were released to the general public. It was not very well received at first; but, later that year, sales increased after an essay, "Alcoholics and God," appeared in *Liberty,* a popular magazine of the day. The financial strain involved in publishing the book eased somewhat after a donation from a Fr. Edward Dowling, who noticed a similarity between A.A.'s twelve step perspective and his Jesuit order. In 1941, a 7,500 word article in the *Saturday Evening Post* resulted in a dramatic increase in sales; and, that same year, the "Serenity Prayer," which was included in the second edition and which has been attributed to one Dr. Reinhold Neibuhr, became a staple of A.A. meetings.

In 1947, the A.A. Preamble became a standard at all meetings, and in 1953, Ebby wrote *Twelve Steps and Twelve Traditions,* a comprehensive and somewhat more cerebral overview of the full meaning and focus of A.A.'s twelve steps and twelve traditions—both of which had been covered rather summarily and without much explanation in *Alcoholics Anonymous.*

The second edition of *Alcoholics Anonymous* included chapters on A.A. principles and was essentially the same as the first edition, including the eight original testimonies from A.A "pioneers" plus twenty-four new stories, which were divided into two sections: "They Stopped in Time" and "They Lost Nearly All."

By 1961, the book had sold more than 50,000 copies, and included translations in Spanish, French, and German. The one-millionth copy was presented to President Richard Nixon in 1973; and, in 1976, A.A. membership topped approximately one million.

The third edition was issued in 1976; and, a year later, it was published in paperback so it could be carried into prisons where hardcover books may not have been permitted.

Sales of the book topped 8 million in 1989, 10 million in 1990, and 20 million in 2000.

The fourth edition came out in 2001; and, although the "doctor's opinion" and Ebby's 164 page discussion were unchanged, it had 24 new narratives, 17 "keepers," and a number of other testimonies intended to appeal to a wider cross-section of readers with diverse experiences, ages, beliefs, and ethnicities.

In 2005, the 25 millionth copy of the book was presented as a gift to San Quentin Prison, whose first A.A meeting was held in 1941. As of this writing, attendance at A.A. national and international conventions has included delegates from countries as diverse as Finland, Samoa, Australia, Guatemala, Malaysia, Cambodia, Malta, Italy, Japan, China, Vietnam, India (where *"The Big Book"* is printed in eight separate languages), Turkey, Russia, Botswana, Zimbabwe, Jerusalem, South Africa, and Sweden.

Although *Alcoholics Anonymous* and *Twelve Steps and Twelve Traditions* are A.A.'s primary texts, it has published a considerable variety of other books on addiction and alcoholism. These books are concerned with a variety of related topics and groups, including Al-Anons (family members and close relatives of alcoholics), individuals who are cross-addicted to other chemicals, A.A. service, and the history and evolution of

A.A. Those who are interested in learning more about the A.A. perspective on alcohol, addiction, and recovery may want to read *Alcoholics Anonymous Comes of Age* (1957), *Youth and the Alcoholic Parent* (1957), *Twelve Concepts for World Service* (Bill W, 1962), *The A.A Way of Life* (1967), *As Bill Sees It* (1971), *Came to Believe* (1973), *Living Sober* (1980), *"Pass It On." The Story of Bill W. and How the A.A. Message Reached the World* (1984), and *Experience, Strength, and Hope,* (2003).

Alcoholics Anonymous and *Twelve Steps and Twelve Traditions* are concerned with matters of recovery, not analysis, and they should not be judged according to their literary merit. They are essentially a call to action, sanity, and sobriety; and their dated style and quaint verbiage have little to do with their impact and universal appeal.

While the first 164 pages and Dr. William Silkworth's "opinion" have remained the same throughout the four editions of *Alcoholics Anonymous,* the Preface and the Foreword have been adapted to account for the various revisions and updates since the first publication in 1938. Chapter 1 of the text begins with Bill Ebby's personal story, although his biography is not entirely complete and contains a number of omissions and contradictions. This should in no way detract from the book or from Ebby's story, his budding career as a stock broker, his terrifying bouts with alcohol, and his gradual return to sobriety.

Chapter 2 picks up the story, discussing the common peril that faces so many alcoholics, Ebby's work and friendship with other alcoholics, and his decision to publish an anonymous volume on alcoholism.

Chapter 3 describes the various, unsuccessful strategies most alcoholics have used in their futile efforts to attain sobriety and the difference between "normal" drinking and alcoholic drinking. It also describes the experiences of a number of confirmed alcoholics, their return to sobriety, and the importance of certain spiritual principles in helping a candidate attain sobriety.

Chapter 4 is addressed to agnostic readers concerning their spiritual doubts and the importance of recognizing a *"Power greater than ourselves."* It goes on to discuss the role of faith in attaining sobriety and the impossibility of denying the existence of some kind of higher power in the overall scheme of things.

Chapters 5, 6, and 7 describe Ebby's twelve step program in detail. These three chapters are the cornerstone of the entire book. Chapter 5, "How It Works," is concerned with the first four steps of the program and how they relate to alcoholic delusions of self-management, the importance of a rigorous personal inventory, and the necessity of making amends where the candidate may have harmed others.

It is interesting to note that Ebby's twelve step discussion is always presented in second person "we" in order to suggest a commonality of interest and concern with his readers.

Chapter 6, "Into Action," describes steps five to twelve. It begins with the Fifth Step when a candidate admits to himself, a fellow human being, and to God the exact nature of his offenses. It stresses the importance of rigorous honesty and suggests various means by which the step can be completed. The Sixth Step requires that the candidate be entirely willing to have God remove his defects of character; and, in the Seventh Step, the candidate "humbly" asks God to remove those defects. In the Eighth and Ninth Steps, the candidate makes a list of all persons he had harmed so that he can make direct amends "whenever possible, except when to do so would injure them or others." The chapter has a number of suggestions regarding strategies that might be carried out in making amends, especially regarding instances of debt, criminal offenses, broken commitments and promises, and unreceptive listeners.

Step Ten requires that the candidate continue to take a personal inventory of his conduct and promptly admit his mistakes when he was wrong; Step Eleven suggests that the candidate seek to improve his conscious contact with God *as he understands him,* asking only for knowledge of His will and the power to carry it out; and Step Twelve encourages the candidate to carry the A.A. message to other still-suffering alcoholics while practicing A.A. principles in all his affairs.[3]

The twelve steps are a difficult order; they can by no means be completed perfectly; and they typically require at least a year to fulfill. Spirituality is a key element of the program, and seven of the twelve steps require a spiritual commitment or contact of some sort, although it is clear that a candidate can—and should—deal *only* with a God or power of his own understanding.

Chapter 7, "Working with Others," is primarily concerned with the Twelfth Step discussed earlier. It suggests methods for dealing with practicing alcoholics who may be candidates for A.A. and a sober life, how to outline a program of action, and the importance of helping others as a foundation for one's own, continuing recovery. It is also concerned with domestic issues and strategies for dealing with them. Finally, it discusses methods for dealing with the temptation to drink in a world where alcohol is constantly available and notes how to avoid difficult or "slippery" situations and events.

Chapter 8, "To Wives," describes the alcoholic household before and after sobriety—including the pain, confusion, financial problems, and loneliness that are an inevitable consequence of an alcoholic marriage. It goes on to describe the common strategies and struggles faced by most spouses, the evolving nature of the disease, and the despair that must ultimately ensue. This is followed by a series of strategies for dealing with an addicted spouse and notes the importance of supporting his or her commitment to sobriety, the possibility that even the most apparently hopeless situation might be remedied, and the fact that alcoholism is a disease, not a failure of will or moral character.

The chapter concludes with comments relating to employers, children, issues of commitment to the program, jealousy, and the fellowship of Al-Anon, which uses A.A. principles as a guide for husbands, wives, relatives, friends, and children of alcoholics.

Chapter 9, "The Family Afterward," is about the nature of recovery once a candidate has stopped drinking, the importance of moving beyond "past occurrences," and the necessity of assuring anonymity and not discussing the stories and problems of fellow alcoholics when at home or in public.

As with so many of the previous chapters, the discussion is filled with examples, including the testimonies and experiences of a broad range of individuals, some of whom were alcoholics and some who were Al-Anons.

Chapter 10, "To Employers" advocates support and tolerance of the recovering alcoholic and notes various ways in which an employer can work with a candidate to help him remain sober. Chapter 11, "A Vision for You," is perhaps one of the most popular chapters in the text, assuring sobriety and promising a better life that could not possibly have been imagined in the worst of times. It concludes with a promise of fulfillment and fellowship that echoes the final words of Walt Whitman's poem "Leaves of Grass." Ebby writes,

> Give freely of what you find and join us. We shall be with you in the Fellowship of the Spirit, and you will surely meet some of us as you trudge the Road of Happy Destiny.
>   My God bless you and keep you-until then.[4]

The second part of the book is concerned with various exemplary histories and testimonials in which a member of A.A. describes his life as a practicing alcoholic, his discovery of A.A., and his life (and the rewards) after sobriety. They include the "pioneers" of A.A., the narratives of individuals who "stopped in time," and finally those who "lost nearly all."

Twelve Steps and Twelve Traditions offers a somewhat more cerebral approach to the Twelve Step method of recovery. It is not necessarily intended for employers, families of alcoholics, or interested parties, as in the case of *Alcoholics Anonymous*. Most of the discussions are relatively simple in style and content, and the majority of chapters or twelve step discussions are approximately ten pages in length. The book speaks directly to the reader while developing most of the concepts presented in *Alcoholics Anonymous* in a somewhat more detailed format that minimizes confusion and assures perhaps a somewhat more comprehensive level of understanding. However, while it spells out the various steps in considerable detail, some readers feel that this is unnecessary and prefer to rely on *Alcoholics Anonymous*. Others prefer the no-nonsense approach of *Twelve Steps and Twelve Traditions* and appreciate its detailed suggestions and insights.

The second half of the book discusses A.A.'s Twelve Traditions, and most candidates for sobriety are encouraged to familiarize themselves with its principles, which deal with the common welfare of A.A., governance, membership, autonomy, the purpose of A.A., affiliations, financial support, professionalism, politics, the media, and the importance of placing principles before personalities.

Appendix 5

Suggested Additional Reading

A.A. and the Alcoholic Employee. New York: Alcoholics Anonymous World Services, 1962.

Alcoholics Anonymous: The Story of How Many Thousands of Men and Women Have Recovered from Alcoholism. New York: Alcoholics Anonymous World Services, 1976.

At Last...AA. Atlanta: Metro Atlanta Alcoholics Anonymous, n.d.

Came to Believe. New York: Alcoholics Anonymous World Services, 1991.

Covington, Stephanie S. *A Woman's Way through the Twelve Steps.* Center City, MN: Hazeldon, 1994.

Goodwin, Donald W. *Is Alcoholism Hereditary?* New York: Oxford UP, 1976.

Jackson, Charles. *The Lost Weekend.* New York: Farrar and Rinehart, 1944.

Jellinek, E.M. *The Disease Concept of Alcoholism.* New Haven, CT: Hillhouse Press, 1960.

Johnson Vernon E. *I'll Quit Tomorrow.* Rev. ed. San Francisco: Harper and Row, 1980.

London, Jack. *John Barleycorn.* New York: Grosset and Dunlap, 1913.

Milam, James R. and Katherin Ketcham. *Under the Influence: A Guide to the Myths and Realities of Alcoholism.* Seattle: Madrona Publishers, 1981.

Robertson, Nan. *A.A.: Inside Alcoholics Anonymous.* New York: Morrow, 1988.

Rudy, David R. *Becoming Alcoholic: Alcoholic's Anonymous and the Reality of Alcoholism.* Carbondale: Southern Illinois UP, 1986.

Valiant George E. *The Natural History of Alcoholism.* Cambridge, MA: Harvard UP, 1983.

Notes

Foreword

1. This book (sometimes called "The Big Book") is the primary reference for the Twelve Step program of recovery of Alcoholics Anonymous. It is intended for individuals interested in recovery, those who are trying to find some way to deal with a friend, relative, or spouse who is alcoholic, and employers of alcoholics. It does not attempt to explain the causes of alcoholism or the nature of the disease.

Chapter One   The Foundations of Alcoholic Thinking and the Role of Fantasy, Alienation, and Rebellion

1. For an additional, comprehensive definition of the disease, please see chapter 2, note 2, p. 156.
2. Thomas Gilmore, in his book *Equivocal Spirits*, notes that of the American Nobel Prize winners, five of them, Lewis, O'Neill, Faulkner, Steinbeck, and Hemingway, were alcoholic or drank alcoholically. In his book, *The Thirsty* Muse, Tom Dardis provides an extensive list of alcoholic writers, including Edward Arlington Robinson, Jack London, Edna St. Vincent Millay, F. Scott Fitzgerald, Hart Crane, Conrad Aiken, Thomas Wolfe, Dashiell Hammett, Dorothy Parker, Ring Lardner, Djuna Barnes, John O'Hara, James Gould Cozens, Tennessee Williams, John Berryman, Carson McCullers, James Jones, John Cheever, Jean Stafford, Truman Capote, Raymond Carver, Robert Lowell, and James Agee.
3. The entire prayer is as follows:
   God grant me the serenity to accept the things I cannot change,
   The courage to change the things I can,
   And the wisdom to know the difference.
4. Some professionals and certain members of A.A. do not regard alcoholism as an addiction. However, since the primary features are essentially the same. I will use the terms "alcoholism" and "addiction" interchangeably where appropriate.

Chapter Two   Alcoholism in Ernest Hemingway's
The Sun Also Rises: A Wine and Roses
Perspective of the Lost Generation

Revised from the original as published in *The Hemingway Review* 14.2 (Spring 1995): 64–79.

1. See also chapter 1, p. 2.
2. According to Johns Hopkins Hospital in Baltimore, an individual may be an alcoholic if his drinking, among other things, leads to irritability, carelessness, personality changes, impulsiveness, decreased self-control, and moodiness. The questions they pose ask the individual to consider whether he drinks to relieve feelings of inadequacy, to seek an inferior environment, and whether or not his drinking leads to marked likes and dislikes. Johns Hopkins Hospital believes that an affirmative to any three of these characteristics raises a very good possibility that the examinee is an alcoholic (see Weston, 39–40).

   Another questionnaire by the Christopher D. Smith Foundation asks in part whether the lack of a drink leads to tension and whether drinking is used to relieve tension, to escape worries, to escape guilt, feelings of inferiority, and shyness, and whether alcohol is used to relate to others. It further asks whether drinking makes the subject irritable, unambitious, detached, self-centered, and resentful (see Smith Foundation, 212–213). The catalog of questions posed by Alcoholics Anonymous is similar. In any case, it is obvious that Brett, Jake, and Mike match these profiles in no small measure.

   Finally, my own observations, experiences, and studies have led me to believe that,

   a. The practicing alcoholic suffers from low self-esteem that will very likely be disguised in a mask of grandiosity. That is, most alcoholics have a massive, all-absorbing ego accompanied by an inferiority complex that threatens to undermine the core of their self-esteem.
   b. The practicing alcoholic is likely to feel powerless over events, over the behavior of others, and over the conduct of his own life.
   c. This feeling of powerlessness can lead him to try to erect a fantasy of control over people, places, and things.
   d. It can also lead him to rebel against any symbol of authority, whether perceived or real.
   e. Finally, it can lead him to the illusion that, because he has his external life is seemingly under control, he himself is under control.
   f. Thus, he will try to manipulate people and circumstances to excess, and he will try to "use" others in the expectation that they will somehow make his world congruent with his needs.
   g. It also seems to me that the practicing alcoholic suffers from a great deal of repressed anger. This anger is a mask disguising his fear about

his value as a human being and his inability to control events external to himself. In that regard, it is a defense, a response to the belief that his most intimate needs cannot or will not be satisfied. Of course, the anger is likely to be directed against those held responsible for withholding gratification.

    h. Such anger can become depression—anger turned inward—or sullenness and emotional rigidity. It can also erupt violently when the inability to control exterior events becomes obvious and he becomes frustrated.

    i. The practicing alcoholic also has difficulty understanding and sharing his feelings. Consequently, he feels isolated; and, indeed, he is often a loner and has difficulty making any kind of stable or long-term commitment to others.

    j. Finally, it is not at all unusual for a practicing alcoholic to see life in black and white terms. He cannot compromise: small problems and momentary setbacks may frustrate him and appear catastrophic. He may then become childish and self-pitying and, ultimately, seek release from his feelings in the euphoria and desensitizing effects of liquor (see also chapter 1, p. 2.

3. Among recovery groups such as Alcoholics Anonymous, there is considerable discussion and attention given to the problems of individuals who have chosen not to drink any more, but who insist on behaving much the same as an intoxicant. That is, they manifest feelings of loneliness, anger, resentment, perfectionism, control, denial, and intolerance in much the same manner as if they were drinking to excess. Such people are commonly referred to as "dry drunks."

Chapter Three   Addiction and Spirituality in Contemporary American Poetry: Frustration and Paradox

Revised from "Addiction and Spirituality in Contemporary American Poetry." *Dionysos* 11.1 (Spring 2001): 5–17.

1. See John Milton's *Paradise Lost, Book IV*, l. 73 in which the fallen angel, Lucifer, complains, "Which way I fly is hell; myself am hell;...." This line is unquestionably derived from Virgil who wrote, "Each of us bears his own hell" (*Aeneid*, VI, l. 743).

2. The final lines of the poem, "Goodfriday, 1613. Riding Westward," are as follows:

    O Saviour, as thou hang'st upon the tree
    I turne my backe to thee, but to recieve
    Corrections, till they mercies bid thee leave.
    O thinke mee worth thine anger, punish mee,

Burne off my rusts, and my deformity,
Restore thine Image, so much, by thy face,
That thou may'st know mee, and I'll turne my face. (36–42)
3. Jonathon Edwards was an eighteenth-century defender of New England
Calvinism. His grim, Puritan idealism and orthodoxy relied on fundamentalist insights and mysticism as much as rational argument. Although he
placed a great deal of emphasis on sin and the nature of God's wrath, he
also argued that God's grace was freely extended to all repentant sinners.
4. The entire poem is as follows:

Huswifery

Make me, O Lord. thy Spin[n]ing Wheele compleate.
    Thy Holy Worde my Distaff make for mee.
Make mine Affections thy Swift Flyers neate
    And make my Soule thy holy Spoole to bee.
    My Conversation make to be thy Reele
    And reele the yard thereon spun of thy Wheele.

Make me thy Loome, then, knit therein this Twine:
    And make thy Holy Spirit, Lord, winde quills:
Then weave the Web thyselfe. The yarn is fine.
    Thine Ordinances make my Fulling Mills.
    Then dy the same in Heavenly Colours Choice,
    All pinkt wih varnisht Flowers of Paradise.

Then cloath therewith mine Understanding, Will,
    Affections, Judgement, Conscience, Memory
My Words, and Actions, that their shine may fill
    My wayes with glory and Thee glorify.
    Then mine apparell shall display before yee
    That I am Cloathed in Holy robes for glory
                                1685 (?)

It is interesting to note that Taylor's poem is an unqualified petition to
be the instrument of God's will—perhaps he had an unquestioning comfort and absolute trust in God and in his Calvinist faith to support him.
Roethke's poem, however, is a good deal more qualified and reveals more
of a twentieth century perspective on the workings of Divine Will and the
nature of God's plan in human affairs.

Chapter Four   John Berryman's "Phase Four" and His Precarious Attempt to Find a Compromise between Drunkenness, Sobriety, and the A.A. Twelve Step Program of Recovery

Revised from "John Berryman's 'Phase Four' and His Precarious Attempt to
Find a Compromise between Drunkenness, Sobriety, and the A.A. Twelve
Step Program." *Dionysos* 8.2 (1999): 17–27.

1. For a comprehensive overview of the A.A. Twelve Step Program, see Appendix 3, "Twelve Step Programs and the Literature of Addiction."
2. The first three steps are as follows:
   1. We admitted that we were powerless over alcohol—that our lives had become unmanageable.
   2. Came to believe that a Power greater than ourselves could restore us to sanity.
   3. Made a decision to turn our will and our lives over to the care of God *as we understood Him.*
3. Berryman's battle with alcohol, his personal nomenclature of addiction, and his ongoing efforts at recovery at Hazeldon are well documented in his biographical novel, *Recovery*, and in much of his other poetry— most especially those involving the retrograde alcoholic persona, "Mr. Bones."
4. In its most common form, "two-stepping" is the act of skipping from Step One (in which the candidate admits powerlessness over alcohol and the unmanageability of his life) to Step Twelve (at this point, having had a spiritual awakening, the candidate carries the A.A. message to other alcoholics and tries to practice the A.A. Twelve Step Program in all of his affairs)." "Two-stepping," then, is a way of skipping those steps that are too rigorous or that may not appear all that pleasant. Berryman is reported to have "two-stepped" when he was in rehabilitation. Apparently, he may have even done some "thirteenth stepping," the act of taking an inordinate interest in members of the opposite sex during A.A. meetings and the like.
5. Thomas Gilmore suggests that the first "phase" is awareness, but I think that the majority of alcoholics who are "aware" of their drinking problem are not yet prepared to attempt recovery. The "bottoming out" phase, in which the consequences of abusive drinking have become so painful and so intolerable that the alcoholic is compelled to seek recovery, is probably "phase one."
6. The entire poem is as follows:

The Pulley
by
George Herbert
When God at first made man,

Having a glasse of blessings standing by;
Let us (said he) poure on him all we can:
Let the worlds riches, which dispersed lie,
Contract into a span.

So strength first made a way;
Then beautie flow'd, then wisdome, honour, pleasure:
When almost all was out, God made a stay,
Perceiving that alone of all his treasure
Rest in the bottome lay.

For if I should (said he)
Bestow this jewell also on my creature,

He would adore my gifts in stead of me,
And rest in Natuture, not the God of Nature;
   So both should losers be,

   Yet let him keep the rest,
But keep then in repining restlessness:
Let him be rich and wearie, that at least,
If goodnesse leade him not, yet weariness
   May tosse him to my breast.

7. Laurel was commonly a symbol of victory given to poets as well as athletes and heroes.

Chapter Five   The Grand Illusion: Evasion, Survival, and Self-Hate

1. Born in Saginaw, Michigan, Roethke was the son of a florist, and his childhood experiences in the family greenhouse influenced him profoundly. While many of his peers wrote of lost values and cynicism following World War II, Roethke became increasingly involved in the rediscovery of man's aboriginal sources of being: the inert rock, the roots of plants, the soil, and the flesh of humanity.
2. Note the similarity to Roethke's "The Waking" in which Roethke claims that "We think by feeling."

Chapter Six   The Alcoholic Isolation and Fall to Self-Destruction in Edwin Arlington Robinson's "Mr. Flood's Party"

Revised from "The Alcoholic Isolation and Fall to Self-Destruction in Edwin Arlington Robinson's 'Mr. Flood's Party.'" *Popular Culture Review* 14.2 (Spring 1955): 64–78.

1. In a letter to Witter Bynner written on October 14, 1921, Robinson wrote that he had a "prejudiced liking" for Flood and was glad Bynner approved of his creation (see page 127 of *Selected Letters*). In an earlier letter to Louis Ledoux on December 14, 1920, he writes that Flood had made his "disreputable debut" in *Nation*, the poem having been turned down by *Colliers* for alcoholic reasons (see page 123 of *Selected Letters*). Robinson seems here to reveal both an element of rebellion against the social order and a feeling of kinship with his creation.
2. It is interesting to note that Robinson has chosen to name the little hamlet back down the road for a light, two wheeled carriage without a top. The

very name suggests a certain openness and vulnerability—as is any positive relationship with society or any kind of human communion. In this
case, however, the old curmudgeon will have none of such exposure or
vulnerability—indeed, we may suppose that he has discerned all too well
that such vulnerability is integral with the nature of human affairs and the
price of social intercourse.

3. The bottle that is cradled and that Eben lays down might also be perceived
   as Eben's own "cradle." It is also interesting to note that Eben has developed
   a very curious personal relationship with his jug; and, on the particular evening that we meet him, the old man has been drinking a a good deal from it
   and is way over his limit. Our first reaction might involve some degree of
   sympathy. After all, he is a rather pathetic though inebriated old pilgrim who
   has very little to look forward to, who feels quite maudlin, and who has been
   left to grow old in an uncaring world. But this is not entirely the case. Eben's
   intoxication and isolation are very much of his own making; and, in fact, it
   appears that the old man has chosen to leave the village and live a solitary
   life in order to grow old and self-destruct in alcohol unobserved.

4. Joseph Harkey rationalizes Flood's two moons as symbolic of a dual time
   frame. He feels that a man of Flood's integrity would not get drunk and
   would not see double (20). Harkey thus seems to think that moral fiber
   and willpower are adequate defenses against excessive drinking. This may
   be true for most people; but will power and integrity have nothing to do
   with alcoholic attitudes, except that they do not work. Harkey thinks that
   he proves his point by noting that Flood has only (!) three drinks during
   the party. Besides, he argues, Flood is trying to escape his loneliness, and
   he is bitter because his life is uncertain. Harkey does not seem prepared to
   admit that loneliness, bitterness, and a fear of loss of control are the hallmarks of alcoholism. It is ironic that, while Harkey thinks he has given
   reasons why Flood is not an alcoholic, he has provided a truckload of
   evidence suggesting that Eben *is* an alcoholic.

5. *Alcoholics Anonymous* describes the puzzling nature of alcoholism (see
   pages 2, 12, 115) and the numerous excuses and alibis that an alcoholic is
   likely to conjure up (see pages 4, 7, 116).

6. Although Robinson was a known alcoholic, the effects of his disease on his
   thinking and on his writing are frequently discounted and, in some cases,
   even politely ignored. The words "alcohol" or "alcoholism" are rarely
   indexed in Robinson's critical canon, and his life-long battle with alcohol is
   usually given short shrift in his biographies. If alcohol is mentioned, it is
   frequently dismissed with a superficial rationale or an apology or two. One
   of the poet's finest critics, Yvor Winters, wrote that Robinson's brother,
   Herman, was "something of an alcoholic" (9), as if there was such a thing
   as quasi-alcoholism. In writing of Robinson, Winters says that the poet was
   "not dangerously addicted" to alcohol (11). In my opinion, there is no such
   thing as not being *dangerously addicted* to alcohol. Alcohol addiction is
   always dangerous. Winters goes on to write that although Robinson
   resumed drinking after prohibition, alcohol would no longer be a problem

for the poet (11). It seems to me that, for the alcoholic, liquor is always a problem. Full recovery is usually impossible; alcoholics are always *in* recovery because their battle with liquor is invariably a lifelong affair (*Alcoholics Anonymous* 43).

7. Consider, for example, "Miniver Cheevy" who felt he was a hopeless failure, but who excused himself because he thought he was born in the wrong age—see Chapter 1, pp. 7–8.

Chapter Seven   Sex and Promiscuity: Conjugal Detachment and the Fear of Intimacy

1. One does wonder, of course, how the narrator could have known all this, since he was—in his own words—"passed out."

2. Most chronic alcoholics appear to be incapable of restricting their sexual appetites, and most have indulged in adulterous affairs that tested the limits of decency and self-respect. Sometimes their sexual histories consisted of little more than an astonishing number of shabby relationships; and, sometimes, they were confounded by specific marital problems, sexual violence, and issues of drunkenness in their immediate families. Still, the profile is much the same regardless of the individual: self-serving behavior, unrestrained appetites a total disregard for moral and ethical parameters, and issues of codependence that are confused with intimacy.

Chapter Nine   The Contaminated Vision: The Alcoholic Perspective in Hart Crane's "The Wine Menagerie"

Revised from "The Contaminated Vision: The Alcoholic Perspective in Hart Crane's 'The Wine Menagerie.'" *Popular Culture Review* 14.2 (Winter 2006): 59–66.

1. See, for example, Lewis, 195.

Chapter Ten   Clowns and Bedlam: The Dark Side of Alcoholic Humor

1. Watson had inherited a good deal of wealth and was part owner of the *Dial*. He participated in the literary life of Harvard Yard.

Chapter Eleven   Through a Glass Darkly: Death and Dissolution

1. Although a self-destructive obsession with death and risk-taking are not particularly unique to alcoholics, they are typically preoccupied with the prospect; and, indeed, death by suicide is much more common than among the population as a whole.
2. As noted in the previous chapters, all three of the fiction writers discussed here—Fitzgerald, Hemingway, and Faulkner—achieved a certain amount of notoriety because of their alcoholism and alcoholic mindset. Regardless of whether they deal directly with alcohol, the mindset and perspective of these three authors is clearly evident in the peculiar fascination with the death, morbidity, and evasion that are integral with the stories discussed in this chapter.
3. In Chapter LXI of *Moby Dick,* Herman Melville describes the death of a whale in particularly vivid terms:

   > When reaching far over the bow, Stubb slowly churned his long sharp lance into the fish, and kept it there, carefully churning and churning, as if cautiously seeking to feel after some gold watch that the whale might have swallowed, and which he was fearful of breaking ere he could hook it out. But that gold watch he sought was the innermost life of the fish. And now it is struck; for, starting from his trance into that unspeakable thing called his "flurry," the monster horribly wallowed in his blood, overwrapped himself in impenetrable, mad, boiling spray,...And now abating in his flurry, the whale once more rolled out into view, surging fro side to side; spasmodically dilating and contracting his spout-hole, with sharp, cracking, agonized respirations. At last, gush after gush of clotted red gore, as if it had been the purple lees of red wine, shot into the frightened air; and falling back again, ran dripping down his motionless flanks into the sea. His heart had burst!
   >
   > "He's dead, Mr. Stubb," said Daggoo.

   This is unquestionably the bloodlust, the horror, and the guilt that Lowell is referring to in his poem; and it is Lowell's comment on human indifference and the love of killing and death—the utter lack of empathy—that is so integral with human sin and perhaps his ultimate damnation.

Appendix 4   A.A.'s Primary Texts: *Alcoholics Anonymous* and *Twelve Steps and Twelve Traditions*: A Review

1. The Oxford Group was a Christian sobriety movement of the1920s and 30s and a precursor to A.A., which adopted many of its principles. To be

spiritually reborn and attain sobriety, it was essential that a candidate share his sins and temptations with another Christian, surrender his life to God's care, perform acts of restitution to all who had been harmed, whether directly or indirectly, and listen for God's guidance.

The group also placed special emphasis on confidence, confession, conviction, conversion, and continuance, which were known as the "Five C's."

2. James' *Varieties of Spiritual Experience* is concerned with existential judgments regarding man's spiritual health and his capacity to maintain a naturally positive outlook on life. James believed that positive thinking was a cure for depression while assuring a productive and healthy union with God. James cited the work of Walt Whitman (see his extended poem, "Leaves of Grass") as a perfect example of a healthy mind at work.

3. It is interesting to note that the use of masculine pronouns throughout both texts has prompted some readers to regard the two books as "sexist."

4. Whitman's long poem, "Leaves of Grass," ends with the lines,

I depart as air, I shake my white locks at the runaway sun,
I effuse my flesh in eddies, and drift it in lacy jags.
I bequeath myself to the dirt to grow from the grass I love,
If you want me again look for me under your boot-soles.
You will hardly know who I am or what I mean,
But I shall be good health to you nevertheless,
And filter and fibre your blood.

Failing to fetch me at first keep encouraged,
Missing me one place search another,
I stop somewhere waiting for you.

(1855, 1881–1882)

Bibliography

Aiken, Conrad. "The Room." *The New Oxford Book of American Verse.* Ed. RichardEllman. New York: Oxford UP, 1976. 618.

Alberti, A.J. "Sam Johnson Meets the Oklahoma Kid on the Road to Heaven: A Reading of the Last Dream Song." *John Berryman Studies: A Scholarly and Critical Journal* 3 (i–ii): 84–92.

Alcoholics Anonymous: The Story of How Many Thousands of Men and Women Have Recovered from Alcoholism. 3rd ed. New York: Alcoholics Anonymous World Services, 1976.

Arpin, Gary Q., ed. "A Symposium on the Last Dream Song." *John Berryman Studies: A Scholarly and Critical Journal* 3 (i-ii), Special Issue, "Anabasti": 5–7.

Axelrod, Steven Gould. "Between Modernism and Postmodernism: Cold War Politics and Bishop, Lowell, and Ginsberg." *Pacific Coast Philology* 42 (2007): 1–23.

Bahr, Howard M. *Skid Row: An Introduction to Disaffiliation.* New York: Oxford UP, l973.

Baker, Carlos. *Ernest Hemingway: A Life Story.* New York: Charles Scribner's Sons, 1969.

Banerjee, Amitava. "The 'Marriage Poems' by Lawrence and Lowell." *Kobe College Studies* 38.3 (1993): 15–36.

Barbara, Jack V. "Pipe Dreams, Games, and Delusions." *Southern Review* 13.2 (1980): 120–128.

———. "Under the Influence." *John Berryman Studies: A Scholarly and Critical Journal* 2 (ii): 56–65.

Barnes, Gordon E. "The Alcoholic Personality." *Alcoholism: Introduction to Theory and Treatment.* Ed. David A. Ward. Rev. 2nd ed. Dubuque: Kendall/Hunt, 1980: 148–192.

Beaver, Harold. "Despondency and Madness." *Parnasses: Poetry in Review* 12.1 (1984): 123–131.

Berndt, Susan G. "The Last Word." *John Berryman Studies: A Scholarly and Critical Journal* 3 (i-ii): 75–83.

Berryman, John. *77 Dream Songs.* New York: Farrar, Strauss, and Giroux, 1989.

———. *Collected Poems, 1937–1971.* New York: Farrar, Strauss, and Giroux, 1964.

———. *Henry's Fate and Other Poems, 1967–1972.* New York: Farrar, Straus, and Giroux, 1977.

Bier, Jesse. "Liquor and Caffeine in *The Sun Also Rises.*" *American Notes and Queries* 18 (nd): 143–144.

Blackmur, R.P. "New Thresholds, New Anatomies: Notes on a Text of Hart Crane." *Hart Crane: A Collection of Critical Essays.* Ed. Alan Trachtenberg. Englewood Cliffs: Prentice-Hall, 1982. 49–64.

Blake, David Haven. "Public Dreams: Berryman, Celebrity, and the Culture of Confession." *American Literary History* 13.4 (2001): 716–736.

Bold, Alan, ed. *Drink to Me Only.* London: Robin Clark, 1982.

Buttitta, Tony. *After the Good Gay Times.* New York: Viking Press, 1974.

Cervo, Nathan. "Robinson's 'Miniver Cheevy.'" *Explicator* 62.4 (Summer 2004): 213–215.

Challener, Scott A. "Do I Contradict Myself? Crisis in the Reader's Imagination." *Journal of Contemporary American Poetry* 6 (October 2006): 86–97.

Christopher D. Smith Foundation, Inc. *Understanding Alcohol: for the Patient, the Family, and the Employer.* New York: Charles Scribner's Sons, 1969.

Coleman, Philip, ed. *New Essays on John Berryman.* Amsterdam, Netherlands: Rodolphi, 2007.

Conarroe, Joel. "After Mr. Bones: John Berryman's Last Poems." *The Hollins Critic* 13 (1976): 1–12.

Cooper, Brendan. "We Want Anti-Models: John Berryman's Eliotic Inheritance." *Journal of American Studies* 42.1 (2008): 1–18.

Coulombe, Charles A., ed. *The Muse in the Bottle: Great Writers on the Joy of Drinking.* New York: Citadel Press, 2002. [anthology of poetry, short stories, etc. on the pleasures of drinking]

Crane, Hart. *Complete Poems and Selected Letters and Prose of Hart Crane.* Ed. Brom Weber. New York: Liveright, 1966.

Cummings, E.E. *Complete Poems, 1904–1962.* Ed. Jeorge J. Firmage. New York: Liveright, 1991.

Dardis, Tom. *The Thirsty Muse: Alcohol and the American Writer.* New York: Ticknor and Fields, 1989.

deRoche, Joseph, ed. *The Heath Introduction to Poetry.* 4th ed. Lexington, MA: D.C. Heath, 1988.

Djos, Matts. "Addiction and Spirituality in Contemporary American Poetry." *Dionysos* 11.1 (Spring 2001): 5–17.

———. "The Alcoholic Dilemmas of Marriage, Impotence, and Objectification in the Poetry of John Berryman and Robert Lowell." *Dionysos* 10 (2000): 23–32.

———. "The Alcoholic Isolation and Fall to Self-Destruction in Edwin Arlington Robinson's 'Mr. Flood's Party." *Popular Culture Review* 14.2 (Summer 2003): 117–125.

———. "Alcoholism in Ernest Hemingway's *The Sun Also Rises*: a Wine and Roses Perspective on the Lost Generation." *Hemingway Review* 14.2 (Spring 1995): 64–79.

———. "The Contaminated Vision: The Alcoholic Perspective in Hart Crane's 'The Wine Menagerie.'" *Popular Culture Review* 15 (Winter 2006): 59–66.

Djos, Matts. "John Berryman's 'Phase Four' and His Precarious Attempt to Find a Compromise between Drunkenness, Sobriety, and the A.A. Twelve Step Program." *Dionysos* 8.2 (1999): 17–27.

———. "John Berryman's Testimony of Alcoholism through the Looking Glass of Poetry and the Henry Persona." *The Languages of Addiction*. Ed. Jane Lilienfield and Jeffrey Oxford. New York: St. Martin's Press, 1999. 193–203.

Donaldson, Scott. "Writers and Drinking in America." *Sewanee Review* 98.2 (1990): 312–324.

Doreski, William. " 'My Mind's Not Right': The Legacy of Robert Lowell." *Arizona Quarterly* 49.3 (1993): 93–106.

Dugan, Alan. *Collected Poems, 1969*. New Haven, CT: Yale UP, 1969.

———. *New and Collected Poems, 1961–1983*. New York: Eco Press, 1983.

Ferguson, Margaret, Mary Jo Salter, and Jon Stallworth, eds. *The Norton Anthology of Poetry*. 5th edition. New York: W.W. Norton, 2004.

Fitzgerald, F. Scott. *The Crack-Up*. Ed. Edmund Wilson. New York: New Directions, 1945.

———. *Tender Is the Night*. New York: Simon and Schuster 1934, 1995.

———. *The Great Gatsby*. Preface and notes by Matthew J. Bruccoli. New York: Scribner Paperback Fiction, Simon and Schuster, 1925, copyright renewed 1953.

Forseth, Roger. "Alcohol and the Writer: Some Biographical and Critical Issues (Hemingway)." *Contemporary Drug Problems* 13 (1986): 361–386.

———. "The Alcoholic Writer and the Modern Temper: Transcendence Downward." *Dionysos* 9.1 (1999): 36–41.

Gelderman, Carol. "Hemingway's Drinking Fixation." *Lost Generation Journal* 6 (1979): 12–14.

Gilmore, Thomas B. "A Happy Hybrid." *Dionysos* 3.1 (1991): 19–23.

———. *Equivocal Spirits: Alcoholism and Drinking in Twentieth Century Literature*. Chapel Hill: University of North Carolina Press, 1987.

———. *The Life of John Berryman*. Boston: Routledge and Kegan Paul, 1982.

Ginsberg, Allen. *Collected Poems, 1947–1980*. New York: Harper and Row, 1984.

Goedde, H. Werner, and Dharam P. Agarwal, eds. *Alcoholism: Biomedical and Genetic Aspects*. New York: Pergamon Press, 1989.

Goodwin, Donald W. *Alcohol and the Writer*. Kansas City: Andrews and McMeel, 1988.

———. *Is Alcoholism Hereditary?* 2nd ed. New York: Ballantine, 1988.

Gornick, Vivian. "Wild at Heart." *American Poetry Review* 5.2 (2006): 4–6.

Grant, Marcus. "Drinking and Creativity: A Review of the Alcoholism Literature." *British Journal on Alcohol and Alcoholism* 16 (1981): 88–93.

Haffenden, John. "Drink as a Disease, John Berryman." *Partisan Review* 44: 565–583.

Haffenden, John. *The Life of John Berryman*. Boston: Routledge and Kegan Paul, 1982.

Hagood, Taylor. "Faulkner and Cultural Conflict." *Modern Fiction Studies* 54.4 (Winter 2008): 837–843.

Harbaugh, Jim. "Literature (and Other Arts): What We Talk about When We Talk about Spirituality and Recovery." *Dionysos* 11.1 (2001): 35–46.

Hart, Henry. "Robert Lowell and the Psychopathology of the Sublime." *Contemporary Literature* 32.4 (1991): 496–515.

Hassel, Holly Jean. *Wine, Women, and Song: Gender and Alcoholism in Twentieth Century American Women's Fiction*. Dissertation Abstracts International, Section A: The Humanities and Social Sciences 63.6 (2002): 2241.

Hazo, Samuel. *Hart Crane: An Introduction and Interpretation*. New York: Barnes and Noble, 1963.

Hemingway, Ernest. *The Sun Also Rises*. New York: Charles Scribner's Sons, 1926.

Hyde, Lewis. "Alcohol and Poetry: John Berryman and the Booze Talking." *Recovering Berryman: Essays on a Poet*. Ed. J. Kelly and Alan K. Lathrop. Ann Arbor: Michigan UP, 1993, reprinted from *American Poetry Review* 4 (1975): 7–12. Response by George F. Wedge, "The Case of the Talking Brews: Mr. Berryman and Dr. Hyde," 229–243. Reply by Lewis Hyde, "Berryman Revisited: A Response," 269–272.

Irving, Donald C. "Poets on the Edge." *Dionysos* 3.2 (1991): 36–41.

Jackson, Charles. *The Lost Weekend*. New York: Farrar and Rinehart, 1944.

Jarrell, Randall. *The Complete Poems*. New York: Farrar, Strauss, and Giroux, 1969.

Johnson, Manly. "John Berryman: A Note on the Reality." *World Literature Today* 64 (1990): 422–425.

Lang, Alan R., Laurie D. Verret, and Carolyn Watt. "Drinking and Creativity: Objective and Subjective Effects." *Addictive Behaviors* 9 (1984): 395–399.

Lansky, Ellen. "Female Trouble: Dorothy Parker, Katherine Ann Porter and Alcoholism." *Literature and Medicine* 17.2 (1998): 213–230.

Leibowitz, Herbert A. *Hart Crane: An Introduction to the Poetry*. New York: Columbia UP, 1968.

Leigh, David. "Addiction and Modern Spiritual Biography." *Dionysos* 10.2 (2000): 20–33.

Lewis, R.W.B. *The Poetry of Hart Crane: A Critical Study*. Princeton, NJ: Princeton UP, 1968.

Lieberman, Laurance. "Corkscrew of the Eternal: Three Essays on Robert Lowell's Later Poems." *The American Poetry Review* 14.6 (1985): 28–46.

Living Sober. New York: Alcoholics Anonymous World Services, 1977.

Locklear, Gloriana. "Robinson's 'The Mill.'" *Explicator* 51.3 (1993): 175–179.

London, Jack. *John Barleycorn*. New York: Macmillan, 1913.

Lowell, Robert. *Poems, 1938–1949*. London: Faber and Faber, 1950.

———. *Selected Poems*. New York: Farrar, Strauss, and Giroux, 1976.

Lynn, Kenneth. *Hemingway*. New York: Simon and Schuster, 1987.

Manning, Jennifer. "Torn Between Knowledge and Desire." *Dionysos* 2.1 (1990): 27.

Mariani, Paul. "Lowell on Berryman on Lowell." *Gettysburg Review* 4.4 (1991): 581–592.

———. "Robert Lowell and Jean Stafford." *Gettysburg Review* 6.3 (1993): 457–474.

Martz, William J., ed. *The Achievement of Robert Lowell: A Comprehensive Selection of His Poems with a Critical Introduction*. Glenview, IL: Scott, Foresman, 1966.

McCarron, Kevin. "Spiritus Contra Spiritum: The Recovery Narrative on 'Spirituality.' " *Dionysos* 2.1 (1999): 33–41.

McClatchy, J.D. "Feeding on Havoc: The Poetics of Edna St. Vincent Millay." *American Scholar* 72.2 (2003): 45–53.

———. "John Berryman: The Impediments to Salvation." *Modern Poetry Studies* 6: 246–277.

McClelland, David C., and William N. Davis. *The Drinking Man*. New York: Free Press, A Division of Macmillan Company, 1972.

Meade, Marion. *Bobbed Hair and Bathtub Gin*. Orlando, FL: Harcourt, 2005.

Mellow, James R. *Invented Lives: F. Scott Fitzgerald and Zelda Fitzgerald*. Boston: Houghton Mifflin, 1984.

Mendelson, Jack H., and Nancy K. Mello. *Alcohol: Use and Abuse in America*. Boston: Little, Brown, 1985.

Millay, Edna St. Vincent. *Collected Poems*. Ed. Norma Millay. New York: Harper and Row, 1956.

Moore, Lorrie. "Burning at Both Ends" *New York Review of Books* March 14, 2002: 12–14. [Edna St. Vincent Millay]

Mullaney, William. "Uncle Tom's Flophouse: John Steinbeck's "Cannery Row" as a (Post Feminist) Sentimental Novel." *Steinbeck Review* (Fall 2007): 41–50.

Newlove, Donald. *Those Drinking Days: Myself and Other Writers*. New York: Horizon Press, 1981.

O'Reilly, Edmund B. *Sobering Tales: Narratives of Alcoholism and Recovery*. Amherst: Massachusetts UP, 1997.

Pearson, Gabriel. "For Lizzie and Harriet: Robert Lowell's Domestic Apocalypse." *Modern American Poetry*. Ed. R.W. Herbie Butterfield. Totowa, NJ: Barnes and Noble, 1984. 187–203.

Pooley, Roger. "Berryman's Last Poems: Plain Style and Christian Style." *Modern Language Review* 76.2 (1981): 291–297.

Poulin, Jr. A., ed. *Contemporary American Poetry*. 5th ed. Boston: Houghton Mifflin, 1991.

Provost, Sarah. "Eratos Fool and Bitter Sister: Two Aspects of John Berryman." *Twentieth Century Literature* 30 (1984): 69–79.

Quinn, Vincent. *Hart Crane.* New York: Twayne, 1963.

Robinson, Edwin A. *Collected Poems.* New York: Macmillan, 1937.

Roethke, Theodore. *Collected Poems.* New York: Doubleday, 1966.

Royce, James. *Alcohol Problems and Alcoholism: A Comprehensive Survey.* New York: Free Press, A Division of Macmillan Company, 1981.

Ruiz, Antonio. "Cumming's Dark Night: Symbolic Design of Fall and Rise in the Poetry and Prose."*Journal of the E.E. Cummings Society* 10 (Fall 2001): 31–43.

———. "Sons of Excess: Cummings, Hyperbole, and the American Adamic Tradition." *Journal of the E.E. Cummings Society* 9 (Fall 2000): 73–95.

Simic, Charles. *Selected Poems, 1963–1983.* New York: G. Braziller, 1985.

Smith, Dave. "Playing for Grace." *Georgia Review* 59.4 (2005): 777–793.

Spencer, Luke. " 'The pieces sat up & wrote': Art and Life in John Berryman's *DreamSongs.*" *Critical Quarterly* 29 (1987): 71–80.

Stevens, Wallace. *Collected Poems.* New York: Knopf, 1954.

Stitt, Peter. "On Extended Wings: the Last Dream Song." *John Berryman Studies: A Scholarly and Critical Journal* 3 (i–ii): 122–127.

Twelve Steps and Twelve Traditions. New York: Alcoholics Anonymous World Services, 1981.

Ward, Brian. *Alcohol Abuse.* New York: Franklin Watts, 1987.

Weston, Drake. *Guidebook for Alcoholics: How to Succeed without Drinking.* New York: Exposition Press, 1964. 39–40.

Wyatt-Brown, Bertram. "William Faulkner: Art, Alienation, and Alcohol." *Bridging Southern Cultures: An Interdisciplinary Approach.* Ed. Nobuko Ochner. Baton Rouge: Louisiana State UP, 2005.

Zeck, Gregory. "Hart Crane's 'The Wine Menagerie': The Logic of Metaphor." *American Imago: A Psychoanalytic Journal of Culture, Science, and the Arts* 36 (1979): 197–214.

Index

GUIDES FOR THE JOURNEY

John Macmurray
Bernard Lonergan
James Fowler

University Press of America, Inc.
Lanham • New York • London

Copyright © 1996 by
University Press of America,® Inc.
4720 Boston Way
Lanham, Maryland 20706

3 Henrietta Street
London, WC2E 8LU England

Library of Congress Cataloging-in-Publication Data

Creamer, David G.
Guides for the journey : John Macmurray, Bernard Lonergan, James
Fowler / David G. Creamer.
p. cm.
Includes bibliographical references and index.
1. Macmurray, John, 1891-. 2. Self (Philosophy) 3. Lonergan,
Bernard J. F. 4. History--Philosophy. 5. Philosophy. 6. Theology,
Doctrinal. 7. Fowler, James W. 8. Christian education--Philosophy.
9. Faith development. I. Title.
B1647.M134C74 1996   191--dc20   95-45294 CIP

ISBN 0-7618-0181-2 (cloth: alk: ppr.)
ISBN 0-0-7618-0182-0 (pbk: alk: ppr.)

To the Creamer family
from whom I continue to learn about
the journey of life and faith

To my brothers in the Society of Jesus
fellow pilgrims with Ignatius

Table of Contents

Tables

Preface

I have written this book as an introduction to the lives and thought of John Macmurray, Bernard Lonergan, and James Fowler. I think their congruent thought is helpful in interpreting our lives and the world in which we live them at this juncture in human and earth history. Their work ought to be made more generally accessible.

Specifically, I have in mind my students in Education and Religion at the University of Manitoba and others I have met in workshops, talks, and small adult faith communities. Accordingly, I am *not* presuming the reader has a familiarity with philosophy or the meaning of technical terms used. So as not to interrupt the flow of the text I have provided a glossary of names and key terms.

I use quotations from Macmurray, Lonergan, and Fowler in my presentation because I want to give the reader a flavor for the texture and depth of their work. I have included endnotes as guides for further reading as well as a bibliography and index. A list of abbreviations used in the book is also provided.

My thanks to J. Bowler, R. Boys, J. Costello, F. Crowe, G. Drobot, J. Emslie, J. English, E. Frigo, G. Leach, P. Malone, M. Matic, D. Swirsky, & J. Veltri for reading various drafts of this book and offering constructive suggestions. Special thanks to my colleague D. Lenoski for grammatical corrections, to M. Matic and G. Broesky for carefully checking quotations, and to M. Caligiuri for his computer wizardry.

David G. Creamer, S.J.
October, 1995

vii

Acknowledgments

Permission to quote from John Macmurrray's *The Self as Agent* and *Persons in Relation* has been granted by Humanities Press International, Inc., Atlantic Highlands, NJ. Permission to quote from Bernard Lonergan's *Method in Theology* has been granted by the Lonergan Trustees.

The poem Bernard Lonergan, S.J. is reprinted with the permission of John F. Kinsella, S.J. and America Press, Inc., 106 West 56th Street, New York, NY 10019; originally published in *America*'s September 11, 1993 issue. The author thanks Ruth McLean for permission to quote sections of her poem "Awoken."

John Macmurrray's photograph (12) is courtesy of the John Macmurray Collection, Regis College, University of Toronto. The photograph of Bernard Lonergan (50) is used with the permission of the Lonergan Archives, 15 St. Mary Street, Toronto. James W. Fowler kindly supplied his photograph (112).

List of Abbreviations

Becoming: Fowler, James W. *Becoming Adult, Becoming Christian: Adult Development and Christian Faith.* San Francisco: Harper & Row, 1984.

Collection: Lonergan, Bernard. *Collection.* Volume 4 of the *Collected Works of Bernard Lonergan.* Edited by Frederick E. Crowe and Robert M. Doran. Toronto: University of Toronto Press, 1988. *Collection* was first published in 1967.

Desires: Gregson, Vernon, ed. *The Desires of the Human Heart: An Introduction to the Theology of Bernard Lonergan.* Mahwah, NJ: Paulist Press, 1988.

Enterprise: Crowe, Frederick E. *The Lonergan Enterprise.* Cambridge, MA: Cowley Publications, 1980.

Freedom: Macmurray, John. *Freedom in the Modern World.* Atlantic Highlands, NJ: Humanities Press International, 1992. *Freedom in the Modern World* was first published in 1932.

Insight: Lonergan, Bernard. *Insight: A Study of Human Understanding.* Volume 3 of the *Collected Works of Bernard Lonergan.* Edited by Frederick E. Crowe and Robert M. Doran. Toronto: University of Toronto Press, 1992. *Insight* was first published in 1957.

Interpreting: Macmurray, John. *Interpreting the Universe.* London: Faber & Faber, 1933.

Lonergan: Crowe, Frederick E. *Lonergan.* Outstanding Christian Thinkers Series. Series Editor Brain Davies, OP. Collegeville, MN: The Liturgical Press, 1992.

Method: Lonergan, Bernard. *Method in Theology.* Toronto: University of Toronto Press for Lonergan Research Institute, 1990. *Method in Theology* was first published in 1972.

Old & New: Crowe, Frederick E. *Old Things and New: A Strategy for Education.* Atlanta: Scholar's Press, 1985.

Passages: Droege, Thomas A. *Faith Passages and Patterns.* Philadelphia: Fortress Press, 1983.

Pastoral: Fowler, James W. *Faith Development and Pastoral Care*. Philadelphia: Fortress Press, 1987.

Pensées: Pascal, Blaise. *Pensées*. London: Penguin Books, 1966. *Pensées* was first published soon after Pascal's death in 1662.

Persons: Macmurray, John. *Persons in Relation*. Atlantic Highlands, NJ: Humanities Press International, 1991. *Persons in Relation* was first published in 1961 by Faber & Faber, London.

Promise: Palmer, Parker. *The Promise of Paradox: A Celebration of Contradictions in the Christian Life*. Notre Dame, IN: Ave Maria Press, 1980.

Search: Macmurray, John. *Search for Reality in Religion*. Swarthmore Lecture Pamphlet. London: Friends Home Service Committee, 1969. The Swarthmore Lecture was first published in 1965, the year of its presentation, by George Allen and Unwin Limited.

Second Collection: Lonergan, Bernard. *A Second Collection*. Edited by William F.J. Ryan and Bernard J. Tyrrell. Philadelphia: The Westminster Press, 1974.

Self: Macmurray, John. *The Self as Agent*. Atlantic Highlands, NJ: Humanities Press International, 1991. *The Self as Agent* was first published in 1957 by Faber & Faber, London.

Stages: Fowler, James W. *Stages of Faith: The Psychology of Human Development and the Quest for Meaning*. San Francisco: Harper & Row, 1981.

Third Collection: Lonergan, Bernard. *A Third Collection: Papers by Bernard J. F. Lonergan, S.J.* Edited by Frederick E. Crowe, S.J. New York: Paulist Press, 1985.

Topics: Lonergan, Bernard. *Topics in Education*. Volume 10 of the *Collected Works of Bernard Lonergan*. Edited by Frederick E. Crowe and Robert M. Doran, revising and augmenting the unpublished text prepared by James Quinn and John Quinn. Toronto: University of Toronto Press, 1993. These lectures were delivered at Xavier University, Cincinnati, in August, 1959.

Transforming: Liddy, Richard M. *Transforming Light: Intellectual Conversion in the Early Lonergan*. Collegeville, MN: The Liturgical Press, 1993.

Understanding: Lonergan, Bernard. *Understanding and Being.* Volume 5 of the *Collected Works of Bernard Lonergan.* Edited by Elizabeth A. Morelli and Mark D. Morelli; revised and augmented by Frederick E. Crowe with the collaboration of Elizabeth A. Morelli, Mark D. Morelli, Robert M. Doran, and Thomas V. Daly. Toronto: University of Toronto Press, 1990. *Understanding and Being*, the Halifax Lectures on *Insight*, was first published in 1980.

Chapter 1

Introduction

If the modern world has begun our emancipation from magic, superstition, and arbitrary belief, it has also brought us to the foot of a bridge over a great abyss. Behind us lies the comfortable world of secure belief. Some who have caught a glimpse of the abyss will want to return to the world of security; they will give themselves, uncritically, once again to the faith of their childhood. . . . Others, more critical in their judgments, will refuse to go back. Some of these will attack the precipice *without* a bridge, believing naively in their own invincibility, and some will but stare into the pit of empty endlessness and wait out their lives.

But most, I suspect, will close their eyes and busy themselves with the endless tasks of daily life . . . but without much real sense of what life is all about. And — what is worst of all — without much real passion for the lives they live.

This . . . is for those who refuse to abandon the quest and are willing to test out some bridges, shaky though they may be, to see where they will lead.[1]

Overview

The past quarter century has been one of unprecedented change in the world in which we live and the understanding we have of our place in it. In 1969, human beings walked on the moon for the first time and

looked back to see a world without any borders; the earth as a beautiful but tiny and fragile blue and white ball suspended in the black void of space. Today, jet travel puts any spot on that globe just a day away and with e-mail and the Internet those same places are just seconds away! This shrinking of our world makes us aware of a whole range of complex issues and problems that heretofore were not part of our consciousness. Traditional groupings and relationships between people are in flux, cancer and AIDS loom as major killers, and the gap between rich and poor nations continues to grow. Moral questions are becoming increasingly complex. We do not even have agreement on when human life begins or ends. Ecological issues ranging from the disposal of toxic waste to the depletion of the stratospheric ozone layer and the disappearance of countless plant and animal species are paramount. For the first time, the entire planet faces an ecological crisis largely brought about by over consumption and exploitation on the part of the Western world:

> If today is a typical day on planet earth, humans will add fifteen million tons of carbon to the atmosphere, destroy 115 square miles of tropical rainforest, create seventy-two square miles of desert, eliminate between forty to one hundred species, erode seventy-one million tons of topsoil, add twenty-seven hundred tons of CFCs to the stratosphere, and increase their population by 263,000. Yesterday, today, and tomorrow.[2]

Added to all of this is the questioning and confusion within our religious traditions. It is commonplace to point out that Western civilization is now "post-Christian" and suffers from a "crisis of meaning." How are we to understand the past few decades; have we lost our way? The Hebrew scriptures caution that "where there is no prophecy, the people cast off restraint" (Proverbs 29:18) and the prophets in our midst today warn that "the major actions to stabilize the vital signs of earth and stop the hemorrhaging of life must be made within the next decade or two."[3]

During the Rubik's Cube craze several years ago one of my friends discovered that each little square got its color from a sticker that could be peeled off. And so, when twisting and turning could not quite achieve uniform color on each of the six sides of the cube, he completed the puzzle by peeling and sticking little squares of color as required! There is this tendency in all of us, it seems, to look for simple solutions as our response to complex situations and problems.

This tendency promotes reductionism — religious fundamentalism at one extreme and secularism at the other. Within my own faith tradition, the Roman Catholic church, we seem to be polarizing into two camps. Reminiscent of Popes Pius IX and Pius X who censured the "world" and things "modern," some withdraw into a Catholic fundamentalism seeking to "restore" the church to its earlier triumphal power and glory. Others adapt to the modern, secular world to the point where they begin to wonder, 'Do we even need religion?' There appears to be a clash between conserving religious tradition and opening ourselves to things contemporary and scientific. And then there are those few still faint voices — this book introduces three of them — who call us to journey far beyond both *classicism* and *modernism* towards a world community rich in diversity but living harmoniously with one another and the planet.

Twenty-five years ago I was introduced to the thought of Bernard Lonergan in an undergraduate philosophy course and several years later, during graduate school, to the philosophy of John Macmurray and the developmental approach to faith put forward by James Fowler. Over time I have come to appreciate the potency and broad applicability of their respective critical investigations. I believe that these three scholars are helpful in discerning the path along which human beings are called to travel as we approach the new millennium.

The Roman philosopher and statesman Boethius (c. 480–c. 524) observed that 'each age is a dream that is dying *and* one that is coming to birth.' Looking back over the history of human thought we see that, as one way of making sense of the world proved inadequate to the task at hand and began to collapse, another was already beginning to appear. So, as the European medieval religious synthesis (Scholasticism) proved unable to accommodate the findings of Copernicus, Newton, and Darwin, modern philosophical and scientific approaches emerged. Today, by and large due to the growth of modern science and our awareness of human subjectivity and historical consciousness, contemporary Western culture no longer rests on the certainty of absolute truth. But we still have a *desire* for certitude, at the same time recognizing the limitations of science and technology when it comes to providing answers for our spiritual hunger. We live, as it were, in an age when the old dream, while dying, is not yet dead and the new dream, having been conceived, is not yet born. So what is the way forward?

It is my conviction that the works of John Macmurray, Bernard

Lonergan, and James Fowler represent something of the new ways of 'knowing' and 'being' that are coming to birth in our day. Each one recognizes that there need not be a clash between living in continuity with tradition *and* openness to authentic creativity. Real knowledge is not a choice between *what was* and *what is* but is a paradoxical relationship between both old and new. An exploration of the new *both/and* convergence in their thought, in opposition to earlier *either/or* approaches to human knowing, will be a major focus of this book.

Personal Stories

> The life of each of us is a story in progress — a story taking form and living out a narrative structure (*Becoming* 135).[4]

My mentor from graduate school, Dr. Edmund V. Sullivan, wrote at the end of the Acknowledgments section of one of his books: "I depart from the usual 'I do not hold all of those listed above responsible for my ideas.' I hold them all responsible. My ideas are formed by the company I keep."[5] Dr. Sullivan's words sum up my sense of how I have come to hold and teach the views I do. A major influence on my thinking, Dr. Sullivan's courses at the Ontario Institute for Studies in Education (OISE) in Toronto introduced me to the work of John Macmurray and James Fowler. Moreover, Dr. Sullivan re-acquainted me with the thought of Bernard Lonergan which I had earlier dismissed as obscure and irrelevant to real life. What you will be getting in these pages, therefore, is an introduction to the company I have kept with Macmurray, Lonergan and Fowler over the past quarter century. I write about their lives and their thought, not from a neutral or disinterested stance, but, with the conviction that they have something worthwhile to say to us as we journey through life in the last years of the twentieth century.

What I offer in these pages is also influenced by the company I kept before arriving at this point in my life; my youth in Saint John, New Brunswick; undergraduate days at St. Mary's University in Halifax, Nova Scotia; teaching as a young Jesuit at Gonzaga High School, St. John's, Newfoundland; studying theology in the ecumenical context of the Toronto School of Theology (TST); and more recently as a high school administrator in Winnipeg and now professor in Education and Religion at St. Paul's College, the University of

Manitoba.

Accordingly, I want to begin by sharing four of *my* stories; four of "the strange and fateful 'moments'"[6] which say something about who I am, what I have brought to my reading and study of these three figures, and the difference they have made in my life. I do this at the outset because I believe that my personal history; my religious, cultural, and educational milieu have shaped my voice. In these pages, my selection of topics, my weighing of evidence and evaluation of people and events, my vision and values will constantly be heard. Ultimately, I believe, there is no such thing as a neutral approach to meaning questions — the central themes of this work reflect, and in part arise from, the central themes and movements of my life. I am formed by the company I keep!

My first story begins with twelve years of Catholic education in Saint John. As a boy growing up, I went to Catholic schools not because Catholicism was a strong influence on our family but because, in New Brunswick where one had to choose between a Catholic and 'Protestant' school, we certainly knew we were not Protestant! My religious education was provided by the *Baltimore Catechism*,[7] the prime vehicle used for the moral and religious instruction of North American Catholics before the Second Vatican Council (1962–65). This formal, rather dry and authoritarian, albeit clear and concise, book set forth the basic beliefs of Catholics. We were required to memorize and give intellectual assent to "The Faith" thus expressed. In those days before Jean Piaget revolutionized the way we understand childhood, it was believed that a child of seven or eight could be taught the same things as an adult. A teacher might have to use simpler language but abstract concepts could be taught; after all, children were just "miniature adults." Accordingly, in Miss Luney's Grade 2 class at St. Peter's School (1953–54), I memorized the truths of the Catholic faith about the Trinity.

Related to this point about rote learning is the fact that as I graduated from St. Malachy's High School (1964) in Saint John, I won an award for Religion. The award had nothing to do with how I lived my faith but was for successfully answering questions on an examination paper. An ability to memorize, not religious practise, seemed to be the measuring stick of my Catholicism. It struck me as odd, even then.

In the fall of 1976, as part of my divinity studies, I enrolled in the 'Trinity' course at Regis College in the Toronto School of Theology. I recall that the professor, Frederick Crowe, S.J., a published expert

on the subject, opened his first lecture by saying that he 'really didn't know much about the Trinity — the Trinity is a mystery.' It popped into my head that he should have met Miss Luney because she knew *everything* about the Trinity! Looking back, I think I left Grade 2 believing God was a triangle or shamrock; God was Irish in any case! What was missing from much of my religious education in Catholic schools was a sense of life as a faith *journey* and a sense of the ineffable mystery of God's self communication and desire for a personal relationship with me.

A second story, related to these earlier incidents from school days, comes from my early teaching experience (1971–74) as a young Jesuit at Gonzaga High School, St. John's, Newfoundland. I taught Chemistry, General Science, World History, Geography, and Religion at various grade levels. As part of the school's Grade 11 religion program, we designed a program (Awareness Day) around the Last Judgment passage in Matthew's gospel dealing with the separation of sheep from goats on the basis of their treatment of the "least ones" (Matthew 25:31–46). Once during the year, each class would be divided into small groups to spend a morning visiting selected local government and church related service agencies. After a "poverty lunch" in various settings, the students returned to the school to spend the afternoon in a large group sharing of the experiences of the day. Each Awareness Day ended with Mass (focusing on the theme of social justice as integral to faith) and a simple communal supper.

Over the next decade I returned to St. John's on various occasions and often met with students from my teaching days at Gonzaga. Invariably, they would speak with great affection about their Awareness Day experience. Hardly ever was there any reference to their Religion *classes*; on occasion I met students who couldn't even remember that I had taught them Chemistry! This experience says something profound to me about the limits of knowledge that is not used or lived — it is one thing to *know* the truth; it is quite another to *live* it.

My third story concerns my interest in, or more accurately lack of interest in, Philosophy. As a science undergraduate at St. Mary's University (1964–68) I was required to take two philosophy courses during the four year degree program. I hated the experience. While I can still recall the boring lectures in the introductory course (Philosophy 201, 1965–66), I needed to check my transcript to make sure I had, in fact, taken a second philosophy course. I had (Philosophy

302 in 1966–67). My transcript reveals that I passed only after a supplemental examination in September, 1967, which probably accounts for my lack of memory of the experience!

In August, 1969, I joined the Jesuit Order and soon found that philosophical studies were a required part of the regimen. Fortunately, my two courses at St. Mary's did not go for naught and I was required to take just one semester at the University of Guelph, Ontario (Winter, 1971). One of those courses was on the philosophic thought of a Canadian Jesuit, Bernard Lonergan. I passed the course but it made little sense to me and seemed totally irrelevant. I had read somewhere that philosophy offered 'unintelligible answers to insoluble problems' and adopted that characterization as my own. My negative evaluation of philosophy, and of Lonergan in particular, was only confirmed when I heard the great man himself give a lecture at Ignatius College, Guelph (1970), on the 'Meaning of Meaning' — it was totally beyond me! As I moved from Guelph I hoped I had moved away from philosophy forever!

My fourth story explains my reacquaintance with the thought of Bernard Lonergan through that of Macmurray and Fowler. It begins with a workshop I attended at Ewart College, Toronto (February, 1978), while I was doing graduate studies at OISE. It was my introduction to James Fowler and his theory of "faith development." I was immediately drawn to Fowler's work because I saw his field of study as of practical value. Because of my own eclectic studies in science, humanities, and education, I was also attracted by its interdisciplinary character, blurring the artificial boundaries we have erected between disciplines. In the case of Fowler's research interests, the boundary was between psychology and religion and much of my own work in recent years has been at this interface.

At OISE, Dr. Sullivan introduced me to the philosophy of John Macmurray which initially held no fascination.[8] I applied Macmurray's belief that "it is always legitimate to ask, of any theory which claims to be true, what practical difference it would make if we believed it" (*Self* 23)[9] to philosophy and concluded that it made no practical difference to me! Over time, however, I came to see that Macmurray's work sought to replace the modern idea of philosophers ʻas thinkers isolated from the world, their philosophy a "bubble floating in an atmosphere of unreality" (*Self* 78), with a personalist philosophy emphasizing relationship and action. Macmurray took seriously the questions (and answers) of earlier philosophers (notably the rational-

ism of René Descartes and the idealism of Immanuel Kant) but he also took *my* experience seriously: "When philosophy is alive it grows straight out of human life" (*Freedom* 44).[10] Macmurray's was a philosophy with *practical* implications. I was hooked![11]

Armed with this background, I returned to Bernard Lonergan and found a methodology adequate to the task of continuing Macmurray's effort to elucidate the nature of personal existence. As I began teaching graduate students in the Faculty of Education at the University of Manitoba, their initial reaction to the idea of studying philosophy was negative (as was mine before them) but they were soon won over by Macmurray, Lonergan, and Fowler, none of whom they had previously encountered. I have since introduced elements of the thought of all three thinkers into my undergraduate teaching with positive results. This encouraging response to my classes is in part responsible for this work.

Conclusion

Each of these personal stories say something to me about a shift that is taking place in my lifetime, both within Western culture and the Christian tradition to which I belong — a shift from the pre-modern, classical, worldview to the modern, historically conscious, worldview. The acceptance and integration of this shift has not come easily in my own life and, if my interaction with people tells me anything, it is that this is not an easy paradigm shift for most of us. But it is a transition we must make to get on with the journey of life. It has been, for me, a movement from *uncritical* reliance on authorities and dogma, to an appreciation of what Lonergan calls the "new learning" (*Topics* 16–17)[12] and the importance of living with, and learning from, one other in community. John Macmurray, Bernard Lonergan, and James Fowler have been three of my mentors in this process; their lives and work are testimony to the importance, necessity, and value of the shift. They come from different times and places and are the product of different religious and educational backgrounds, yet they communicate a complementary vision of the human project. In each case, their vision extends beyond the shift out of classicism and into modernity to a way of living in harmony with one another and the planet that in times past was the dream of a few visionaries and even now is grasped by only a few.

Because I believe that the central themes and resonances of the work of Macmurray, Lonergan, and Fowler reflect, and in part arise from, the central themes and movements of their lives and times, my consideration of each will begin with a biographical sketch followed by an exposition of their basic thought. A concluding chapter will attempt to draw the basic themes of the book together into a parcel convenient for carrying on life's journey.

Notes

1. Russell Pregeant, *Mystery Without Magic* (Oak Park, IL: Meyer Stone Books, 1988), 17.
2. David W. Orr, *Ecological Literacy: Education and the Transition to a Post-modern World* (Albany, NY: State University of New York Press, 1992), 3.
3. David W. Orr, *Ecological Literacy: Education and the Transition to a Post-modern World* (Albany, NY: State University of New York Press, 1992), 20.
4. The reference in brackets (*Becoming* 135) is to James W. Fowler, *Becoming Adult, Becoming Christian: Adult Development and Christian Faith* (San Francisco: Harper & Row, Publishers, 1984), 135. Quotations from this work will henceforth be indicated as here (*Becoming* 135).
5. Edmund V. Sullivan, *Critical Psychology and Pedagogy: Interpretation of the Personal World* (Toronto: OISE Press, 1990), xvii. Currently, Dr. Sullivan is Coordinator of a program in Community and Global Transformation Studies (an interdisciplinary approach to global ecological and social issues and global education) in the Department of Curriculum at the Ontario Institute for Studies in Education, Toronto, Canada.
6. Paul Tillich as quoted by Robert Coles in *Walker Perry: An American Search* (Boston: Little, Brown & Company, 1978), x.
7. See chapter 7, notes 18 and 19.
8. I never met John Macmurray. In graduate school, at Dr. Sullivan's invitation, I attended a meeting of the John Macmurray Society (founded 1971 in Toronto) which soon broke up as the keynote speaker was taken away by ambulance after suffering a suspected heart attack.
9. The reference in brackets (*Self* 23) is to John Macmurray, *The Self as Agent* (Atlantic Highlands, NJ: Humanities Press International, 1991), 23. Quotations from this work will henceforth be indicated as here (*Self* 23).
10. The reference in brackets (*Freedom* 44) is to John Macmurray, *Freedom in the Modern World* (Atlantic Highlands, NJ: Humanities Press International, 1992), 44. Quotations from this work will henceforth be indicated as here (*Freedom* 44).

11. I agree with E. F. Schumacher who quotes St. Augustine as writing "Man has no reason to philosophize except with a view to happiness" (E. F. Schumacher, *A Guide for the Perplexed* (London: Sphere Books Ltd, 1978), 5.

12. The reference in brackets (*Topics* 16–17) is to Bernard Lonergan, *Topics in Education*, vol. 10 in the *Collected Works of Bernard Lonergan*, ed. Frederick E. Crowe and Robert M. Doran (Toronto: University of Toronto Press, 1993), 16–17. Quotations from this work will henceforth be indicated as here (*Topics* 16–17). By "new learning" Lonergan does not just mean an *addition* to accumulated knowledge in a subject area but a *transformation* of our very understanding of the nature of the discipline in question. The physics of Albert Einstein, for instance, is not just an addition of material to Newtonian physics but a transformation of the very nature of what we mean by "physics."

John Macmurray (c. 1958)

Chapter 2

John Macmurray (1891–1976)

> I want to say something just in passing about the world we are living in, which is the really important period of history. We can regard this period of our history, I should say, as far greater than the Elizabethan period, but more like the period of the Ancient Greeks — the greatest period of history that the world has known. Lots of things are happening that have never happened before. It makes me wish I had not been born so early — I wish I had been born about now (John Macmurray, June 12, 1949).[1]

Early Years

John Macmurray was born in 1891 in Maxwellton, Kirkcudbright, in the extreme southwest of Scotland. While he was still a boy, his family moved to Aberdeen where he was educated at the Grammar School and Robert Gordon's College. Science was an interest from his teens and as a university student he took courses in science whenever he could. Later in life he allowed that a "solid grounding in science and scientific method has been of the greatest possible use to me not only as a philosopher . . . but at least as much in the religious field" (*Search* 11).[2] Summarizing his thoughts as a young man, Macmurray asked: "Could we not hope that through testing and modification we should arrive at a religion which science need not be ashamed to serve?" (*Search* 14).

Macmurray's religious upbringing was the traditional Calvinism of the Scottish church; he described his family as "deeply religious" and desirous of traveling to foreign mission lands. Filled with Christian fervor, he joined the Student Christian Movement (SCM) in 1909 when he enrolled as a student at Glasgow University. He organized bible study groups among students and addressed open air evangelical meetings. When his father died without achieving his goal of working in foreign missions, Macmurray volunteered for a mission career but was turned down.[3] It was while studying in Glasgow that he matured into the conviction that *reality is religious*, in that "religion is about human beings in relation,"[4] a view he was to live and defend throughout his life.

In October 1913, equipped with an honors degree in Classics from Glasgow, Macmurray went on to Balliol College, Oxford University, to study Philosophy. The outbreak of World War I interrupted his degree program.

World War I

Because he was struggling with the pacifist option (he was attracted to Quaker philosophy), Macmurray chose to serve with the Royal Army Medical Corps as a nursing orderly on the Western Front. Later, having discovered that a medic was as much a part of the fighting machine as any soldier, he accepted a commission as a lieutenant with the Queen's Own Cameron Highlanders. Wounded in the defense of Arras during the final German attack in 1918, he was awarded a Military Cross and sent home. As the war ended he returned to Oxford to finish his interrupted studies, taking his final Master of Arts examinations in the summer of 1919.

Reflecting on the war years, Macmurray tells us that he and many of his contemporaries "went into war in a blaze of idealism, to save little Belgium and to put an end to war" only to discover "stage by stage . . . that war was simply stupidity, destruction, waste and futility." "We became," he says, "critical, skeptical and sometimes cynical" (*Search* 18–19).

A key event in the life of John Macmurray occurred during home leave in the autumn of 1916.[5] He had been invited to preach in a church and took advantage of the occasion to speak (in full uniform) on the need for reconciliation among warring parties following the

cessation of hostilities. His words were met with a hostile and cold reaction from the congregation. It is to this unhappy event that Macmurray traces his refusal to be associated with denominational Christianity: "I spoke and wrote thereafter in defense of religion and of Christianity; but I thought of the churches as the various national religions of Europe" (*Search* 21). "I stand as a Christian," he said, "but outside all the Churches."[6] Macmurray explains this bold statement:

> When I say that I am a Christian I mean, therefore, that I stand in the contemporary world for and with the movement that Jesus originated. When I say that the effect of this is to set me outside all the Churches, I mean to imply that at the present time, and in their contemporary condition, the Churches do not stand in and with that movement.[7]

The war years had a significant impact on the development of Macmurray's thought. War was an alienating, destructive experience, quite opposite to that of personal relationship ("friendship") which is the underlying motif of his writings. Further, his negative experience in the wartime pulpit caused him to live on the fringes of organized religion throughout his professional life even as he championed Christian ideals.[8]

Professor of Philosophy

Following demobilization, Macmurray considered working with the newly formed League of Nations[9] but, believing that his emerging philosophical ideas were relevant to daily life, he decided on a career as a professor of philosophy. In a letter written ten years later to Rev. Richard Roberts (an early mentor), Macmurray wrote: "I think I am entering a field which is absolutely virgin soil for the philosopher, and calling for a reconstruction of modern philosophy from top to bottom. . . . I'm only trying to pioneer and blaze a philosophical trail in this new continent of being"[10] He was aware as he set out that he was taking "the road less travelled"[11] and that his work would probably be rejected or at least ignored by his contemporaries. Harboring no illusion about doing more than pointing the way towards an adequate modern philosophy, he accepted a one year appointment as a lecturer in Philosophy at Manchester University (1919–20). Then, between

March, 1921 and November, 1922, Macmurray taught Philosophy at the University of Witwatersrand, Johannesburg, South Africa.

From 1922–28 he was Fellow and Classical Tutor at Balliol College, Oxford where his first essay was issued by the Aristotelian Society in 1925.[12] In subsequent publications during this period, his enduring interest in the relationship between science and religion is already evident.[13]

In 1928 Professor Macmurray accepted a position in Philosophy at London University College where he lectured and wrote until 1944. During his London tenure he became a BBC radio celebrity and began publishing in earnest.

Typical of a number of British intellectuals in the 1930s, Macmurray undertook a serious study of the writings of Karl Marx. Over the next several years, in a series of articles and books highlighting the Marxist emphasis on action and social relations, he argued that a synthesis of the key elements in Marxism and Christianity was not only possible but desirable.[14] In later works from the period, a fading of sympathy towards Marxism is apparent in his critique of the Marxist understand-ing of religion ("opiate of the people") as incorrect. Dialectical materialism was an inadequate tool for interpreting the world which Macmurray had come to know as essentially *personal*. As a result of these interests and writings, throughout the 1930s and 1940s Macmurray maintained connections with British labor unions and even acted as the spokesperson for a group called The Christian Left. The preeminent position his philosophy gives to action over knowledge can be traced to these years.

Radio Personality and Author

During the summer of 1930, in an attempt to take philosophy to the people, Macmurray delivered a series of twelve BBC Radio talks relating to the philosophical questions of the times. Titled "Reality and Freedom," they were surprisingly well received:

> Few would have expected that at the height of a beguiling summer and at the unlikely hour of eight of the evening twelve broadcast talks on Philosophy would have produced a miniature renaissance among thousands of English listeners. In that sense, at least, the talks made broadcast history. The pamphlet which introduced them . . . became a 'best-seller.'[15]

In large part due to the considerable correspondence these and a subsequent series of four talks on "The Modern Dilemma" (January, 1932) generated, they were published as Macmurray's first book, *Freedom in the Modern World*, which appeared in the Spring of 1932.[16] In 1935 he published a second collection of lectures, *Reason and Emotion*, which went through several editions.[17]

Macmurray has said that the whole of his adult life was concerned to explicate the character of Christianity. *Clue to History*,[18] for instance, one of Macmurray's early and most difficult works, unfolds how Christianity, ensnared in a Greco-Roman understanding of consciousness (theoretical, aesthetic, technical, pragmatic), had conceived of Jesus as a kind of Greek philosopher. Macmurray offers the corrective that Jesus, in continuity with Hebrew consciousness and the Hebrew prophetic tradition (religious, communal, practical), was not a philosophical *thinker* according to the Greek ideal but a person who *acted*.

Macmurray studied Descartes, Kant and Hegel, concluding that idealist religion is *unreal*, and he found kindred spirits in Soren Kierkegaard and Martin Buber. In his introduction to *Reason and Emotion*, John E. Costello, S.J. tells this anecdote about Macmurray and Buber: "In his one and only meeting with Martin Buber, after three hours of conversation Buber is reported to have said, 'I see no point on which we differ. It is simply that you are the metaphysician and I am the poet.'"[19] Of Buber, Macmurray wrote, "I met him once and was wholly at one with him."[20]

Communal experiments in education were another focus of his attention, particularly at Wennington, a Quaker school in Yorkshire (founded 1940). In its "effort to make the school itself a society of friends," Macmurray wrote, "the development of the personal lives of their pupils" was the primary focus at Wennington.[21] Seeking, as did the faculty at Wennington, to bridge the gap between "intellectual achievement" (thinking) and "admirable character" (doing) proved to be a major theme of Macmurray's life.

Lecturer

From 1944–57 Macmurray was Professor of Moral Philosophy and later Academic Dean at Edinburgh University. As in London, students overflowed his lectures. World War II veterans were especially

attracted to his thought.

During his tenure in London and Edinburgh, Professor Macmurray traveled extensively to present lectures; notably, at Yale University in the United States[22] and Queen's University in Kingston, Ontario, Canada.[23] At the apex of his career, Macmurray was invited to deliver the prestigious Gifford Lectures for 1953–54 which he titled "The Form of the Personal." These were subsequently published as *The Self as Agent* (1957)[24] and *Persons in Relation* (1961).[25] They represent Macmurray's mature philosophical thought and will be the major focus of the next chapter of this book.[26]

Retirement

John Macmurray retired from Edinburgh University in 1957 after almost four decades of teaching and writing. Although he had been familiar with the Society of Friends since the period between the wars, it was only after retirement that he formally applied for and was accepted into full membership. "I became increasingly unsatisfied in my isolation," he reported (*Search* 28). In 1965, speaking "not as a philosopher but as a person to persons, as a Christian to Christians and . . . as a Quaker to Quakers" (*Search* 3), Macmurray delivered his Swarthmore Lecture, "Search for Reality in Religion," a moving personal confession of faith. A major focus in this lecture was the perennial question as to the relationship between faith and reason. In the next chapter we will consider in some detail Macmurray's understanding of the philosopher as "necessarily involved in a commitment which has itself a religious quality" and the argument set forth in his Swarthmore Lecture that "faith and reason have more in common than we are inclined to allow" (*Search* 2 & 3).

Macmurray moved to Buckinghamshire, England, in the late 1960s. He died in Edinburgh on June 20, 1976 and was buried in the Quaker village of Jordans. A year later, a friend and student of his thought wrote:

> We keenly miss the presence of this *real* person. Our toothy video-tape world has all too few of his kind whose only ulterior motive in communicating is to do the truth, textured with seasoned experience, expert research, and the wisdom born of wide-ranging, unhurried and unflinching reflection.[27]

John Macmurray is remembered as a deep but clear and original twentieth century philosopher of ethics and religion. With the reissuing of five of his most important works between 1991 and 1993 there is a renewed interest in his thought which we try to unpack in the next chapter.

Notes

1. This quotation is from a transcript of an address delivered by John Macmurray during a Sunday evening assembly at Wennington School, June 12, 1949. It is part of the John Macmurray Collection, Regis College, University of Toronto, Canada.

2. The reference in brackets (*Search* 11) is to John Macmurray, *Search for Reality in Religion*, Swarthmore Lecture Pamphlet (London: Friends Home Service Committee, 1969), 11. Quotations from this work will henceforth be indicated as here (*Search* 11). The Swarthmore Lectures are sponsored by Swarthmore College, a Society of Friends foundation in Swarthmore, Pennsylvania. The title of the Lecture, "Search for Reality in Religion," is "virtually descriptive of Macmurray's philosophical career" (A. R. C. Duncan, "No Man is an Island . . .," *Listening: Journal of Religion and Culture* 10, no. 2 [Spring, 1975]: Note 4, 53). See also, Thomas E. Wren, "John Macmurray's Search for Reality," *Listening: Journal of Religion and Culture* 10, no 2 (Spring, 1975): 1 which views Macmurray's Swarthmore Lecture as "virtually descriptive of his entire life." Macmurray describes himself as "having always been a staunch supporter of science" (John Macmurray, "Science and Objectivity," *Listening: Journal of Religion and Culture*, [Spring, 1975]: 8). He credits his scientific training for his ability to reject the dogmatic claims of theology which do not stand up to critical analysis.

3. Albert H. Nephew, "The Personal Universe," *Listening: Journal of Religion and Culture* 10, no. 2 (Spring, 1975): 99. In this respect, as in others, it strikes me that Macmurray's life parallels that of Eric Liddell, the 1924 Olympic sprinter from Scotland, the subject of the 1981 Academy Award winning film, *Chariots of Fire*.

4. This quotation is taken from a 1967 BBC radio talk of John Macmurray, "What Religion is About." It is found in Kenneth Barnes, Kathleen Lonsdale, and John Macmurray, *Quakers Talk to Sixth Formers: A Series of Broadcasts* (London: Friends Home Service Committee, 1970), 51. Clearly, Macmurray does not intend the term *religion* to be understood as synonymous with theology or any system of beliefs (*Search* 14–15).

5. On an earlier leave in 1916 he married Betty who survived him. The Macmurray's had no children.

6. John Macmurray, "Here I Stand," a somewhat autobiographical talk found in the John Macmurray Collection, Regis College, University of Toronto, Canada. It is not dated. Macmurray's critique of religion at this time in his life recalls Lonergan's comment: "I for one would object to the identification of religion with self-centered religion. . . . the function of religion is not to make man self-centered but to complete his self-transcendence" (*Second Collection* 158–59). Human authenticity lies in this self-transcendence (*Second Collection* 155).

7. John Macmurray, "Here I Stand," John Macmurray Collection, Regis College, University of Toronto, Canada.

8. As we shall see more clearly in our exploration of his philosophical thought in the next chapter, "Macmurray held firmly to a personal faith in Christ and in the power of the Christian gospel as the single most potent force available to transform human hearts and human society in the direction of the justice and love that our human nature desired and required" (John E. Costello, S.J., Introduction to *Reason and Emotion* by John Macmurray [Atlantic Highlands, NJ: Humanities Press International, Inc., 1991], x).

9. He had great hope that the League of Nations could prevent future war. See A. R. C. Duncan, "No Man is an Island . . .," *Listening: Journal of Religion and Culture* 10, no. 2 (Spring, 1975): 43.

10. John E. Costello, S.J., Introduction to *Reason and Emotion* by John Macmurray (Atlantic Highlands, NJ: Humanities Press International, 1992), xi and xiii. In this attitude, Macmurray was like Bernard Lonergan who set out to reconstruct a methodology for Roman Catholic philosophy and theology. Both Macmurray and Lonergan can be thought of as "personalist" philosophers (*See* **Personalism/ist** in Glossary).

11. This is the title of a Robert Frost poem which was echoed in the classic best-seller *The Road Less Traveled* by M. Scott Peck (New York: Simon & Schuster, 1978).

12. John Macmurray, "Is Art a Form of Apprehension or a Form of Expression?," *Proceedings of the Aristotelian Society* (Supplement 5, 1925): 173–89. Macmurray remained active in the Aristotelian Society until the late 1930s.

13. For example, in "Objectivity in Religion" (in *Adventure: The Faith of Science and the Science of Faith*, ed. B. H. Streeter [London: Macmillan, 1927]), Macmurray sets forth questions about the nature of religion which were to prove central in later publications.

14. In part, this same sympathy motivates Liberation Theology, a largely Roman Catholic phenomenon originating in Latin America. Liberation Theology combines Biblical and Marxist themes in its critique of oppressive social, economic, and political structures.

15. C. A. Siepmann, Foreword to *Freedom in the Modern World* by John Macmurray (Atlantic Highlands, NJ: Humanities Press International, 1992), xxxvi.

16. A second edition of *Freedom in the Modern World* was published in 1935 and various editions appeared down to 1968. In 1992, Humanities Press International reissued the book "in the belief that the problems Macmurray examines and his close reasoning towards a solution, are just as relevant today" (back cover of 1992 edition). In addition to the 1930 and 1932 lecture series, the book included the pamphlet distributed by the BBC as preparatory reading to the 1930 lectures, "Today and Tomorrow: A Philosophy of Freedom," and an original concluding essay, "The Final Summary: Self-Realization," in which Macmurray tackles his critics. Macmurray's last BBC radio series, during Lent 1964, evidenced that the main mission of Jesus was to free human beings from fear.

17. Other publications by Macmurray in the 1930s and 1940s include: *Interpreting the Universe* (1933), *Philosophy of Communism* (1933), *Creative Society* (1935), *Structure of Religious Experience* (1936), *The Boundaries of Science* (1939), *Challenge to the Churches* (1941), *Constructive Democracy* (1943), all first published by Faber & Faber Limited, London, England. *The Clue to History* (1938) was published by the Student Christian Movement Press in London.

18. John Macmurray, *The Clue to History* (London: Student Christian Movement Press, 1938).

19. John E. Costello, S.J., Introduction to *Reason and Emotion* by John Macmurray (Atlantic Highlands, NJ: Humanities Press International, 1992), xix.

20. Letter to Stanley Peck, July 21, 1972, in the John Macmurray Collection, Regis College, University of Toronto, Canada.

21. This is taken from the concluding paragraph of "They Made A School," a handwritten manuscript by Macmurray, dated December 4, 1968. It is found in the John Macmurray Collection, Regis College, University of Toronto, Canada. The same collection also contains an "Address to Wennington Students," dated June 12, 1949. See also Kenneth C. Barnes, *Energy Unbound: The Story of Wennington School* (York, England: Williams Sessions Ltd., 1980). Wennington School is now closed.

22. Macmurray's Terry Lecture at Yale was published as *The Structure of Religious Experience* (London: Faber & Faber Limited, 1936). The Terry Lecture for 1937, "Psychology and Religion," was delivered by Carl Jung. In 1950, Erich Fromm was the Terry lecturer on "Psychoanalysis and Religion."

23. In 1949, Macmurray came to Canada to present "Conditions of Freedom," a set of lectures sponsored by the Chancellor Dunning Trust at Queen's University in Kingston. They have been published as John Macmurray, *Conditions of Freedom* (Toronto: The Ryerson Press, 1949) and reprinted in 1977 by the John Macmurray Society, Toronto.

24. John Macmurray, *The Self as Agent* (Atlantic Highlands, NJ: Humanities Press International, 1991).

25. John Macmurray, *Persons in Relation* (Atlantic Highlands, NJ: Humanities Press International, 1991). In a letter to Kenneth Barnes (founder and first headmaster of Wennington School), November 27, 1973, Macmurray, with reference to the Spanish translation of the Gifford Lectures, remarked "my clientele is broadening" (John Macmurray Collection, Regis College, University of Toronto, Canada).

26. In the first set of lectures, using a complex metaphysical argument, he demonstrates the primacy of action over thinking. In the second set of lectures he shows how the mutuality of persons ("'I' exist as only one element in the complex 'You and I'") brings doing (and not thinking) to center stage in human affairs. At the end of the lectures, having carefully developed his own philosophical standpoint, Macmurray tackles the key questions Gifford Lecturers are charged with answering: "What contribution does this philosophical study make to the problem of the validity of religious belief? Are there, or are there not, rational grounds for a belief in God?" (*Persons* 206). He argues that his new "more inclusive" philosophical standpoint ("I do" as including "I think") does indeed provide "rational grounds" for understanding that the world is personal and that God is the "Agent" whose "action" *is* the world; that is, we live in "a personal universe in which God is the ultimate reality" (*Persons* 224).

27. Philip Mooney, "Freedom Through Friendship, John Macmurray: In Memoriam (1891–1976)," *Friends Journal* (January 1, 1977): 4.

Chapter 3

Macmurray's Characterization of the Personal Life

All meaningful knowledge is for the sake of action, and all meaningful action for the sake of friendship (John Macmurray in *Self* 15).

Task of Philosophy

We have seen that Macmurray's choice of career as a professor of Philosophy was influenced by his earnest belief that "real philosophy . . . is the understanding of real human experience, and springs hot out of life itself" (*Freedom* 67). He understood and practiced philosophy, not as an intellectual exercise but in an effort to understand the meaning of the experience of real people struggling in this very real world to live together in community. Further, his philosophical positions grew out of the very fabric of his life; a strict Presbyterian youth and later abandonment of *organized* Christianity, wartime experiences and struggles, years spent in the university milieu, flirtation with Marxist thought and unions, and countless other experiences that helped shape his person. "Instead of saying that a philosophy is a way of life," he wrote, "it would be better to say that any way of life implies a philosophy" (*Self* 24). Because he believed that traditional academic philosophy had reached an impasse (unable to account for two world wars or

come to satisfactory answers to the key questions of life), he brought a fresh philosophical approach to bear on the questions of his age, contributing to a philosophical Copernican Revolution.

The nature of the personal life was, for John Macmurray, the central issue of the twentieth century: "That we are living through a period of revolutionary change is already a commonplace. . . . To me it seems certain that the scale of change must dwarf the transformation of medieval into modern Europe" (*Self* 26).

The Gifford Lectures on Natural Theology, 1953–54[1] represent Macmurray's mature exposition of this new philosophical conceptualization — "the form of the personal" (*doing* is a more fundamental human category than *thinking*). In the Introductory to the Spring 1953 lectures (*The Self as Agent*), Professor Macmurray says: "The simplest expression that I can find for the thesis I have tried to maintain is this: All meaningful knowledge is for the sake of action, and all meaningful action for the sake of friendship" (*Self* 14–15). This chapter is an effort to uncover the profound meaning embedded in this deceptively simple sentence.

Macmurray maintained that "it is always legitimate to ask, of any theory which claims to be true, what practical difference it would make if we believed it" (*Self* 23); a question to ask yourself about *his* philosophical ideas as they unfold in these pages.

Survey of Western Philosophical Tradition

Contemporary philosophical positions can only be appreciated in the context of the history of philosophy.[2] Accordingly, Macmurray's thought must be situated within the Western philosophical tradition. We will begin with his analysis of modern Western philosophy as already having passed through two distinct phases, respectively dominated by a mechanistic metaphor (we are complicated machines) and an organic metaphor (we are complex animals).

Mechanical Metaphor

The first phase in modern Western philosophy, roughly corresponds to the growth of the physical sciences; Galileo Galilei (1564–1642) and Sir Isaac Newton (1642–1727) being two of the better known figures of the period. In philosophical terms, Macmurray

says, this phase covers the period from René Descartes (1596–1650) to David Hume (1711–1776).[3] It is to this philosophical tradition, with roots in fourth century B.C. Greece (Plato and Aristotle), that we owe our tendency to identify rationality as *the* peculiarly human attribute.

During this first period, according to Macmurray's analysis, the central concern of philosophy was to understand and explain matter (i.e., its *form*). The essence of human nature was *thinking* (the human being was a thinking thing, a "mind in a machine") and knowledge of the external world resided in the human mind. According to this view, what we knew as a result of contemplative thought was *objective* and real; what we knew only from sense experience was *subjective* and, hence, unreliable, illusory or imaginary. The universe was viewed as a collection of inert chunks of matter (stars and planets) and tiny particles (atoms) operating "mechanically;"[4] philosophy was theoretical and analytic (deductive) with "substance" (thing) as its key concept. A concrete example may help to clarify the point.

Our eyes tell us that the sun circles the earth, rising in the east and setting in the west (just watch it!), yet we *know* that the earth moves around the sun. Accordingly, sense experience is unreliable. What we have come to see, however, is that both of these views, in their respective spheres are correct. To say that the sun rises and sets is to *describe* in ordinary language the movement of the sun as it *appears* to my eyes. To say that the earth moves around the sun in an elliptical orbit is to *explain*, in technical (i.e., mathematical) language, the *real* relationship between the earth and sun.

René Descartes (1596–1650)

Often called the father of modern philosophy, René Descartes approached his discipline with the understanding that to *think* was to *know*. This rational approach to philosophy discounted the senses as a reliable means for discovering truth. Employing a method of doubt (doubt is a form of thinking), Descartes' methodological skepticism led him to the one indubitable declaration "Cogito ergo sum" (I think, therefore I am). This "axiom" came to be viewed as the starting point for modern philosophy.[5]

All knowing was considered to be philosophy for the ancient Greek thinkers (*philosophos*, lover of wisdom), but with Descartes we see an effort to distinguish between philosophy and theology. Philosophy

was the domain of human *reason* and theology, based on divine revelation, was the domain of *faith*.[6] Note that for Descartes, this distinction was not meant to discredit God or religion; he was in fact a believer, and his whole philosophical approach rested on God — because God is perfect, God could not deceive us and so the exercise of true reasoning will lead to truth. Descartes even offered a "proof" for God's existence (God is the Cause of the idea we have of God as Perfection).

David Hume (1711–1776)

In the work of the Scottish enlightenment philosopher David Hume, we see philosophy (already distinct from theology) further divided from science.[7] Hume attacked Descartes' rationalism and supported the view that knowledge can be derived through sense experience, i.e., empirically. Truth can be known in the physical world through the senses — *empirical* knowledge is knowledge of what is real. *Only* in the scientific realm, through the use of an inductive methodology, can we derive sure knowledge. The deductive relationship in rational philosophy between cause and effect, Hume argued, is not "necessary" but based on custom or habit.[8]

Note, however that although Descartes and Hume differ as to how the connection between the knowing subject and the object known is made (for Descartes, *mind* is the link, for Hume the link is *sense experience*) they hold in common the notion that, in the process of knowing, I (a subject) stand apart from the material world I seek to know (an object). It is this idea of the knower as radically distinct from what is to be known (subject/object split) which will be the focus of Macmurray's critique of the first phase of Western philosophy.[9]

Organic Metaphor

Over the seventeenth and eighteenth centuries it became apparent that while science and mathematics were appropriate for predicting and explaining events in the physical world, it was quite another thing to use material and mechanical categories as descriptive and predicative of the activity of living beings. Accordingly, a second phase of European philosophy can be discerned, roughly corresponding to the growth of the biological sciences; Robert Hooke (1635–1703) and Charles Darwin (1809–1882) being symbolic of the spirit of the age.

As representative of the second phase of philosophy, Macmurray chose the thought of the German idealist, Immanuel Kant (1724–1804), who sought to build a bridge between rationalism and empiricism, at the same time defending both from romanticism (emphasis on feeling over thinking). Before tackling Kant, we need to acquaint ourselves with this important antecedent.

Romanticism

The Romantic period in Western cultural history has its origins in the seventeenth century and extends into the nineteenth century. For the Romantics "reason" was that within us which produced science but it was "faith," our capacity for aesthetic experience, which really mattered and distinguished us from lower animals.[10] A 1930 publication expressed the essence of the Romantic critique of rational and empirical philosophy quite well:

> We are quite willing to be told that we are curiously carved pieces of the earth's crust, or strange dust-wreath vortexes, if we may add to the account *the something more which we know we are*. The whirling dust-wreaths of the street do not have longings. The bits of earth-crust which we throw about with our shovel do not yearn for what is not and then forthwith construct it. Desires and strivings, visions and ideals, emotions and sentiments, are as much a genuine part of us as are the iron and lime and phosphorus in our bodies. We have insights of what ought to be, appreciations of beauty, convictions of truth, experiences of love, and these things are not part of the earth's crust. They are not physical realities. They are not *results* of masses of matter in motion. They cannot be adequately explained mechanically.[11]

As the basis for our knowledge of the real, the Romantics, as it were, substituted the artist's point of view (ideas about the "true," the "good," the "beautiful") for the rationalist's mind and the scientist's empirical method. Neither rationalism nor empiricism leave any room for affectivity (feelings, emotion). The productive spontaneity of the imagination (an artistic activity which combines elements of experience in a way that is not given in experience) underlies all experience, the Romantics said, and particularly all cognitional activity (knowing). It is this synthetic and artistic movement which is the wellspring of knowledge for the Romantics.

Immanuel Kant (1724–1804)

According to John Macmurray, Kant's publications represent "the most adequate of modern philosophies" for two reasons — because Kant was correct in his critique of rational thinking which dominated the first phase of philosophy, and because modern philosophies since Kant are derivative of his thought (*Self* 39).[12] Before proceeding with Macmurray's critique of this second, "organic," phase of Western philosophy we must consider, briefly, Kant's idealist philosophy. At the outset, however, I should remind you that Kant is reported to have sent an early draft of his *Critique of Pure Reason*[13] to a colleague who returned it unfinished with the comment that he was afraid if he went on to the end he might become insane. You are warned!

Critical of the classical philosophical position (rationalism), Kant held that it was not possible to gain knowledge of the world by thought alone. However, he also knew, contrary to the views expounded by British empiricists, that sense experience by itself does not give true knowledge of the world either. For Kant, knowledge comes as a result of a *synthesis* between what we experience by means of our senses ("phenomena") and concepts ("categories") of pure thought which exist in our minds and are imposed on phenomena to make sense of the world. It is true, Kant says, that unless an object is apprehended by the senses we could not even become aware of it but at the same time it is equally true that there is more to knowing than just taking a good look at what is already out there — without interpretation, sense experience is blind! Further, we can *think* as we please but if we are trying to get at truth there is only one way to proceed and that, Kant contends, is to acknowledge that we think according to categories existing in the mind. One can say, for instance, that '1 + 1 = 3,' but to count correctly there are rules that prescribe the method and describe the process to be followed.

In his *Critique of Pure Reason*, Kant first proposed that "space" and "time" are given to everyone as "*a priori* pure intuitions;" i.e., they are absolute, independent of, and prior to, any sense impression. Second, serving as a kind of basic conceptual apparatus for making sense of the world, he proposed twelve "categories of thought" organized according to quantity (unity, plurality, totality), quality (reality, negation, limitation), relation (substance, causality, interaction), and modality (possibility, existence, necessity). We "construct" the world we know (i.e., knowledge is "synthetic") but we do so in

accordance with laws of thought. Without categories of understanding we would not be able to form a concept of the object out there and hence not be able to *know* it. An example may prove helpful at this point. David Hume had used a game of billiards to illustrate that there was no *necessary* connection between cause and effect. It is a habit of mind, he said that makes us assume that one ball striking another in a particular spot will move it in a predictable direction. Kant, concerned to preserve a role for reason in the knowing process, understands the billiard shot quite differently. For Kant, the intuitions of space and time allow the sense impression of one ball on the table being struck by another to be conveyed to the mind. Here the quantitative category "plurality" registers the two balls, the qualitative category of "reality" registers that one ball strikes the other in a certain way, the relational category of "causality" understands that the struck ball will go in a certain predictable direction, and the modal category of "necessity" understands that this will occur in the same way each time one ball strikes another in the same way.

Even if the example has not proven to be helpful, I trust it makes clear that according to Kant, knowing depends on an integration of sense data about what is "out there" with categories of understanding. But there is a catch! Kant's view is that the categories of understanding are in the *mind* of the knower rather than features of things as they are in themselves. Accordingly, what we know through this process is the world only as it *appears to us* (the practical world of phenomena) and not the world as it *is in itself* (the real world of noumena) which is beyond the limits of human knowledge. Yet, although Kant denies the Cartesian view that we can have knowledge of *things in themselves*, he does not repudiate reason as such but just points out its limitations.

Further, Kant says that, although reality cannot be perceived in experience, the existence of an absolute moral law or "categorical imperative" must be presumed: "Two things fill the mind with ever new and increasing admiration and awe," Kant wrote in *The Critique of Practical Reason*, "the starry heavens above and the moral law within."[14] Traditional metaphysical arguments for the existence of God, the soul, immortality, free will and similar issues, Kant pointed out, were also beyond the limits of reason which is legitimately employed only in knowing the phenomenal world.

So, for Kant, knowing is not the simple, straightforward, mechanical activity it was for Descartes (pure reason) and Hume (sense experience). His complex understanding of the knowing process involves *both* sense experience of an object out there *and* a knowing of that object by means of inner categories of the mind. In this way he sought to stake out a middle ground which held together the positive elements in rationalism and empiricism and at the same time defended both from the attacks of romanticism which argued that feeling was a more basic human category than was thinking.

This achievement accounts for Macmurray's assessment of Kant's thought as the "most adequate of modern philosophies." The philosophical problem Kant wrestled with, as Macmurray formulates it, was the "form" or conceptualization of the "organic" (it is more than just mechanical "thing") and his answer to the question was a synthesis of elements of both rationalism and empiricism. But, in his efforts to defend rationality against the influence of romantic sensitivity (heart before head), Kant is not able to make the connection between a thing as it *is* in itself and that same thing as it *appears* to me. He is forced to conclude that although there is indeed a real, noumenal, world "out there," as mere "thinking things" we can never know it but only the phenomenal world of appearances. Macmurray summarizes Kant's predicament as follows:

> Knowledge is, in some sense, the discovery of what exists independently of any activity of ours. If we construct our knowledge, if it depends at all upon a spontaneous, inventive activity of the mind, then there is no escape from the conclusion that we can never know the world as it is in itself, independently of our ways of apprehending it. . . . Reality as it is in itself is unknowable. This is the famous doctrine of the Thing-in-itself, of the noumenal world, and it is Kant's denial of knowledge (*Self* 46).

Kant is correct, Macmurray contends, to critique rationalists for their attachment to the mind of the subject and the empiricists for their fixation on the object as known through the senses. He is even correct in his explanation that the object we have grasped through the senses is at least partially known in terms of categories of the mind (i.e., subjectively) but, and this is Kant's difficulty, he is not able to show that the *real* object out there and the knowledge of that object which I have in my mind correspond. Kant's distinction between what is real 'out-there' and what is real 'only in the mind' is unacceptable for Mac-

murray because it makes the mind a place of unreality and illusion where each of us is, as it were, locked up like a prisoner in solitary confinement (*Self* 39–61).[15]

Note that Kant, like his predecessors, primarily understands the knowing subject to be separate from what is to be known. It is a critique of this separation of subject and object which lies at the heart of Macmurray's effort to rethink the starting point of philosophy as that of the self as an *agent* (involved with and for others in action) rather than that of the self as an isolated *thinker* absorbed in thought.

Insights derived from nineteenth century evolutionary biology, helped to move us away from perceiving human beings as simply "thinking things" to understanding them as "organisms" actively involved in their knowing. To have arrived at this point is a great achievement but, as Macmurray points out, we were too easily seduced by the ability of the new organic metaphor to explain human behavior. A powerful advance on the understanding of what it is to be a human being offered by the earlier mechanical model, the organic metaphor, Macmurray insists, is also limited because of its attempt (denying 'self' and 'human consciousness') to explain the human person exclusively in organic categories:

> The root of the error is the attempt to understand the field of the personal on a biological analogy, and so through organic categories. . . . We are not organisms, but persons. The nexus of relations which unites us in a human society is not organic but personal (*Persons* 45–46).[16]

We will now turn to a consideration of Macmurray's critique of our Western philosophical tradition and his understanding of the "personal."

Macmurray on the Western Philosophical Tradition

Macmurray's Gifford Lectures begin with a general statement that they focus on his two major criticisms of our Western philosophical tradition (applicable to both the mechanical and organic metaphors) — it is "theoretical" and "egocentric."[17]   In turn, we will unpack each of these appraisals.

Modern Philosophy as "Theoretical"

Modern philosophy is *theoretical*. It assumes that a human being ('self') is primarily a *thinking* 'subject' for whom the world is the 'object' to be *known*. Against this "presupposition," Macmurray argues that a thinking subject is derivative of a doing subject (an 'agent'). By proposing[18] that we substitute "I do" for "I think" as our starting point, *The Self as Agent* seeks to "shift the center of gravity in our philosophical tradition" from the theoretical to the practical (*Self* 85).

Macmurray's foundational critique of our Western philosophical heritage centers on our habitual understanding of the knower as being distinct from the object to be known in the human knowing process. For Descartes, the knower stood apart from the object, thinking about it. For Hume, the knower stood apart from the object, collecting empirical data about it through the senses. For Kant, the knower took sense data from out there into his/her mind where the mind's categories processed the raw data in order to understand it. Although each of these positions came under attack by the Romantics, they also stood apart from the object to be known, merely substituting feeling as the basis for human knowing.

Rationality, Macmurray agrees is *one* human quality; it is "the capacity for objectivity, and . . . it is the possession of this capacity which distinguishes persons from whatever is sub-personal" (*Interpreting* 127–28).[19] And, even though he speaks of rationality as "the essential characteristic of personal consciousness," for Macmurray, rationality means much more than just thinking: "It is the essence of personal consciousness as such. Rationality is not a peculiar characteristic of the intellect. It is equally characteristic of the emotional life. . . . art and religion are just as rational as science or philosophy" (*Interpreting* 131). *Being* is more foundational than knowing; who we *are* is far more important that what we *know*. Here, of course, Macmurray is integrating the insights of the Romantics into his position (something Kant was loathe to do).

Knowing, then, for Macmurray, is more than mere intellectual activity; *knowing what to do* certainly involves more than just interpreting sense experience (empiricism). Feeling is integral to knowing and acting: "there is no *a priori* reason . . . why at the personal level, feeling should not be as much an element in cognition as sense. For it is a person who knows in acting, not his mind or his thought, and

feeling, like sense, is a necessary element in any personal consciousness" (*Self* 126).

Accordingly, Macmurray proposes *action*, not thought, as the
fundamental category for understanding what it is to be human. In
ordinary speech when we absentmindedly make a mistake we say, 'I'm
sorry, I wasn't thinking about what I was doing' — the implication
being that if I *was* thinking about what I was doing I would have done
it right! "Knowledge is that in my action which makes it an action,"
Macmurray says, "and not a blind activity" (*Self* 129). Our very use
of language, then, lends support to Macmurray's argument that while
thought does not include action, action by its very nature includes
thinking. The "I do" contains the "I think," of necessity; we solve our
day-to-day problems by "taking thought." Moreover, the "I do" includes the "I *know* that I do." In fact, as he points out, thinking is not
something that just happens to me but something that I *do*![20] In
Macmurray's view, and here is where the practicality of his philosophical approach is apparent, our theoretical activities *ought* to have their
origin in practical requirements and theoretical results, if they are
meaningful at all, are solutions to *practical* problems. Macmurray
refers to "purely theoretical" activities as "purely imaginary" (*Self*
21).[21] To sum up, action is an *inclusive* concept whereas thought is an
exclusive concept.

Macmurray's philosophy, then, is not just a theory of knowledge
but of action! Action is a full concrete activity of the Self employing
all our capacities whereas thought is constituted by the exclusion of
some of our powers and a withdrawal into an activity which is less
concrete and less complete. It is important to remember, however, that
a theory of knowledge is derived from and included within a theory of
action. Avoiding the dualism of theoretical philosophies (subject as
separate from object), Macmurray points out that the self that reflects
and the self that acts is the same self; action and thought are *contrasted* (not split) modes of its activity.

Table 3.1

I DO	=	I KNOW	+	I MOVE
ACTION	=	KNOWLEDGE	+	ACTIVITY (*Self* 128)

Modern Philosophy as "Egocentric"

Macmurray's second criticism of our European philosophical tradition is that it is *egocentric*. Logically, he deduces, we ought to expect that the emergence in our century of a scientific human *psychology* would be paralleled by a transition from an organic to a *personal* philosophy. Resting on the assertion that *the Self is neither a substance nor an organism, but a person* (person is inclusive of both substance and organism), the "form of the personal" would be the "emergent problem" (*Self* 37). This is the transition Macmurray champions but it is not easy to achieve because his interpretation of the term "personal" involves a letting go of the egocentric point of view. Simply put, the self does not exist in isolation but as part of the unit 'You and I.'

In my teaching I use an example which may help to clarify what Macmurray means by his use of the term *personal*. As I understand it, if you were placed at birth on a deserted island where you were the only human being and somehow grew to maturity, you would know that you were a different kind of creature from the rats and chimpanzees; you might know too that this difference consisted in your rationality. But according to Macmurray's understanding, although you might know what it is to be *human* (rational) you could not know what it is to be a *person* until another human being arrived on the island and befriended you. The notion of person is only realized in relationship with at least one other human being.

Having established in the 1953 Gifford Lectures that the self exists not as a thinking subject but as 'agent' (actor, doer), Macmurray argued in the following year's lectures that the 'agent self' can exist only in dynamic relation with other human beings who are also agents. The thesis he defended is "that the Self is constituted by its relation to the Other; that it has its being in its relationship; and that this relationship is necessarily personal" (*Persons* 17).

> The idea of an isolated agent is self-contradictory. Any agent is necessarily in relation to the Other. Apart from this essential relation he does not exist. But, further, the Other in this constitutive relation must itself be personal. Persons, therefore, are constituted by their mutual relation to one another. 'I' exist only as one element in the complex 'You and I' (*Persons* 24).

To substantiate this view, *Persons in Relation* (Gifford Lectures, Spring, 1954) sets out Macmurray's criticism of *egocentrism*. For Macmurray, a foundational problem with the traditional point of view adopted by our philosophy is the idea that a human being is, in essence, a 'self' in the moment of *private reflection*, by definition cut off from the world he/she seeks to know. A formal dualism is thus created between the subject and any object of his/her concern; between thought and action, between reason and emotion, between theory and practice. Any philosophy which takes the 'I think' as its first principle, Macmurray contends, must remain formally a philosophy without a second person; a philosophy which cannot be conceived relationally; 'You *and* I.' Against this understanding of the 'self' as a solitary and isolated thinking thing,[22] Macmurray sets forth the view that the 'self' is a *person*, and that human existence is *constituted* by the relationship of persons.[23]

Thinking about another person or seeing another person in terms of the organic metaphor, for example, can never amount to *personal knowledge of* that other person. The possibility of persons *in relation* (involving action, emotion and practice) is therefore unattainable. But, when we start from the standpoint of action, Macmurray argues, there is an *essential* relation between thought and action (theory and practice) which is that thought is included in action.

Form of the Personal

Macmurray begins his argument with a consideration of the prototypical relationship in our lives, that between a mother and her baby.[24] He does this, in part, to counter the "widespread belief . . . that the human infant is an animal organism which becomes rational, and acquires a human personality, in the process of growing up" (*Persons* 44). If the organic metaphor can be proven inadequate as an explanation for human behavior at infancy, he reasons, then it follows that it must also be inadequate as an account of human maturity.

Macmurray's argument is that the new born baby's "total helplessness" indicates that infants are "made to be cared for." Animals are more or less endowed instinctually with what they need for survival in the environment into which they are born. We might similarly expect new born babies to be endowed with what they need for survival in the environment into which they are born. But, because the organic

metaphor is not an exhaustive description of humanness, a baby's adaptation is to "a complete dependence upon an adult human being." Further, this need which the baby has for care, Macmurray points out, "is not simply biological but personal, a need to be in touch with the mother, and in conscious perceptual relation with her."[25]

Relationship is *constitutive* of human living for Macmurray: "We need one another to be ourselves. This complete and unlimited dependence of each of us upon the others is the central and crucial fact of personal existence" (*Persons* 211). The idea of an isolated agent is self-contradictory; any agent is necessarily in relationship. Apart from this essential relation an *agent* does not exist. Further, personal relationship is not only a possibility, in action, but necessary. We act with and for others.[26] Morality, Macmurray points out, "is essentially social" (*Persons* 116).

Persons are *constituted* by their mutual relation to one another. 'I' exist only as one element in the community 'You and I' which constitutes both the 'You' and the 'I.' You tell me who I am as a *person*. "I need you to be myself" (*Persons* 150). The emerging ecological worldview supports this principle of the *mutuality* of the personal; we are who we are only in and through our relationships with other human beings, all creatures, and the planet itself. The intrinsic value of community is honored and there is a growing recognition in the emerging world order that the best way to serve individuals is to improve community.

"Friendship," the word Macmurray prefers to love as descriptive of the true nature of personal relationships, is a central concept in his exposition of the "form of the personal." Friendship is "the real relationship of one person with another independently real person."[27] Friends can take off their masks and be wholly themselves in the presence of others. "To be a friend," as Macmurray puts it, "is to be yourself for another person."[28] One characteristic of friendship which he holds dear is the freedom inherent in the relationship: "All knowledge of persons is by revelation. My knowledge of you depends not merely on what I do, but upon what you do; and if you refuse to reveal yourself to me, I cannot know you, however much I may wish to do so" (*Persons* 169). Friendship is not forced. Macmurray's second set of lectures survey the field of the personal from the standpoint of action, the distinguishing quality which sets us apart as human beings. The aim of *Persons in Relation* is to discover how this ultimate fact can be generalized in reflection. For Macmurray, meaningful relation-

Table 3.2

	PRE-MODERN Classical Greece Descartes to Hume	MODERN Kant Rousseau/Hegel	POST-MODERN[30] John Macmurray Bernard Lonergan
HISTORY OF WESTERN PHILOSOPHY AS REVELATORY OF THREE LEVELS OF HUMAN CONSCIOUSNESS [29]			
Self as . . .	SUBSTANCE	ORGANISM	PERSON
Reality as . . .	SCIENTIFIC	ETHICAL	SPIRITUAL[31]
Philosophical Problem	FORM OF THE MATERIAL	FORM OF THE ORGANIC	FORM OF THE PERSONAL
Philosophy	MATERIALISTIC	IDEALISTIC	EXISTENTIAL
Science	PHYSICAL/ MATHEMATICAL	BIOLOGICAL	HUMAN/ PSYCHOLOGICAL
Scientist	GALILEO	DARWIN	FREUD
World view	MECHANICAL	ORGANIC	PERSONAL
Primacy of the . . .	THEORETICAL (THINKING)		PRACTICAL

ship depends upon meaningful action; the two are symbiotically related. I can know another person *as a person* only by entering into a
personal relationship with that other person. Without this I can know
that person only by observation and inference; only as an object or
thing. An activity of reflection is never completed until it is *expressed*
and "a morally right action is an action which intends community"
(*Persons* 119).[32]

The question which underlies any philosophical inquiry into action
is not the organic question, 'How can we *know* what is right to do?'
but the personal question, 'How can I *do* what is right?' Implicit in
this, Macmurray proposes, is the idea that without another human
being no *action* (Action = Knowledge +Activity) is possible: "The
possibility of action depends upon the Other being also agent, and so
upon a plurality of agents in one field of action" (*Self* 145). To *act* is
to work cooperatively with others and it is impossible to live rationally
and communally without such cooperation.

Science

Several of Macmurray's early essays dealt with his abiding interest
in the relationship between science and religion. One, titled "Christianity — Pagan or Scientific?" is critical of traditional Christianity with
its emphasis on the certainty and unchangeable nature of dogma and
sympathetic towards what he calls "scientific Christianity:"

> . . . a Christianity which lives experimentally, holding all its doctrines
> as liable to modification or even rejection, accepting all its rules of
> organization and its laws of conduct, as simply so much result of
> human experience to be used as working hypotheses and experi-
> mented with incessantly for their own development and reshaping.[33]

"Beyond Knowledge"[34] goes even further, arguing that the attitude
of science is, in fact, the attitude of genuine faith. Science was the
topic of one of John Macmurray's last published essays, "Science and
Objectivity."[35] Here, he presents two points about the nature of science: (a) the scientific method by its very nature is a "paradigm of
self-transcendence"[36] and (b) the findings of science are not certain[37]
but always tentative, probable, "radically hypothetical."[38]

One of the more important theoretical consequences of the shift in
John Macmurray's philosophy from the theoretical (thinking) to the

practical standpoint (action) is that we no longer see the sciences as independent bodies of truth but as human performances, as something that human beings do.

This is a relatively new understanding of science. In the nineteenth century, for example, the German atheistic philosopher, Ludwig Feuerbach, after referring to Copernicus as the "first revolutionary of modern times" proclaimed that the natural sciences had "dissolved the Christian world view in nitric acid."[39] Until well into our own century, science more or less lived by Feuerbach's condescending attitude, secure in its belief that *only* science could know reality with certainty. Today few scientists make this claim.

Classical physics (Isaac Newton) understood matter to be comprised of tiny material atoms which in turn contained still smaller particles (electrons revolving around a nucleus composed of protons and neutrons). In many respects the inner world of the atom, like the planetary system, was understood to operate mechanically according to precise mathematical laws. Since theoretical physicist Albert Einstein (1879–1955) authored his generalized theory of relativity (1915), science has abandoned the mechanical model of reality and is busy revising its theory. The world is no longer understood in terms of tiny material particles moving with mathematical precision but in terms of relationship between entities, no longer in terms of certainty but in terms of probability. This new attitude towards scientific inquiry provides crucial support for Macmurray's argument and is a point of congruence between his philosophy and that of Bernard Lonergan.

Religion and God

Search for Reality in Religion[40]

Characteristic of philosophy and theology in Macmurray's day was the widespread acceptance of an impassable gulf between *faith* and *reason* (traceable to Descartes). Outside of the narrow confines of religion, the supremacy of reason was taken for granted and it was more or less agreed (often even within religion) that knowledge of the divine, if there was such a thing, could only be attained in transcendent religious experiences. Because "religious" experiences were considered by rationalist definition to be "non-rational," there was no point

at which faith and reason could meet. Faith was *un*-reasonable, then, and atheism the only logical conclusion a *reasonable* person could hold; religion was an "illusion," Sigmund Freud said,[41] echoing the sentiments of his age. Macmurray disagreed:

> The view that there is no path from common experience to a belief in God; that religion rests upon some special and extraordinary type of experience apart from which it could not arise — this seems to me hardly credible (*Self* 19).

Where atheistic existentialism finds human relationship an insoluble problem and all human projects doomed to frustration and ultimate meaninglessness, the theistic alternative, Macmurray avows, issues from the hope of an ultimate unity of persons in fellowship, which gives meaning to human effort. His philosophy's very conceptualization of the personal directs our attention to *real* religion. Religion, as Macmurray understands it, is a universal *human* experience "bound up with that in our experience which makes us persons and not mere organisms" (*Persons* 156).

Drawing on an understanding of a progressive unfolding of Western philosophy through material, organic, and personal phases, Macmurray advances the view that reality unfolds in three spheres, scientific, aesthetic (ethical), and religious (spiritual). In his view, the first two are subordinate to (but included within) the third, religion, which is essentially "interpersonal." In fact, for Macmurray, "religion is about the community of persons" (*Persons* 157). True religion, he says, is about working to achieve an all embracing world community.

The field of personal relationships is the field of religion, for Macmurray. In *Search for Reality in Religion*, he goes so far as to speak of community not only as the friendship which ought to exist among human beings but also as our proper relationship with God.[42] Moreover, friendship ought to characterize the relationship between humanity and the God given natural world (*Search* 34).[43] Friendship is not just the ideal relationship among human beings but it is also the paradigm for right relationship to the planet. Both are forms of the community of all existence: "The two forms of dependence — upon other people and upon nature — are interwoven and inseparable. They constitute the community of all existence."[44]

God

"Objectivity in Religion" (*Adventure* 177–215)[45] sets forth questions and principles which were to prove central to Macmurray's later thought. Having dismissed the traditional proofs for God's existence, Macmurray asks: "Is the supreme reality of the world properly described as God or as matter or as life, or in some other way?" (*Adventure* 182–83). Arguing, as we have seen, that reality is essentially religious (i.e., interpersonal) and understanding that "the whole of religion is rooted in the idea of God" (*Adventure* 181), Macmurray argues that to describe the supreme reality of the world as God is to say that "the ultimate reality of the universe is such that it can satisfy religious demands. God is therefore necessarily personal. . . . There can be no question of an impersonal God. The phrase is a contradiction in terms" (*Adventure* 183).

Our understanding of God as caring about creation implies that God is to be grasped as necessarily personal and the religious life as necessarily about personal relations, Macmurray maintains. Further, the shift in his philosophy from *I think* to *I do*, from the viewpoint of a disembodied thinker to that of a social, historical, embodied subject or agent, shifts the understanding of God from First Cause or Unmoved Mover to Person or Actor. The aim of Macmurray's Gifford Lectures was to set the stage for this new understanding of God: "In its full development, the idea of a universal personal Other is the idea of God" (*Persons* 164).

In his last lecture, Macmurray turns to the question set before each Gifford lecturer: "'What contribution does this philosophical study make to the problem of the validity of religious belief? Are there, or are there not, rational grounds for a belief in God?'" (*Persons* 206).

Macmurray begins to answer the question not with God but with human beings, specifically the Hebrew people, "the uniquely religious people of history" (*Search* 35). Note that he speaks of the Jewish people as *being* religious, not *having* a religion, as being in relationship with one another, with God, and with God's creation. God is creator of heaven and earth and all that exists including human beings made in the very *imago Dei* (image of God). God, in Macmurray's terminology, is the "original, unlimited and universal agent," an actor or doer. Human beings made in God's image are also free and creative agents. Of course, the relationship between ourselves as free and creative agents and God, the "original, unlimited and universal agent"

is personal (*Search* 44). God's first covenant with his people established this relational pattern: "I will be your God and you shall be my people" (Jeremiah 7:23).[46]

Macmurray's philosophy, as we have seen, is in reaction to the *theoretical* point of view. Accordingly, he begins his discussion of the reality of God with a dismissal of earlier theoretical and egocentric "proofs." It is clear to him that metaphysical proofs for God's existence make very little impact; they prove not the existence of God but the existence of an *idea* or conception of God. At best, they arrive at God as the Unmoved Mover, First Cause or Necessary, Intelligent and Perfect Being[47] totally removed from our sphere of activity (dualism) and lacking "any quality deserving of reverence or worship" (*Persons* 206–07).[48]

That we are not alone in the world is, for Macmurray, the "central and crucial fact of personal existence." "We need one another to be ourselves" (*Persons* 211).

> In ourselves we are nothing; and when we turn our eyes inward in search of ourselves we find a vacuum. . . . It is only in relation to others that we exist as persons; we are invested with significance by others who have need of us; and borrow our reality from those who care for us. We live and move and have our being not in ourselves but in one another; and what rights or powers or freedom we possess are ours by the grace and favor of our fellows (*Persons* 211).

Furthermore, what we know of another person we know because they tell us. It is only a small step to transpose this notion to the Judaeo-Christian understanding of God as one who has revealed God's self as one who is with us; YaHWeH, Emmanuel.

To this point, we have traced Macmurray's argument that the dynamic that makes the process of "mutual self-revelation" possible is love (i.e., "friendship") through to his position that such love is the "field of religion." He goes on, then, to point out that "from the standpoint of the agent, which is the presupposition of our whole argument, the question whether the world is personal is the question whether God exists" (*Persons* 214). The question, Macmurray says, is not 'Does God exist?' but 'Is what exists personal?' Resting on the proposition that *doing* is more fundamental than *thinking* and that as human beings we act in mutual relationship, his entire philosophy aimed to demonstrate the "inadequacy of any impersonal conception of the world" (*Persons* 218). Further, he established that the universe

itself must be personal (human beings are personal and part of the universe; therefore the universe is personal): "By shifting our standpoint from the 'I think' to the 'I do,' we have restored the reference of thought to action, and in the result have found that we are driven to conceive a personal universe in which God is the ultimate reality" (*Persons* 224).

Macmurray concludes his Gifford Lectures by recalling that philosophy in the Greek tradition left us with a theoretical and impersonal God lacking "any quality deserving of reverence or worship" (*Persons* 206–07) and modern philosophy, following in that tradition, "had been driven by its own logic in the direction of atheism" (*Persons* 224). He reminds us that shifting philosophy's starting point from the theoretical and egocentric to the personal led to the inevitable conclusion that there is "only one way in which we can think our relation to the world, and that is to think it as a personal relation, through the form of the personal." Of course for Macmurray, to see the world through this lens is to see it as the *act* of God. And, if God acts, God is Personal: "A personal conception alone is fully theistic and fully religious" (*Persons* 223). We are impelled, he says finally, "to conceive a personal universe in which God is the ultimate reality" (*Persons* 224).

Notes

1. The Gifford Lectures were later published as *The Self as Agent* and *Persons in Relation* and dedicated to his wife Betty. They were first published in London by Faber and Faber, in 1957 and 1961 respectively.

2. This is not the case for all disciplines; one can be a successful chemist, for instance, without knowing anything about the historical development of chemistry.

3. Bernard Lonergan also saw an initial phase of modern philosophy where "the primary focus of attention was cognitional activity." It was the period "from Descartes to Kant" who was a transitional thinker to the second phase where "there was a notable shift in emphasis" (*Third Collection* 242).

4. On the roof of the old observatory in Beijing, I marveled at various large mechanical representations of the solar system. How different this mechanical version of the universe is from James E. Lovelock's hypothesis that the planet is alive! See James E. Lovelock, *Gaia: A New Look at Life on Earth* (Oxford: Oxford University Press, 1979).

5. But how did Descartes get to be this thinking being? Macmurray would say that Descartes became a thinker as a result of his interactions with people and the world; i.e., relationally. Note that not all seventeenth century

thinkers were in total agreement with Descartes. Blaise Pascal (he and Descartes met) was drawn to science but he also knew that human beings were substantially more than calculating machines and that there is more to being human than rationality. He considered the heart (not mind) to be the core of human personality and in his *Pensées* wrote that "the heart has its reasons of which reason knows nothing" (*Pensées* 154).

6. In the thirteenth century, Thomas Aquinas had already made a clear distinction between philosophy (the work of human reason unaided by revelation) and theology (which takes revealed truth as its data) but he understood philosophy to be the handmaiden to theology, the 'queen of the sciences.' Descartes further distanced philosophy from theology but did not differentiate between philosophy and science.

7. The value of philosophy, for Hume, lies precisely in its ability to free us from the unhappy grasp of theology. In contrast with Descartes, Hume saw no philosophical arguments for God's existence because we cannot have empirical "experience" of God. Hume's most significant work, *A Treatise of Human Nature* (1739), was published when he was only twenty-eight. It was, however, a later and shorter work, *Inquiry Concerning Human Understanding* (1748), that was to attract the attention of Immanuel Kant (representative of the next phase of Western philosophy). Bernard Lonergan's *Insight* has been described as a modern day equivalent to Hume's *Inquiry Concerning Human Understanding*.

8. Bernard Lonergan uses David Hume to point out the contradiction between "a mistaken cognitional theory and the actual performance of the mistaken theorist." Lonergan wrote: "Hume thought the human mind to be a matter of impressions linked together by custom. But Hume's own mind was quite original. Therefore, Hume's own mind was not what Hume considered the human mind to be" (*Method* 21).

9. The mechanical world view is far from dead. During the 1991 Persian Gulf War the killing of human beings was referred to as "collateral damage." And, of course, we speak of the people working for a given company as "human resources."

10. Jean Jacques Rousseau (1712–1778) is representative of the romantic approach. His novel *Émile* (1762) champions education built on a child's natural interests and sympathies and *Confessions* (1782) describes Rousseau's romantic feelings of affinity with nature.

11. David M. Wulff, *Psychology of Religion: Classic and Contemporary Views* (New York: John Wiley & Sons, 1991), 153–54. Wulff is quoting Rufus Jones from William P. King, ed., *Behaviorism: A Battle Line* (Nashville, TN: Cokesbury Press, 1930), 21.

12. Some modern philosophers adopt Kantianism and some reject it outright. Others, while acknowledging Kant's contribution to the development of philosophy, critique and expand upon his thought in their efforts to take philosophy in new directions. Macmurray and Lonergan are in this category.

13. The problem for philosophy, as Kant saw it, was to distinguish science and morality from aesthetics. For this reason Kant wrote three critiques: the first about science (*The Critique of Pure Reason*), the second about morality (*The Critique of Practical Reason*) and the third about art (*The Critique of Judgment*). Throughout, he was concerned to defend rationality against attack from the Romantic and "faith" philosophers.

14. Macmurray argues that Kant's philosophy is flawed in that it appeals only to an *internal* rational principle or rule ("categorical imperative") for truth and right action. In Macmurray's view, it is possible for human beings to arrive at *real* truth and to make *real* decisions about what good actions to perform without recourse to law. As we shall see in chapter 5, Bernard Lonergan agrees with Macmurray.

15. Bernard Lonergan's critique of Kant (in *Insight*) is that, although he was well aware that knowing involved an understanding of experience, he did not move to the next level of consciousness where a judgment as to the validity of his understanding would bring him to truth, to reality. Lonergan and Kant are compared in Giovanni Sala, "The *A Priori* in Human Knowledge: Kant's *Critique of Pure Reason* and Lonergan's *Insight*," *The Thomist* 40, no. 2 (April 1976): 179–221.

16. The reference in brackets (*Persons* 45–46) is to John Macmurray, *Persons in Relation* (Atlantic Highlands, NJ: Humanities Press International, 1991), 45–46. Quotations from this work will henceforth be indicated as here (*Persons* 45–46).

17. *The Self as Agent* deals with Macmurray's first criticism and *Persons in Relation* with the second. The very titles of these works suggest something of the approach Macmurray will take in his critique of modern philosophy.

18. Note that what Macmurray sets forth is a *proposal*, the choice of which cannot be demonstrated but which will be verified in its unfolding power to explain.

19. The reference in brackets (*Interpreting* 127–28) is to John Macmurray, *Interpreting the Universe* (London: Faber & Faber, 1933), 127–28. Quotations from this work will henceforth be indicated as here (*Interpreting* 127–28). Macmurray first explores his more complete notion of rationality in chapter 6 of *Interpreting the Universe* and more succinctly in "The Nature of Reason," *Proceedings of the Aristotelian Society* 35 (1934–35): 137–48.

20. This is the conclusion of "Logic and Psychology," an unpublished paper in the John Macmurray Collection, Regis College, University of Toronto, Canada.

21. Macmurray also said that "the purely spiritual is the purely imaginary" (Postscript to *Green Pastures* by Mark Connelly [London: Delisle, 1963], 111) and elsewhere, "a purely spiritual world is a purely imaginary one" (Kenneth C. Barnes, *Energy Unbound: The Story of Wennington School* [York, England: William Sessions Limited, 1980], 29).

22. "When a person is 'thinged' only one aspect, or group of aspects, of his existence is recognized as real" (George R. Bach and Ronald M. Deutsch, "Of People, Images and Things," *Pairing* [New York: Avon Books, 1971], 76).

23. The agent-self, Macmurray states, is a logical abstraction and can only exist as a community of personal agents.

24. In support of the intersubjective nature of community, Bernard Lonergan writes that we were born of our "parents love" and "grew and developed in the gravitational field of their affection." He specifically mentions the primordial "bond of mother and child" (*Insight* 237). In the Western world today, we recognize that the "mother" might not be the biological mother but another loving primary care giver.

25. The quoted elements in this paragraph are all found in *Persons in Relation* between pages 47 and 49.

26. This is reminiscent of the work of Brazilian educator, Paulo Freire. Freire's thesis is that education is not a neutral process and ought to be cultural action for freedom. *Pedagogy of the Oppressed* (New York: Seabury Press, 1970), his most famous work, introduces the need for a pedagogy that liberates the oppressed and elaborates Freire's basic theme that, to be fully human, men and women must become subjects, agents.

27. Philip Mooney, "Freedom Through Friendship, John Macmurray: In Memoriam (1891–1976)," *Friends Journal* (January 1, 1977): 4. Because of Macmurray's Quaker background, "friendship" is a word charged with religious connotations of relationship, community, and love.

28. John Macmurray, "Ye Are My Friends," a 1943 address to the Student Christian Movement, issued as a pamphlet by the Friends Home Service Committee in 1943 and reprinted many times. It is quoted by Philip Mooney in "Freedom Through Friendship, John Macmurray: In Memoriam (1891–1976)," *Friends Journal* (January 1, 1977): 5. According to Macmurray, the emphasis in modern society on jobs and material goods (all we have left in Western society, it has been said, are *things* to buy) can in part be accounted for as a failure in friendship.

29. While using this chart, keep in mind that each successive historical period or "unity-pattern" of consciousness includes the viewpoint (s) of the previous period(s) or pattern(s) The biological perspective, for instance, is inclusive of the physical sciences and so we can have a discipline like biochemistry. Similarly, the human sciences make use of both the biological and physical sciences. And "organisms and persons, whatever more they may be, are certainly material objects" (*Interpreting* 102). For Macmurray, the central issue was not the historical periods themselves but the history of the development of human consciousness which they represent. It is also important to point out that each of the unity-patterns for seeing and thinking about reality represented by these three historical periods is still with us. *Interpreting the Universe* is an extended discussion of these ideas.

30. Macmurray uses the term "personal" to characterize the third period in the history of Western philosophy (inclusive of both the mechanical and organic). Because we tend to understand the term personal more narrowly than does Macmurray, I have chosen to use the term "postmodern" (*See* **Postmodern** in Glossary) to define the emerging era in philosophy. Although the term "postmodern" is variously defined, I take it to mean that which takes us beyond the failed assumptions of modernity. As I am using the term it refers to a sense that the "modern" is in need of reconception; a revisioning along holistic lines. Thomas Berry and others might use the term "ecozoic" (*See* **Ecozoic** in Glossary) to further emphasize that this intercommunion is not just among human beings but characterizes the entire earth community. In my view, Macmurray's understanding of "personal" and our use of the term "postmodern" are inclusive of "ecozoic."

31. Macmurray uses the term "religious" to describe the understanding of reality emerging in the third phase in western philosophy; religion as "about human beings in relation." In my experience, religion is often considered to be a negative word in contemporary western culture and so I have chosen the word "spiritual" as best capturing what Macmurray means by the term "religious" ("communal" would be another possibility but it lacks the transcendent dimension implicit in "spiritual").

32. This reminds me of M. Scott Peck's definition of love: "The will to extend one's self for the purpose of nurturing one's own or another's spiritual growth" (M. Scott Peck, *The Road Less Traveled* [New York: Simon and Schuster, 1978], 81). According to Macmurray's analysis, we possess two types of knowledge of people: our knowledge of people as *persons* and our knowledge of them as *objects*. The first depends upon and expresses a personal attitude to the other person, the second an impersonal attitude. When our attitude is personal, reflection will be philosophical; when it is impersonal, our reflection will be scientific. The first will yield a philosophy of the personal; the second a science of humankind (an anthropology).

33. John Macmurray, "Christianity — Pagan or Scientific?," *The Hibbert Journal* 24 (1926): 421–33.

34. John Macmurray, "Beyond Knowledge," *in Adventure: The Faith of Science and the Science of Faith*, ed. B. H. Streeter (New York: Macmillan, 1928).

35. John Macmurray, "Science and Objectivity," *Listening: Journal of Religion and Culture* 10, no. 2 (Spring, 1975): 7–23.

36. This phrase is quoted from Thomas E. Wren, "John Macmurray's Search for Reality: Introduction," *Listening: Journal of Religion and Culture* 10, no. 2 (Spring 1975): 3. In a similar vein, Abraham Maslow writes: "Some perceptive liberals and non-theists are going through an 'agonizing reappraisal' very similar to that which the orthodox often go through, namely a loss of faith in their foundational beliefs. Just as many intellectuals lose faith in religious orthodoxy, so do they also lose faith in positivistic, nineteenth-century science as a way of life. Thus they too often have the sense of loss,

the craving to believe, the yearning for a value-system, the valuelessness and
the simultaneous longing for values which marks so many in this 'Age of
Longing.' I believe that this need can be satisfied by a larger, more inclusive
science, one which includes the data of transcendence" (Abraham H. Maslow,
Religions, Values, and Peak-Experiences [New York: Penguin Books, 1970],
43–44).

37. Robert Coles challenges the notion of the objective, rational observer
able to arrive at value-free knowledge. Critical thought is itself shaped and
influenced; there can be no such thing as the autonomous rational Self.
Knowing is never separated from the knower, nor does the knower stand apart
from the complex web of society and culture in which he/she is embedded.
The intellectual product is never totally distinct from the interpretive method
that produced it. To appreciate this postmodern spirit is to appreciate the
irony present in contemporary life (Bruce A. Ronda, *Intellect and Spirit: The
Life and Work of Robert Coles* [New York: The Continuum Publishing Company, 1989], 32).

38. John Macmurray, "Science and Objectivity," *Listening: Journal of
Religion and Culture* 10, no. 2 (Spring 1975): 7.

39. Ludwig Feuerbach as quoted in Hans Kung, *Freud and the Problem
of God* (New Haven: Yale University Press, 1990), 3.

40. That Macmurray's religious commitment persisted is supported by
the fact that his last essay, published by the Society of Friends in 1973, was
titled "The Philosophy of Jesus."

41. Sigmund Freud hoped that humankind might one day so progress as
to be able completely to do without the false consolation of religious belief.
Religious doctrines, he wrote, "are illusions and insusceptible of proof. No
one can be compelled to think them true, to believe in them. Some of them
are so improbable, so incompatible with everything we have laboriously
discovered about the reality of the world, that we may compare them . . . to
delusions. . . . The riddles of the universe reveal themselves only slowly to
our investigation; there are many questions to which science today can give
no answer. But scientific work is the only road which can lead us to a
knowledge of reality outside ourselves" (Sigmund Freud, *The Future of an
Illusion*, ed. and trans. James Strachey (New York: W. W. Norton & Company, Inc., 1961), 31–32.

42. Gerald A. Largo, "Two Prophetic Voices: Macmurray and Buber,"
America 128 (March 31, 1973): 286. Macmurray was not alone in arguing
that not *all* religion is illusory. Abraham Maslow concurs: "some others, still
a small proportion, are finding in newly available hints from psychology
another possibility of a positive, naturalistic faith, . . . a 'humanistic faith' as
Erich Fromm called it, humanistic psychology as many others are now calling
it. As John Macmurray said, 'Now is the point in history at which it becomes
possible for man to adopt consciously as his own purpose the purpose which
is already inherent in his own nature'" (Abraham Maslow, *Religions, Values,
and Peak-Experiences* [New York: Penguin Books, 1970], 39).

43. "Man is . . . a part of nature; and we individual men and women are not merely members of the human community but elements of the natural world. We have in the end to face the question of our relation to the world. How is it to be conceived? How must we represent the world and the relation between ourselves and the world?" (*Persons* 212).

44. John Macmurray, *Religion, Art, and Science*, (Liverpool: Liverpool University Press, 1961), 58.

45. The reference in brackets (*Adventure* 177–215) is to John Macmurray, "Objectivity in Religion," in *Adventure: The Faith of Science and the Science of Faith*, ed. B. H. Streeter (New York: Macmillan, 1928), 177–215. The other references to *Adventure* in this paragraph are also to Macmurray's "Objectivity in Religion."

46. Macmurray's discussion of Christianity begins with a reminder that Jesus was a Jew, part of the most "uniquely religious people of history." Jesus lived not as a Greek philosopher in continuity with Plato and Aristotle but as one in continuity with the great Hebrew prophetic tradition of action. His teaching centered on the proclamation of the good news of the inbreaking on earth of the Reign of God coupled with the demand for a transformation in the way human beings relate to each other in keeping with the reality of God's reign. And yet, even in the New Testament we find evidence of the influence of Hellenistic thought on the first "followers of the way." Under the spell of Greek philosophy, the emphasis in the Christian community begins to shift from practice to theory, from action to thought, from following "the way" to professing certain orthodox beliefs. The theological definitions of the Councils of Nicaea, Constantinople, and Chalcedon are, in a real sense, a triumph of the theoretical point of view which comes to us from fifth century B. C. Athens. In the theologies of Augustine and Aquinas we *canonized* or at least *baptized* Plato and Aristotle!

47. This is shorthand for Aquinas' "five proofs" for God's existence.

48. Macmurray does, however, see value in the "argument from design" (*Persons* 207). A book by Brian Davies, *God and the New Physics* (New York: Simon and Schuster, 1983) would have pleased him.

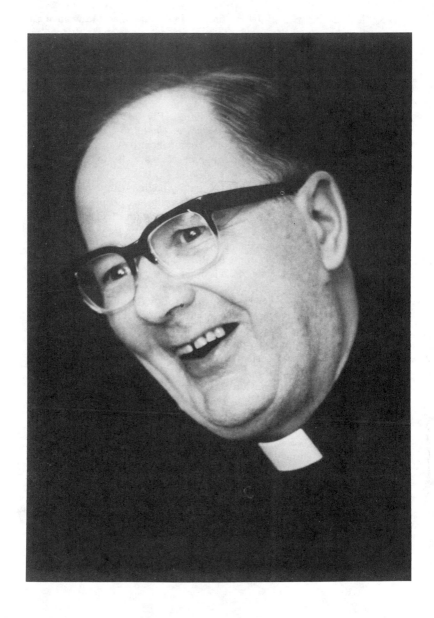

Bernard Lonergan (c. 1970)

Chapter 4

Bernard Lonergan (1904–1984)

> I am certain (and I am not one who becomes certain easily) that I can put together a Thomistic metaphysic of history that will throw Hegel and Marx, despite the enormity of their influence on this very account into the shade. I have a draft of this already written as I have of everything else.
>
> . . . I think this is my work but I know more luminously than anything else that I have nothing I have not received, that I know nothing in philosophy that I have not received through the Society [of Jesus] (1935 Lonergan letter in *Transforming* 110–11, 113).[1]

Early Years

Bernard Joseph Francis Lonergan was born on December 17, 1904 in the town of Buckingham, Quebec. He was the first of three boys.[2] The Lonergans came from Ireland and by 1830 had settled on a farm near Buckingham where, with the exception of Bernard's grandfather, they integrated into the French speaking culture. Bernard's father was a civil engineer. His mother, Josephine Wood, descended from the United Empire Loyalists and was the daughter of a local wheelwright. As Bernard grew up in Buckingham his warm extended family also included his mother's parents and his mother's sister (*Lonergan* 3).[3]

In Lonergan's youth, Buckingham was a prosperous place, domina-

ted by the sawmill at the waterfall on the Lièvre River, made famous in Archibald Lampman's (d. 1899) poem *Morning on the Lièvre*. The population of 3,000 was mostly Roman Catholic (about three-quarters of them French speaking). The Lonergan's were parishioners at the town's only Catholic church, St. Gregory Nazianzen, and Bernard attended St. Michael's, the local Catholic school for boys administered by the Brothers of Christian Instruction. His intellectual ability did not attract particular attention during elementary school although his brothers remembered that even as a boy he liked reading the stock market reports in the newspaper.

In the Fall of 1918, Bernard was sent as a boarder to Loyola College in Montreal, run by the English speaking Jesuits.[4] He completed the four year high school *Cours Classique* in two years, consistently winning the Governor General's Medal for placing first in his class. He was nicknamed "brains Lonergan."

Jesuit Formation

Bernard Lonergan entered the Jesuit Novitiate[5] at Guelph, Ontario, on July 29, 1922. He was in his eighteenth year. He later said that his decision to enter the Jesuit Order was taken on his ride out to a weekend discernment retreat: "I went out to the Sault [Montreal novitiate of the Jesuits of French Canada] to make a retreat, an election, and I decided on the street-car on the way out" (*Lonergan* 6). After two years of spiritual training in the Novitiate and his first vows as a Jesuit, Lonergan completed the traditional two year Juniorate course of classical studies. In the last of his four years at Guelph, he was asked to teach Latin and Greek to the Novices and mathematics to those entering the Juniorate program (*Lonergan* 7–12).

From 1926–29 he and other Canadian Jesuits studied Philosophy at Heythrop College,[6] Oxfordshire, England. The following year, with concentrations in classics, mathematics, and French, he completed his B.A. at the University of London (1930).

Formed spiritually over four years at Guelph and intellectually over four years at Heythrop, Lonergan was strengthened for his Regency at Loyola College, Montreal, where he taught a variety of subjects from 1930–33.[7] His teaching and other duties with the boarders allowed little time for creative thinking. He was able, however, to do "some reading" and write for the *Loyola College Review* which he edited

during his three years at the school (*Lonergan* 18).

In the summer of 1933, Lonergan was assigned to theological studies at the Collège de l'Immaculée-Conception, Montreal (seminary of the French Canadian Jesuits). A few months later, and most significantly for Lonergan's future career, his Jesuit Provincial Superior transferred him to the Gregorian University in Rome to study philosophy and theology. He was ordained to the Roman Catholic priesthood on July 25, 1936 in the Jesuit Church of St. Ignatius, Rome, and received his Licentiate (Master's Degree) in Sacred Theology (S.T.L.) in 1937. Lonergan completed his Jesuit formation with Tertianship in Amiens, France (1937–38) before returning to the Gregorian where he pursued a Doctorate in Sacred Theology (S.T.D.) on the thought of Thomas Aquinas.

Lonergan considered his assignment to Rome a "magnificent vote of confidence" in his hopes for an academic career. Years later he would write to friends of his "breathless . . . enthusiasm for Rome" and love for "that 'timelessness' that characterizes life in the 'eternal' city" (*Lonergan* 20). Unfortunately, he was not quite so keen in his evaluation of professors at the Gregorian University who he described as assuming "that we lift static concepts off mental images much as if the mind were a sausage factory. Missing was insight, the notion of development and the personal dimensions of understanding."[8]

Bernard Lonergan left Rome just before the outbreak of war on the Italian peninsula and from 1940–46 taught theology at the College de l'Immaculée-Conception in Montreal. These years were the beginning of a teaching and writing career that was to span forty-three years.[9]

Genesis of *Insight*

From 1946–53 Lonergan taught at the Jesuit Seminary in Toronto and in 1949 began his magnum opus, *Insight: A Study of Human Understanding* (1957) which he wrote in English.[10] Lonergan explained the genesis of *Insight*. In 1945, he had given a course, Thought and Reality, at the newly founded Thomas More Institute for Adult Education in Montreal.[11] As a result of this experience he said "I knew that I had a book." Modestly, he often referred to the 750 pages of *Insight* as his "little book."[12]

In *Insight*, Lonergan sought to "transpose St. Thomas' position to meet the issues of our own day." He points to what these issues were

and the task that needs to be done:

> Modernity lacks roots. Its values lack balance and depth. Much of
> its science is destructive of man. Catholics in the twentieth century
> are faced with a problem similar to that met by Aquinas in the
> thirteenth century. Then Greek and Arabic culture were pouring into
> Western Europe and, if it was not to destroy Christendom, it had to be
> known, assimilated, transformed. Today modern culture, in many
> ways more stupendous than any that ever existed, is surging around
> us. It too has to be known, assimilated, transformed.[13]

That he understood this task would prove to be the work of a lifetime
is clear from a remark in *Insight*: "To strike out on a new line and
become more than a week-end celebrity calls for years in which one's
living is more or less constantly absorbed in the effort to understand."[14] Frederick E. Crowe attests that the example *par excellence*
of such a person is Lonergan himself, "whose whole life has been one
of renouncement of the immediate small gain for the sake of the great
harvest of the future" (*Enterprise* 41).[15]

Insight was well received by religious and secular scholars.[16] It has
been published in Italian and translations are underway in six other
languages. It has achieved the status of a philosophical classic and is
one of those books that many people speak about but few have read
and even fewer have understood. Yet this is not too surprising because, although Lonergan's style is clear, "his dense, elliptical prose,
studded with references to Thomas Aquinas and modern physics,
makes its points in a methodical and mind-wearying manner. One
typical passage hammers home a conclusion with 'In the thirty-first
place . . .'"[17]

By the early 1960's *Insight* had attracted a great deal of attention
on university campuses across North America and study clubs grew up
to assimilate and expand its complex thought. *Time* magazine did two
stories on Lonergan (January 22, 1965 and April 27, 1970). The 1970
article, "The Towering Thought of Bernard Lonergan," opens with:
"Canadian Jesuit Bernard Joseph Francis Lonergan is considered by
many intellectuals to be the finest philosophic thinker of the 20th century."[18]

Generalized Empirical Method Applied to Theology

Gregorian University

In the fall of 1953, while *Insight* was in the editing and publication process, Lonergan returned to his alma mater, the Gregorian University in Rome, where he taught until 1965. Although the Professorship was prestigious, these years were not easy for Lonergan. His thinking had moved far beyond that taught and permitted in Catholic intellectual circles in Rome.[19]

Lonergan himself clearly suffered, during his early career, because of the academic institutions and practices he inherited: "The situation I was in was hopelessly antiquated, but had not yet been demolished. . . . I taught theology for twenty-five years under impossible conditions." These conditions made it difficult not only to teach effectively but also to write creatively. Indeed, Lonergan himself found that most of the Latin theology he wrote early in his career was not "enduring" enough to bother translating into English.[20]

In the static and formal church environment of Rome in the decade before the Second Vatican Council, Lonergan was a ray of light for the scholarly and became an underground legend, a kind of cult figure, among Catholic seminarians who came to his classes in large numbers (650 in a lecture hall). The amusement of new students at "his sing-song voice and unmelodiously flat Latin pronunciation" was soon turned to despair at "his blithe unconcern for the frailties of lesser intellects:"

Once, after failing to get a philosophical point across to his class, Lonergan brightened, said: "I think this will make it clear," [and] proceeded to cover the blackboard with differential equations. During a World War II discussion about the loss to mankind in bomb-gutted libraries, Lonergan argued that the important things were in people's minds, not in books. In answer, someone cited Shakespeare and got out a copy to cite lines at random. In each case, Lonergan identified the quotation, imperturbably reeled off the rest of the passage.[21]

Asked on one occasion where he got his ideas, Lonergan replied, "I read books"; asked how he found the books he answered "Luck."[22] On still another occasion, when queried as to why he didn't bring two

conflicting passages in *Insight* into conformity, he replied: "Because I didn't have a word processor. When is a work finished? Not when it has reached perfection, but when you are sick and tired of correcting it."[23]

In Rome he published his major Latin theological treatises and solidified his interest in foundational questions rather than the day-to-day controversies in the church that seemed to capture the imaginations of other theologians. Lonergan was to devote his life to articulating a generalized method of inquiry and its implications for philosophy and theology, psychology, history, logic, mathematics, and economics. "In constructing a ship or a philosophy," he wrote in *Insight*, "one has to go the whole way; an effort that is in principle incomplete is equivalent to a failure" (*Insight* 7).[24] His own clear vision pointed to the need to overcome the terrible fragmentation of knowledge and life in modern times and the work of his lifetime was an effort to achieve an integrated view.[25]

During the Second Vatican Council (1962–65) he was among the theological experts (*periti*) who acted as teachers of the bishops.[26] Gerald Emmett Cardinal Carter of Toronto had this to say about Bernard Lonergan's contribution to the work of the council:

> I have always maintained that Bernard Lonergan was the hidden, valid source of much of the theology of the Second Vatican Council. I almost used the expression that he lurked in the Vatican Council giving advice to the *periti* who then paraded it in the council, generally through their Bishops. But one could never think of Bernie as lurking! That crazy laugh of his always gave me the impression that he was laughing at the world. And those who laugh at the world don't lurk. But what I would mean to say is that he never paraded his wisdom or for that matter his many contributions to other people.[27]

Method in Theology

Poor health brought Bernard Lonergan back to Canada (1965) to Regis College, the Jesuit Seminary, in Willowdale (a northern suburb of Toronto). It was discovered that he had lung cancer. He never returned to Rome, and after treatment (his right lung was removed) and lengthy recovery in Canada, Lonergan devoted himself mainly to research and writing.

At a plain wooden table in his spartan sixth floor room at Regis College, he drafted the theological sequel to *Insight* which was pub-

lished in 1972 under the title *Method in Theology*. If *Insight* is Lonergan's answer to questions about the possibility and nature of human knowing, *Method* is his answer to a second problem having to do with the inadequacy of intellectual methods in the discipline he knew best, theology. So, despite his shy and somewhat insecure exterior, Lonergan dares to spell out the problem of theological method and offer the solution as well![28] The main ideas in both *Insight* and *Method* will be discussed in the next chapter.

Honors

In 1971–72, Lonergan was the Stillman Professor of Catholic Studies at Harvard University and a few years later (1975) he accepted the post of Visiting Distinguished Professor at Boston College where he conducted seminars, tutored students, and exchanged ideas with faculty.[29]

He received seventeen honourary doctorates (including one awarded at a special convocation for Lonergan and Karl Rahner (1904–1984)[30] at the University of Chicago in 1974) and numerous other awards. He was named a Companion of the Order of Canada in 1970.[31]

In April of 1970, the first major international congress on his work was held at St. Leo's College near Tampa, Florida. For four days, the 77 participants listened to 65 papers comprising more than 700,000 words (a "living *Festschrift*" to honor Lonergan's sixty-fifth birthday). Since 1970, numerous other conferences and workshops on his work have taken place in cities around the world, among them Halifax, Milwaukee, Ottawa, Toronto, Montreal, Boston, Rome, Philadelphia, Edmonton, Dallas, Dublin, and Mexico City.

A Lonergan Center was established in Toronto in the early 1970's (in 1985 it became the Lonergan Research Institute)[32] and Lonergan Centers exist in Montreal, Boston, Santa Clara (California), Sydney and Melbourne (Australia), Naples and Rome (Italy) Manila (Philippines) and Dublin (Ireland).

Since 1974, Lonergan Workshops have been held annually at Boston College.[33] They attract scholars from around the world and aim to expand and apply Lonergan's thought and methodology in new ways and in fields other than theology.

Method: Journal of Lonergan Studies has been published by

Loyola Marymount University of Los Angeles since 1983. It aims to promote scholarly, critical study of the ideas of Bernard Lonergan and to provide a forum for the dissemination of the results of such study. The *Lonergan Studies Newsletter*, initiated to celebrate Lonergan's seventy-fifth birthday, is a quarterly publication of the Lonergan Research Institute in Toronto. It lists publications related to Lonergan and also offers reviews, workshop and conference particulars, as well as news from the various Lonergan centers around the world.

The Lonergan Research Institute in Toronto, in cooperation with the University of Toronto Press, is in the process of editing the Collected Works of Bernard Lonergan in twenty-two volumes.[34]

Retirement Years

In March of 1983, Lonergan moved to the New England Jesuit Infirmary at Campion Center (Weston, Massachusetts) and then, at seventy-eight years of age, and in failing health, he willingly retired to the Canadian Jesuit Infirmary in Pickering, Ontario (his brother Greg joined him a few months later). "Scientist-humanist-philosopher-theologian" (*Enterprise* 2), Bernard Lonergan, died here of multiple ailments, on November 26, 1984 (just three weeks before his eightieth birthday).

At the time of his death Lonergan was largely unknown to the majority of Canadians, yet obituary tributes to his genius appeared in magazines and newspapers around the world from the Los Angeles Times, New York Times, Times of London, to the Hong Kong Sunday Examiner.

Bernard Lonergan has been acclaimed as one of the greatest thinkers of the twentieth century, a man "whose shadow has already fallen far into the next century."[35] *Insight* is routinely referred to as one of the most important works to be published in the world in this century. He is credited with having "closed a seven century gap in Catholic thought."[36] Many unabashedly call Lonergan one of the greatest thinkers of all time.

Although Lonergan spent eleven years of his life "reaching up to the mind of Aquinas" he once said that he did not think he had succeeded in climbing more than halfway up the mountain of Aquinas' achievements (*Insight* 769). In my view, we are not even halfway up the mountain of Lonergan's achievement and ten years after his death

his thought still points us towards an intellectual, moral, and religious self-transcendence that we have yet to fully embrace.

Notes

1. This quotation is from a letter, dated January 22, 1935, which Bernard Lonergan wrote from Rome to his Jesuit Provincial Superior in Toronto. The reference in brackets (*Transforming* 110–11, 113) is to Richard M. Liddy, *Transforming Light: Intellectual Conversion in the Early Lonergan* (Collegeville, MN: The Liturgical Press, 1993), 110–11, 113. Quotations from this work will henceforth be indicated as here (*Transforming* 110–11, 113).

2. The second boy, Gregory, also became a Jesuit. Gregory typed much of the manuscript for *Insight*. Mark, the youngest, studied engineering and worked in industry.

3. The reference in brackets (*Lonergan* 3) is to Frederick E. Crowe, S.J., *Lonergan*, Outstanding Christian Thinkers Series, ed. Brian Davies, OP (Collegeville, MN: The Liturgical Press, 1992), 3. Quotations from this work will henceforth be indicated as here (*Lonergan* 3). *Time* (April 27, 1970, 11) recorded Lonergan as saying: "I've never been lonely. . . . A man is never lonely if he was loved by his mother."

4. In a public interview during the First International Lonergan Congress (1970), Lonergan described Loyola as follows: "The one [Jesuit boarding school] I went to in Montreal, in 1918, was organized pretty much along the same lines as Jesuit schools had been since the beginning of the Renaissance, with a few slight modifications. So that I can speak of classical culture as something I was brought up in and gradually learned to move *out of*" (*Second Collection* 209–10).

5. Jesuit terminology (Novitiate, Juniorate, Regency, and Tertianship) used in this chapter is explained in the Glossary.

6. Now part of the University of London, Heythrop was where English Jesuits took their Philosophy studies. Here Lonergan's first essays were published in the *Blandyke Papers*, the "Journal" of the College (*Lonergan* 12–17).

7. Lonergan was assigned by his Jesuit superiors to an extra year at Loyola, which he considered a serious and unjust rebuke at the time: "I had regarded myself as one condemned to sacrifice his real interests and, in general, to be suspected and to get into trouble for things I could not help and could not explain" (*Lonergan* 17).

8. *Newsweek*, April 20, 1970, 75. *Transforming Light*, by Richard Liddy, a student of Lonergan at the Gregorian in the early 1960s, charts Lonergan's early life including his "intellectual conversion" in the 1930s and the genesis of *Insight*.

9. Lonergan's work was *not* narrowly focused on Roman Catholic philosophy and theology. Essays and notes found among Lonergan's papers dating from the 1930s, ("File 713–History") make it clear that he was build-

ing a "philosophy of history" which, he wrote, "is as yet not recognized as the essential branch of philosophy that it is." Because his Roman studies were in theology, this philosophy of history project was put on a back burner (*The Lonergan Research Institute Bulletin*, no. 4, November 1989, 3). "File 713–History" further indicates "his interests to lie in the field of culture, philosophy of history, human sciences such as sociology, politico-economic questions, and the like" (*Lonergan* 24). A 1959 series of lectures on the philosophy of education (*Topics in Education*, vol. 10 in the *Collected Works of Bernard Lonergan*) which focused on the "new learning" testify to his relevancy in this field. A work on economics consumed the last years of Lonergan's life; it will be published as part of the *Collected Works of Bernard Lonergan*, University of Toronto Press.

10. Bernard Lonergan, *Insight: A Study of Human Understanding*, vol. 3 in the *Collected Works of Bernard Lonergan*, ed. Frederick E. Crowe and Robert M. Doran (Toronto: University of Toronto Press, 1992). Newsweek (April 20, 1970, 75) quotes Lonergan as saying: "Had 'Insight' been written in Latin . . . I might never have been allowed to publish it." The same article, "A Great Christian Mind," offered the following: "When he submitted his early treatise on the Trinity to Vatican censors for the church's traditional *nihil obstat* (a judgment that a book contains no doctrinal error), the unsigned manuscript finally was referred to the only scholar thought capable of judging it — Bernard Lonergan — who promptly stamped his approval."

11. The Thomas More Institute had been founded by his Jesuit friend, Eric O'Connor, an accomplished mathematician. Lonergan regularly offered courses and workshops there.

12. Lonergan was a quiet, shy, man who avoided personal publicity. Friends knew him as "an inveterate film goer . . . a man who loved music, Beethoven in particular, a hand of bridge, and who relaxed at night with a copy of *The New Yorker* magazine" (*The Toronto Star*, July 10, 1990, M4).

13. *Compass*, March, 1985, 19.

14. Quoted from The Lonergan Research Institute *Bulletin*, no. 4 (November 1989): 4.

15. The reference in brackets (*Enterprise* 41) is to Frederick E. Crowe, S.J., *The Lonergan Enterprise* (Cambridge, MA: Cowley Publications, 1980), 41. Quotations from this work will henceforth be indicated as here (*Enterprise* 41). The quotation continues: "We should be clear on the degree of sacrifice involved in such a decision. To withdraw from the hunt when there is quarry immediately before one and to postpone the pursuit while giving oneself to the forging of a new and vastly superior instrument; to be willing to spend one's entire life at the task, hoping that the long-term benefits will make it worthwhile, but knowing with certainty that one will not see the full harvest and realizing that at best one's efforts will be appreciated only by a small band of attentive readers and students; to live the long years perseveringly, hopefully, unwaveringly, in the labor of creating an adequate organon of incarnate spirit — that withdrawal, renouncement, willingness, decision,

and perseverance is not the act of a drifter or a self-seeker. It is an act of notable self-transcendence, one that we who share Fr. Lonergan's estimate of the momentousness of our times and of the magnitude of the task before us, should be able to appreciate."

16. *Insight* has been described as an "awe-inspiring" documentation of Lonergan's contribution to that job of knowing, assimilating, and transforming modern culture. One Lonerganian offered the following testimony as to the importance of *Insight*: "There are times I become quite discouraged with the state of the world, the church, and especially with the state of theology. I feel as though we've lost our bearings and aren't about to get them back. At such moments, there is only one remedy: I must return to my room and pick up Lonergan's *Insight*. I open it at random and read. Any section will do, just a few pages. Then I can sleep" (Bernard F. Swain, "Lonergan's framework for the future," *Commonweal* 112, no. 2 [January, 1985]: 46). In 1970, *Newsweek* called it "a philosophic classic comparable in scope to Hume's *Inquiry Concerning Human Understanding*" (*Newsweek*, April 20, 1970, 75). *Time* called it an "authentically towering masterpiece" which alone would have secured Lonergan a place in the history of thought (*Time*, January 22, 1965, 46). *Insight* has left its impact on philosophy and theology, education, mathematics, economics (a work nearing completion at the time of his death), sociology, (Lonergan wrote an article in 1935 arguing for a "Summa Sociologica.") and history ("File–713" in the Lonergan Archives).

17. *Time*, January 22, 1965, 46. The quote from *Insight* is on page 747.

18. *Time*, April 27, 1970, 10. Lonergan's obituary appeared in *Time* on December 10, 1984.

19. Lonergan was a strong defender of the need for intellectual freedom in the Catholic church: "one might as well declare openly that all new ideas are taboo, as require that they be examined, evaluated, and approved by some hierarchy of officials and bureaucrats; for members of this hierarchy possess authority and power in inverse ratio to their familiarity with the concrete situations in which the new ideas emerge; they never know whether or not the new idea will work; much less can they divine how it might be corrected or developed; and since the one thing they dread is making a mistake, they devote their energies to paper work and postpone decisions" (*Insight* 259–60).

20. Bernard F. Swain, "Lonergan's framework for the future," *Commonweal* 112, no. 2 (January, 1985): 47.

21. *Time*, January 22, 1965, 47.

22. *The Lonergan Research Institute Bulletin*, no. 5, November, 1990, 3.

23. *The Lonergan Research Institute Bulletin*, no. 6, November, 1991, 3.

24. The reference in brackets (*Insight* 7) is to Bernard Lonergan, *Insight: A Study of Human Understanding*, vol. 3 in the *Collected Works of Bernard Lonergan*, ed. Frederick E. Crowe and Robert M. Doran (Toronto: University of Toronto Press, 1992), 7. Quotations from this work will henceforth be indicated as here (*Insight* 7).

25. Lonergan seems to have worked all of his life as if he were preparing for another major shift in consciousness such as that involved in the transition from a classical to modern worldview. "His vision of the distant future was clear, his sense of the need [for a complete restructuring of knowledge] compelling, and his life's labor designed to meet that need at its most fundamental level" (*The Lonergan Research Institute Bulletin*, no. 5, November, 1990, 1).

26. Lonergan saw himself as "a Roman Catholic with quite conservative views on religious and church doctrines" (*Method* 332).

27. "Address by His Eminence Gerald Emmett Cardinal Carter," July 30, 1991, in *Companions of Jesus: Pilgrims with Ignatius* (Toronto: Canadian Institute of Jesuit Studies, 1991), 30.

28. A systematic Lonergan theology, he half-jokingly insisted, would be left for second-rate minds (*Time*, January 22, 1965, 47). Lonergan was reluctant to popularize or publish applications of his methodology to specific problems. A recent example of such an application is the collection of ten scholarly essays in *Lonergan and Feminism*, ed. Cynthia S. W. Crysdale (Toronto: University of Toronto Press, 1994). With regard to the general topic of applying Lonergan's thought, "The Genus 'Lonergan and' . . . and Feminism" by Frederick E. Crowe, in *Lonergan and Feminism*, is of particular interest.

29. During this period at Boston College, Lonergan got to know Hans-Georg Gadamer (they both lived in the Jesuit residence). In a conversation reported in *Method: Journal for Lonergan Studies*, Gadamer explains his relationship with Lonergan as follows: "He could talk; he was a fascinating talker. But he really couldn't discuss. But on a friendship-basis, we got along with one another very well" (M. Baur, "A Conversation with Hans-Georg Gadamer," *Method: Journal of Lonergan Studies* 8, no. 1 (March 1990): 2.

30. Lonergan and Rahner were born in the same year and both died in 1984. They were both Jesuit theologians.

31. Other awards and honors include: the Spellman Award from the Catholic Theological Society of America in 1949; the Aquinas Medal from the American Catholic Philosophical Association in 1970; the John Courtney Murray Award from the Catholic Theological Society of America in 1973; and the Aquinas Award from Aquinas College in 1974. Lonergan served as a theological expert during the Second Vatican Council, 1962–65, was a member of the International Theological Commission, 1969–74, and appointed as a consultor of the Vatican's Secretariat for Non-Believers in 1973. In 1975 he was named a Corresponding Fellow of the British Academy.

32. Lonergan Research Institute, 10 St. Mary Street, Suite 500, Toronto, ON, M4Y 1P9. The idea of an Institute was proposed (1984) by Robert M. Doran, S.J. Its first major project is the publication of the *Collected Works of Bernard Lonergan* (*Collection* xvii).

33. That same year (1974) Loyola College and Sir George Williams University merged to form Concordia University. Aware that gigantic universities can suffer, rather than profit, from their size, Lonergan College was established on the Loyola Campus in 1979. Operating at the undergraduate level, it teaches courses in the thought of Bernard Lonergan and offers its students an interdisciplinary seminar, unique in North America for its success. The seminar is based on Lonergan's method which not only includes but demands cross-disciplinary learning. To do otherwise is to contribute to the "pool of misunderstanding" that in Lonergan's thought lies at the source of so many of humankind's woes. Each year in the Lonergan College Seminar, a classic work is chosen for study (Bernard Lonergan, Northrop Frye, Carl Jung, Niccolo Machiavelli, Theresa of Avila, Charles Darwin). Every second Monday afternoon the College Fellows (15 professors from diverse departments and disciplines) meet with the year's seminar leader to discuss a segment of the classic, while the college undergraduates listen in. On the alternating Mondays, students meet in small groups with an assigned Fellow to extend the discussion of the previous week.

34. Five volumes (*Insight* 3, *Collection* 4, *Understanding and Being* 5, *Philosophical and Theological Papers* 6 and *Topics in Education* 10) have been released. The night before Bernard Lonergan died, Robert M. Doran (Associate Director of the Institute and co-editor of the Collected Works) told him that an agreement had been reached with the University of Toronto to publish his work (*America* July 27, 1991, 46).

35. One of his doctoral students in Rome said: "Not since Robert Bellarmine have so many been influenced by one Roman thinker." Another offered: "He's still 30 years ahead of his time" (*Time*, January 22, 1965, 47).

36. *Dictionary of Jesuit Biography: Ministry to English Canada 1842–1987* (Toronto: Canadian Institute of Jesuit Sources, 1991), 191.

Chapter 5

Lonergan's Understanding of Understanding

*Thoroughly understand what it is to understand, and not only will
you understand the broad lines of all there is to be understood but
also you will possess a fixed base, an invariant pattern, opening upon
all further developments of understanding* (Bernard Lonergan in
Insight 22).

Introduction

As Bernard Lonergan studied and taught in Rome and Canada, he
came to a deepening awareness that the Roman Catholic scholastic
theological tradition, a paradigmatic representative of the classical
worldview, was "obsolete," "finished," "done for" and that a reconstructed theology was required. Further, he recognized that it was
impossible to rebuild theology correctly until it was first established
on a viable philosophical foundation. And so, by the time Lonergan
had finished his doctoral studies at the Gregorian University in Rome,
he was committed to nothing less than the total reconstruction of both
Roman Catholic philosophy and theology. *Insight: A Study of Human
Understanding* and *Method in Theology*, the major fruits of that effort
to enhance the old with the "new learning," will be the main sources
of our account of Lonergan's ideas in this chapter.

Basic to the thought of Bernard Lonergan is his effort to understand the nature of the human act of understanding; *insight* being the
key to unlocking the basic pattern whereby the fundamental nature of
reality is revealed to human beings. His analysis is of intentionality,
human acts informed by meaning — experiencing, imagining, remembering, desiring, wondering, inquiring, understanding, conceiving,
reflecting, evaluating, judging, deliberating, deciding, acting, loving.
More simply, the work of Lonergan's lifetime was to clarify and
unfold a methodological answer to the question 'What does it mean to
know?' Lonergan assumes that we *do* have an experience of knowing
because to claim that we do not know is at least to *know* that we do not
know, proving that knowledge is possible:

> Am I a knower? The answer yes is coherent, for if I am a knower,
> I can know that fact. But the answer no is incoherent, for if I am not
> a knower, how could the question be raised and answered by me? No
> less, the hedging answer 'I do not know' is incoherent. For if I know
> that I do not know, then I am a knower; and if I do not know that I do
> not know, then I should not answer.
> Am I a knower? If I am not, then I know nothing. My only
> course is silence (*Insight* 353).

Our initial focus in this chapter will be Lonergan's answers to four
questions: 'What am I doing when I am knowing?' (his cognitional
theory), 'Why is doing that knowing?' (his epistemology), 'What do
I know when I have done that?' (his metaphysics), and 'How am I to
decide what to make of myself?' (his existential ethics).[1]

Human Knowing

What am I doing when I am knowing? (cognitional theory)

Bernard Lonergan's investigation into the dynamics of human cognition (our "conscious intentionality") led him to propose that all conscious and intentional operations of knowing occur by means of a
dynamic interlocking pattern of experiencing, understanding, judging,
and deciding.[2]

Using a spacial metaphor, Lonergan speaks of four *levels* through
which the dynamic of conscious intentionality unfolds: the *empirical*
level of conscious attention to data, characterized by the operations of

our senses (seeing, hearing, touching, smelling, tasting) but including as well the interior senses (perceiving, imagining, anticipating, feeling, remembering); the *intellectual* level of consciousness, characterized by inquiry, insight (the act of understanding) and conceptualizing;[3] the *rational* level of consciousness, characterized by all operations of reflecting, grasping the evidence, and judging which are involved in verifying our understanding and judging the truth of what is; and the *responsible* level of consciousness characterized by deliberating, evaluating, and deciding about what good action ought to be done. This process brings us to a knowledge of reality. The real world for Lonergan is not simply the object of our understanding of experience (this is just thinking) but the object of judgments and decisions made in light of our understanding of this experience.

Before moving on, we will pause to consolidate our appropriation of the unfolding of what Lonergan refers to as the "generalized empirical method." I hope these two concrete illustrations of cognitional theory will suggest others to the reader.

First, consider how television star Peter Falk, as Lieutenant Columbo,[4] solves a murder case. What is unusual about a *Columbo* mystery is that at the outset we see the murder being planned and executed; we know who did it, as well as when, where, and how. Over the time remaining, we see Lieutenant Columbo's painstaking efforts to collect and assess evidence. His detective work moves from cigar puffing and head scratching at the complexity of the clues through a logical series of questions for intelligence — What happened? Why is this here? How does this fit? Where did that come from? Who could have done that? Columbo records *data* in his little black book, struggling to fathom how seemingly random pieces of evidence fit together. He goes off on tangents but endless questions raise suspicions and solve small puzzles until the penny drops and a flash of *insight* clarifies his *understanding* of the data. As he continues to scratch his head, search for matches in his shabby coat, and drive around in his old car, he surfaces questions for reflection (Is that really so? Am I certain?) and forms and tests hypotheses. Methodically he builds a case until he arrives at a possible, then probable, and finally certain *judgment* as to the true identity of the guilty party. In the final scene, he makes the arrest. Since we viewers know the identity of the guilty party from the very beginning of the show, why do we bother to watch *Columbo*? In my view, it is because of our fascination with the dynamics of human knowing, with the relentlessness of the process of understanding the

evidence and arriving at the precise judgment that fits all of the facts beyond any doubt. *Columbo*, Lonergan would say, gives us an insight into insight.

The second example that I want to use is that of the film *Lorenzo's Oil*.[5] It begins in 1984 with the Odone family's growing consciousness of their five year old son Lorenzo's rare illness as its debilitating effects manifest themselves (*experience*). We follow them in their efforts to *understand* adrenoleukodystophy (ALD), initially in conversation with doctors and then in medical research libraries sifting through abstruse papers. The Odone's arrive at the stark realization that there are conflicting explanations for the cause and treatment of Lorenzo's rare disease. No consensus exists in the medical profession for how they ought to proceed. Lorenzo grows weaker and his family continues to try to understand the disease. At a turning point in the film, Lorenzo's father states that *understanding* is not enough. Although the Odone's have become experts and even organized an international conference on ALD, Lorenzo continues to weaken. The awareness dawns that they need to reflect on what they have understood and make a *judgment* about which explanation for Lorenzo's illness is correct and then *act* on it. They enter into a process of deliberation and assessment leading to the judgment that a particular by-product of common oils is the best course of treatment as it at least inhibits the progress of ALD. In the final minutes of the film the Odone's take the steps necessary to carry out their *decision*; Lorenzo begins to improve. Their discovery is communicated to other sufferers and what has become known as 'Lorenzo's oil' is still the best available treatment for adrenoleukodystophy.

From what we have seen to this point, I think it is clear that each step in the generalized empirical method builds on the preceding one: without the data of experience there is no possibility of inquiry and understanding; without a proper grasp of intelligibility (relationships and meanings), correct judgment is impossible; without having made a judgment as to what is so, no proper decision can be taken. According to Lonergan, as we achieve the goal of a particular level we go on, spontaneously, to the next. We don't go on, or at least can't *satisfactorily* go on, until the goal of a given level has been reached. So, every question for reflection presupposes that we have arrived at an answer to a question for intelligence; every question requiring deliberation and decision presupposes that we have answered yes or no to the reflective question, 'Is our understanding of the data correct?'[6]

These three levels are solidary. Without the first there would be no base for the second and no precise meaning for the third. Without the second the first could not get beyond elementary statements, and there could be no punch to the third. Without the third the second would be regarded as incredible, and the first would be neglected (*Insight* 7).

We are impelled to move from one level of consciousness to the next by wonder, by our intellectual curiosity, by means of that inborn human need to find answers to questions, all of which Lonergan calls our "detached, disinterested, unrestricted desire to know" (*Insight* 659).

A few years ago, I had occasion to meet a young university student from the former Soviet Union who was in Canada studying for the Orthodox priesthood. He explained to me that with the parting of the Iron Curtain his closed, controlled world had exploded. After only a few months in Canada he discovered so much that had happened in the world and even within Orthodox Christianity of which he was unaware. He told me that he "needed to know" and when I asked, "know what?" he replied "things; anything, everything, I just want to know." I immediately thought of Lonergan's detached, disinterested, unrestricted desire to know!

Each level of consciousness, according to Lonergan's account, is open to reality from a different standpoint. "The first level is open to reality as it can be experienced. The second level is open to reality as it is intelligible. The third level is open to reality as it is true. The fourth level is open to reality as it is *good*" (*Desires* 25).[7] In Lonergan's vision we human beings have within ourselves deep longings and desires for what is beautiful in our experience, for what makes sense, for what is true, and for what is good.

These four interlocking levels of human consciousness are "a rock on which one can build" (*Method* 19);[8] they constitute human consciousness and the *pattern* of the operations involved is *normative*. By this Lonergan means that in order to disprove what he is saying you would necessarily have to appeal to a *judgment* you have made that your *understanding* of a particular set of *data* is correct; in other words, you would *necessarily* have to use the process to disprove the process and so Lonergan concludes that "the possibility of a revision presupposes this analysis" (*Understanding* 143):[9]

If it is true that this is a structure that excludes the possibility of a revision, in the sense that any future revision in any concrete sense of

'revision' would presuppose knowing to be precisely a structure of this type, we have arrived at a fundamental invariant pattern. Any future advance in self-knowledge may fill out this pattern with further details, may enrich it with all sorts of conclusions; but to be a revision it has to preserve this pattern (*Understanding* 144).

The dynamic of the generalized empirical method grounds what Lonergan calls the "transcendental precepts" which guide the gradual expansion of human consciousness: *Be attentive, Be intelligent, Be reasonable, Be responsible*. There is, he suggests, an imperative quality to the dynamics of human consciousness. But, to suggest that human consciousness naturally unfolds attentively, intelligently, reasonably, and responsibly does not mean that we can't pass over or just pay cursory attention to one or another of the levels. We often do. We can, for instance, be unwilling to gather all of the data and seek to understand with the probability of an incomplete or erroneous insight. We can refuse to reflect reasonably and thereby make false judgments. We can choose not to act, to act apathetically, or even choose to do what is wrong. We can "impede or derail the deepest desires" of our human minds and hearts (*Desires* 22). For Lonergan, neglect of these transcendental precepts leads to alienation (*Method* 55).

Note that the spontaneous drive operating at each level of consciousness is in the form of a *precept* or imperative and not *necessity*; although we are called to be attentive to data, to probe intelligently, to reflect reasonably, and to decide responsibly, we need not respond to the call; we can choose to be inattentive, unintelligent, unreasonable, and irresponsible. Human freedom lies in that capacity for choice.

Why is doing that knowing? (epistemological theory)[10]

Medical researchers can dissect the human ear and see its intricate workings but they cannot *see* the inner act of hearing. Similarly, because the world of human consciousness (like hearing) is not something *out there*, it cannot be investigated empirically. Yet, even though human consciousness is not verifiable from *outside*, because the levels which constitute the process of human knowing are conscious (we are aware in our experiencing, aware in our understanding, aware in our judging, aware in our deciding), the human knower can answer this question about the validity of the knowing process from *inside*. Because the activity of knowing takes place within the consciousness of human beings who claim to have knowledge, knowers

must decide whether their knowing is merely *subjective* (i.e., unreliable) or answer that they can know the truth about things as they exist apart from their own perceptions, i.e., *objectively* (reliably).

Lonergan's position on this question is rooted in an awareness that human consciousness is characterized by both outer and inner components. To focus, for example, on the dynamic operating on the empirical level, we are conscious of *what* we are attending to and we are conscious that *we* are attending to it. We are present *both* to the object of our inquiry *and* to ourselves. There is never just an isolated experience of something out there (rationalism, empiricism), but there is also a person, a *subject*, aware of doing the experiencing. The role of the human subject in the knowing dynamic is, as we shall see, key to Lonergan's argument for the possibility of *objectivity* in human knowing.

Before we proceed, allow me to offer one other example of this knowing process at work. When I completed my basic science degree I worked with two senior high school chemistry classes. The teacher assigned to teach chemistry had never taken a university science course and accordingly had no real *understanding* of the scientific method or of basic chemical procedures, reactions, and interconnections. But he had more or less memorized the textbook and did a credible teaching job except when it came to answering a student's question arising from confusion about definitions or explanations in the text. The only answers the teacher knew were those in the book; in fact, he had extraordinary recall. However, he was tied to the text and could not use different language to *explain* concepts or give alternative examples. He did not really understand the concepts himself and what was worse, he knew it; he *knew* that he didn't understand chemistry. It was at this point that I came onto the scene armed with my new Bachelor of Science degree in chemistry; i.e., armed with an *understanding* of the scientific method and the procedures of chemistry as well an acquired ability to offer alternative explanations and weigh the appropriateness of a student's rewording of a definition. The teacher I replaced would agree wholeheartedly with Lonergan that "until I have understood something, I haven't understood it, and I know I haven't understood it, and no amount of self-deception is going to really satisfy me" (*Desires* 19).

This story, I trust, helps to make the point that Lonergan's inquiry into the dynamic of human inquiry involves "self-appropriation;" we attend to the data of our consciousness (inside) even as we focus on

data 'out there' which happens to be of interest. Key to a proper understanding and appreciation of Lonergan's achievement is this notion — all real knowledge requires that we *make our own* the structure of experiencing, understanding, judging, and deciding:[11]

> The dynamic cognitional structure to be reached is . . . the personally appropriated structure of one's own experiencing, one's own intelligent inquiry and insights, one's own critical reflection and judging and deciding. The crucial issue is an experimental issue, and the experiment will be performed not publicly but privately. It will consist in one's own rational self-consciousness clearly and distinctly taking possession of itself as rational self-consciousness. Up to that decisive achievement, all leads. From it all follows. No one else, no matter what his knowledge or his eloquence, no matter what his logical rigor or his persuasiveness, can do it for you (*Insight* 12–13).

Thus, in *Insight* we are counseled not to learn from the book but from reflection on our own human consciousness at work. For Lonergan, philosophy is what occurs in us; the *history* of philosophy is found in books. The philosophic evidence for Lonergan's position, then, lies within each one of us. The dynamic structure of knowing he has carefully uncovered is not *his* theory nor that of a philosophical school, nor is it something we can be taught, but it is *us*; it is ourselves as we search for an understanding of our experience, ourselves as we strive for what is true and good, ourselves as we engage in all aspects of life. Lonergan insists that there is no such animal as a "Lonerganian." His work is a way of challenging human beings "to discover themselves and be themselves" (*Second Collection* 213).[12] Accordingly, in the Introduction to *Insight*, Lonergan says:

> Though I cannot recall to each reader his personal experiences, he can do so for himself and thereby pluck my general phrases from the dim world of thought to set them in the pulsing flow of life. . . . the point here . . . is appropriation; the point is to discover, to identify, to become familiar with, the activities of one's own intelligence . . . (*Insight* 13–14).

As we follow the steps of the generalized empirical method, as we move from one level of human consciousness to another, the *quality* of our consciousness is enlarged. For Lonergan, the data of philosophy (human consciousness) and the methodology used in doing it (intentionality analysis) are coincidental. As questions move us from

level to level "it is a fuller self of which we are aware and the awareness itself is different" (*Method* 9). We are conscious, not only that our operations are different, but that *we* are different. In other words, more of ourselves, more of what it is to be human, is at risk as we go from experiencing to understanding to judging to deciding.[13] For example, as a professor correcting examination papers, I find it quite easy to admit that through oversight I missed a student's answer or added up grades incorrectly. As students come to my office to discuss their work, it is a little more difficult to acknowledge that I have misunderstood them, and to concede that I misjudged their motives would necessitate an admission of some personal failure. Finally, to say that I made a mistake and followed a wrong course of action in my dealings with a student is tantamount to confessing to some serious flaw in my very character.

What is significant, for Lonergan, about the movement through the levels of consciousness, then, is not just the growing complexity of the operations involved but the change in ourselves as we move from receptivity, to inquiry, to verification, to decision:

> [As human beings] we are so endowed that we not only ask questions leading to self-transcendence, not only can recognize correct answers constitutive of intentional self-transcendence, but also respond with the stirring of our very being when we glimpse the possibility . . . of oneself as a moral being, the realization that one not only chooses between courses of action but also thereby makes oneself an authentic human being or an unauthentic one (*Method* 38).

But, how do we know that this many-leveled subject really exists? Lonergan, of course, replies that we must answer that question for ourselves. His own answer is unequivocal: "I do not think that the answers are in doubt. . . . There exist subjects that are empirically, intellectually, rationally, morally conscious" (*Collection* 210).[14]

Questions about truth and objectivity are forms of the epistemological question in philosophy. For Lonergan, it is answered, as I hope is becoming clear, by reflecting on the *process* of knowing; i.e., reflecting on the dynamic structure of human consciousness as experiencing, understanding, judging, and deciding.

> If knowing is a conjunction of experience, understanding, and judging, then knowing knowing has to be a conjunction of (1) experiencing experience, understanding and judging, (2) understanding one's experience of experience, understanding, and judging, and (3) judging

Table 5.1

A GUIDE FOR UNDERSTANDING THE SET OF TERMS LONERGAN HAS DEVELOPED IN HIS ANALYSIS OF HUMAN CONSCIOUSNESS					
LEVELS OF CONSCIOUSNESS	QUESTION	TRANSCENDENTAL ACTIVITIES	TRANSCENDENTAL PRECEPTS	OPEN TO REALITY AS IT IS . . .	
THE LOVING	IS IT LOVABLE?	LOVING/CARING	BE IN LOVE!	LOVABLE	
THE RESPONSIBLE	IS IT OF VALUE? OUGHT I TO DO IT?	DECIDING DELIBERATING	BE RESPONSIBLE!	GOOD/OF VALUE WORTHWHILE	
THE RATIONAL	IS IT SO?	JUDGING REFLECTING	BE REASONABLE!	TRUE	
THE INTELLECTUAL	WHAT IS IT?	UNDERSTANDING INQUIRING CONCEIVING	BE INTELLIGENT!	INTELLIGIBLE	
THE EMPIRICAL	NONE (PRIOR TO INQUIRY)	REMEMBERING PERCEIVING SENSING	BE ATTENTIVE!	EXPERIENCED	
THE ELEMENTAL	NONE	DREAMING		PRE-CONSCIOUS	

one's understanding of experience, understanding, and judging to be correct (*Collection* 208).

Knowing knowing, then, is just a reduplication of Lonergan's basic cognitional structure. The answer to the question 'Why is doing that knowing?' is, simply, 'because *I* know it to be so!'[15] Such reflective knowledge of the framework of human knowing puts us in touch with its very drive or dynamism — human beings by their very nature desire to know. And what is it that we want to know? Like my Orthodox seminarian friend, we want to know *what is* and *what is* is another way of speaking about the 'real' or the 'true'. In philosophical language, human knowing intends *being*. This Lonergan calls "the epistemological theorem" — "namely, that knowledge in the proper sense is knowledge of reality or, more fully, that knowledge is intrinsically objective, that objectivity is the intrinsic relation of knowing to being, and that being and reality are identical" (*Collection* 211).

Intellectual Conversion

In ordinary daily life when we ask someone 'How do you know?' and they respond with a definitive 'Because I saw it!' the issue is normally settled. We often behave as if seeing is knowing (naive realism) or, in a more sophisticated manner, as if the real is what we *know* through sense experience (empiricism). Lonergan does not claim that the empiricist point of view is wrong, only that it is incomplete; it takes just one of the components of knowing (experiencing) and treats it as if it were the whole of knowing. Inquiry, insight, formulation, reflection, judgment, truthfulness, goodness, trust, fidelity, caring, and love cannot be grasped by means of the senses and are therefore pejoratively labeled "subjective" (unreliable) by empiricists, yet these activities are at the very *heart* of the knowing process.

Lonergan asks that we be present to the pattern of our own experiencing, understanding, judging, and deciding as we evaluate his viewpoint. Can we give up the myth that knowing is just taking a "super-look" (*Insight* 658) at the "already-out-there-now-real" (*Second Collection* 272)? Can we discover the intelligible structure of our own dynamic pattern of consciousness, and then affirm the truth about it? To do so, for Lonergan, is to be intellectually converted.

Intellectual conversion is a radical clarification and, consequently, the elimination of an exceedingly stubborn and misleading myth concerning

reality, objectivity, and human knowledge. The myth is that knowing is like looking, that objectivity is seeing what is there to be seen and not seeing what is not there, and that the real is what is out there now to be looked at (*Method* 238).

Intellectual conversion, then, is an awakening to the realization that we will only discover what is true when we use our most personal human capacities, when we devote ourselves to experiencing, understanding, and judging with *all* of the resources available to us. Intellectual conversion implies the realization that the personal, interpersonal, and social dimensions of our existence in this world are made up not principally of sense data but by human understandings, judgments, and decisions. The world in which we live is *constituted by human meaning*. Lonergan's claim is that there is a subjective component to *all* knowing and, far from making our knowing suspect, subjectivity is integral to the correct unfolding of the knowing process. In fact, he argues that *all* knowing *is* subjective and in an often quoted phrase points out that "genuine objectivity is the fruit of authentic subjectivity. It is to be attained only by attaining authentic subjectivity" (*Method* 292).

As a simple illustration of what Lonergan means by this significant but perhaps enigmatic expression, consider an x-ray.[16] Knowing what an x-ray means is certainly more than just *looking* at shades of light and dark on a sheet of plastic. A radiologist practicing his/her craft *knows* how to interpret (understand) these shadows and to judge that a certain tiny line on the film *means* that the patient has a fractured rib. The radiologist's trained subjectivity arrives at an objectivity that I, by *looking* at the x-ray, cannot reach. Knowing is not just taking a good look; knowing is an interlocking process of attending (sensing, perceiving, and imagining), understanding (inquiring, gaining insight, and formulating), reflecting and judging. To *know* that this is so and to operate in this way is for Lonergan to be intellectually converted.

At this point in our survey of Lonergan's thought, it may be helpful to recall John Macmurray's remark (chapter 2) that "it is always legitimate to ask, of any theory which claims to be true, what practical difference it would make if we believed it" (*Self* 23). Lonergan may look to you like an ivory-tower philosopher, offering incomprehensible answers to insoluble problems (to borrow a definition I heard somewhere). He was certainly aware that "in the minds of some" he dwelt in a "cocoon of abstractions" (*Transforming* 209). In my opinion, Lonergan *isn't* an abstract, ivory-tower thinker but a prophetic

interpreter of our transition from the classical age that is dying, through the modern age, and into the one that is coming to birth. As this summary of his thought unfolds, *you* ought to be able to see the practicality of his approach. As will presently become apparent, Lonergan's analysis bears on significant contemporary questions about the nature of reality.

Metaphysics: What do I know when I have done that?

At least implicitly, we have already answered the metaphysical question. For Lonergan, knowledge is knowledge of *reality*; whatever I can grasp intelligently and affirm as reasonable through the use of the generalized empirical method, is *what is*. Knowing *what is* is knowing the 'real' or 'being,' for *the real* is *what is*.[17]

Note that reality, for Lonergan, is not some *object* totally outside of myself which I know with absolute certitude by use of reason (rationalism) or by taking a good look (naive realism). Nor is reality unknowable (idealism) or merely a matter of opinion (relativism). Lonergan's answer (critical realism) is that *we can know reality* and we do so through the dynamic and conscious process of experiencing, understanding, judging, and deciding.

To see how the critical realist understanding of the dynamic of human consciousness unfolds in a concrete instance, allow me to propose for your consideration the meaning of a recurrent expression from the Hebrew scriptures, describing the Promised Land as "flowing with milk and honey" (Exodus 33:3, Deuteronomy 27:3, et. al.). California has always been my image of a land flowing with milk and honey and so when I visited Israel during the course of my Jesuit formation, I was surprised to discover a landscape quite unlike California. Much of the land of the Bible, bordered on the south by the Sinai Desert and on the east by the vast Arabian Desert, is desert-like wilderness with very little vegetation. Some areas, like Jerusalem itself, are mountainous and at the other geographic extreme we find the lowest point on earth, the lifeless Dead Sea. Except for a relatively small area of productive agricultural land (along the Mediterranean coast and in a few broad valleys), the Bible's "flowing with milk and honey" designation seems hardly appropriate!

In terms of Lonergan's elaboration of the generalized empirical method, this biblical text ("a land flowing with milk and honey") is

given to us on the level of experience as a datum to be understood. In my efforts to understand, I consulted the endnotes to various editions of the Bible and found nothing specific. I read several commentaries on scripture which either passed over the expression or said it refers to the fertility of the Promised Land, as compared to the aridity of the desert where the Hebrew people had been wandering for decades. Even though part of Israel is far superior to desert, much of it is, in fact, quite unlike my image of the Promised Land as flowing with California-like "milk and honey." I didn't really understand this "milk and honey" image and I knew that I didn't understand it.

Then, a few years ago I heard a talk on the geography of the Promised Land by a cultural geographer, Dr. James Fleming, from the Hebrew University in Jerusalem. With photographic slides and maps he built up a case for the words "milk" and "honey" as descriptors of two life styles supported by the Promised Land; i.e., the lifestyle of herding in the mountainous areas and on the edges of the deserts (goat's "milk") *and* farming on the broad coast plain and fertile valleys along the Mediterranean (fruit trees give jam or "honey"). The key word in the expression, as it turns out, is the conjunction "and." Peoples living in the areas surrounding the Promised Land were *either* herders *or* farmers. The significance of the Promised Land of "milk *and* honey" is that it is a land supporting *both* herding *and* farming; a very special place indeed!

Based on this scholarly lecture and my own personal experience and study, I made a judgment that Dr. Fleming's explanation of "milk and honey" is the correct one and have even used it in my preaching. Does that mean that this understanding is absolutely certain truth? No! But it is much more than just an opinion, or even a particular scholar's opinion. It represents the accumulated wisdom of many scholars (archaeologists, cultural geographers, climatologists, linguists, anthropologists) and is the consensus of biblical scholarship at the present time. It is a *highly probable explanation*. Note, however, that a highly probable explanation is not *THE* TRUTH (God's Truth) because new evidence from an archaeologist or a textual critic may lead to a somewhat nuanced understanding of the expression which in turn will lead to a slightly different judgment as to its correct interpretation. In more formal terminology, Lonergan says that although the *formally* unconditioned (God's Truth) is beyond our grasp in knowing (*we* cannot know *absolutely*, because *all* possible questions have not been answered), we do reach a *virtually* unconditioned (as much as is

humanly possible the relevant questions have been answered). We can make a *reasonable* affirmation as to what is the truth. So, even though what I achieve as a result of the process of experiencing, understanding, judging and deciding is not absolute certainty (classicism) neither am I left with the polar opposite extreme of mere opinion (relativism). What I reach is knowledge of *what is*. It is *truth*. I like to characterize what is known by this transcendental process as being *relatively* absolute!

In addition, truth, for Lonergan, is necessarily *my* truth; truth which *I* arrive at by means of the pattern of human consciousness expanding through empirical, intellectual, *and* rational, and responsible levels. Truth is not something *apart* from me, carved into granite or preserved in an illuminated manuscript, passed down and accepted uncritically by subsequent generations, because, unless I have made it *my* stone or *my* book, it represents the work of another person's mind. *I* do not yet know it as truth (until the stone or manuscript become data I judge with sufficient evidence to be true in light of my own understanding and critical reflection).

Despite the emphasis above on the word *my*, I trust that you can see why Bernard Lonergan is not open to the charge of being a relativist.[18] The choice for Lonergan is not between the *classical* stance supporting eternal, unchanging, absolute truth and what many people take to be the *modern* view that everything is just a matter of opinion or relative. There is, he argues, a third alternative (critical realism); what is absolute or normative in knowing is *not* so much the *object* I am trying to know but the *process I follow* in coming to know. It is the *pattern* of my conscious and intentional operations which forms the "rock" on which I can build truth.

Existential Ethics

How am I to decide what to make of myself?

> The individual grows in experience, understanding, judgment, and so comes to find out for himself that he has to decide for himself what to make of himself (*Method* 79).

At the beginning of this chapter I said that our focus would be on two of Lonergan's works, *Insight* and *Method in Theology*. Our discussion in this section marks the transition from one to the other.

Lonergan's three level description of cognitional activity (empirical, intellectual, rational) governs *Insight* whereas the overarching motif in *Method* is the four level structure which includes responsibility. To this point, our discussion of Bernard Lonergan's achievement has been (like *Insight* itself) highly cognitional. *Method* reflects a decisive shift in his approach in that it emphasizes the central importance of affectivity and love in knowing and doing at the higher levels of conscious intending. "Experience, understanding and judgment without feeling," Lonergan says, "are paper-thin."[19]

Affectivity is at the center of the fourth level of human intending. It is critical to authenticity at this level; it is in feelings that possible values are *first* apprehended and it is largely in negotiating our feelings that deliberation about decision takes place. The addition of the affective dynamics of *heart* to the cognitional dynamics of *mind* leads to a corresponding shift in decision making from doing what is reasonable to acting responsibly.

What is clear in *Method* is that responsible decision making is a level of consciousness quite distinct from experiencing, understanding and judging. Lonergan variously refers to this level of conscious intentionality as the *responsible* level, as existential consciousness, as the level of authenticity or unauthenticity, and the level where "we emerge as persons" and "meet one another in a common concern for values" (*Method* 10).

Lonergan argues (as does Macmurray) that as human beings we are more than mere *knowing* subjects (mind), we are *agent*-subjects imbued with a built-in spontaneous drive to seek congruence between what we know and what we do. So while cognitional theory, epistemology, and metaphysics are *necessary* in understanding human consciousness, they are not *sufficient*: "They have to be subsumed under the higher operations that integrate knowing with feeling and consist in deliberating, evaluating, deciding, acting" (*Second Collection* 204). And how do we arrive at this level? Just as questions calling for understanding move us from the empirical to the intellectual level of consciousness, and questions for reflection move us from the intellectual level to the level of judgment, so questions for deliberation move us from the rational level to the existential level. For Lonergan, there is in us "an internal compass," a fundamental or innate drive, targeted to what is true and worthwhile, and we know when we have arrived there. Because more than mind is involved in our "detached, disinterested, unrestricted desire to know," we are drawn beyond cognition to

a fourth level of human consciousness where affectivity (heart) joins with knowledge (head) in responsible decision-making about the values by which we will live (hands and feet).[20] To quote Blaise Pascal, as Lonergan often does, "the heart has its reasons of which reason knows nothing" (*Pensées* 154).[21]

So, as we move beyond the third level of consciousness where we reach a judgment of fact about what is *true* or *real*, we reach a fourth level where we ask about what course of action to follow — 'Is this or that particular project or goal really of value?' In essence, at this level of consciousness we come face to face with the basic ethical question — 'Why be moral at all?' 'Is doing the truth worthwhile?' Lonergan would say that an affirmative answer to this question presupposes "moral conversion,"[22] i.e., presupposes that I desire to put the interests of others ahead of my own, group satisfaction before personal satisfaction. This, of course, leads to further questions: 'Why would I want to do that?' and 'How would I accomplish that even if I wanted to?'

To treat these questions in summary form, Lonergan would answer the *why* question by saying that responsible action is what we human beings, having been created *imago Dei* (in the image of God), are made for; right action is the path to human authenticity. Our choices and actions make us who we are, they are the work of free and responsible agents producing the first and only edition of themselves (*Second Collection* 83). He would answer the *how* question with reference to human beings who have been "grasped by ultimate concern," who have fallen in love, who have surrendered themselves totally to God (*Method* 240). This what Lonergan calls "religious conversion;" it grounds both moral and intellectual conversion.[23]

Moral Conversion

To affirm the existence and structure of *four* levels of consciousness, Lonergan says, is to come to a moral question. Why does he say this? It is because, if the pattern we have been considering is indeed the dynamic method of our consciousness, it is our way to be fully human, and to deliberate about whether to follow its injunctions (conscience) is to deliberate about whether to work and grow as individual human beings and with others. To reject mere personal satisfaction and decide to work for the common good is, for Lonergan, *moral conversion*. Moral conversion involves a shift in the criterion

we use for deciding what action we will take; a shift from the criterion of personal satisfaction to that of value (*Method* 240).

The dynamics of human consciousness move us beyond *cognitional* questions of truth to *affective* questions of value, we desire to know because we want to act, and act intelligently. We pay attention to experience and consciousness, inquiry intelligently into the meaning of our experience, and exercise critical judgment, because we want to make responsible decisions, thereby to become *moral* — "to become moral practically, for our decisions affect things; to become moral interpersonally, for our decisions affect other persons; to become moral existentially, for by our decisions we constitute what we are to be" (*Third Collection* 29).[24] The endpoint of the knowing process is ethical, *not* just cognitional. True judgments generate a "peaceful" or "good" conscience and the "uneasy" or "nagging" conscience is the result of false judgment (*Method* 40, *Third Collection* 174). Conscience, for Lonergan is the necessity to make our doing consistent with our knowing.

There is, therefore, a dual creation in our knowing and doing; we not only create objects, we create ourselves (i.e., form character). This critical juncture in our increasing autonomy is where we discover in ourselves and for ourselves that it is ultimately up to ourselves to determine who we are to be (*Third Collection* 230). Lonergan refers to this appreciation as the "existential moment," "the realization that one not only chooses between courses of action but also thereby makes oneself an authentic human being or an unauthentic one" (*Method* 38).[25]

Authenticity, then, involves more than just *knowing* the truth; it is knowledge of truth as oriented towards decision for action, towards *doing* the truth and deciding to live that way habitually. This is a tall order and for Lonergan only possible when we have been "grasped by ultimate concern" (God, for believers). For Christians this "fated acceptance of a vocation to holiness" (*Method* 240) is the experience of God's love having been "poured into our hearts through the Holy Spirit that has been given to us" (Romans 5:5). Lonergan is quick to point out that authenticity is never a permanent, once and for all, achievement:

> Human authenticity is not some pure quality, some serene freedom from all oversights, all misunderstandings, all mistakes, all sins. Rather it consists in a withdrawal from unauthenticity, and the withdrawal is never a permanent achievement. It is ever precarious,

ever to be achieved afresh, ever in great part a matter of uncovering still more oversights, acknowledging still further failures to understand, correcting still more mistakes, repenting more and more deeply hidden sins (*Method* 252).

The path to authenticity, then, is not an easy one and many choose to live unauthentic lives; others "authentically realize unauthenticity." Lonergan explains this, perhaps puzzling phraseology, very well:

Divers men can ask themselves whether or not they are genuine Catholics or Protestants, Muslims or Buddhists, Platonists or Aristotelians, Kantians or Hegelians, artists or scientists, and so forth. Now they may answer that they are, and their answer may be correct. But they can also answer affirmatively and still be mistaken. In that case . . . what I am is one thing, what a genuine Christian or Buddhist is, is another, and I am unaware of the difference. My unawareness is unexpressed. I have no language to express what I am, so I use the language of the tradition I unauthentically appropriate, and thereby I devaluate, distort, water down, corrupt that language.

Such devaluation, distortion, corruption may occur only in scattered individuals. But it may occur on a more massive scale, and then the words are repeated, but the meaning is gone. The chair was still the chair of Moses, but it was occupied by the scribes and Pharisees. The theology was still scholastic, but the scholasticism was decadent. The religious order still read out the rules, but one wonders whether the home fires were still burning. The sacred name of science may still be invoked but . . . all significant scientific ideals can vanish to be replaced by the conventions of a clique. So the unauthenticity of individuals becomes the unauthenticity of a tradition. Then, in the measure a subject takes the tradition, as it exists, for his standard, in that measure he can do no more than authentically realize unauthenticity" (*Method* 80).

When we have begun the process of self-constitution from a reflective, critical stance on the responsible level of consciousness, Lonergan asserts, we have come to a critical turning point in our lives — the point at which *spiritual* development, properly speaking, begins. Practical reflection moves us from the realm of fact into that of *value* when we deliberate about the goodness of a possible course of action and right action moves us towards community, towards being-in-love. In other words, just as moral conversion takes us beyond intellectual conversion, so "religious conversion" takes us beyond moral conversion.

Love/Community

Religious Conversion

For Lonergan, love is the fundamental basis for all that we do. To affirm love as a *fifth* level of human consciousness (the ultimate good, love, God), in Lonergan's view, requires *religious conversion* which he defines as "being grasped by ultimate concern," as "other-worldly falling in love," as "total and permanent self-surrender without conditions, qualifications, reservations" (*Method* 240). From the viewpoint of causality, Lonergan would say that *first* there is God's freely given gift of love.[26] He was fond of quoting St. Paul's letter to the Romans: "Hope does not disappoint us, because God's love has been poured into our hearts through the Holy Spirit that has been given to us" (Romans 5:5). Religious conversion brings a joy that the things of this world cannot give and its influence is so pervasive that, in the normal course of events, "once it comes and as long as it lasts, it takes over. One no longer is one's own. Moreover, in the measure that this transformation is effective, development becomes not merely from below upwards but more fundamentally from above downwards. There has begun a life in which the heart has reasons which reason does not know" (*Third Collection* 77)

In Lonergan's analysis, because human beings are created in the image of God, human authenticity means being like God. Christianity is authentic to the degree that it is "a love of others that does not shrink from self-sacrifice and suffering" (*Method* 291). Clearly, authenticity, defined in this way, is *only* possible in response to the prior, more fundamental gift of God's love "from above."

Community

Although we have not specifically called attention to it until now, Bernard Lonergan understands the whole process of coming to know as "the work of many," a "group enterprise" (*Second Collection* 87). Even academic research, generally thought of as a solitary, ivory-tower type of activity, he envisages as a *collaborative* enterprise carried out by a *community* of scholars.

In *Insight*, Lonergan writes that human beings have a primordial sympathy for one another. We don't live together mechanically or like ants in an ant hill; we live with feelings for and commitments to other

persons. Such community is much more than a number of people living in the same geographic area; it is constituted by means of mutual personal relationships of love.

Lonergan explains mutual love as "the intertwining of two lives" in such a way that an 'I' and 'thou' are transformed into a 'we'; a 'we' "so intimate, so secure, so permanent, that each attends, imagines, thinks, plans, feels, speaks, acts in concern for both" (*Method* 33). Relationships of this kind (respectful, intimate, loving) "bind a community together" whereas relationships characterized by contempt, ignorance, exploitation, and enmity divide a community "into factions, or tear it apart" (*Method* 51).[27]

Because religious experience, however personal and intimate it may be, is not an isolated, solitary experience but a gift given to many, we have the basis for religious *community*. Another way Lonergan looks at community is to see it as a means to "sustain one another in . . . self-transformation" (*Method* 130). Accordingly, he proposes that the Christian church, "the community that results from the outer communication of Christ's message and from the inner gift of God's love" (*Method* 361), ought to have as a primary function the promotion and renewal of community; i.e., the promotion of intellectual, moral, and religious conversion.

When encountered for the first time, this may seem to be strange way to speak about the church. Certainly in times past, the task of the church was understood as enabling believers "to assimilate the available religious meanings, make their own the available religious ideals, [and] participate with their fellows in the customary rituals" (*Third Collection* 59). What has brought about this change in emphasis?

Bernard Lonergan recognized that since the transformation of mathematics, natural science, and philosophy during the enlightenment period, a higher differentiation emerged in human consciousness (the "new learning"), a differentiation which raised new questions about the place of the individual in society. In our own day, he says, those questions have brought about a movement towards "world community" (*Third Collection* 65). Lonergan makes his point with a quotation from the philosopher of religion, Robley E. Whitson:

> Without parallel in the past, contemporary civilization is coming to be centered upon consciousness of man as community: the significance of man in personal relationship — not the isolated individual nor the subordinating society. . . .
> . . . And an immediate consequent of even the most rudimentary

> recognition of human community is the further recognition of human
> unity . . . as emerging consciousness of what man really is . . .
>   Yet human unity . . . is still clearly at its beginnings, still mostly
> dream.[28]

Such developments have, in part, contributed to the ecumenical
movement within Christianity and dialogue among world religions.[29]
In 1975, as part of an International Symposium on Belief, Lonergan
presented a paper on the *emerging* religious consciousness of our
time[30] in which he acknowledged (borrowing from Whitson) that the
notion of a world community was still a dream but reminded his audience that a dream emerges from our unconscious "as an intimation of
a reality to be achieved" (*Third Collection* 66).

Today, in addition to our human relationships, that dream increasingly includes our relationship with the eco-systems of the fragile
planet on which we live. According to Bernard Lonergan's analysis,
because the knowing process involves both inner and outer aspects,
not only do we know and make ourselves we also know and make the
world. It is because of this human/earth relationship that we are not
only *individually* responsible for the lives we lead but we are also
collectively responsible for the world in which we lead them (*Second
Collection* 93 & 115). Honest concern for the future life of our planet
begins, Lonergan says, with self-transcendent moral conversion:

> For to know what is truly good and to effect it calls for a self-
> transcendence that seeks to benefit not self at the cost of the group,
> not the group at the cost of mankind, not present mankind at the cost
> of mankind's future. Concern for the future, if it is not just high-
> sounding hypocrisy, supposes rare moral attainment. It calls for . . .
> heroic charity" (*Second Collection* 115–16).

Does such heroism exist? It does for Lonergan because of the
Spirit of God "moving the hearts of the many." It is found in those
whom "ultimate concern has grasped" (*Second Collection* 116 &
Method 240). In Christian terms it exists in those who respond to the
gift of "God's love [which] has been poured into our hearts through
the Holy Spirit that has been given to us" (Romans 5:5). Being-in-
love with God, with Other, with others, is a prerequisite for being-in-
love with Mother Earth. We need love to create an ecological future:
"Being in love is a fact, and it's what you are, it's existential. And
your living flows from it. It's the first principle, as long as it lasts"

(*Second Collection* 229). Can that be proven? Lonergan replies that "if you are in love it doesn't need any justification. It's the justification beyond anything else. . . . Love is something that proves itself" (*Second Collection* 230).

Two Ways of Knowing [31]

So far we have principally focused on the four levels of consciousness as moving *upward* (in terms of Lonergan's spatial metaphor) from experience to understanding to judgment to decision. Our discussion of moral and religious conversion surfaced the fact that generally we don't live our lives in this logical order. It was certainly apparent to Bernard Lonergan that the single structure of human consciousness can be traversed in two complementary ways:

> Human development is of two quite different kinds. There is development from below upwards, from experience to growing understanding, from growing understanding to balanced judgment, from balanced judgment to fruitful courses of action, and from fruitful courses of action to the new situations that call forth further understanding, profounder judgment, richer courses of action.
>
> But there also is development from above downwards. There is the transformation of falling in love: the domestic love of the family; the human love of one's tribe, one's city, one's country, mankind; the divine love that orientates man in his cosmos and expresses itself in his worship. Where hatred only sees evil, love reveals values. At once it commands commitment and joyfully carries it out, no matter what the sacrifice involved (*Third Collection* 106).

According to Lonergan, these two ways of appropriating human interiority are inverse but complementary components of a *single structure* of human consciousness. Two examples may help to make the connection between Lonergan's thought and lived experience.

My first illustration goes back to my days in graduate school. For one course I read Neil Postman's *Teaching as a Subversive Activity*[32] which advocates a novel approach to education in the belief that traditional ways of schooling are inadequate for solving modern problems. According to this book, conventional methods of conducting schools shield students from reality, educate for obsolescence, do not develop intelligence, punish creativity and independence, are based on fear, and induce alienation (*Subversive* xi–xv). In terms of Lonergan's elu-

cidation of two kinds of human development, Postman negates what has been handed down in the educational tradition and proposes "subversive" strategies for change which arise out of his analysis of schools.

In drawing attention to *Teaching as a Subversive Activity* I don't mean to imply that I disagree with its criticisms of current educational practices or the solutions it proposes. For the most part I like the book. My point is that it is one-sided, incomplete (honoring and promoting just one way of knowing); surely not *everything* about traditional education is wrong.[33]

The reason why a reference to Postman is included in this section related to Lonergan's understanding of knowing as *both* "from below upwards" *and* "from above downwards," is the interesting fact that, in 1979, he published a second book entitled *Teaching as a Conserving Activity*[34] which was intended to bring balance to the discussion in his earlier work: "Without at least a reminiscence of continuity and tradition, without a place to stand from which to observe change, without a counterargument to the overwhelming thesis of change, we can easily be swept away . . ." (*Conserving* 21). If my understanding of Postman in terms of Lonergan's two ways is correct, *Teaching as a Subversive Activity* is written as an achievement of the creative process of development as from below upwards, whereas *Teaching as a Conserving Activity* is written from the ecological perspective of development as from above downwards, a healing process involving the conservation of and passing on of traditional wisdom. The second book was needed as a corrective to the lack of balance in the first — testimony to the inverse but complementary temper of the two ways of knowing. While it is true that tradition must be submitted to the critique of progress, it is equally true that progress must issue forth from a tradition (*Old & New* 24).[35]

My second example to illustrate Lonergan's two ways of knowing is drawn from the film *Dead Poets Society*.[36] As it opens, a buoyant new English teacher, John Keating, is beginning his career in a fashionable and traditional prep-school. In the first class he tells his students to throw away their textbook article on poetry (written by an authority on the subject) and *learn* about poetry by writing it themselves based on their experience of the world around them. He represents education as a creative achievement (from below upwards). As you might imagine, a conflict arises between his unorthodox ways and the traditional teaching methods advocated by the school. Mr. Keating

is no match for the weight of tradition and the film ends as he leaves the school and the august headmaster begins to *teach* the poetry class by appealing to the authority of the very textbook article thrown out earlier! The headmaster, of course, represents the continuity and tradition characteristic of knowing from above downwards.

Lonergan would certainly agree that senior high school students ought to be able to learn à la John Keating, but even as he affirms the creative process, he reminds us that human development is more "fundamentally" and more "importantly" a healing process from above downwards.[37]

What we must keep before us, then, as we reflect on human knowing is that it is not a question of either/or but of both/and — we learn *both* by means of the distinct but interdependent path from below upwards *and* by means of the distinct but interdependent path from above downwards. There are serious limitations inherent in focusing on either way to the neglect of the other. If knowing was *only* conceived classically as preserving and passing on the wisdom of the past (from above downwards), there would be no such thing as progress. Carried to its extreme we would still be starting fire with flint. Yet, if knowing was *only* conceived empirically (from below upwards) there would be constant change and development but there would be no sense of accumulating patrimony or wisdom. In its extreme there would be *nothing* classical; no classical music or art, no classic books or cars. As Lonergan puts it, "just as the creative process, when unaccompanied by healing, is distorted and corrupted by bias, so too the healing process, when unaccompanied by creating, is a soul without a body" (*Third Collection* 107). Elsewhere he clarifies the association of the two ways:

> These two modes of development are interdependent. Both begin from infancy. But only through the second does the first take one beyond the earliest prehistoric stages of human development. Only through the first is there any real assimilation and appropriation of the second.
>
> Such interdependence, as it supposes distinction, so too it opposes separation . . . .[38]

A recognition of the interdependence and balance between the two ways, therefore, is required for authenticity. We receive the traditions and wisdom of our ancestors which we adapt to the needs of our times and places; we live by it, we critique it, we modify it, we add to it, and

we pass that on to our descendants.

Lonergan's way of relating to the thought of Thomas Aquinas is an excellent illustration of this balance at work. The generalized empirical method of *Insight* did not drop from heaven but came gradually and with a great deal of effort from Lonergan's study and dialogue with the western philosophical and theological tradition, most significantly with the works of St. Thomas. Having discovered in 1933 that the Angelic Doctor was "not nearly as bad as he is painted" (*Lonergan* 40), Lonergan spent eleven years as an apprentice "reaching up to the mind of Aquinas" (*Insight* 769). This discipleship, combined with his doctoral dissertation on divine grace and human freedom in the thought of St. Thomas might lead you to conclude that Lonergan was a conventional Thomist. Many, in fact, criticized him for being too Catholic and even labeled him a neo-Thomist. In actuality, Lonergan's interpretation of Aquinas was quite unconventional, and dogmatic Thomists were outraged at his unorthodox reappraisal. Lonergan himself has said that:

> The magnitude and brilliance of his [Thomas Aquinas'] achievement permit us to single him out as the example . . . of what was going forward in his day, namely, discovering, working out, thinking through a new mold for the Catholic mind, a mold in which it could remain fully Catholic and yet be at home with all the good things that might be drawn from the cultural heritage of Greeks and Arabs (*Second Collection* 44).

Lonergan's fascination, then, was not with the *answers* Thomas Aquinas gave to theological questions (we have already noted his growing disillusionment with scholasticism) as with his person and the methodology he employed — "the way Aquinas worked and questioned and thought and understood and thought again and judged and wrote" (*Lonergan* 47). In Lonergan's view it was *not* doctrinal content but the intellectual *method* of St. Thomas that was "going forward" (*Second Collection* 160). It was his way of proceeding that shone "as unmistakably as the sun on the noonday summer hills of Italy"[39] and inspired the young Bernard Lonergan to attempt for the twentieth century what Aquinas had done for the thirteenth. "A completely genuine development of the thought of St. Thomas," Lonergan wrote, "will command in all the universities of the modern world the same admiration and respect that St. Thomas himself commanded in the medieval University of Paris."[40] So we see, in Lonergan's engage-

Table 5.2

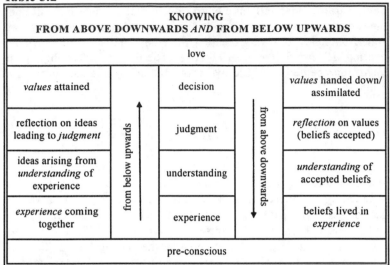

		KNOWING		
FROM ABOVE DOWNWARDS *AND* FROM BELOW UPWARDS				
love				
values attained		decision		*values* handed down/ assimilated
reflection on ideas leading to *judgment*	from below upwards	judgment	from above downwards	*reflection* on values (beliefs accepted)
ideas arising from *understanding* of experience		understanding		*understanding* of accepted beliefs
experience coming together		experience		beliefs lived in *experience*
pre-conscious				

ment with the thought of Thomas Aquinas, new scholarship firmly anchored in the intellectual traditions of the past.

One statement of Lonergan that I often quote reflects this view that one can preserve the best of the old tradition and at the same time be open to the "new learning." Referring to our modern tendency to "brush aside the old questions of cognitional theory, epistemology, [and] metaphysics," Lonergan said, "I have no doubt, I never did doubt, that the old answers were defective" (*Second Collection* 86). Note the balance in this statement; it is not that we have traditionally asked the wrong *questions* (classical science and much that calls itself philosophy today says we did[41]) but that our way of answering them fails to take into account advances (largely in terms of historical consciousness and contemporary scientific approaches) that have been made since the classical answers were carved in stone.[42] Lonergan's "I never did doubt" takes us back to the 1935 letter to his Jesuit Provincial Superior in Canada in which he pointed out inadequacies in current interpretations of Aquinas and his belief that he could show continuity between the medieval synthesis of the Angelic Doctor and ways modern.[43] That he labored almost another fifty years to establish an adequate methodology for the task of recasting philosophy and theology is testimony to his faithfulness to *authentic* tradition![44]

What is important to take away from this discussion is Lonergan's demonstration that authentic human development is dependent upon the successful integration of two seemingly conflictual vector forces; "one from below upwards, creating, the other from above downwards, healing" (*Third Collection* 107–108). The balance and complementarity represented by these two ways of knowing is summarized in Table 5.2.[45]

Method in Theology as Illustrative of the "Two Ways"

Notwithstanding the efforts of Pope Leo XIII (1878–1903) to enshrine Thomas Aquinas as *the* Roman Catholic theologian,[46] Thomism is generally considered passé in our day and "what is going forward in Catholic circles is a disengagement from the forms of classicist culture and a transposition into the forms of modern culture" (*Second Collection* 160). In the decades before and after the Second Vatican Council, scholars worked to construct a "theology of renewal" but, according to Lonergan's analysis, their work of a half century amounted to nothing more than a "scattering of new theological fragments" (*Second Collection* 108). The real task for contemporary Catholic theology, says Lonergan, "is to replace the shattered thoughtforms associated with eternal truths and logical ideals with new thoughtforms that accord with the dynamics of development and the concrete style of method" (*Second Collection* 202). Yet, no new theological *method* appropriate to the contemporary context had been forthcoming. This brings us to a fifth question taken on by Lonergan: "What are we doing when we do theology?" (*Second Collection* 207).

Convinced of the long-term necessity of providing a firmer foundation for the "renewal of theology," Lonergan wrote *Method in Theology*, not really a theological work but a book about the labor of theologians.[47] Specifically, it is an application of the generalized empirical method of *Insight* (called "transcendental method" in *Method*) to the discipline of theology. Described as a "theologian's theologian," Lonergan's entire career was spent developing the *methodology* for this new approach to doing theology.[48]

At the outset, it is important to establish that *Method* does not so much answer theological questions as provide a means for bringing Roman Catholic theology from the thirteenth into the twentieth century.[49] In the medieval world of Thomas Aquinas, theology was

conceived *classically* as a universal and permanent achievement. Within our liberal, scientific, historicist, "modern," mindset, theology is conceived *empirically* as an ongoing process in need of adaptation to varying cultures and circumstances. In this contemporary context for theology what is necessary in order to proceed is clarity about methodology. This is Lonergan's contribution:

> Method is not a set of rules to be followed meticulously by a dolt. It is a framework for collaborative creativity. It would outline the various clusters of operations to be performed by theologians when they go about their various tasks. A contemporary method would conceive those tasks in the context of modern science, modern scholarship, modern philosophy, of historicity, collective practicality and coresponsibility (*Method* xi).

Lonergan's methodology for theology focuses on "functional specialization" which "distinguishes and separates successive stages in the process from data to results" (*Method* 126).[50] There are, he says, eight functional specializations, divided into two phases. In phase one, we investigate the past in order to guide our future and in phase two, enlightened by our study of the past, we take our own stand with regards to the problems of our time. These two phases correspond respectively to Lonergan's understanding of human intentionality as unfolding *both* from below upwards *and* from above downwards (*Method* 133–34).

Each of the two phases of theology has its own set of four functions, paralleling the two ways of knowing represented by the dynamic operating through the four levels of human consciousness. The first phase is concerned to retrieve, interpret, narrate, and evaluate what others have said and done in the discipline of theology and what others in the Christian community (in various contextual situations) have said and done. It is the *reporting* phase of theology. To be specific, *research* is concerned to retrieve what has been done; *interpretation* is concerned to interpret what has been retrieved; *history* narrates the interpretation of what has been retrieved; *dialectic* evaluates in an attempt to find out which issues are important and then mediates disputes.

On the basis of what has been achieved in phase one, theologians in the second phase must stand on their own two feet and come to grips with the issues of their day; given the results of phase one, this is what *I* say, what *I* understand, what *I* hold, what *I* want.[51] *Foundations* sets

forth the horizon out of which I am working, the basis for holding what I believe to be true; *doctrines* expresses what I hold to be true; *systematics* is my attempt to understand what I hold to be true; *communications* is a sharing of my theology with others, including other theologians and other religious traditions. These eight functional specialties, for Lonergan, are the basic structure of theology.

While the four functions in phase one could be carried out by an unbeliever (any textual scholar can decipher biblical texts, for instance), the second phase is, in Lonergan's view, an explication of the faith of a believer. It is also important to point out that he never intended that this theological method would be the work of one person. Theology, for Lonergan, is understood to be a collaborative enterprise carried out by a *community* of scholars.

To illustrate the dynamics of these two phases in action let us consider the highly public and controversial career of American theologian John Courtney Murray, S.J. (1904–1967).[52]

To put Murray's work in its historical context, recall the longstanding opposition of the Catholic church to the concept of religious liberty. Pope Pius IX's *Syllabus of Errors* (July 26, 1855), for instance, stated the position that "the Catholic religion should be [ideally] . . . the only religion of the state, all other worships whatsoever being excluded" (Error # 77). It was not until one hundred years later, during the papacy of Pius XII, that the Catholic church officially declared that democracy was an appropriate form of government for maintaining human dignity.

In the United States of America, founded on the notion of freedom of religion, the separation of church and state had not hindered the functioning of the Roman Catholic church. In fact, without any help from government, the church in America prospered and grew. This positive American experience made John Courtney Murray credible in proposing the idea that the universal church would be better off if it recognized religious freedom as a basic human right.

In the decades before the Second Vatican Council, Murray researched, evaluated, and wrote on questions dealing with the relationship between Church and State. Believing that theologians are not just to shed light on current church teachings (in Lonergan's schema that is the function of the specialty *interpretation* in phase one) but must be on the leading edge of thought, he zeroed in on the issue of religious liberty and tirelessly affirmed it as a basic human right. Murray deliberately said and wrote things that went against current church

teaching. He did so because they were what *he* held to be true and what he believed ought to be the official teaching of his church (*foundations*). He did this at great personal cost (censured in 1955) and for a time was even ordered to stop publishing (which he did). When the ban was lifted, Murray continued to do research and express his unorthodox theological views.

The Second Vatican Council (1962–65) was called by Pope John XXIII to bring the knowledge, wisdom, and experience of the world's bishops and theologians to bear on the great pastoral problems facing both church and world. Although not invited to the first session of the council, Murray served as the personal theologian of Cardinal Spellman of New York during the remaining three sessions where he rose to prominence as America's outstanding theological expert. After much stormy debate, the controversial Vatican II document *Declaration on Religious Freedom* was finally passed towards the end of the council's last session (December 7, 1965). Addressed to the whole world and clearly reflecting the views of John Courtney Murray, it read in part:

> The Vatican Council declares that the human person has a right to religious freedom. Freedom of this kind means that all men should be immune from coercion on the part of individuals, social groups and every human power so that, within due limits, nobody is forced to act against his convictions nor is anyone to be restrained from acting in accordance with his convictions in religious matters in private or in public, alone or in associations with others. The Council further declares that the right to religious freedom is based on the very dignity of the human person as known through the revealed word of God and by reason itself. The right of the human person to religious freedom must be given such recognition in the constitutional order of society as will make it a civil right (# 2).

In this way, Murray's dissenting views on religious freedom became official church teaching. For many, the resolution of this issue, so long resisted by the church, was the climax of the whole council. The Murray Document, as many of the bishops called it, was a great advance in the church's understanding of religious freedom and perhaps *the* major contribution of the American church to Vatican II.[53]

Without going into a further explanation of *Method in Theology*, a largely theological work, it remains to summarize, in chart form (Table 5.3), the relationship between the eight functional specialties essential to theological investigation and Lonergan's generalized em-

Table 5.3

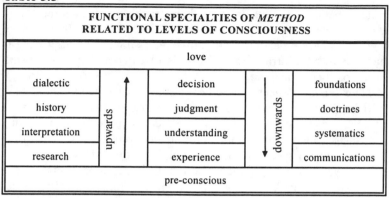

FUNCTIONAL SPECIALTIES OF *METHOD* RELATED TO LEVELS OF CONSCIOUSNESS						
love						
dialectic	upwards	decision	downwards	foundations		
history		judgment		doctrines		
interpretation		understanding		systematics		
research		experience		communications		
pre-conscious						

pirical method of human knowing; i.e., the relationship of *Method in Theology* to *Insight*.[54]

From Classicism to Modernity

Lonergan's explication of the significance of modern historical consciousness is entwined with his analysis of the transition from *classicism* to *modernity*. Focusing on his own religious tradition, Lonergan outlines two basic positions:

> One may be named classicist, conservative, traditional; the other may be named modern, liberal, perhaps historicist. . . . The differences between the two are enormous, for they differ in their apprehension of man, in their account of the good, and in the role they ascribe to the Church in the world. . . . For either side really to understand the other is a major achievement and, when such understanding is lacking, the interpretation of Scripture or of other theological sources is most likely to be at cross-purposes (*Second Collection* 2).

The emergence of modern science (Galileo and Newton) and philosophy (Descartes and Kant), changing economic orientations, political freedoms, and a general secularization of modern western society appeared as a threat to the traditional (classical) understanding of religion. Without much success, Christianity tried to reject, avoid, and then understand modernity.[55]

Referring to his efforts to update Roman Catholic philosophy and theology, Lonergan made an observation that is apropos of our dis-

cussion here about the relationship that ought to exist between old and new, between classicism and modernity, between tradition and achievement:

> I did not think things wrong because they were classicist; on the contrary, I found a number of things that I thought wrong, and, on putting them together, I found what I have named classicism. Again, I do not think things are right because they are modern, but I did find a number of things I thought right and they are modern at least in the sense that they were overlooked in the nineteenth-century Catholic theological tradition.
>
> Here I should like to stress that our disengagement from classicism and our involvement in modernity must be open-eyed, critical, coherent, sure-footed. If we are not just to throw out what is good in classicism and replace it with contemporary trash, then we have to take the trouble, and it is enormous, to grasp the strength and the weakness, the power and the limitations, the good points and the shortcomings of both classicism and modernity (*Second Collection* 98–99).[56]

Historical Mindedness

The classical emphasis on continuity and permanence ignored obvious variation and change of all kind, in favor of what was seen as the more basic, universal, unchanging component of human nature. Given the assumptions of this worldview, it was natural to assume that the future would be just a continuation of the past (we've always done it this way). History was a repetitive cycle of birth, life, and death presided over by the divine authority of Pope and king who preserved and taught objective, unchanging truth. In contrast with this static view of history we have the modern understanding of historical consciousness.

In the nineteenth century a series of thinkers began to study humankind in its concrete self-realization. In making this shift they recognized not only the givenness of human nature but variability in what we have done with that gift in history: "Man is to be known not only in his nature but also in his historicity, not only philosophically but also historically, not only abstractly but also concretely" (*Third Collection* 179). Historical mindedness is a recognition of the fact that to properly understand human beings and their accomplishments we must study their concrete history. Such historical study reveals "the making of man by man" and in particular is interested to discern,

in Lonergan's terminology, what has been "going forward." Accordingly, a modern historian makes a crucial distinction between *data* and *facts*,[57] a distinction Lonergan phrases as between "historical experience" and "historical knowledge" (*Method* chapter 8). An example may help to make the point.

To state that Christopher Columbus sailed westward from Palos, Spain on August 3, 1492, reached land in what we now call the Bahamas on October 12, and returned home to tell about it on March 15, 1493 is a piece of historical data or historical *experience*. But, to say that Columbus *discovered* the New World is a limited Eurocentric interpretation of the data. To say that Columbus was the first person from southern Europe (the Vikings had a settlement in Newfoundland hundreds of years earlier) to encounter the inhabitants of the western hemisphere (the land wasn't *new* to them) is a more accurate interpretation and an example of what Lonergan means by *critical* history leading to historical *knowledge*.[58] I am sure you can see that this approach of modern historians supports Lonergan's illumination of the movement through the levels of conscious intentionality. Their efforts

Table 5.4

COMPARISON OF CLASSICAL AND MODERN WORLDVIEWS[59]		
	classical	**modern**
the real	as what *is*	as *becoming*
truth	as *eternal*: based on immutable principles	as *relative*: based on changing principles
theology	as a permanent achievement	as an ongoing process
science	as rational/certain conceived normatively	experimental/probable conceived empirically
change	as *accidental*	as necessary
history	as *objective* factual	as *subjective* historical consciousness
the world	as *religious*	as *secular*
culture	as *universal* normative	as *particular* empirical
horizon	as *logic*	as *method*

...o understand the data of empirical consciousness inexorably move them to critical judgments about the truth or falsity of their reconstruction and interpretation. Moreover, the concerns and questions about objectivity raised earlier in this chapter, are reformulated in this context as a recognition that there are different versions of what happened in the same historical event. This raises the central question as to whether or not there is a such a thing as *objective* history? Lonergan's discussion of *perspectivism* and *horizons*,[60] show that while at times our histories merely represent different (and complementary) perspectives on the same event at other times, in fact, incompatible and irreconcilable histories can and do arise because of historians working from quite different "basic options" (assumptions and value judgments). These histories all may be unauthentic or some may be authentic and others unauthentic. Only a *conversion*, Lonergan asserts, on the part of one or another historian can bring about compatibility.

Before moving on, another example of modern historical consciousness at work may prove helpful. From this vantage point, what we see going forward in European history is an understanding of one expression of culture (Western as it came to us through Greek philosophical categories) as *the* Culture with a capital "C" (*Second Collection* 101). Another way of putting this is that the Christian churches took a Eurocentric understanding of Christianity and made it *the* version. Missionaries traveling to foreign lands inculcated a Western, Eurocentric interpretation of the Christian message but presented it as *the* one and only expression of Christianity.[61]

My own experience supports this. Traveling in India, I discovered that Fort St. George in Madras is virtually identical in design to the Citadel in Halifax, Nova Scotia; each no doubt commissioned by a military engineer in London who gave no thought at all to climatic variations between South India, Nova Scotia and England.[62] In India, I also visited exact reproductions of English country churches and met native Catholic clergy wearing *Roman* collars!

Related to this discussion of historical consciousness is an incident which occurred during my Jesuit Tertianship in South India. When I was asked by some of the Tamil Novices to "speak some Canadian," I thought they meant French. It took me a while to see that they were asking if I knew an aboriginal language. It was only then that I realized that I was not a *native* Canadian in the sense that they were *native* Indians (descendants of the ancient Dravidians).

Bernard Lonergan's Journey

Our biographical sketch of Bernard Lonergan in chapter 4, has, I am sure, stirred up in you an appreciation for the fact that his life and career can be interpreted as the journey of a person *out of* the classicism in which he was nurtured and *into* historical consciousness (*Second Collection* 210).

In the Scholastic tradition which Lonergan grew out of, the focus of theological reflection was on understanding and communicating basic Church doctrine, the truth of which was a given. Without denigrating the genuine achievements of the past, Lonergan sought to elaborate the intellectual justification for a decisive shift in focus, away from the static *doctrines* which express a person's faith, to the spiritual *experience* of the believer who affirms the doctrine; i.e., away from the way of *tradition* to the way of *achievement*. For too long, he argues, we subordinated the realities of the lived Christian faith to seven century old Scholastic doctrinal formulations that had become *the* formulations. We subordinated *living* the faith to *knowing* the truths of the faith, subordinated religious experience to doctrine. Lonergan's approach to theology, beginning as it does from below upwards is to discover in religious existence (the first four functional specialties) the foundation for religious affirmation (the second four functional specialties). So, for Lonergan, a key component in this shift from a classical to a modern worldview is the "recovery of the subject" who experiences, understands, judges, decides, and loves.[63]

It was clear to Bernard Lonergan that an acceptance of this transition demands the complete rethinking of everything, yet (according to his methodology) in a manner that *preserves a continuity* with the genuine achievements of the tradition (let us not throw out the baby with the bath water) and in a manner that enables us to judge precisely what is genuinely going forward from those achievements.[64]

In light of this discussion, the Second Vatican Council can be viewed as an inspired attempt to move Roman Catholicism from an uncritical maintenance of classicism, "the shabby shell of Catholicism" (*Method* 327), to modern historical consciousness and beyond to ecological postmodernism. In fact, Lonergan has said that "the meaning of Vatican II was the acknowledgment of history" and his own work in theology can be understood as an effort to introduce history into that discipline (*Lonergan* 98). However, in some respects, today's institutional Catholic church appears to be carrying on the

struggle to preserve its "shabby shell" by silencing theologians and restoring static, culturally specific, "correct formulae" as the key to "the unity of faith."[65] This resistance to historical consciousness and a desperate clinging to "a world that no longer exists" exacerbates efforts to make the pastoral and theological changes appropriate to the emerging ecozoic age.

Bernard Lonergan, S.J.

Wisdom comes
not from watching a parade
(he said),
but from marching consciously,
feeling the rhythm and movement in me.

Theology is not carved lapidary
from the quarry of eternal truth
(he said),
but flashes fresh in each new age,
dancing just beyond the horizon of longing.

He made a deft incision in my mind,
as small and as useful as an episiotomy,
midwifing a less painful birth
for the unthinkable,
cutting the umbilical of fixed assumptions,
the tether of unchanging ideas.

A birth but also a death
of the great fumbling heresy
that faith is blind repetition.

In the end
(he said),
if the Word had not flamed up
and tied himself
to the tree of time and place
there would be no fixed point.

But now there is.

John Kinsella[66]

Notes

1. The first three questions are found often in Lonergan; see, for example, *Second Collection* 203 & 241. In this chapter, we shall also consider a fifth question: 'What are we doing when we do theology?' (*Second Collection* 207).

2. *Insight* speaks of three levels of the generalized empirical method (experience, understanding and judgment) with decision included in judgment as an extension of knowing. Not long after *Insight*, Lonergan began to differentiate decision from judgment as a fourth level of human consciousness. By the mid-1960s, his thinking took a turn (David Tracy, *The Achievement of Bernard Lonergan* [New York: Herder and Herder, 1970]), and Lonergan began to refer to *love* as a fifth level. *Method in Theology* (1972) refers to five levels to the "transcendental method" (Lonergan's new name for "generalized empirical method") and in *A Third Collection* (1985) love is essential to Lonergan's understanding of "method." Michael Vertin, "Lonergan on Consciousness: Is There a Fifth Level?," *Method: Journal of Lonergan Studies* 12, no. 2 (Spring, 1994): 1–36) presents an interesting discussion of the pros and cons of a fifth level. Towards the end of his career, Lonergan put forward the notion that the basic dynamic structure of human knowing is open at both ends. He had uncovered six levels in the generalized empirical method; adding love after decision and inserting dreams before experience. For our purposes in this introduction to his thought we will focus on *experience, understanding, judgment* and *decision. Love* and *dreams* will be given brief consideration.

3. Taken together, the first two levels represent *thinking*, not knowing. Our understanding of the world can be mistaken; it is because we can *mis*understand that a third level, judgment, is needed for knowledge. The level of judgment is where we determine how much of our thinking is correct (*Second Collection* 31).

4. The Preface of *Insight* opens with the example of a detective story.

5. Robert M. Doran, S.J. of the Lonergan Research Institute, Toronto, suggested that *Lorenzo's Oil* illustrated Lonergan's transcendental method. A 1992 Universal picture, *Lorenzo's Oil* was directed by George (II) Miller.

6. The two highest levels of consciousness, deliberation about what action to take and the possibility of being-in-love, "sublate" and unify knowing and feeling (*Second Collection* 277). They are the context for the whole knowing project; to use John Macmurray's language, we want to know in order to act responsibly and build a community of love.

7. The reference (*Desires* 25) is to Vernon Gregson, ed., *The Desires of the Human Heart: An Introduction to the Theology of Bernard Lonergan* (Mahwah, NJ: Paulist Press, 1988), 25. Quotations from this work will henceforth be given as here (*Desires* 25).

8. The reference (*Method* 19) is to Bernard Lonergan, *Method in Theology* (Toronto: University of Toronto Press for Lonergan Research Institute, 1990), 19. Quotations from this work will henceforth be given as

here (*Method* 19).

9. The reference in brackets (*Understanding* 143) is to Bernard Lonergan, *Understanding and Being*, vol. 5 in the *Collected Works of Bernard Lonergan*, edited by Elizabeth A. Morelli and Mark D. Morelli, revised and augmented by Frederick E. Crowe with the collaboration of Elizabeth A. Morelli, Mark D. Morelli, Robert M. Doran, and Thomas V. Daly (Toronto: University of Toronto Press, 1990), 143. Quotations from this work will henceforth be indicated as here (*Understanding* 143).

10. I have provided a rather complete answer to the cognitional question. Answers to the epistemological question and the metaphysical question are much more involved philosophically and therefore beyond the scope of this introduction to Lonergan's thought. My treatment of Lonergan's epistemology and metaphysics is merely suggestive of the direction he takes and an invitation to the reader to consult primary sources.

11. At the end of chapter 1 of *Insight*, Lonergan points out that what is important is not the content of the chapter but the experience of our own minds at work as we grappled with that content. See also the Introduction xiii.

12. The reference in brackets (*Second Collection* 213) is to Bernard J. F. Lonergan, S.J., *A Second Collection*, ed. William F. J. Ryan and Bernard Tyrrell (Philadelphia: The Westminster Press, 1974), 213. Quotations from this work will henceforth be indicated as here (*Second Collection* 213).

13. There is a parallel here with John Macmurray's insistence on the primacy of action. It is not *knowing* which is the defining characteristic of being human but right *action* done in congruence with what I know to be true. To know the truth and not to do it is to acknowledge a flaw in our character, i. e., to be less than fully human. This point of congruence in the thought of Lonergan and Macmurray will be developed in chapter 8.

14. The reference in brackets (*Collection* 210) is to Bernard Lonergan, *Collection*, vol. 4 in the *Collected Works of Bernard Lonergan*, ed. Frederick E. Crowe and Robert M. Doran (Toronto: University of Toronto Press, 1988), 210. Quotations from this work will henceforth be indicated as here (*Collection* 210).

15. In using the expression "because *I* say so," I do not in any way mean to imply relativism. *My* truth is not just what is true for *me* but is the best available scholarly conviction which I affirm as mine through experiencing, understanding, judging, and deciding.

16. Bernard Lonergan, *The Way to Nicea: The Dialectical Development of Trinitarian Theology*, a translation by Conn O'Donovan from the first part of *De Deo trino* (London: Darton, Longman & Todd , 1976), viii.

17. *Insight* exhaustively derives what has been summarized here in a few sentences.

18. In chapter 7, as we turn to a consideration of James Fowler's stages of faith development, we will see that this quality of "my-ness," first-hand and not second-hand knowledge of truth, is characteristic of Stage 4 faith.

19. *Time*, April 27, 1970, 11.

20. Lonergan's concern to bring congruence between what we have judged to be true and our decision as to what good action ought to be done, is a significant point of congruence with the philosophy of John Macmurray. The attainment of knowledge is *not* the endpoint for either thinker but is just a step (albeit a crucial step) in the larger process of becoming a full human person capable of good action and love. For Macmurray, as we have seen, knowledge is for the sake of action (and action for friendship). Here Lonergan makes the point that, although knowledge of the truth is the termination of a *cognitional* process, a person is now impelled by further questions to the next level of human consciousness where a decision has to be made about what to do. See chapter 8 for a further discussion of this parallel in the thought of Lonergan and Macmurray.

21. The reference in brackets (*Pensées* 154) is to Blaise Pascal, *Pensées*, trans. A. J. Krailsheimer (London: Penguin Books, 1966), 154. Quotations from this work will henceforth be indicated as here (*Pensées* 154).

22. A perennial question in moral philosophy has to do with justifying the shift from *is* to *ought*. For Lonergan this is the movement from knowing the truth to deciding to do what is good, worthwhile, of value. Moral conversion is required to authentically make the transition.

23. In later writings, Lonergan identifies *deciding* and *being-in-love* as separate levels of consciousness; already hinted at in a 1970 interview in which he stated that "what really reveals values and lets you really see them, is being in love" (*Second Collection* 223).

24. The reference in brackets (*Third Collection* 29) is to Bernard Lonergan, *A Third Collection: Papers by Bernard J. F. Lonergan, S.J.*, ed. Frederick E. Crowe, S.J. (New York: Paulist Press, 1985), 29. Quotations from this work will henceforth be indicated as here (*Third Collection* 29).

25. "In the main it is not by introspection but by reflecting on our living in common with others that we come to know ourselves. What is revealed? It is an original creation. Freely the subject makes himself what he is, never in this life is the making finished, always it is in process, always it is a precarious achievement that can slip and fall and shatter" (*Gregorianum*, 1963 as quoted in *Time*, April 27, 1970, 11).

26. Although the usual order in the conversions is religious, moral, and intellectual, Lonergan preferred to explain them in reverse order as we have done here. See, for example, "Bernard Lonergan Responds," in *Foundations of Theology*, papers from the International Lonergan Congress, 1970, ed. P. McShane (Dublin: Gill and Macmillan Ltd., 1971), 233.

27. "Community coheres or divides, begins or ends, just where the common field of experience, common understanding, common judgment, common commitments begin and end. . . . As it is only within communities that men are conceived and born and reared, so too it is only with respect to the available common meanings that the individual grows in experience, understanding, judgment, and so comes to find out for himself that he has to

decide for himself what to make of himself" (*Method* 79).

28. *Third Collection* 66, quoting Robley Edward Whitson, *The Coming Convergence of World Religions* (New York: Newman, 1971), 17–18.

29. The modern ecumenical movement, with origins in the World Missionary Conference in Edinburgh (1910), took definite shape in 1948 with the founding of the World Council of Churches. Headquartered in Geneva, the WCC is an international association of about 300 Protestant, Anglican, Eastern Orthodox and other Christian traditions committed to the promotion of unity among Christians. In 1960, Roman Catholicism joined the effort as Pope John XXIII established a Secretariat for Christian Unity at the Vatican and subsequently invited "separated brethren" to participate as observers during the Second Vatican Council which produced ground breaking ecumenical documents. More recently, and of great significance in terms of inter-faith dialogue, Pope John Paul II joined leaders of major world religions at Assisi for a day of prayer for peace (October 27, 1986).

30. Bernard Lonergan, "Prolegomena to the Study of the Emerging Religious Consciousness of Our Time," paper presented at the Second International Symposium on Belief, Baden/Vienna, January, 1975. It is reprinted in *Third Collection* 55–73.

31. After *Method*, Lonergan is explicit about there being "two vectors" in the functioning of transcendental method. This is most clearly stated in Bernard Lonergan, "Healing and Creating in History," *Third Collection* 100–109.

32. Neil Postman, and Charles Weingartner, *Teaching as a Subversive Activity* (New York: Dell Publishing Co., Inc., 1969). Quotations from this work will henceforth be given as *Subversive* followed by a page number.

33. I am reminded of a distinction I have heard between "tradition" and "traditionalism" — tradition is the living faith of the dead whereas tradition-alism is the dead faith of the living.

34. Neil Postman, *Teaching as a Conserving Activity* (New York: Delacorte Press, 1979). Quotations from this work will hence forth be given as *Conserving* followed by a page number.

35. The reference in brackets (*Old & New* 24) is to Frederick E. Crowe, S.J., *Old Things and New: A Strategy for Education* (Atlanta: Scholar's Press, 1985), 24. Quotations from this work will henceforth be indicated as here (*Old & New* 24). Moral education is characterized by an ongoing debate as to whether morality is *taught* or *caught*. My sense of Lonergan's two ways of knowing is that the way from above downwards represents morality as *taught* and the way from below upwards represents morality as *caught*. More precisely I would say that, according to the way down, because we love our children we teach them values and the truths on which the way of life implied by those values is predicated. We hope that they will accept what has been given, understand it and put it into practice in their own lives. According to the way up, experiences are given and understanding facilitated, with the hope that students with catch the truth and decide to live in harmony with it.

36. A 1989 film by Touchstone Pictures, *Dead Poets Society* was directed by Peter Weir.

37. *Dead Poets Society* presents us with an either/or choice, the good guy (Keating) versus the bad guy (headmaster); creative and independent thinking versus the boring three Rs. We are left with the impression that there is nothing of value from the past which is worthy of being passed on or made part of the data of experience we work with (reminiscent of the old conflict between science and religion). A critique of the views expressed by the expert on poetry as a prelude to poetry writing, or a critical reading of the article after experience in writing a few poems, represent *balanced* alternatives to the either/or approach reflected in the film.

38. Bernard Lonergan, "Questionnaire on Philosophy," *Method: Journal of Lonergan Studies* 2, no. 2 (October 1984): 10.

39. Bernard Lonergan, *Verbum: Word and Idea in Aquinas*, ed. David B. Burrell (Notre Dame: University of Notre Dame Press, 1967), 219.

40. Bernard Lonergan, *Verbum: Word and Idea in Aquinas*, ed. David B. Burrell (Notre Dame: University of Notre Dame Press, 1967), 220.

41. E. F. Schumacher wrote: "The philosophical maps with which I was supplied . . . failed to show large 'unorthodox' sections of both theory and practice in medicine, agriculture, psychology and the social and political sciences . . . The maps produced by modern materialistic scientism leave all the questions that really matter unanswered. More than that, they do not even show a way to a possible answer: they deny the validity of the questions" (E. F. Schumacher, *A Guide for the Perplexed* [London: Sphere Books Ltd., 1978], 11–12 and 13).

42. I am reminded of a similar comment by the American humanist, Abraham Maslow: "It is increasingly clear that the religious questions themselves . . . are perfectly respectable scientifically, that they are rooted deep in human nature, that they can be studied, described, examined in a scientific way, and that the churches were trying to answer perfectly sound human questions. Though the answers were not acceptable, the questions themselves were and are perfectly acceptable, and perfectly legitimate" (Abraham H. Maslow, *Religions, Values, and Peak-Experiences* [New York: Penguin Books, 1970], 18).

43. In this letter, Lonergan writes: "I can prove out of St. Thomas himself that the current interpretation is absolutely wrong." See chapter 4, note 1.

44. An understanding of the *two ways* of knowing is central to my use of Lonergan's epistemology to shed light on Fowler's faith development theory. Lonergan's *way of tradition* is parallel to Fowler's Stage 3 faith (characteristically *classical*, conservative and based on authority) and his *way of achievement* to Stage 4 faith (characteristically *modern*, liberal, and quite individualistic). As we will see in chapter 7, Fowler's understanding of Stage 5, Conjunctive faith, arises out of a need to bring elements from the two earlier faith patterns together.

45. This chart is adapted from Frederick Crowe's *Old Things and New*, 14. The diagrams and discussion of Lonergan's thought presented in this paper have been simplified to highlight the main upward and downward dynamics of human development. But it is important to recall that the two ways are used in tandem and that there is a horizontal dynamic operating as well. To give just one example from the chart, our reflection on the values that have been handed down to us may lead to the formation of judgments about what we hold to be true.

46. On August 4, 1879, Pope Leo XIII issued the encyclical *Aeterni Patris*, on the restoration of Christian philosophy. It declared that the theology of Thomas Aquinas (Thomism) was to be the standard against which all Catholic philosophy and theology would be judged. The pronouncement gave impetus to the revivals of Neo-Thomism and Neo-Scholasticism. The theology of Thomas Aquinas was foundational in Catholic seminary teaching for eight centuries.

47. "I am writing not theology but method in theology. I am concerned not with the objects that theologians expound but with the operations that theologians perform" (*Method* xii).

48. Answering a question from German theologian Karl Rahner, Lonergan recognized the applicability of *Method* beyond the theological sphere: "Clearly functional specialties as such are not specifically theological. Indeed, the eight specialities we have listed would be relevant to any human studies that investigated a cultural past to guide its future. Again, since the sources to be subjected to research are not specified, they could be the sacred books and traditions of any religion" ("Bernard Lonergan Responds," in *Foundations of Theology*, ed. Philip McShane (Dublin: Gill and Macmillan, 1971), 233. In a later paper, Rahner himself indicated that Lonergan's methodology need not be confined to the theological enterprise but "could be applied to any human science that was fully conscious of itself as depending on the past and looking towards the future" (*Second Collection* 210).

49. *Method in Theology* frankly acknowledges the fact that Roman Catholic theology (i.e., Scholasticism) had not kept pace with humanity's intellectual evolution (*Method* 279 & 311) and takes seriously the shift from classicism to the "new learning" representative of the modern worldview (*Topics* 131).

50. Traditionally, theology has been divided according to departments or subjects (for example, languages of the Near East or Hellenistic history), or in more recent years according to narrow fields or topics. A theologian is no longer an expert in scripture but in the Synoptic gospels, no longer a Patristic scholar but a specialist in the thought of Augustine. In this vein, Lonergan speaks of a specialist as "one who knows more and more about less and less" (*Method* 125).

51. Much of academia holds to the view that scholars are not supposed to (and good scholars don't) enter into the second phase Lonergan describes. It seems clear to me that they do in fact do it; they just don't admit it!

52. In 1992, a two-part conference on John Courtney Murray's thought was held at Notre Dame University, South Bend, Indiana (April 3–5) and Georgetown University, Washington, DC (October 30–November 2). A good selection of Murray's writings can be found in,John Courtney Murray, *Bridging the Sacred and Secular: Selected Writings of John Courtney Murray*, ed. J. Leon Hooper (Washington, DC: Georgetown University Press, 1994).

53. Towards the end of Vatican II, Pope Paul VI quite deliberately invited a group of controversial theologians, John Courtney Murray among ·them, to concelebrate Mass with him before the assembly of bishops. Branded as rebellious in the decades before the Council, they were vindicated in their own lifetimes!

54. Historical consciousness is a major theme in many of the items in *A Second Collection* (dated between 1966 and the publication of *Method in Theology* in 1973). See, for example, Bernard Lonergan, "The Transition from a Classicist World-View to Historical-Mindedness" (*Second Collection* 1–9); "The Dehellenization of Dogma," (*Second Collection* 11–32) and "Belief: Today's Issue" (*Second Collection* 87–99).

55. This is the process I see occurring during the reigns of Popes in the nineteenth and twentieth centuries. Hostile to modern trends, Gregory XVI (1831–46) banned railways (*chemins de fer* in French) in the Papal States calling them *chemins d'enfer* (roads to Hell). Following the loss of the Papal States in the unification of Italy, Pius IX (1846–78) retired to the Vatican as a "prisoner" from where he proclaimed his Syllabus of Errors (1864) and had Papal Infallibility defined by Vatican I (1869–70). Pius X (1903–14) condemned biblical scholar Alfred Loisy (1857–1940) and "modernism." With *Divino Afflante Spiritu* (1943) Pius XII (1939–58) belatedly allowed Catholic scholars to make use of modern developments in the study of scripture. John XXIII (1958–63) convoked the Second Vatican Council and ushered in *aggiornamento* (updating). John Paul II even pardoned Galileo, albeit three hundred and fifty years after his death!

56. In "The Absence of God in Modern Culture" (*Second Collection* 101–16), Lonergan points out that the *aggiornamento* (bringing up to date) called for by Pope John XXIII "is not desertion of the past but only a discerning and discriminating disengagement from its limitations. *Aggiornamento* is not just acceptance of the present; it is acknowledgment of its evils as well as of its good" (113). The idea that the Roman Catholic Church, indeed the western world, has polarized between two world views is accounted for in Lonergan's analysis of human consciousness. The modern empirical notion of reality rests on his explication of the way from below upwards and, as we have seen, since the birth of scientific methodology, knowing has not been a static permanent achievement but an ongoing, developmental process (*Method* xi). The classicist view is rooted in Lonergan's analysis of human

consciousness as also moving from above downwards. This prior movement in a person and in human history is often considered (notably among religious fundamentalists) to be the *only* way of knowing.

57. An empiricist would identify the facts with the data. An idealist would say that although we can make interconnections in the sense data, we can never really get to the facts. A critical realist (Lonergan) would say with the empiricist that an historian is in immediate contact with real data but would acknowledge the necessity of a prolonged period of reconstruction and thought (first with respect to the authenticity of sources and then with a view to understanding what was going forward) in order to reach the facts. Facts include the interconnections in the data that have been reconstructed.

58. What I think this example makes clear is that we don't know *in our time* what is going forward in our time. What is going forward is a function of intention as well as mistakes and failures; it may be either progress or decline. Only from the perspective of the passage of time do people come to know what was really going forward in time.

59. Many of the terms in this table are found in "The Absence of God in Modern Culture," *A Second Collection*, 101–16.

60. Although a discussion of "perspectivism" and "horizon" are beyond the scope of this book (See *Method*, chapter 9 and *Topics in Education*, chapter 4), I do want to introduce Lonergan's definition of "horizon." There are questions that I can ask and answer (the *known*) and there are questions I can ask but do not yet have answers for (the *known unknown*). Further, there is "the range of questions that I do not raise at all, or that, if they were raised I would not understand, or find significant" (the *unknown unknown*). "Horizon" is the boundary between the *known unknown* and the *unknown unknown* (*Topics* 89).

61. On a visit to the continent during his papacy, Paul VI called, not for a Christian Africa, but for an African Christianity. The Church is no longer to be European but global. It is still Roman Catholic but authentically local. The pertinent question is, 'Who is Jesus Christ for *Africa*?'

62. A few years back a student responded to my defense of the use of English in the liturgy with, "If Latin was good enough for Jesus it is good enough for me."

63. A clear exposition of Lonergan's thought on human subjectivity is found in "The Subject," *Second Collection*, 69–86.

64. C. S. Lewis has said that our uncritical belief that things modern are superior to the past just because they are *new* is "chronological snobbery"(C. S. Lewis, *Surprised by Joy* [London: Collins Fount, 1977], 166).

65. The *Catechism of the Catholic Church*, published in 1992 arises within this viewpoint. According to Lonergan, there can be unity without the uniformity of "correct formulae." Such a unity lies in the structure of our human consciousness as it moves from culturally and situationally limited experience, through insight and conceptualization to judgment, and from judgment on the facts as they are to deliberation and decision making

regarding the real world and the self as they ought to be. For the believer, of course, this also presupposes and demands "being in love with God."

66. *America* 169, no. 6 (September 11, 1993): 13.

James W. Fowler

Chapter 6

James Fowler (b. 1940)

> What is there in common between Athens and Jerusalem?
> What between the Academy and the Church?
> *Tertullian*

Early Years

James Wiley Fowler III was born October 12, 1940, in Reidsville, North Carolina where his father, James W., Jr., was an ordained Methodist minister (his mother was a Quaker from Indiana). When he was twelve the family moved to Lake Junaluska, in the Great Smoky Mountains of Western North Carolina, because his father has just been named Executive Director of the Methodist Summer Conference Center. This particular corner of God's earth has great significance for Fowler and he continues to maintain a residence there.

With regards to his own faith journey, Fowler recalls that his Christian commitment was "very much a process of gradual formation . . . an ongoing process of growth in grace." In a 1986 interview, he provided a few tantilizing details of this journey:

> I can remember as early as 8 going to a small revival and answering an altar call. This happened again at 15 at a Billy Graham crusade.

I was sitting in the top row of the choir, in front of everyone. Reverend Graham got to the climax of the sermon, gave the invitation, and I stood up before 3,000 people, tears streaming down my face. I spent that night walking, crying, and praying, trying to sort out what this meant, and somehow realizing this didn't finish my business with God."[1]

Newly graduated with a Bachelor of Arts degree from Duke University, he married Lurline P. Locklair on July 7, 1962. They have two grown daughters, Joan and Margaret.

My family is a key commitment and major source of joy in my life. Our two daughters continually pull me out of books and writing, reminding me of the vitality of music, dance, and horseback riding. My wife pursues a career that parallels mine and works with me at the challenging adventure of finding vitality in a lasting marriage. We have a retreat in the mountains of western North Carolina where, with friends, family, and in solitude, we periodically recover the rootedness in Spirit which gives purpose and power to our demanding lives.[2]

Following marriage, Fowler entered Drew Theological Seminary (Madison, New Jersey) from which he graduated (*magna cum laude*) in 1965 with his Bachelor of Divinity degree. He continued his studies (concentration on ethics) at Harvard University Divinity School from which he graduated with a Master's degree in 1968 and was ordained in the United Methodist church of America.

Origins of Faith Development Theory

For nearly two years after completing divinity studies (1968–69) Fowler was Associate Director of Interpreters' House, a Methodist retreat center located above Lake Junaluska in his beloved Great Smoky Mountains. Established by Fowler's friend and mentor, Carlyle Marney (*Becoming* 33),[3] Interpreters' House is "an unusual religious and cultural center . . . a place of conversation — a meeting place where interreligious, interracial, interpersonal engagements of real depth and honesty could occur" (*Stages* 37).[4] Marney took the name of the center from John Bunyan's *Pilgrim's Progress* where the 'house of the interpreter' was a place where pilgrims would break their journey and he spelled it as a possessive plural to indicate that any participant in the conversations, staff or pilgrim, could offer an

"interpretation"(*Stages* 37).

The program at Interpreters' House featured interfaith seminars for clergy and laity. A key component of such seminars was an opportunity for pilgrims to share something of their life histories. This faith sharing (and subsequent sorting out of its various dynamics) proved to be a powerful instrument in helping participants, many of whom had reached a point where the struggle and pain of living had become too difficult to handle, begin to put broken lives together again. As these stories unfolded, Fowler, under the tutelage of Marney, learned a great deal about the dynamics of faith. He recalls coming to Marney on one occasion frustrated at not being able to get through to a middle-aged, rigid, and aggressive fundamentalist. Marney's sage advice was to "let him be" because "there are some bales of hay you don't cut the wires on, or you're going to have hay scattered all over the room."[5]

It was at Interpreters' House that faith development theory was born:

> The listening at Interpreters' House usually began with our hearing something of each person's life journey. As I listened to some two hundred men and women that year I began to hear patterns. The particular relationships and events of their lives differed, to be sure, but there did seem to be some important commonalities in the stories. I shall never fully know to what degree my search for and attention to common turning points in life stories were shaped by my immersion in the writings of Erik Erikson. What is certain is that I devoured his work that year, finding him to be an extraordinary teacher and companion as I tried to process the overwhelmingly rich data people shared (*Stages* 38).[6]

Erik Erikson proved to be the major influence on Fowler as faith development theory initially emerged. Although Erikson's theory of eight ages in the life cycle makes no direct appeal to belief in God, he certainly would affirm "the importance and even the necessity" of what Fowler calls *faith* "in the sustaining of lives of meaning and devotion" (*Becoming* 29).[7]

In the fall of 1969, Fowler returned to Harvard Divinity School, Cambridge, Massachusetts, as a doctoral student in theology, at the same time lecturing and serving as the director of continuing education (*Becoming* 98). After successfully defending his dissertation on the thought of the American theologian, H. Richard Niebuhr,[8] Fowler received a Ph.D. from Harvard University in 1971. From 1971–74 he was assistant professor and chairperson of the Department of Church

at Harvard Divinity School and associate professor of applied theology from 1974–76.[9] He was Director of the Research Project on Moral and Faith Development (1973–79), funded by a grant from the Joseph P. Kennedy, Jr., Foundation. This research, conducted first in Boston and later in Atlanta, involved indepth interviews with almost 400 people (age 4 to 80) representing various religious groups as well as agnostics and atheists. It provided the basis for his ground-breaking work in faith development theory, *Stages of Faith.*

It was while teaching applied (pastoral) theology to graduate students at Harvard Divinity School, that Fowler put forward his tentative theory about something like stages in faith (with echoes of Erikson's eight ages in the life cycle). At their prompting he began to read the cognitive development research of Jean Piaget and was introduced to Lawrence Kohlberg's work in moral development.[10] He spent 1973 in postdoctoral study at Harvard where he read in the field of pastoral care while continuing his study of Erik Erikson and the cognitive developmentalists. During this time too, Lawrence Kohlberg and his associates helped Fowler to structure his insights from Interpreters' House into the nature of our growth in faith:

> In my effort to become literate in these new areas I found the friendship and colleagueship of Kohlberg. In the circle of associates that I met through his work my tourist's approach to developmental psychology began to become more systematic and committed. A citizen reared in the land of theology began to try to earn dual citizenship in the new world of the psychology of human development. . . . I want to communicate some of the immense richness I have found in the worlds of Jean Piaget, Lawrence Kohlberg and Erik Erikson. I have read and learned from many other theorists of human development, but as regards the timbers and foundations of my own work these three keep proving most fundamental (*Stages* 38–39).[11]

It was in Boston, too, that Fowler faced a personal faith crisis. Although he was firm in his belief in God and in God's unconditional love, the college years had given rise to "real struggles about how God related to the church and how the church related to Jesus Christ." He began to see a Jesuit spiritual director and followed the *Spiritual Exercises of Ignatius of Loyola,*[12] another influence on his subsequent work. These experiences helped him get his Christology "straightened out" and introduced him to a form of prayer compatible with what he understands as Conjunctive (Stage 5) faith:[13]

Not until I was in my thirties, undergoing my first experience of spiritual direction in the tradition of St. Ignatius's *Spiritual Exercises*, did I begin to learn a method of working with scripture that breathed more of the spirit of Stage 5. The Ignatian approach did not require me to give up or negate my critical skills, but it did teach me to supplement them with a method in which I learned to relinquish initiative to the text. Instead of *my reading*, analyzing and extracting the meaning of a Biblical text, in Ignatian contemplative prayer I began to learn how to let the text *read me* and to let it bring my needs and the Spirit's movements within me to consciousness (*Stages* 185–86).

In the fall of 1976, Fowler crossed the Charles River to Boston College, a Jesuit institution in Chestnut Hill, where he was associate professor of theology and human development for one year — for the first time in his career teaching undergraduates. Seventy freshmen and sophomores enrolled in "Faith and the Life Cycle," a theology course Fowler designed to test out some of his ideas relating the faith journey to Erikson's research on the eight ages in the life cycle and Kohlberg's work in cognitive moral development.

My academic career unfolded as I sought to pursue issues that concerned and interested me most. It should not be surprising that interdisciplinary pursuits have claimed me; I was fated by commitment and interest to live in interaction between university and church, and I was inclined by my time, place, and circumstances of birth and early childhood to be one who lives on boundaries.[14]

Emory University

In 1977 Fowler moved to Emory University, Atlanta, Georgia, to establish and direct the Center for Faith Development (renamed in 1988 as the Center for Research in Faith and Moral Development)[15] and teach in the Candler School of Theology:[16]

My chief satisfaction as a teacher and writer has come from the way some early work I did on faith development, based on listening to some two hundred life stories at Interpreters' House, ignited the interests of a wide range of religious and non-religious folk. With some splendid associates across eight years, I have pursued research in this area. To my surprise, the resulting body of theory shows signs of becoming a field of inquiry itself. At Emory University we are

founding the Center for Faith Development where this research will continue and where we will expand our work in the direction of experimentation — on behalf of church, education and counseling — with modes of formation and transformation in faith.[17]

In 1979, Fowler was a key participant in a week long International Symposium on Moral and Faith Development. Fittingly scheduled at a conference center in the former twelfth-century Cistercian Abbey of Senanque (southern France), the symposium was a dialogue among distinguished European and North American scholars on the cutting edge of moral and faith development research. The symposium provided a stage on which Fowler was able to present his faith development model to a broad audience. His work was well received.[18]

On a semester's leave from Emory University (1979–80), Fowler drafted a book length manuscript on faith development research and theory. As work on the book proceeded, he was faced with a major career choice between accepting a senior administrative position in a major theology school, or continuing with research, teaching, and completion of the half finished book. It was not an easy decision but Fowler opted to continue along the path opened up for him at Interpreters' House ten years earlier. *Stages of Faith: The Psychology of Human Development and the Quest for Meaning* was one of the impressive results.[19] Other books followed, notably *Becoming Adult, Becoming Christian: Adult Development and Christian Faith* (1984), *Faith Development and Pastoral Care* (1987), and *Weaving the New Creation: Stages of Faith and the Public Church* (1991).

Although Fowler had written articles[20] and conducted workshops[21] on faith development theory in the 1970's, it was not until the publication of *Stages of Faith* in 1981,[22] that the full range of information arising from more than four hundred faith interviews could be systematically presented. Lawrence Kohlberg welcomed *Stages of Faith* as opening up "a whole new area in the study of human development, with wide ranging implications" and acclaimed Christian educator, Thomas Groome, allowed that, "what Piaget and Kohlberg did for cognitive and moral development respectively, Fowler has done for faith development."[23]

Faith Development: Fifteen Years Later

Since its publication in 1981, *Stages of Faith* has undergone six

printings (more than 60,000 copies sold) and has been translated into German, Portuguese, and Korean. Summaries of its theory of faith development have appeared in several university textbooks in psychology and psychology of religion[24] and *Stages of Faith* has itself been used as a textbook. To date, four volumes of critical essays on the faith development model have appeared[25] and more than 220 research projects related to the theory have been conducted.[26] The bibliography of secondary literature is growing.[27]

Fowler himself points to several characteristics of faith development theory which help to account for its durability and diverse secular and religious acceptance. Among these are: the definition of "faith as a generic, universal, and dynamically unfolding phenomenon;" the empirical basis of the theory in social science research; its integration of the *development* metaphor from Piaget and Kohlberg and life-cycle research of Erikson; its use as a "comparative and critical hermeneutic theory for studying the reception of traditions;" and its practical use in designing religious education curricula and as a diagnostic tool in counseling.[28]

In my view, Fowler's genius is that he works both as a social scientist and a Christian theologian. His faith development theory is cross-disciplinary, straddling the boundaries between psychology and religion. His application of insights from psycho-social psychology and cognitive developmental approaches to knowing have enriched our understanding of the faith journey. And his inclusion of the affective side of human beings in his concept of rationality allows traditional understandings of religion to be taken seriously by his theory.

New Directions

Two of Fowler's recent books, *Faith Development and Pastoral Care* (1987) and *Weaving the New Creation: Stages of Faith and the Public Church* (1991), as well as a 1994 article, "Keeping Faith with God and Our Children: A Practical Theological Perspective"[29] show less of Fowler the social scientist and more of Fowler the Christian theologian seeking to make a practical contribution to church ministry. His views on the Christian vocation or, more precisely, his "Christian conviction about the *human* vocation" are very much in harmony with the thinking of both John Macmurray and Bernard Lonergan:

From a Christian standpoint, at the heart of what it means to be a human being is the conviction that we are called into being by God for partnership with God. This is . . . a Christian conviction about the *human* vocation.

. . . vocation is the response a person makes with his or her total life to the call of God to partnership. . . .

. . . God does not call us to our vocations in individualistic isolation. God calls us into covenanted relations in community with others. . . . we are called by God into covenant solidarity with all God's children — and more radically, with all of God's creation.[30]

But, because we all fall short of the fullness of that call, Fowler has begun to articulate an outline of a "theory of shame" and its relationship to our sinful condition. The myth of the Western world, he suggests, is that we will *individually* achieve and succeed. Many do, Fowler grants, but the dark side of this myth is shame at not reaching the ideal. For some it may be shame at dropping out of medical school and having to work as a nurse. For another it may be shame at not having a swimming pool in the backyard. For those living in the "permanent underclass" this shame, Fowler argues, moves beyond tolerable limits. Denial and suppression of their deep, pervasive, unacknowledged shame allows them to slip into a shame of apparent shamelessness. In modern "post-Christian" Western society it is young people in particular, he says, who fall into this destructive pattern.

In keeping with his growing conviction that our approach to religious and ethical questions needs to be grounded in a practical theological perspective,[31] Fowler accepted a position as the Human Development Director of the Center for Ethics in Public Policy and the Professions at Emory University (1994). He also continues as the Charles Howard Candler Professor of Theology at Emory.

Notes

1. "Fowler on Faith," in *Christianity Today* (June 13, 1986): 8-1.

2. Some of the biographical material in this account is taken from the entry on Fowler, James W(iley) III in *Contemporary Authors* 104, ed. Frances C. Locher (Detroit: Gale Research Company, 1982), 154.

3. Fowler understands a mentor as "a person usually seven to twenty years older than the one being mentored" who "takes an active interest in the life and dream of the younger adult and develops with him or her a quality of

love relationship that constitutes a special kind of friendship" (*Becoming* 33). This book is dedicated "to James Luther Adams and Carlyle Marney, Mentors and Exemplars in Vocation." In the Acknowledgments (149), Fowler describes Marney as "special beyond words to me from my age seventeen till his death in 1978" at age sixty-one.

4. The reference in brackets (*Stages* 37) is to James W. Fowler, *Stages of Faith: The Psychology of Human Development and the Quest for Meaning* (San Francisco: Harper & Row, Publishers, 1981), 37. Quotations from this work will henceforth be given as here (*Stages* 37).

5. Linda Lawrence, "Stages of Faith," *Psychology Today* 17, no. 11 (November 1983): 56–58.

6. As a divinity student, Fowler had read Erik Erikson's *Young Man Luther: A Study in Psychoanalysis and History* (New York: W. W. Norton & Company, 1958) and with this introduction began an indepth study of his psychosocial theory of development.

7. "It is not the psychologists job to decide whether religion should or should not be confessed and practiced in particular words and rituals. Rather the psychological observer must ask whether or not in any area under observation religion and tradition are living psychological forces creating the kind of faith and conviction which permeates a parent's personality and thus reinforces the child's basic trust in the world's trustworthiness. . . . it seems worth while to speculate on the fact that religion through the centuries has served to restore a sense of trust at regular intervals in the form of faith . . .

Whosoever says he has religion must derive a faith from it which is transmitted to infants in the form of basic trust; whosoever claims that he does not need religion must derive such basic faith from elsewhere" (Erik H. Erikson, *Identity and the Life Cycle* [New York: W. W. Norton & Company, 1980], 66–67).

8. It was published in 1974 as *To See the Kingdom: The Theological Vision of H. Richard Niebuhr* (Nashville: Abingdon Press, 1974) and republished in 1985 by University Press of America, Inc.

9. In 1976, Fowler won the distinguished teaching award from the Associated Alumni of Harvard Divinity School.

10. Fowler says it was 1972 when he "first became seriously aware of Lawrence Kohlberg's structural-developmental research" (*Stages* 270).

11. Fowler "worked closely" with Lawrence Kohlberg and considered him a "good friend." Kohlberg was reported missing on January 17, 1987 and his body was found near Boston's Logan Airport on April 6, 1987. Friends said he took his own life after having suffered many years from a disease caused by an intestinal parasite. In May, 1987, Fowler spoke at a memorial service for Kohlberg. He had occasion to meet Erik Erikson and hear him lecture (*Stages* 41). "I have found it easier to put on paper the influence of Piaget and Kohlberg on our work than I have that of Erikson. I believe this is because Erikson's influence on me has been both more pervasive and more subtle; it has touched me at convictional depths that the

structural developmentalists have not addressed. As unsystematic and unsatisfactory as it may seem, I simply have to say that Erikson's work has become part of the interpretive mind-set I bring to research on faith development" (*Stages* 110).

12. Spiritual experiences at Manresa, Spain (1522–23) provided Ignatius with the essential elements of his *Spiritual Exercises*. If Manresa was the school where Ignatius was taught by God, then the *Spiritual Exercises*, arising out of his mystical experiences, are the school of Ignatius of Loyola. Although the sixteenth century language and form of expression may be somewhat foreign to us, Ignatius' purpose in writing the *Spiritual Exercises* is clear. It is not a book to be read but a practical methodology to be followed by those seeking to discover God's will for their lives and the steps they ought to take to conform their lives to the divine will. A modern English version of the *Spiritual Exercises* is found in D. L. Fleming, S. J., *The Spiritual Exercises of St. Ignatius: A Literal Translation and a Contemporary Reading* (St. Louis: The Institute of Jesuit Sources, 1978). Annually, the Guelph Center of Spirituality (Guelph, Ontario) sponsors a symposium on Ignatian Spirituality. James Fowler will be a presenter during the 1996 symposium on the ministry of the Spiritual Exercises and Ignatian spirituality as we approach the third millenium.

13. Quoted phrases in this paragraph are from "Fowler on Faith," in *Christianity Today* (June 13, 1986): 8-1.

14. *Contemporary Authors* 104, ed. Frances C. Locher (Detroit: Gale Research Company, 1982), 154.

15. In 1988, Dr. John Snarey joined the Center for Faith Development and Emory University. His presence strengthened the Center's research and theory construction work in faith development. Fowler writes that the new name reflects "new levels of engagement and broadened foci in our corporate enterprise" and "the special emphasis which John Snarey's leadership in the Center enables us to advance" (Newsletter of the Center for Research in Faith and Moral Development, no. 7 (January 1989), 1.

16. Fowler has lectured extensively and presented workshops in the United States and abroad. After coming to Emory in 1977 he remained an associate in education at Harvard University. Fowler is a member of the American Academy of Religion, Religious Education Association, and Phi Beta Kappa.

17. *Contemporary Authors* 104, ed. Frances C. Locher (Detroit: Gale Research Company, 1982), 154.

18. The Senanque Papers have been published as *Toward Moral and Religious Maturity* (Morristown, NJ: Silver Burdett Company, 1980). James W. Fowler and Antoine Vergote are senior authors.

19. Fowler describes the complexities of this choice in the Introduction to *Becoming Adult, Becoming Christian*, ix–x.

20. Fowler has contributed chapters to several books addressing faith development theory and his articles and reviews have appeared in various religious magazines and journals, including *Religious Education, Journal of Religion, Christian Century, Religion in Life,* and *Perkins Journal.*

21. My introduction to Fowler and his theory was one such workshop: "Continuing Education Programme," Ewart College, Toronto, Ontario, February, 20–24, 1978.

22. At times, Fowler's style has an almost poetic quality to it, not unusual because he admits to writing blank verse at times (*Stages* 26).

23. "In Praise of *Stages of Faith,*" promotional literature for *Stages of Faith.*

24. Fowler's theory is included in a text I use in my teaching at the University of Manitoba: David M. Wulff, *Psychology of Religion: Classic and Contemporary Views* (New York: John Wiley & Sons, 1991), 399–402.

25. James W. Fowler, Antoine Vergote, et al., *Toward Moral and Religious Maturity* (Morristown, NJ: Silver Burdett, 1980); Craig Dykstra and Sharon Parks, eds., *Faith Development and Fowler* (Birmingham, AL: Religious Education Press, 1986); James W. Fowler, Karl Ernst Nipkow, and Friedrich Schweitzer, eds., *Stages of Faith and Religious Development: Implications for Church, Education, and Society* (New York: The Crossroad Publishing Co., 1991); and Jeff Astley and Leslie Francis, eds., *Christian Perspectives on Faith Development: A Reader* (Grand Rapids, MI: William B. Eerdmans Publishing Company, 1992).

26. Among these is a thesis in the Department of Sociology at the University of Manitoba: Dennis Wayne Hiebert, "Schools of Faith: The Effect of Liberal Arts, Professional, and Religious Education on Faith Development" (Ph.D. diss., University of Manitoba, 1992).

27. Much of this information is summarized in James W. Fowler, "Stages of Faith: Reflections on a Decade of Dialogue," *Christian Education Journal* 13, no. 1 (Autumn 1992): 13.

28. James W. Fowler, "Stages of Faith: Reflections on a Decade of Dialogue," *Christian Education Journal* 13, no. 1 (Autumn 1992): 14–15.

29. James W. Fowler, "Keeping Faith With God and Our Children: A Practical Theological Perspective," *Religious Education* 89, no. 4 (Fall, 1994): 543–60.

30. James W. Fowler, "Keeping Faith With God and Our Children: A Practical Theological Perspective," *Religious Education* 89, no. 4 (Fall, 1994): 546–47.

31. Former U. S. President, Jimmy Carter, a man of deep faith (Fowler has suggested that he may be at Stage 6 in his faith development schema), is partial inspiration for Fowler's effort to articulate a practical theological vision. See "Keeping Faith With God and Our Children," 559–60.

Chapter 7

Fowler's Faith Development Theory

> The Lord your God, who goes before you, is the one who will fight
> for you, just as he did for you in Egypt before your very eyes, and in
> the wilderness, where you saw how the Lord your God carried you,
> just as one carries a child, all the way that you traveled until you
> reached this place (Deuteronomy 1:30–31).

Introduction

What is faith? What words or images come to mind? As you begin
to read this chapter exploring James Fowler's model of faith development, pause and take a minute to get in touch with your own understanding of faith.

In the previous chapter, we saw that research into the notion of
faith as a developmental process has been done by James Fowler and
associates — at Harvard University in the seventies and more recently
at the Center for Research in Faith and Moral Development, Emory
University, Atlanta. This chapter will begin with an introduction to
Fowler's understanding of faith and then consider how the faith development dynamic typically operates in people's lives.

Faith is a Human Universal

Faith, as Fowler understands it, is a universal human reality, a feature of the lives of all people: "a *human phenomenon, an apparently generic* consequence of the universal human burden of finding or making meaning" (*Stages* 33). Human beings are "creatures who live by faith. We live by forming and being formed in images and dispositions toward the ultimate conditions of our existence" (*Becoming* 50). Fowler's understanding of faith is almost equivalent to our orientation to life, our meaning-making; in fact he refers to the human person as "the meaning-maker."[1] Our faith answers life's deep philosophical questions: Why does the universe exist? Why do human beings exist? Is there a purpose to life? Why is there suffering? What happens when we die? Why do we have deep heartfelt longings and desires?

Faith, then, having "to do with the making, maintenance, and transformation of human meaning,"[2] is our attempt to hold together a coherent vision of the world. According to Fowler, "we do not live long or well without meaning" (*Becoming* 50).[3]

Faith is a Verb

Faith is also an active, dynamic process, involving not just the mind or heart but the whole person. As such, Fowler speaks of faith as more like a *verb* than a noun: "it is an active mode of being and committing, a way of moving into and giving shape to our experiences of life" (*Stages* 16). Fowler's stage theory, drawing as it does on developmental psychology, centers on the *process* by which we come to hold our beliefs and not on the beliefs as such. His primary usage of the term faith, then, is not focused on the *content* of faith but on the *act* of faith; theistic faith is primarily an act of *trusting* God. Accordingly, because faith development theory is not narrowly focused on beliefs but on believers as actively engaged in forming the content of their faith,[4] people holding different theological positions or with no theology at all may share the same faith stage and, conversely, believers who make the same doctrinal affirmation may be at quite different faith stages.

Before proceeding, it is important to point out that, although Fowler understands faith to be a universal human phenomenon and focuses

on the process of faith growth (as opposed to specific content), he recognizes that "no person can be religious in general" (*Stages* 292)[5] and does not intend to exclude faith being understood theologically and given a substantive content.[6] In a 1991 work, for instance, Fowler writes that faith development theory, far from denigrating religion, provides religion with an empowering role. He concludes his essay with this thought: "it is appropriate to describe this work, in both its status as a general theory, and in its contribution to practical theology, with the . . . language of Johannes Metz: It *is* a theory of our 'becoming subjects before God.'"[7] Accordingly, we can speak of religious faith as concerned with God[8] and Christian faith with God's self-revelation in Jesus Christ. Our focus in this chapter will be a specific application of Fowler's theory to the Christian tradition.

Faith is "Knowing"

Fowler speaks of faith as a special kind of knowing: "Faith . . . is an active mode of knowing, of composing a felt sense or image of the condition of our lives taken as a whole" (*Stages* 25). Later he adds: "Faith is imagination as it composes a felt image of an ultimate environment" (*Stages* 33). Faith knowing, to recall a maxim of St. Anselm of Canterbury (c. 1033/34–1109), is 'faith seeking understanding;' reflection or thinking about our "relationship of trust and loyalty to the God who promises love and life" (*Passages* 46).[9]

Clearly, when Fowler describes faith as a type of *knowing*, he intends a deeper and more encompassing process than the largely cognitive pattern we normally associate with knowing.[10] Like Lonergan, Fowler would agree with Pascal that "the heart has its reasons of which reason knows nothing" (*Pensées* 154).

Faith is Relational

Central to Fowler's faith development theory is the notion that faith is necessarily relational — "there is always *another* in faith. 'I trust *in* and am loyal *to* . . .'" (*Stages* 16). We do not live lives of faith in a vacuum but in interaction with other people as well as to "centers of value," "images of power," and shared "master stories." Faith is interactive and social: "we are fundamentally social creatures" and "the

community of faith, at its best, is an 'ecology of vocations'" (*Becoming* 113 & 126).[11] To have faith is to be related with one's whole being to someone, or something, in a way that one's heart is committed to and one's hope and trust focused on another. For Fowler, this relational quality of faith is *triadic* or *covenantal* in shape, involving self, others, and God[12] (or, for non believers, a transcendent center or centers of meaning and value): "We are not alone. We are created for interdependence and partnership — with each other and with God."[13]

That being fully human is deeply grounded in a relationship to others and a transcendent center of meaning and value is a basic tenet of faith development theory.[14] Fowler uses the following prayer of unknown origin, written on the wall of a Nazi concentration camp, as illustrative of the power of this triadic love relationship with God and neighbor:

> O Lord, when I shall come with glory into your kingdom, do not remember only the men of good will; remember also the men of evil. May they be remembered not only for their acts of cruelty in this camp, the evil they have done to us prisoners, but balance against their cruelty the fruits we have reaped under the stress and in the pain; the comradeship, the courage, the greatness of heart, the humility and patience which have been born in us and become part of our lives, because we have suffered at their hands.
>
> May the memory of us not be a nightmare to them when they stand in judgment. May all that we have suffered be acceptable to you as a ransom for them (*Becoming* 121–22).

Faith is Believing and Trusting

There is a long Christian tradition of distinguishing between two major aspects of faith. In the thirteenth century theology of St. Thomas Aquinas, for example, this distinction was phrased as that between faith as knowledge of revealed truth — 'fides *quae* creditur' (the faith *which* I believe) — and faith as a personal, trusting relationship with God — 'fides *qua* creditur' (the faith *by which* I believe).

Simply put, the distinction is between *believing **in** God* (an activity of the head) and *believing God* (an affective or gut response). A line is drawn, therefore, between the intellectual assent one gives to objective doctrinal propositions about God, Scripture, church, Jesus, for example, and the affective, personal way in which believers encounter and respond to God's mysterious action in their lives. On the one

hand, we encourage one another to 'keep the faith' and Roman Catholics even speak of the church as being the guardian of the 'deposit of faith' (the creeds and dogmas which are objective, flat descriptions of that which is believed). On the other hand, in contrast to this formal, intellectual understanding of faith, we find a parallel tradition in which faith is experienced and understood as a personal response to God's freely given grace, a human response to God's self-revelation, measured in terms of love, trust, reliance, loyalty, and commitment.[15]

Past Catholic and Protestant Emphases

In the writings of Saint Cyril of Jerusalem we already see much of the language of faith that is so familiar to older Roman Catholics:

> Since not everyone has both the education and the leisure required to read and know the Scriptures . . . we sum up the whole doctrine of the faith in a few lines. . . . For the present, just listen and memorize the creed as I recite it, and you will receive in due course the proof from Scripture of each of its propositions. . . . Take heed . . . and hold fast to the teachings which are now delivered to you. . . .
>
> Guard them with care else by chance the enemy may despoil those who have grown remiss, or some heretic may pervert the traditions entrusted to you. Faith is like opening a deposit account at the bank . . . keep this faith which is delivered unto you . . .[16]

Since the Protestant Reformation, *the faith which I believe* has been associated with the Roman Catholic tradition. Catechisms,[17] manuals of doctrine usually in a question and answer format, were the main tool used for the moral and religious instructions of Catholics going back to the *Roman Catechism* of the Council of Trent (1566). This *Roman Catechism* served as the model for the *Catechism of the Third Plenary Council of Baltimore*, (first printed in 1885), commonly called the *Baltimore Catechism*. This formal, rather dry and authoritarian, albeit clear and concise, manual was the chief instrument of catechetics among Roman Catholics in North America until the Second Vatican Council. It set forth basic Catholic beliefs (the faith which we believe) which were memorized and given intellectual assent by generations of students. Such training was considered essential so that Roman Catholics would be able to 'defend the faith' in the face of the many hostile critics assumed to be gathered against the church.[18] I

recall learning the *Baltimore Catechism* definition: "Faith is the virtue by which we firmly believe all the truths God has revealed, on the word of God revealing them, who can neither deceive nor be deceived."[19]

The second dimension of faith, *the faith by which I believe*, came to be identified with Martin Luther and the Protestant reform movement in Christianity. The emphasis here is not on the objective content of faith (creeds, doctrine, catechisms, confessional statements) but on faith understood as an activity of God. In the words of St. Paul, Christian faith is the work of the Holy Spirit: "no one can say 'Jesus is Lord' except by the Holy Spirit" (1Corinthians 12:3). Martin Luther's commentary on the Third Article of the Apostles' Creed is illustrative of this second movement in faith:

> I believe that I cannot by my own understanding or effort believe in Jesus Christ, my Lord, or come to him. But the Holy Spirit has called me through the Gospel, enlightened me with his gifts, and sanctified and kept me in true faith. In the same way he calls, gathers, enlightens, and sanctifies the whole Christian church on earth, and keeps it united with Jesus Christ in the one true faith (*Passages* 11).

Blaise Pascal (1623–1662), French mathematician, physicist, and renegade religious thinker,[20] also supports Luther's understanding of faith. There are only two kinds of reasonable people, he wrote, those who serve God with all their heart because they know God, and those who seek God with all their heart because they don't know God (*Pensées* 160). To Catholic believers of his day who had substituted a safe and coolly rational faith for the original, radical message of Jesus, Pascal proclaimed that religion is ultimately of the heart, not of the mind:

> And that is why those to whom God has given religion by feeling of the heart are very happy and legitimately persuaded. But to those who have it not [in this way] we cannot give it except by reasoning, while waiting for God to give it them by feeling of the heart, without which faith is only human, and useless for salvation.[21]

It should be emphasized, however, that both aspects of faith (*fides quae* and *fides qua*) are integral to the Christian tradition even though, in the past, Roman Catholics tended to stress the *confessional* dimension of faith and the Reform traditions put the emphasis on faith as *trust* and *commitment*.

Synthesis of Faith as Believing and Trusting

A more complete understanding of faith, then, involves an interweaving of these two differing aspects — they cannot really be separated. American philosopher of religion, Paul Tillich, stated the synthesis as follows: "Faith is neither mere *assensus*, nor mere *fiducia*. But in every belief-ful *assensus* there is *fiducia*, and in every belief-ful *fiducia* there is *assensus*."[22]

Aware too of this organic unity of the two aspects of faith, the Second Vatican Council (1962–65), a momentous and profound event in the life of the Roman Catholic Church, sought to reintegrate the intellectual and *cognitive* dimensions of faith; faith as conceptually formulated in belief, doctrine and assent (faith as confession), with the personal[23] and *affective* dimension; faith as existentially realized in trust, fidelity, and love (faith as commitment):

> "The obedience of faith" (Rom. 16:26; cf. Rom. 1:5; 2 Cor. 10:5–6) must be given to God as he reveals himself. By faith man freely commits his entire self to God, making "the full submission of his intellect and will to God who reveals," and willingly assenting to the Revelation given by him. Before this faith can be exercised, man must have the grace of God to move and assist him; he must have the interior helps of the Holy Spirit, who moves the heart and converts it to God, who opens the eyes of the mind and "makes it easy for all to accept and believe the truth."[24]

To draw some conclusions:

a) Religious faith has an *essential* content component of belief, knowledge, and doctrine.

b) It is not that this knowledge, and doctrinal component is not important, it is that it is *not sufficient*! Faith also involves trust, commitment and relationship with God (the most fundamental, prior, sense of faith). Referring to Wilfred Cantwell Smith, Fowler writes: "Faith . . . is the relation of trust in and loyalty to the transcendent about which concepts or propositions — beliefs — are fashioned" (*Stages* 11). Fowler is certainly conscious of the interplay of these two dimensions in faith: "Faith . . . involves rationality and passionality; it involves knowing, valuing and committing" (*Stages* 272).

c) The challenge is for us to effect a synthesis of these two dimensions of faith (form and content) leading to a living out of personal faith in daily life.

Faith is Doing

As is clear in both Macmurray's understanding of what it is to be a person and Lonergan's understanding of the fourth and fifth levels of human consciousness, there is an *actional* element that we must take into account in trying to understand the human faith journey. The performative component of faith, the *deeds* of faith, doing the truth, service to the entire human community, may have been too much neglected in the past but it is integral to a holistic understanding of faith.[25]

We see God as a *doer* in the Exodus event, a foundational experience for the Hebrew people. Yahweh sees the oppression of his chosen people and awakens Moses to his vocation as liberator:

> Then the Lord said, "I have observed the misery of my people who are in Egypt; I have heard their cry on account of their taskmasters. Indeed, I know their sufferings, and I have come down to deliver them from the Egyptians . . . I have also seen how the Egyptians oppress them. So come, I will send you to Pharaoh to bring my people, the Israelites, out of Egypt." (Exodus 3:7–10)

In recent years Liberation Theology has reminded Christians that Jesus is the one, par excellence, who works for radical, liberating change:[26]

> [Jesus] unrolled the scroll and found the place where it was written: "The Spirit of the Lord is upon me, because he has anointed me to bring good news to the poor. He has sent me to proclaim release to the captives and recovery of sight to the blind, to let the oppressed go free, to proclaim the year of the Lord's favor." (Luke 4:18–19)

Recall, too, that in Matthew's gospel Jesus explains that it is not everyone who professes "Lord, Lord" who enters the kingdom of heaven but only the one who *does* the will of God in heaven (Matthew 7:21). And, of course, the classic New Testament statement on this third dimension of faith is found in the letter of James:

> What good is it, my brothers and sisters, if you say you have faith but do not have works? Can faith save you? If a brother or sister is naked and lacks daily food, and one of you says to them, "Go in peace; keep warm and eat your fill," and yet you do not supply their bodily needs, what is the good of that? So faith by itself, if it has no

works, is dead. . . . For just as the body without the spirit is dead, so faith without works is also dead. (James 2:14–17, 26)

An often quoted statement from a 1971 Synod of Roman Catholic Bishops, expresses the same faith/action linkage:

Action for the sake of justice and participation in the transformation of the world fully appear to us to be a constitutive element of the preaching of the Gospel, that is, of the mission of the Church for the redemption of the human race and its liberation from every state of oppression.[27]

Faith, then, is more than intellectual assent to beliefs about God and/or heartfelt trust in God; it is a reorientation of the whole person, of one's thoughts, feelings, and actions in the struggle against all forms of injustice and oppression. The following graphic description promotes this actional component of faith:

Daniel Berrigan, always colorful and always deep, had his own way of putting this. Asked in an interview to pin-point faith's deepest seat, he states something to this effect: Where does your faith reside? Your faith is rarely where your head is at. Or your heart. Your faith is where your ass is at! Where are you sitting? What are you involved in? Are you faithful to anything? That will show, or not show, the quality of your faith.[28]

This actional component of faith, the *deeds* of faith, doing the truth, service, is integral to faith. A faith belief or experience which is not lived, which does not express itself, is not really full faith.

Holistic Faith is Believing, Trusting, and Doing

Before moving on, let me offer three additional way of understanding the dimensions that characterize holistic faith, one from the experience of the primitive church and two drawn from the writings of contemporaries.

There is a Syrian catechetical manual, dating from the end of the first century, known as the *Didache* (teaching)[29] which is an early attempt to formalize *the faith which is believed*. The Greek word *koinonia* (companionship), used to describe the faith fellowship in the Holy Spirit of the earliest Christians, is illustrative of *the faith by*

which they believed. And we have the Greek word *diakonia* (service) to illustrate the third dimension of faith.

Table 7.1

THREE MOVEMENTS IN FAITH		
HEAD	*HEART*	*HANDS*
fides *quae* creditur	fides *qua* creditur	
content	form/process	
believing *in* God	believing God	doing God's will
intellectual	affective	actional
objective	subjective (personal)	
assensus	*fiducia*	
belief	trust/commitment	deeds
didache	*koinonia*	*diakonia*
conviction	trust	commitment
intellectualist	fiducial	performative
professed	celebrated	lived

Richard McBrien's comprehensive exercise of theology in the post-Vatican II context, *Catholicism*, offers this thought about faith:

> Faith can be understood as *conviction*, as *trust*, and as *commitment*. The first is an *intellectualist* approach; the second a *fiducial* approach; the third a *performative* approach. In the classical tradition, Catholics have tended to emphasize the first, Protestants the second; today both increasingly support the third.[30]

In the same vein, the acclaimed religious educator, Thomas Groome, writes about faith as follows:

> Lived Christian faith has at least three essential activities: believing,

trusting and doing. While they can be distinguished for the sake of clarity, they cannot be separated in the life of the Christian community as if any one of them could exist alone or have priority over the others. . . . As a lived reality, the faith life of the community, and to some extent the faith life of every Christian must include all three activities.[31]

To sum up, then, holistic faith is an interconnected reality involving all three aspects we have considered, the three being so entwined that they cannot be separated. Faith has a cognitive dimension (faith as confessional or as *believing* in doctrinal content), an affective and relational dimension (that *trusting* which enables one to believe), as well as an actional dimension (the concrete *living* out of one's belief and trust in relationship with others in one's daily life). Holistic faith is a movement of the head (*professed*), the heart (*celebrated*), and the hands (*lived*).

This leads us into a final way of looking at faith; as evolving or developing. It is here that Fowler makes an important and unique contribution to our understanding of the journey of life.

Faith is Developing

Until not so long ago, conventional wisdom was that human beings went directly from childhood to adulthood. The works of the great sixteenth century Flemish painter, Pieter Bruegel (c. 1525–1569), for instance, clearly show children as tiny adults (Peasant Dance, Peasant Wedding). I recall learning in primary school that just a century ago children worked ten and twelve hour shifts in the coal mines of England under appalling conditions; a shocking idea to me as a boy but in England at the time it was thought very practical to have short children working under the low ceilings of mines. Cruelty would have been forcing tall adults to work in the mines! It was believed that a child of seven or eight could be taught anything that could be taught to an adult. Smaller, simpler words might have to be used but the concept could still be taught; children were, after all, just miniature adults. Human growth and development was broadly understood as just getting bigger and older.

Until quite recently our image of human development was like putting a jigsaw together; a process of fitting together the pieces of life, completing the puzzle as young adults, and living by the pattern

of the completed product for the rest of our days.[32] We more or less held this sort of view until the arrival of the field of developmental psychology in our own century.

Beginning with the cognitive development research of Jean Piaget earlier in this century, and continuing with the work of Lawrence Kohlberg, Erik Erikson, and others, psychology has added substantially to our understanding of the dynamics involved in the ongoing human process of development. According to the developmental view, *all* stages of life hold out the possibility of growth and learning — we are not fully grown-up until we take our last breath. Today, this notion of development across the life span is more or less accepted — we are familiar with adult learning, mid-life crisis,[33] and geriatrics as more than a medical speciality. But, while we accept the notion of development generally, I think it is still unusual to find people who understand their *faith* as *developing*.

Drawing on Erik Erikson's psychosocial theory of development across eight ages in the life cycle, Jean Piaget's cognitive-structural approach to human knowing, Lawrence Kohlberg's theory outlining stages of moral development, Robert Kegan's notion of the "evolving self,"[34] as well as his own study and research, Fowler holds that "faithing" is a dynamic way of perceiving, trusting and valuing that can evolve through seven stages, in concert with other aspects of the whole person, in the maturation process.[35]

Like Piaget and Kohlberg before him, Fowler sees his different faith structures as necessarily sequential, invariant, and hierarchical, each stage building upon and incorporating into its more complex pattern the operations of previous stages:[36]

> We are part of a small but growing field of structural-developmental research and theory building. Jean Piaget is considered the founder of this field. . . . The colleague who has influenced me most is Lawrence Kohlberg . . . but I have also been deeply influenced by Erik Erikson, and through him by the tradition of psychoanalytic ego psychology.[37]

Note, however, that unlike the developmental "myths of becoming" of Piaget and Erikson, movement from one faith stage to another is not automatic or inevitable and not directly age related (*Stages* 50). While biological maturation, chronological and mental age and psychological development are all *necessary* factors in determining a person's readiness[38] to make a faith stage transition, for Fowler they are not

sufficient. Movement from one stage to another is not automatic but only occurs when challenges, new information, and crises shake the stability of a given stage and expose its inadequacy. Transition, Fowler points out, is a time when "everything nailed down is coming loose" (*Becoming* 58).[39] The faith development dynamic is both "evolutionary" and "revolutionary" (*Stages* 34).

Consequently, transitions from one stage of faith to another "are often protracted, painful, dislocating and/or abortive" (*Stages* 274). We must let go of old ways of making meaning before we can build a new way of faith knowing; the new rising, as it were, like the mythical phoenix from its own ashes.[40] Because of the distress involved, we often resist the developmental path of faith growth, choosing to hold onto limited ways of faith knowing so as not to "lose" our faith.

A few verses from "Awoken," a poem by Ruth McLean, convey something of the flavor of what is involved in faith stage transition:

> . . . the firm beliefs and solid suppositions
>   that ordered my daily decisions . . .
> had evaporated before my eyes . . .
>
> . . . the props i used
>   to keep me strong
>   now seemed obsolete
> and strangely out of synchronization.
>
> . . . caught and helpless,
>   uprooted and airborne,
>   i existed . . .
>   dangling in space
>   between the old
>   and the new . . .
>
> one eye was fixed with longing to the past,
>   the other,
>   with an urgent expectancy,
>   to what might lie ahead . . .
>
> one hand was clutching
>   at what had been so easy and certain,
>   the other

Guides for the Journey

Table 7.2

Era and Ages	PIAGET Cognitive Development	ERIKSON Psycho-Social Stages	KOHLBERG Moral Development	FOWLER Faith Development
Infancy (0–1½)	Sensorimotor	Trust v. Mistrust		Primal
Early Childhood (2–6)	Preoperational	Autonomy v. Shame & Doubt Initiative v. Guilt	Pre-conventional *reward/punish*	Intuitive-Projective
Childhood (7–12)	Concrete Operational	Industry v. Inferiority		Mythic-Literal
Adolescence (13–21)	Formal Operational	Identity v. Role Confusion	*reciprocal relativity* Conventional *approval disapproval*	Synthetic-Conventional *ideology borrowed & supported by external authority*
Young Adulthood (21–35)		Intimacy v. Isolation	*law & order* Post-Conventional *social contract*	Individuative-Reflective *construct own rationalized worldview*
Adulthood (35–60)	Post-formal Operational	Generativity v. Stagnation	*golden rule*	Conjunctive *validity of other systems; paradoxical*
Maturity (60+)		Integrity v. Despair		Universalizing *often prophetic*

grasped at what might fill
the freshly-opened void. . . .[41]

Perhaps you are asking, 'Why bother with the process if it is so painful?' It is because, although the ending of an old way of faith knowing is painful, the possibility of a new, more satisfactory way of living one's faith lies ahead.[42]

Cautions

Before outlining the styles of faith Fowler has discovered, five cautions are in order:[43]

(1) Fowler presents his theory quite tentatively and not as carved in stone or as Gospel! Just as Lonergan speaks of his cognitional structure as not open to revision, Fowler would argue for the normativity of the broad pattern of his faith development schema without claiming infallibility for the specifics.

(2) It is important to keep in mind that Fowler's research is looking at faith from *our* side of the I and Other relationship:

> Faith development theory, focusing resolutely on the human side of the faith relationship, comes up against the fact that the transcendent other with whom we have to do in faith is not confined by the models we build or to the patterns we discern (*Stages* 302).

(3) The movement through the stages is *not* like climbing steps or a ladder. Fowler is much more attracted by Daniel Levinson's metaphor of journeying through "seasons" (*Becoming* 30–33). In fact Fowler diagrams his stages of faith as a "rising spiral movement" where "each successive spiral stage [is] linked to and adding to the previous ones." There is "a movement outward toward individuation, culminating in Stage 4" and then the movement "doubles back, in Stages 5 and 6, toward the participation and oneness of earlier stages" (*Stages* 274).[44] The stages in the process Fowler describes are interwoven like an intricate tapestry and what he offers us are seven windows that look in on particular junctures of the faith journey, that freeze the human person, as it were, in moments of a typical developmental pattern. Accordingly, "Fowler's stage descriptions should not be taken for portrait photographs of a 'still life' but rather as impressionistic paintings of a subject in motion."[45] And the transitions

between stages are at least as important as the equilibrated stages. In the descriptions that follow, keep in mind too that the movement through Fowler's stages is not as mechanical as my presentation which will deliberately exaggerate the distance and differences between the stages for the purpose of explanation.

Table 7.3

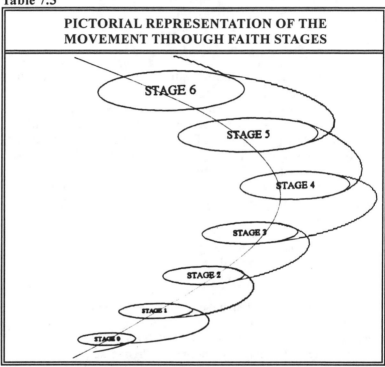

PICTORIAL REPRESENTATION OF THE
MOVEMENT THROUGH FAITH STAGES

STAGE 6

STAGE 5

STAGE 4

STAGE 3

STAGE 2

STAGE 1

STAGE 0

(4) In harmony with other developmental stage theories, higher faith stages can be considered "better" in the sense that they offer more encompassing and complex, more differentiated, more "adequate," forms of being in faith. Growth in faith cannot add years to one's life but can add life to one's years! It is important to point out however that the higher stages are *not* better in the sense that people living out of higher faith stages are more loving or more open to the "mysterious and unpredictable vector of [God's] extraordinary grace" than those living out of the lower stages (*Stages* 303). To love and self-transcend are *not* characteristics of the faith development process

but characteristics of human authenticity, possible at any faith stage: "Each stage has the potential for wholeness, grace and integrity and for strengths sufficient for either life's blows or blessings" (*Stages* 274). Theologian Karl Rahner sheds further light on this key point. On the distinction between "steps in the development of the spiritual life" and "grades of perfection," Rahner writes:

> The stages of the spiritual life make sense (and the sense they are actually intended to make) only if it is presupposed that these steps in the development of the spiritual life are actually separate *from one another*, really follow *one after the other*, and that *those* phases which in this theory come *before* another, can also not be skipped over in practice . . . similarly to the way in which the steps of the biological development of a living being follow one another in proper sequence, each clearly having its proper place in the total curve of life, and each later stage essentially presupposing the previous one. The phases of the spiritual life and the grades of perfection of the classes of moral acts are not the same. . . . For it is impossible to see, either in theory or practice, why precisely the higher kind of acts should not be possible on the lower step of the spiritual life . . . [46]

(5) As I write about faith development theory, I tend to refer to Stage 3 *people* or Stage 4 *people*. This is really a shorthand way of saying that the responses in a given Faith Interview (Fowler's way of collecting data)[47] exhibit patterns of thinking, relating, acting, and believing, which can on average be understood to reflect the attributes of a particular stage construct.

Stage 0: Primal Faith

Fowler refers to the faith of the new-born as Stage 0 (not really a stage as such), Primal faith. Primal faith, he suggests, "arises in the roots of confidence that find soil in the ecology of relations, care, and shared meanings that welcome a child and offset our profound primal vulnerability" (*Becoming* 53).

A recent viewing of the birth scene (loving mother and father and caring doctor) in the film *My Life*[48] impressed upon me Fowler's description of this pre-natal and infancy faith stage: "We are bruised and squeezed into life; we gasp our way into community" (*Becoming* 52). Early conscious contact by infants with the world out-there-now

is characterized by seeing, hearing, smelling, tasting, and touching things which are immediately present. In Lonergan's terminology the infant lives in a "world of immediate experience" (*Collection* 233).[49]

From this trusting family environment the infant forms a sense of self (strongly affected by its parent's sense of self and life) and the elements from which initial images of God are constructed.

Stage 1: Intuitive-Projective Faith

The transition to Intuitive-Projective faith takes place with the emergence of language and inquiry. A whole new world opens up, one where words have a meaning. The infant's world of immediacy gives way to a world "mediated by meaning" (*Collection* 233). A few minutes in the presence of a five year old child's endless questions brings us up against their exuberant imagination and awakening spirit of wonder. It is this questioning which propels children from the world of immediacy into a world of common meaning.

The most dramatic example I can think of to illustrate this transition is from the life of blind and deaf Helen Keller (1880–1968). During a pivotal incident in her life (at age seven in Tuscumbia, Alabama), she comes to know that Anna Sullivan's touches on her hand (the Manual Alphabet) conveyed the name of the water in which it is immersed. With great rapidity Helen learns the names for things around here (as well as learning that Anna is a teacher!); her introduction to a remarkable career as an author and lecturer in a world mediated by meaning.

Pre-school children at this Intuitive-Projective stage of faith development see God as similar to those with authority in their lives. Their thinking about God, in fact, is largely affected by their relationship to their parents — the biggest most powerful people they know in the world. When taken to church they often point to the clergyperson as God. Their image of Satan (tied in with monsters, ghosts, and scary fairy tales), as one from whom we need to be protected, is also formed during this stage.

Strongly influenced by the stories and images of faith provided by family, children at this stage use their fertile imagination, and sense of fantasy and magic, to construct deep, more or less permanent, faith images and stories. Because we do not leave faith stages behind, these faith images of childhood surface throughout life, especially during

times of crisis. There are periods in adulthood when a sense of our own smallness, vulnerability, and powerlessness cause us to turn anew to our childhood image of God's consoling and protective power:

> At such times what we need is a God who is *Abba*, meaning father, a God who is able to be and do what only *Abba* can do. To such a God we can respond not only with trust but also with love and obedience, willing to follow wherever he may lead, no matter how filled with shadows and terrors that way may be (*Passages* 52).

Stage 2: Mythic-Literal

At the Mythic-Literal faith stage, children are far clearer and more logical about their faith experience. They can now distinguish between fantasy and reality, wondering if Santa Claus is "real" and knowing that a clergyperson is not God but God's representative.

Children exhibiting Stage 2 faith are beginning to develop a sense of place, a sense of belonging to a particular family grouping, a neighborhood, a school community, a religious denomination. And they want to know the stories associated with these people, places, and associations. Because they are now able to take the perspective of another person, children can repeat their favorite stories (Stage 1 children may have stories told to them repeatedly but are still unable to retell them).

Stage 2 youngsters have constructed a dependable universe in which God always rewards the good and punishes the bad. Simple stories about good and evil hold a great attraction for children at this stage. I can't help but recall my carefree, childhood Saturday afternoons (in the Regent theater on Main Street in Saint John) cheering on Roy Rogers and The Lone Ranger. In the end, the bad guy always got the punishment he deserved at the hands of the good guy in the white hat. The experience was so satisfying, so right! When I first saw *Star Wars*,[50] I recall the children in the audience cheering for the same reasons that I did as a boy! A parent, teacher or church minister will have great success introducing children to similarly themed bible stories, such as Moses and the Ten Commandments.

The concept of fairness looms large in a person's way of faith knowing at this faith stage: fairness understood, not in any abstract way, but concretely as a way of knowing what to expect from others and as a way of bringing order into one's world. There are times when

those around us are not fair and when we ourselves are not being fair but God is seen as always fair. From this it should be obvious why a bible story like the Parable of the Laborers in the Vineyard (Matthew 20:1–16), who all received the same pay even though some worked all day and others only one hour, doesn't meet with much comprehension from Stage 2 people: 'the story is so unfair.'

The absence of 'fairness' in the Vineyard parable helps us to see how some children, coming to a realization that life is not always black and white, can exhibit what Fowler refers to as "11-year-old atheism."[51] Adults who remain fixated at the Mythic-Literal faith stance can develop an exaggerated, unhealthy sense of law and sin. On the one hand they can live in fear of God's judgment condemning them to Hell for one tiny mistake, one weak moment and conversely develop an unhealthy self-righteousness — 'Thank you God that I am not a sinner like the rest of people: I don't smoke or drink, I tithe, I am at church every Sunday morning, I'm saved!'

Stage 3: Synthetic-Conventional

As one reaches adolescence, the ability to think abstractly and reflectively provides a new awareness of oneself in relation to others. A sense of past, present, and future, both as regards the world and people 'out there' and one's own inner self, is also present and one is able to articulate these distinctions.

At Stage 3, I am no longer completely egocentric, no longer living out of a framework where I just want what is good for me, but now I am in touch with other people and their needs, expectations and demands. I have developed the ability to see myself as others see me — a transforming event in interpersonal relations (mutual perspective-taking). I struggle to integrate conflicting self-images into a coherent identity and I seek out a package of beliefs and values to support that identity and connect me emotionally with others.

Stage 3 faith is often characterized as the *conformist* stage because this faith stance is deeply influenced by significant others (individuals and groups) and tends to conform to their expectations and judgments. Fowler has labeled Stage 3, Synthetic-Conventional. Faith development research shows that many adults remain in Stage 3 throughout their lifetime.

Characteristically, at Stage 3, my worldview or meaning-system,

my faith, comes from certain trusted others. That authority in my life might be parents, teachers, religious figures, the magisterium of the church, peer group, gang leader, television advertising, or cult guru. It might even be a sacred text like the Bible or Koran. Basic to faith at Stage 3 is the notion that I choose someone or something as my authority, and give that authority unquestioned, uncritical, adherence.[52] In a very real sense, my faith is *second hand.*

We can say, too, that at Stage 3 my identity comes from my relationships: "There is not as yet a self that *has* roles and relations without being fully identical with or fully expressed by them. The self, rather, is a function of its significant social ties" (*Pastoral* 66).[53] At Stage 3, I *am* the Smith boy, I *am* Bill's wife, I *am* the vice president of IBM, I *am* Dr. Jones, I *am* a good Episcopalian. The policeman Javert in the musical, *Les Miserables,* sings "I am the law and the law is not mocked."[54] At Stage 3, I *am* these roles; at Stage 4, I *have* these roles. At this stage of faith development, Fowler says, I am "*embedded* in the interpersonal." To illustrate this quality of embeddedness in faith and lack of critical faculties, Fowler likes to quote a remark of the Spanish-American philosopher George Santayana: "we don't know who first discovered water but we can be sure it wasn't the fish."

In the cohesive society (blending of the secular and religious) of my youth in Eastern Canada, the priests, my teachers, my parents, the druggist, the barber and the family who owned the candy store on the corner all shared the same basic faith consensus. Even my peers all knew the same faith content. A network of significant others (parents, family, neighbors, peers) supported the faith consensus and helped to bolster me/us in Stage 3 faith.[55]

As I reflect on my own Catholic upbringing in light of faith development theory, I think it is fair to say that in the decades before the reforms of the Second Vatican Council the Roman Catholic church reinforced Stage 3 thinking and behavior in its members. The following description of Holy Mother Church is a classic Stage 3 image:

> "Mother Church" . . . is, in many ways, an admirable and dedicated person, deeply concerned about her children, endlessly and tirelessly careful for every detail of their welfare. Her long experience has taught her to understand her family very well. She knows their capabilities and she knows their weakness even better. . . . there are no lengths to which she will not go to help those who turn to her in their need. She is also well able to educate her family. She has a

huge fund of stories, maxims and advice, all of them time-tested, and usually interesting as well. She is very talented, skilled in creating a beautiful home for her children; she can show them how to enrich their lives with the glory of music and art. And there is no doubt that she loves God, and wishes to guide her children according to his will.

On the other hand, she is extremely inclined to feel that her will and God's are identical. In her eyes there can be no better, no other, way than hers. . . . She knows her children's limitations so well that she will not allow them to outgrow them. . . . she uses her authority "for their own good" but if it seems to be questioned she is ruthless in suppressing revolt. She is hugely self-satisfied, and her judgment, while experienced, is often insensitive and therefore cruel. She is suspicious of eccentricity and new ideas, since her own are so clearly effective, and non-conformists get a rough time . . .[56]

Today adolescents and adults at Stage 3, even within the religious sphere, find themselves surrounded by people whose expectations and judgments are often very different, making them restless with their Synthetic-Conventional faith orientation. The result is that as they grow they can withdraw into a rigid Stage 3 (fundamentalism) or succumb to the attraction of relativism, one possible interpretation of Stage 4 faith.

Research has shown that if people stay at Fowler's Stage 3 too long, then a move to Stage 4 is not a normal evolutionary process but a real disruption. Joan Chittister, the well known Benedictine prioress and feminist theologian, spoke of how she moved into the Stage 3-Stage 4 transition slowly and painfully:

> What was it like when the Order went through renewal? That's easy; it was a walk through the outskirts of hell. Absolutely everything that you had ever been taught, everything you ever saw, everything you ever believed, was now up for grabs. . . . The entire symbol system had gone . . . so seduced had we been by the symbols that we couldn't imagine that you could have the faith without them.[57]

It is important to point out here that Stage 3 faith has substantial strengths. Potentially, Stage 3 faith can provide a stable and well-organized meaning system within which one can find equilibrium and live a productive faith life. Clarity of teaching and solid well-defined structures are hallmarks of Stage 3 faith. "Tradition," the opening song in *Fiddler on the Roof*,[58] superbly conveys this stable sense of Stage 3 faith.[59] Among us there are Stage 3 voices expressing concern

about the loss of tradition, mystery, and meaning in today's secular and religious culture. These voices need to be heard.

As you might expect, this strong need to obey the letter of the law and/or please significant others can at times place one under what has been called the "tyranny of the *they*."[60] The "Brodie girls" in the film *The Prime of Miss Jean Brodie,* whom she considers the "creme de la creme," are in fact so under her dangerous control that one girl dies senselessly as a result of following Miss Brodie's lead. An example from history of a person rejecting the tyranny of misguided Stage 3 faith is (Saint) Thomas More, executed for high treason on June 6, 1535 because he refused to go against his (Stage 4) conscience and take the required oath about Henry VIII's divorce.

Living out of Stage 3 faith, adult Catholics go to Mass because the third commandment tells them to keep holy the Sabbath day and there is a precept of the church requiring that they "attend Mass on Sundays and holy days of obligation." In the case of youth it is more common to obey some authority figure who tells them they are going to church! I am sure many readers have heard the Stage 3 parental rejoinder, 'As long as you are living in our house you will go to church on Sunday!' And your reaction may have been like one of my student's who said 'they made me *go* but they couldn't make me *pray*!'

The Synthetic Conventional stage of faith, then, exhibits right and wrong as a matter of the expectations of the others, most sophisticatedly in terms of an *uncritical* regard for law and order.[61] In the 1961 film, *Judgment at Nuremberg*,[62] one of the German judge defendants offered the following Stage 3 faith statement in defense of his actions during the Third Reich:

> I have served my country throughout my life and in whatever position I was assigned to; in faithfulness, with a pure heart and without malice. I followed the concept that I believed to be the highest in my profession; the concept that says to sacrifice one's own sense of justice to the authoritative legal order; to ask only what the law is and not to ask whether or not it is also justice. As a judge I could do no other. I believe your honors will find me, and millions of Germans like me who believed they were doing their duty to their country, to be not guilty.[63]

There is a significant limitation to Stage 3 faith. It is that my regard for the authority figure(s) and law is *un*examined, *un*critical. I may have no problem articulating *what* I believe (remember the

Baltimore Catechism) but I have great difficulty offering anything beyond 'because that is what the book says' or "its what my guru teaches' as an answer to *why* I believe what I believe. I can be quite eloquent in expressing what I believe, feel very strongly about those beliefs but still be unable to think *critically* about them. Stage 3 faith remains unexamined.

Reliance on external authority ('the Bible says' or 'my youth pastor says') is needed for the formation and maintenance of my faith. Let me tell you two brief stories to illustrate the point.

As a university professor, I try to give adult answers to my students at this stage, and though they often don't really understand my explanation, I often hear from them a 'thank you Sir/Father;' a puzzling response until I realized that they are not saying thank you for explaining things but thank you (an authority figure) for reassuring me: 'If you're not worried, then I'm not worried.'

A few years ago, I was a resource person at a workshop for advanced spiritual directors at Loyola House, Guelph. During a coffee break one of the participants, a Roman Catholic nun, told me that when she was a novice in her religious order she worked at cleaning a retreat house. After a few months at the task she came to realize that there were better ways to organize the work. Attempting to outline her thinking to her superior, she was stopped short with the rejoinder, "Now, sister, *we* don't think. We leave that to Mother General and her Council."[64]

It is important to remind people at Stage 3, especially if you have hope of sponsoring them towards Stage 4, that something is not wrong because God has given us a commandment against it but because it is inherently wrong God forbids it. The realization of the seemingly subtle difference in this expression is an important step towards appreciating the *intrinsic* moralism which characterizes Stage 4 faith. Enough said about Stage 3 for the moment!

Stage 4: Individuative-Reflective

The question as to whether or not I have an identity apart from the authority I respect or the roles I play initiates the movement towards Stage 4 which Fowler calls Individuative-Reflective faith.

The movement from Stage 3 to Stage 4 is a movement from conformity to individuality, a movement from unexamined faith to critical

faith, a movement from being who others want me to be to being who I really am (*Passages* 58).[65] It is an awareness that I and others like me are part of a larger social system, heretofore beyond my horizon. It is an awareness that I must ultimately assume responsibility for making choices of ideology and lifestyle.

It is only in the late teens or early adulthood that I am ready to make the identity I have been given by my socio-cultural milieu my own or ready to begin the process of becoming a new person, i.e., developing a new identity for which I can assume responsibility. I reach a point where I need to know not only what the authority figure or the law says, but the law or authority must correspond to my own experience and be assimilated in a personal way or, alternatively, I need to 'do my own thing.' I need to know who I am for myself, I can't live out of second-hand faith.[66]

In my experience as a professor on a large secular university campus, the move from the shelter of home to the openness of university is often accompanied by a readiness on the part of students to move from Stage 3 to Stage 4 faith.[67] Two brief stories make the point.

A young woman who had come to the noon Mass one day told me that it had not been convenient to get to church on the weekend and so she had decided to attend a weekday Mass. She also said that her mother, clearly Stage 3, told her not to bother because "it won't count" — it's *Sunday* Mass or nothing!

I recall, too, speaking with a student who had appeared at the Sunday Mass on campus for the first time. He told me that although his home in the city was quite near the parish church, he had decided not to go to Mass with his family any more because he was tired of being referred to as so and so's son. He said that he was a person in his own right who was going to Mass as himself, by himself, and for himself and not just because his family insisted upon it. At Stage 4 I go to Mass because *I choose* to go.

On just this point about the qualitative difference between faith Stages 3 and 4, Viktor Frankl's remarks about religion, in *The Unconscious God*, are instructive:

> Being human is not being driven but "deciding what one is going to be."
>
> . . . Authentic existence is present where a self is deciding for himself, but not where an id is driving him (26–27).

> Genuine religiousness has not the character of driven-ness [Stage 3]
> but rather that of deciding-ness [Stage 4]. Indeed, religiousness
> stands with its deciding-ness — and falls with its driven-ness (64–65)
> Religion is genuine only where it is existential, where man is not
> somehow driven to it, but commits himself to it by freely choosing to
> be religious (72).

> Unlike an animal, man is no longer told by drives and instincts what
> he must do. And in contrast to man in former times, he is no longer
> told by traditions and values what he should do. Now, knowing
> neither what he must do nor what he should do, he sometimes does
> not even know what he basically wishes to do. Instead, he wishes to
> do what other people do — which is conformism — or he does what
> other people wish him to do — which is totalitarianism (91).[68]

A *critical* attitude toward authority, toward law, emerges as one
moves into Stage 4. The term "critical," as Fowler uses it in describing Individuative-Reflective faith, does not necessarily mean negative
and harsh judgment but an attitude characterized by careful and exact
evaluation. It is as if Santayana's fish develops the ability to jump out
of the water and look back at the tank in which it had just been
swimming around. An example may help to illustrate what is meant.
I am a fan of the Toronto Blue Jays baseball team and as a Jay's fan I
am *not* careful and exact in my evaluation of their performance. I
readily make excuses for their losses and exaggerate the significance
of their wins. My attitude towards them is *uncritical*! But, I do have
friends who are more balanced, more careful and realistic, more *critical*, in their evaluation of the team.
    Note that the development of this critical faculty does not *neces-
sarily* mean throwing out authority or stability or law or loyalty to
institutions. What it does involve, however, is a growing awareness
that nothing — no person, no book, no authority — can lift from my
own adult shoulders the ultimate responsibility for what I say and do.
I must decide for myself who I am, what I believe, and what I am
going to do.[69] The following exchange between Jesus and his apostles
is an example of the movement from a Stage 3 to a Stage 4 question:

> [Jesus asked] "Who do people say that I am?" And they answered
> him, "John the Baptist; and others, Elijah; and still others, one of the
> prophets." He asked them, "But who do you say that I am?" Peter
> answered him, "You are the Messiah" (Mark 8: 27–29).

Stage 4, therefore, is characterized by *autonomous* faith; i.e., self-directed or *first hand* faith:

> There is a movement from conformity to individuality, from strongly felt but unexamined trust and loyalty to objective reflection on different points of view, from being what others want them to be to being the person they are and can become. This is the shift from Stage 3 to Stage 4 (*Passages* 58).

Further, Stage 4 faith, to borrow Gordon Allport's distinction, is "intrinsic" as opposed to "extrinsic."[70] A doctoral dissertation applying Allport's categories of religious motivation to faith development found that "at Stage 4 and beyond, the incidence of extrinsic motivation . . . virtually disappears."[71]

It is important to point out that in growth from Stage 3 to Stage 4, the *content* of my faith does not necessarily change. My beliefs can remain the same but the reasons I give for holding those beliefs will have changed significantly. Second hand Stage 3 faith gives way to a faith that is becoming my own. This individual responsibility or ownership so characteristic of Stage 4 faith is in sharp contrast to the conformity required of Stage 3 faith.[72] When someone begins to say things following the pattern 'I know that they say . . . but I think . . .' it is likely that such a person is in transition[73] to Stage 4 faith. Another story may help to throw light on the Stage 4 viewpoint on faith.

A few summers ago I had occasion to speak about faith development to a group of young adult counselors at an Anglican church camp. At the end of the day, one young man came up and told me that he appreciated hearing about the difference between the stages and saw himself at Stage 5. He said he was not under the tyranny of any *they* (neither of the church or peer group variety) and he certainly didn't just believe the things he found to his liking (his understanding of the meaning of Stage 4). He said he believed the things that "made sense" to him and went on to illustrate with reference to church doctrine which he accepted and teachings which he didn't think made sense and so were rejected (still Fowler's Stage 4!).

There are limitations however to the Stage 4 faith stance, one being that it is often as much a reaction against Stage 3 as it is a movement towards a new meaning system. Accordingly, a person is likely to see things in terms of polarities — external authority v. personal freedom, church v. conscience, law v. love. Stage 4 people often look down on Stage 3 people (and vice versa) and tension often characterizes these

relationships as well as relationships with the wide range of people at Stage 4.

A second limitation of Stage 4 faith is its tendency towards a heroic individualism, the critique of which is a central theme in the work of the thinkers we are considering in this book. If "Tradition," from *Fiddler on the Roof,* captures something of Stage 3, then, Frank Sinatra's song "My Way" is an appropriate theme for Stage 4. Behind "My Way" is "the individualistic assumption that we are or can be *self-grounded persons*," which Fowler calls "our most serious modern heresy" (*Becoming* 101).[74]

> This assumption means believing that we have within us — and are totally responsible for generating from within us — all the resources out of which to create a fulfilled and self-actualized life (*Becoming* 101–02).

I have heard James Fowler say that the nicest thing that can happen to a person at Stage 4 is that they move on to Stage 5 and his research clearly shows that Stage 4 rational autonomy[75] is not the final goal of faith development but just a rest stop on a longer journey to a paradoxical integration of the best elements of Stages 3 and 4. The following metaphor vividly captures the limitations of both Stage 4 and Stage 3 faith respectively and the consequent need for Stage 5, *conjunctive* faith: "A window stuck open is as useless as a window stuck shut. In either case, you've lost the use of the window."[76]

The move towards Stage 5 faith is stimulated by a restlessness and uncomfortableness with the tough individuality and apparent clarity and coherence of Stage 4 faith ('I know *they* say . . . but *I* think . . .'), coupled with a re-examination of and pull towards the sense of belonging and loyal participation in something bigger than myself characteristic of Stage 3 faith. Fowler see Stage 5 faith as moving beyond the liberal, individualistic assumption underlying the Stage 4 stance to the paradoxical view that "we are called to personhood in relationships:"

> There is no personal fulfillment that is not part of a communal fulfillment. We find ourselves by giving ourselves. We become larger persons by devoting ourselves to the pursuit of a common good. From the standpoint of vocation, fulfillment, self-actualization, and excellence of being are by-products of covenant faithfulness and action in the service of God and the neighbor (*Becoming* 102).

As we saw earlier, one image that Fowler uses to conceptualize the sequence of faith stages is a rising spiral; "each successive spiral stage linked to and adding to the previous ones" (*Stages* 274). At Stage 5, to capture the re-examination of "the participation and oneness of earlier stages," the spiral "doubles back" (*Stages* 274). It is in the tension of this felt need (having achieved an awareness of the limitations of the individuation so characteristic of Stage 4) to double back and recapture something of collective dimension of Stage 3 faith, that the dynamic balance of Stage 5 faith originates.

Stage 5: Conjunctive Faith

Fowler calls Stage 5, Conjunctive Faith.[77] Paradox and the tension of polar opposites, are at the heart of Stage 5 faith.

In *A Guide for the Perplexed*,[78] E. F. Schumacher sought to "look at the world and try and see it whole" (15). His efforts to deal with pairs of opposites (for example, tradition and innovation, stability and change, justice and mercy, freedom and order) reflect, in my view, an awareness of what Fowler means by Stage 5 faith:

> A pair of opposites — like freedom [Stage 4] and order [Stage 3] — are opposites at the level of ordinary life, but they cease to be opposites at the higher level [Stage 5], the really *human* level, where self-awareness plays its proper role. It is then that such higher forces as love and compassion, understanding and empathy, become available . . . as a regular and reliable resource. Opposites cease to be opposites; they lie down together peacefully like the lion and the lamb . . . (146)

To take an example from religion, many people see the contradiction between their commitment to a religious tradition that has been handed down through the centuries (Stage 3) and openness to the experience of others who are not part of that tradition (Stage 4) as too great to be bridged (Stage 5). Some resolve the tension by keeping the world at a distance and living in safe situations (the Catholic church before Vatican II encouraged this Stage 3 form of Catholicism), others by abandoning the "illusion" (Sigmund Freud) of religion and God and choosing to live in the real (i.e., secular, scientific) Stage 4 world. But Stage 5 is a third, more encompassing, alternative. In the words of Parker Palmer:

> There is a third way to respond. A way beyond choosing either this
> pole or that. Let us call it "living the contradictions." Here we refuse
> to flee from tension but allow that tension to occupy the center of our
> lives. And why would anyone walk this difficult path? Because by
> doing so we may receive one of the great gifts of the spiritual life —
> *the transformation of contradiction into paradox.* The poles of
> either/or, the choices we thought we had to make, may become signs
> of a larger truth than we had ever dreamed. And in that truth, our
> lives may become larger than we had ever imagined possible! (*Prom-
> ise* 19).[79]

A contradiction is a statement containing components logically at
variance with one another, whereas a paradox is a statement which
seems self-contradictory but on investigation may prove to be essentially true. The character of paradox then is that both poles (Stages 3
and 4 in faith development theory) are true. When either extreme is
taken alone, the reality of what it is to be a full adult human being is
distorted. Only when the poles are held in creative tension with each
other is the fullness of humanity adequately expressed. In the words
of the psalmist, we are made "a little lower than God" and "crowned
. . . with glory and honor" (Psalm 8:5) but we are also "like the animals that perish" (Psalm 49:12) In Isaiah we hear God say: "I form
light and create darkness, I make weal and create woe" (Isaiah 45:7).
Jesus said "Those who find their life will lose it, and those who lose
their life for my sake will find it." (Matthew 10:39)

At faith Stages 3 or 4, people discussing a controversial point in
religion are likely to end up in an argument, each one convinced that
his or her viewpoint is the only correct one. At Stage 3 their conflicting views as to the truth (with a capital 'T') can be thought of (from
the Stage 5 faith stance) as fundamentalist and sectarian. The liberalism and relativism which can characterize Stage 4 faith (there is no
such thing as truth with a capital 'T') would produce at best an answer
like 'You hold on to what you think is true and I'll hold on to what I
think is true and we'll still be friends.' Two Stage 5 people in the
same discussion are able to *dialogue*; there is real interchange, real
listening, even openness to change of heart; certainly an expectation
of learning something new from the exchange.[80] A person must have
great confidence in his or her faith stance in order to freely and openly
engage in such dialogue.

> One of the purposes of our thinking is to provide us with a map
> — call it an image or a picture — of what we experience. So it is also

in our faith-thinking. . . .

Stage 5 persons discover that their maps are not only incomplete and limited in capturing the depth and beauty of the landscape, but they also sense that something in addition to maps is needed to put one in touch with the fullness of what has been revealed. . . .
Imagine an encounter between two Stage 5 persons who have mapped the territory of faith experiences. As distinguished from a person at Stage 4, they will be ready to compare their maps without prejudgments, will make corrections where these seem warranted, and may even withhold final judgment where there seems to be irreconcilable differences between the maps (*Passages* 60–61).

As you might expect, Stage 5 faith is characterized by an openness to genuine dialogue with communities and traditions quite different from our own:

Truth is more multiform and complex than most of the clear, either-or categories of the Individuative stage can properly grasp. In its richness, ambiguity, and multidimensionality, truth must be approached from at least two or more angles of vision simultaneously (*Becoming* 65).

Fowler goes on to say that what he means by conjunctive faith is analogous to the discovery in physics of the necessity for two different and unreconcilable models (packets of energy and wave theory) to adequately explain the behavior of light. Related to this, Abraham Maslow comments: "Isolating two interrelated parts of a whole from each other, parts that need each other, parts that are truly 'parts' and not wholes, distorts them both, sickens and contaminates them".[81]

To live Stage 5 faith, then, means that we hold onto the gains of independence, autonomy, and personal responsibility made at Stage 4 but take a fresh look at Stage 3 — at the stability, at the loyalty, at the respect for law and authority, and ask whether it has to be either/or — can't it be both/and? We now try to live in the creative tension between those polarities, i.e., with paradox.[82] Fowler doesn't think we reach Stage 5 until at least age thirty.[83]

Three concrete examples of the Stage 5 faith phenomenon may help to clarify the way in which it is an advance over faith Stages 3 and 4.

My first example is taken from Paul's letter to the Galatians in the Christian scriptures. The following passage conveys something of the shift from the Stage 3 authoritarian faith stance to the inclusive and

paradoxical faith of Stage 5:

> Now before faith came, we were imprisoned and guarded under the law until faith would be revealed. Therefore the law was our disciplinarian until Christ came, so that we might be justified by faith. But now that faith has come, we are no longer subject to a disciplinarian, for in Christ Jesus you are all children of God through faith. As many of you as were baptised into Christ have clothed yourselves with Christ. There is no longer slave or free, there is no longer male and female; for all of you are one in Christ Jesus. And if you belong to Christ then you are Abraham's offspring, heirs according to the promise (Galatians 3:23–29).

A second example of the movement from Stage 3 to Stage 5 faith is found in Ari Goldman's *The Search for God at Harvard*.[84] A religion writer with *The New York Times*, Goldman spent a year at Harvard Divinity School studying comparative religions. Raised "in a warm cocoon of Orthodox [Jewish] observance" (6), Goldman feared "the threat of the pagan and Christian worlds" (4) and imagined that his tenure at Harvard might lead to religious conversion or even abandonment of religion. He did not convert; in fact his Orthodox Jewish identity was strenghtened. What he experienced in Fowler's terminology was a transition from Stage 3 faith through to Stage 5.

> No, I did not convert. . . . But what did happen was an extraordinary dialogue, one between the religious ideas that I encountered and the Jewish ideas within myself. The dialogue continued every day in the classroom, in the words of the New Testament, the Koran, the Upanishads and in fellowship at my own Sabbath table, around which I assembled people of various faiths. As a result of these encounteres, I learned how others experience their faith. But more important, I developed a richer and fuller understanding of myself and my own Judaism (8).

It was five years after his Harvard experience that Goldman wrote *The Search for God at Harvard*. It concludes with a Fowler Stage 5 expression of his renewed faith:

> Today, when I go on assignment to a church, synagogue, mosque or temple, I no longer go as a stranger, an outsider. The ideas preached and the rituals practiced are familiar, unthreatening and, ultimately, enriching to me. The amazing dialogue that began at Harvard between the Judaism within me and other faiths I encountered continues

at St. Paul Community Baptist Church in a black section of Brooklyn, at St. Patrick's Cathedral on Fifth Avenue, at a Reform temple in Cincinnati, at a Zen retreat center in Los Angeles, at a Sunni mosque in Detroit.

. . . In each case I leave as a Jew, rooted in the richness of my own faith but nourished by the faith of others (282–83).

My third and final illustration of the journey to Stage 5 faith is Trappist monk, Thomas Merton (1915–1968).[85] In light of Fowler's finding that Stage 5 is rare before age thirty, what impresses me about Merton's faith journey is the contrast between his early writing and later works. *The Seven Story Mountain*,[86] an autobiographical work describing the process of his conversion, shows Merton as a narrow and somewhat self-satisfied Catholic, intolerant of other Christian churches and overly self-righteous about his Trappist vocation as the most authentic form of Christianity. A few years later, in the Prologue to *The Sign of Jonas*, Merton has changed. He writes, "The life of every . . . Christian is signed with the sign of Jonas . . . but I feel that my own life is especially sealed with this great sign . . . because like Jonas himself I find myself traveling toward my destiny in the belly of a paradox."[87] And still later in life Merton satirizes and distances himself from the pious "modern [Saint] Jerome" image he painted in *The Seven Story Mountain* speaking of himself as a "man in the modern world:"

> This is simply the voice of a self-questioning human person who . . . struggles to cope with turbulent, mysterious, demanding, exciting, frustrating, confused existence in which almost nothing is really predictable, in which most definitions, explanations and justifications become incredible even before they are uttered, in which people suffer together and are sometimes utterly beautiful, at other times impossibly pathetic. In which there is much that is frightening, in which almost everything public is patently phoney, and in which there is at the same time an immense ground of personal authenticity that is right there and so obvious that no one can talk about it and most cannot even believe that it is there.[88]

At the time of his death, Merton was building ecumenical bridges between the great religious traditions of both East and West referring to a "hidden wholeness" in inner experience where "we are already one."[89] Merton's writings themselves document the journey of "a very public hermit" (itself a paradoxical expression) from Stage 3 to Stage

5 faith. That he was aware of this paradoxical character of his faith journey is clear from the following reflection:

> I . . . accept the fact that my life is almost totally paradoxical. . . . It is in the paradox itself, the paradox which was and is still a source of insecurity, that I have come to find the greatest security. I have become convinced that the very contradictions in my life are in some ways signs of God's mercy to me . . . (*Promise* 17).

Thomas Merton, Ari Goldman, and Paul of Tarsus illustrate Fowler's conviction that the capacity to accept paradoxical but complementary thought patterns is a hallmark of this stage of faith development. Further, at Stage 5, faith knowing is more open to the numinous and an affective sense of the world which takes us to levels of awareness well beyond the capacity of our intellect. To recall again an often quoted phrase from Blaise Pascal's *Penseés*, at Stage 5 "the heart has its reasons of which reason knows nothing" (*Penseés* 154). Unusual before full adulthood, Conjunctive faith is born of "the sacrament of defeat and the reality of irrevocable commitments and acts."[90]

We do not give up the individuality and intellectual gains of Stage 4 but instead can consolidate them in a rich paradoxical, affective, personal, other-directed experience of the world and the elements of mystery and paradox inherent in it. Stage 5 faith is a realization that I am not able to do everything on my own. I need others, I need the Other, in order to realize my own full human potential:[91]

> A Christian view of the human vocation suggests that partnership with the action of God may be the single most fruitful way of finding a principle to orchestrate our changing adult life structures (*Becoming* 105).[92]

As Fowler's friend and mentor, Carlyle Marney said (quoting Martin Luther): "We serve God, we love God, we serve and love our neighbors *in commune per vocatione — in community, through vocation*" (*Becoming* 93).

Fowler's research has shown that only 7% of the adult population attain Stage 5 faith and fewer than 1% can be categorized as Stage 6. Accordingly it has been argued that practically and realistically Stage 5 is the normative endpoint of Fowler's faith development theory (*Becoming* 72–73). In our discussion of Fowler's theory in the concluding chapter, we will focus on faith Stages 3 through 5, the stages

that typically characterize adults. My reading of Fowler has led me to diagram and highlight the relationship between faith Stages 3, 4 and 5 as in Table 7.4.

Table 7.4

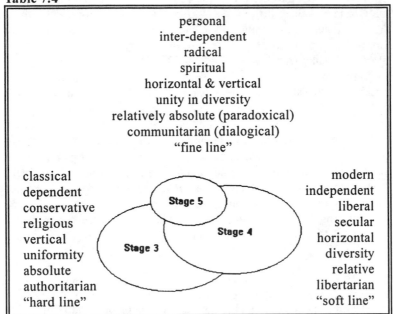

personal	
inter-dependent	
radical	
spiritual	
horizontal & vertical	
unity in diversity	
relatively absolute (paradoxical)	
communitarian (dialogical)	
"fine line"	

classical	modern
dependent	independent
conservative	liberal
religious	secular
vertical	horizontal
uniformity	diversity
absolute	relative
authoritarian	libertarian
"hard line"	"soft line"

Stage 5

Stage 4

Stage 3

Stage 6: Universalizing Faith

If the movement through faith Stages 0–5 can be seen as a *natural* process of development, the movement to Stage 6 Universalizing faith introduces a new factor to the developmental process which Fowler identifies as "grace." The movement from Conjunctive faith to Universalizing faith is a radical leap made only by a few (there is practically no empirical data on Stage 6) and, as Fowler understands it, this leap seems to require a religious, if not theistic, orientation (*Becoming* 72–74).

The words "I have a dream," from Martin Luther King, Jr's famous speech, delivered from the steps of the Lincoln Memorial in Washington, D.C. at the height of the civil rights movement, conjure up one image of Stage 6 faith. The speech focused the thoughts and feelings

of a nation which was slowly, and often painfully, coming to realize the evils of racial discrimination. They are powerful words just because they are spoken by Martin Luther King, Jr., a living symbol of the peace, justice, unity and love for which he gave his life. It is the Christian doctrine of the cross, the condition of true discipleship. In the words of Jesus: "If any want to become my followers, let them deny themselves and take up their cross daily and follow me. For those who want to save their life will lose it, and those who lose their life for my sake will save it" (Luke 9:23–24).

Mahatma Gandhi, Abraham Heschel, Dag Hammarskjold, and Archbishop Oscar Romero were also such people. But you don't have to be a great leader and/or a saint to be a candidate for Stage 6, *Universalizing* faith. One can be less than perfect (as were Martin Luther King, Jr. and Mahatma Gandhi, for example) and one can also at times regress to lower stages of thinking and behaving (especially in situations that one feels one cannot handle). What shines forth, though, in the Stage 6 person is a special grace that makes them a living, breathing representation of the God who is always at work transforming the world and people's lives. Brief excerpts from the writings of Mohandas K. Gandhi and Martin Luther King, Jr. provide a sense of Stage 6 faith:

> To see the universal and all-pervading spirit of Truth face to face one must be able to love the meanest of creation as oneself. And a man who aspires after that cannot afford to keep out of any field of life.[93]

> The old law of an eye for an eye leaves everybody blind. It is immoral because it seeks to humiliate the opponent rather than win his understanding; it seeks to annihilate rather than to convert. Violence is immoral because it thrives on hatred rather than love. It destroys community and makes brotherhood impossible. It leaves society in monologue rather than dialogue. Violence ends by defeating itself. It creates bitterness in the survivors and brutality in the destroyers.[94]

Faith development theory claims[95] that the normative end point to the faith development process is not the individualistic autonomy so characteristic of Western society but an inclusive universal human community living in harmony with the earth. "Pioneers in the commonwealth of love and justice" is one way Fowler describes those visionaries in our midst who live out of universalizing, Stage 6, faith.[96]

Notes

1. James W. Fowler, Karl Ernst Nipkow, and Friedrich Schweitzer, eds., *Stages of Faith and Religious Development: Implications for Church, Education, and Society* (New York: The Crossroad Publishing Company, 1991), 92; referring to "Commonalities of Faith in Religious Pluralism: An Encounter with Wilfred Cantwell Smith," Unpublished Paper, 1987.

2. James W. Fowler, "Faith and the Structuring of Meaning," in *Toward Moral and Religious Maturity*, J. Fowler and A. Vergote , eds. (Morristown, NJ: Silver Burdett, 1980), 53. Fowler understands that "God has prepotentiated us for faith" (*Stages* 22). See also *Faith Development and Pastoral Care* 54.

3. This statement reminds me of Rollo May's view that *true* religion "is essential to a healthy personality." Every genuine atheist with whom he had worked, he says, had shown "unmistakable neurotic tendencies," for each lacked an integrating sense of purpose and direction (David M. Wulff, *Psychology of Religion* [New York: John Wiley & Sons, 1991], 619–20).

4. Ideally, the content of our faith does not come to us passively but we are *agents* (John Macmurray) in the process. Bernard Lonergan's understanding of what it is to move towards authentic adulthood is that of an agent subject knowing for oneself that one has to decide for oneself what one is going to make of oneself.

5. He is quoting the Spanish-American philosopher George Santayana (1863–1952). Fowler says: "As a theologian I never lost sight of the crucial importance of the 'contents' of faith — the realities, values, powers and communities on and in which persons 'rest their hearts'" (*Stages* 273). *Stages of Faith* seriously addresses the "interplay of structure and content in the life of faith" (*Stages* 273).

6. Fowler's understanding of faith, in fact, owes much to the theological tradition represented by Paul Tillich (1886–1965) and H. Richard Niebuhr (1894–1962). Historian of religion, Wilfred Cantwell Smith, helped him to distinguish between *faith, belief*, and *religion* in formulating his understanding of the universality of faith. It is important to highlight the fact that Fowler does not intend to exclude religious content from his faith development theory. This is made quite clear in the opening sentences of the final section of *Stages of Faith*, "On Grace—Ordinary and Extraordinary:" "There is a limit to how much one can talk about faith and development in faith without acknowledging that the question of whether there will be faith on earth is finally God's business. Faith development theory, focusing resolutely on the human side of the faith relationship comes up against the fact that the transcendent other with whom we have to do in faith is not confined by the models we build or to the patterns we discern. . . . God is recognized as sovereign reality — as creator, ruler, and as redeemer of *all* being" (*Stages* 302).

7. James W. Fowler, "The Vocation of Faith Development Theory," in James W. Fowler, Karl Ernst Nipkow, and Friedrich Schweitzer, eds., *Stages of Faith and Religious Development: Implications for Church, Education, and Society* (New York: The Crossroad Publishing Company, 1991), 36.

8. Religious faith, in the language of American theologian Paul Tillich, is concerned with *the* Ultimate Environment; God defined by Tillich as "our ultimate, unconditional concern." Faith, therefore, is universal among humans (i.e., everybody has faith) and everybody even holds to a *religious* faith if we accept Tillich's definition. Such a broad definition prompted Abraham Maslow to ask: "If, as actually happened on one platform, Paul Tillich defined religion as 'concern with ultimate concerns' and I then defined humanistic psychology in the same way, then what is the difference between a supernaturalist and a humanist?" (Abraham H. Maslow, *Religions, Values, and Peak-Experiences* [New York: Penguin Books, 1976], 45).

9. The reference in brackets (*Passages* 46) is to Thomas A. Droege, *Faith Passages and Patterns* (Philadelphia: Fortress Press, 1983), 46. Quotations from this work will henceforth be given as here (*Passages* 46).

10. It seems to me that Lonergan's understanding of the role of feelings in human cognition and decision making is helpful in understanding what Fowler intends by saying that faith knowing involves the *whole* person, not just the intellect. Also pertinent to this discussion is a quotation attributed to American author Evelyn Scott (1893–1963) — "I realized a long time ago that a belief which does not spring from a conviction in the emotions is no belief at all."

11. "Covenant existence" is discussed in *Stages* 33 and *Becoming* 110.

12. Here Fowler is drawing on American theologian H. Richard Niebuhr, the subject of his own doctoral dissertation (1974). See James W. Fowler, *To See the Kingdom: The Theological Vision of H. Richard Niebuhr* (Lanham, MD: University Press of America, 1985), 207–08.

13. Linda Lawrence, "Stages of Faith," *Psychology Today* 17, no. 11 (November 1983): 61.

14. "The covenantal structure of our significant human relations is often made visible as much by our betrayals and failures of 'good faith' as by the times when we are mutually loyal and faithful" (*Stages* 33). A footnote to the quotation tells us that Fowler explores this idea in chapter 5 of *To See the Kingdom*.

15. John Macmurray's study of scripture led him to conclude that *faith*, which he contrasts with *fear*, might "be better translated, 'Trust'" *(The Philosophy of Jesus*, a pamphlet published by the London Friends Home Service Committee in 1973, 5).

16. *The Works of Saint Cyril of Jerusalem*, vol. 1, trans. Leo P. McCauley, S.J. and Anthony A. Stephenson (Washington, DC: The Catholic University of America Press, 1968), 146–47. These lines are from a catechetical instruction by the fourth century bishop.

17. Ironically, Martin Luther's was perhaps the first!

18. "How does a Catholic sin against faith? A Catholic sins against faith by not believing what God has revealed, and by taking part in non-Catholic worship" (*The New Saint Joseph Baltimore Catechism* [New York: Catholic Book Publishing Co., 1964], 79).

19. This is the answer to question 122 in the Baltimore Catechism asking, "What is faith?" (*The New Saint Joseph Baltimore Catechism*, no. 2 [New York: Catholic Book Publishing Co., 1969], 64). In *Evangelization and Catechesis*, Johannes Hofinger, S.J., a well-known Catholic educator, defined faith as "the divine virtue by which we assent to the truths revealed by God, since God cannot deceive or be deceived" (New York: Paulist Press, 1976, 17).

20. Already at age nineteen, Pascal had invented a calculating machine that worked and his research into hydrodynamics and fluid mechanics is preserved in Pascal's Law which is the basis for hydraulics. His religious thought, which emphasized the reasons of the heart over those of rationalism or empiricism, is found in *Pensées* (*Thoughts*) published posthumously by his friends. He felt that metaphysical proofs for God's existence had very little impact on people. "Pascal's wager" (*Pensées* 149–53) recommends that we bet on God because if we win we win everything and if we lose we really lose nothing because religious people are happier anyway.

21. Quoted by Robert Coles in *Irony in the Mind's Life: Essays on Novels by James Agee, Elizabeth Bowen, and George Eliot* (New York: New Directions, 1974), 25. See Bruce A. Ronda, *Intellect and Spirit: The Life and Work of Robert Coles* (New York: The Continuum Publishing Company, 1989), 24.

22. Paul Tillich, *What is Religion?* (New York: Harper Torchbooks, 1973), 76.

23. Vatican II saw *personal* faith as complementary to purely *intellectual* faith. Macmurray's use of the term personal is inclusive of both meanings.

24. *Dogmatic Constitution on Divine Revelation* (*Dei Verbum*), November 18, 1965, chapter 1, # 5. The *Dei Verbum* quotation is taken from Austin Flannery, ed., *Vatican Council II: The Conciliar and Post Conciliar Documents*, New Revised Edition (Boston: St. Paul Books and Media, 1992), 752.

25. For several years I have presented Fowler's understanding of faith as involving the three components of head, heart and hands. I am not sure that the third (action) is as explicit in his work as I will make it seem here.

26. Fowler tells the moving story of a twelve year old boy's "pure and strongly held theism" which reflected an understanding of God as Liberator and Redeemer. "We will never know," the boy said, "how much God *does* [emphasis mine] every day to keep our world working as well as it does" (*Becoming* 88).

27. The quotation is from the document *Justice in the World*, # 5, produced by the Second ordinary World Synod of [Roman Catholic] Bishops meeting in Rome in the fall of 1971. For a discussion of this specific passage, see Charles M. Murphy, "Action for Justice as Constitutive of the

preaching of the Gospel: What did the 1971 Synod Mean?" in *Theological Studies* 44, no. 2 (June 1983): 298–311.

28. Ronald Rolheiser, "Chronicle," *Catholic Herald* (London: Herald House, June 3, 1994): 10.

29. Literally, *didache* means "a teaching." This document is also called the "Teaching of the Twelve Apostles."

30. Richard P. McBrien, *Catholicism*, Study Edition (San Francisco: Harper & Row, 1981), 967.

31. Thomas H. Groome, *Christian Religious Education* (San Francisco: Harper & Row, 1980), 65–66.

32. My puzzle image comes from the fact that on holidays I enjoy working on jigsaw puzzles. Fowler speaks of the "teepee model" which he attributes to his late friend and mentor, Carlyle Marney. The poles represent education, profession, associations, religion, state of life, life style, and so on. In our mid-twenties, we tie the poles together at the top, wrap a skin around them, and crawl inside to spend the rest of our lives (*Becoming* 11–13).

33. Once, I spoke to a group of professional men and women over breakfast at the Carleton Club in Winnipeg. During the meal, and before my talk, a few of them were discussing a new board game called Midlife Crisis.

34. Robert Kegan, *The Evolving Self: Problem and Process in Human Development* (Cambridge, MA: Harvard University Press, 1982).

35. Fowler's faith development model makes use of seven facets of faith that provide insight into the form of faith at a given stage. Briefly, they deal with the way we think (Jean Piaget), perspective taking (Robert Selman), moral judgment (Lawrence Kohlberg), our sense of faith community, authorities, worldview, and use of symbols. Fowler is both a social scientist and a Christian theologian. His faith development theory is cross-disciplinary, straddling the boundaries between developmental psychology and pastoral theology. Here, for instance, it is Fowler's inclusion of the affective side of human beings in his concept of rationality that allows traditional understandings of religion to be taken seriously by faith development theory.

36. See *Stages* 98–105. There has not been enough cross-cultural research completed to claim "universality" for the faith stages (James W. Fowler, Karl Ernst Nipkow, and Friedrich Schweitzer, eds., *Stages of Faith and Religious Development* [New York: Crossroad Publishing Company, 1991], 10).

37. Linda Lawrence, "Stages of Faith," *Psychology Today* 17, no.11 (November 1983): 62.

38. "Readiness" is the term favored by Ronald Goldman in conjunction with stage transition; see Ronald Goldman, *Readiness for Religion: A Basis for Developmental Religious Education* (London: Routledge & Kegan Paul, 1965).

39. Here Fowler is quoting a character in *Green Pastures* by Mark Connelly. John Macmurray wrote a Postscript to the 1963 edition of *Green Pastures* (published in London by Delisle). It occurs to me that "Dark

Nights of the Soul" as described in the writings of Spanish mystic St. John of the Cross (1542–1591) correspond to the transitions between Fowler's higher faith stages.

40. The phoenix is a legendary bird (according to Herodotus only one existed at a time, living for five hundred years) which built its own funeral pyre out of aromatic materials. The dying phoenix was consumed by fire and from its ashes a new bird arose. In early Christian art and writings the phoenix is a symbol for resurrection and immortality.

41. A poem by Ruth McLean as quoted by John A. Veltri S.J., *Orientations: A Collection of Helps for Prayer*, vol. 1 revised (Guelph, ON: Loyola House, 1993), 21–22. Orientations can be found on the Internet at *http://www.oise.on.ca/~rboys/veltri.html*. This poem reminds me of an image of stage transition as like jumping from a cliff without wings trusting that you'll be able to grow them before you hit the ground; wings that will take you to new heights far above the top of the cliff from which you jumped.

42. This process might be referred to as one of "positive disintegration." Khalil Gibran is quoted as saying: "Your joy is your sorrow unmasked. The self-same well from which your laughter rises was sometimes filled with tears" (*Celebration*, January 1991 [Epiphany]: 19). I am reminded of Fowler's remark that the Chinese ideogram for *crisis* is a combination of the characters for *danger* and *opportunity* (*Pastoral* 103). *Global Brain* by Peter Russell (London: Routledge & Kegan Paul, 1982) also makes use of this image.

43. Constructive critiques of Fowler's theory have helped clarify the issues involved. I have found the work of Mary Ford-Grabowsky particularly helpful. See "The Concept of Christian Faith in the Light of Hildegard of Bingen and C. G. Jung: A Critical Alternative to Fowler" (Ph.D. diss., Princeton University, 1985); "What Developmental Phenomenon is Fowler Studying?", *Journal of Psychology & Christianity* 5, no. 3 (1986): 5–13; "The Fullness of the Christian Faith Experience: Dimensions Missing in Faith Development Theory," *Journal of Pastoral Care* 41, no. 1 (1987): 39–41; "Flaws in Faith Development Theory," *Religious Education* 82, no. 1 (1987): 80–93; and "The Journey of a Pilgrim: An Alternative to Fowler," *The Living Light* 24, no. 3 (March 1988): 242–254.

44. This description reminds me of a sentence from T.S. Eliot's poem *Little Gidding*:

> We shall not cease from exploration
> And the end of all our exploring
> Will be to arrive where we started
> And know the place for the first time.

T. S. Eliot, *Collected Poems: 1909–1962* (London: Faber and Faber, 1963), 222.

45. *How Faith Grows: Faith Development and Christian Education*, A Report to the General Synod [Church of England]. London: National Society/Church House Publishing, 1991), 17. What I see as a major contribution

of Fowler is his organization of the order or pattern in which the developmental features of faith appear.

46. Karl Rahner, *Theological Investigations*, vol. 3, The Theology of the Spiritual Life (London: Darton, Longman & Todd, 1967), 13–14.

47. For detailed information on the administration and analysis of faith development interviews, see Romney M. Moseley, David Jarvis, and James W. Fowler, *Manual for Faith Development Research* (Atlanta: Center for Research in Faith and Moral Development, Emory University, 1986).

48. A 1993 film by Columbia Pictures, *My Life* was directed by Bruce Joel Rubin.

49. For adults, beyond the world "we know about, there is the further world we make," the "larger world mediated by meaning" (*Collection* 233).

50. A 1977 Twentieth Century Fox film, *Star Wars* was directed by George Lucas.

51. "Fowler on Faith," *Christianity Today* (June, 1986): 7-I–8-I.

52. A 1968 Twentieth Century Fox film (directed by Robert Neame), *The Prime of Miss Jean Brodie* shows some students, at least at the outset, uncritically accepting Miss Brodie's worldview. In the title role, Maggie Smith won the 1969 academy award as best actress.

53. The reference in brackets (*Pastoral* 66) is to James W. Fowler, *Faith Development and Pastoral Care* (Philadelphia: Fortress Press, 1987), 66. Quotations from this work will henceforth be as here (*Pastoral* 66).

54. Based on the novel by Victor Hugo, *Les Misérables* is a musical by Alain Boublil and Claude-Michel Schönberg. It opened at the Palais des Sports in Paris in 1980.

55. The television serials, *Little House on the Prairie* and *The Waltons* are examples of positive Stage 3 faith culture.

56. Rosemary Haughton, *The Catholic Thing* (Springfield, IL: Templegate Publishers, 1979), 9.

57. Peter Occhiogrosso, *Once A Catholic* (New York: Ballantine Books, 1987), 12–13.

58. The Broadway musical *Fiddler on the Roof* was written by Jospeh Stein.

59. The musical also conveys the limitation of Stage 3 faith in that it portrays two parallel but conflicting religious world views in the same village (Judaism and Ukrainian Orthodoxy).

60. Sharon Parks, *The Critical Years* (San Francisco: Harper & Row, 1986), 76. Fowler first quotes her in *Stages* 154.

61. In terms of Lawrence Kohlberg's stages of moral development, a person living out of Stage 3 faith exhibits Stage 4 "conventional" morality.

62. *Judgment at Nuremberg* is a 1961 film from MGM, directed by Stanley Kramer.

63. This quotation is transcribed from a videotape of the film. The statement is made just before the judges retire to deliberate on the verdict and sentencing.

64. Teaching faith development theory in classes and workshops, I have been struck by how often the interest of participants and their questions arise, not out of their professional involvements, but from the depths of their own faith journey. This ability of faith development theory to "engage its readers' own memories, convictions, and core intuitions" (James W. Fowler, "Stages of Faith: Reflections on a Decade of Dialogue," *Christian Education Journal* 13, no. 1 [Autumn 1992]: 16.) is also reminiscent of the personal involvement and self-appropriation called for by John Macmurray and Bernard Lonergan.

65. If we stay at Fowler's Stage 3 too long, the move to Stage 4 is not a normal evolutionary process but a real disruption. An example comes to mind. Many Jesuits left the Order in the years following the Second Vatican Council (1962–65). Personally, I suspect that a number of them identified the prevailing Stage 3 form of the Jesuit vocation (characterized by a strict hierarchical governance structure and rigid rules of dress and behavior) as *the* Jesuit life. When the reforms of the Council urged us forward in faith, their identity was so tied to externals like clerical dress and conformist behavior that, as these fell away, they found it quite easy to leave the community. More than once in my early days as a member of the Society of Jesus I heard variations on the theme, 'I didn't leave the Jesuits, the Jesuits left me.'

66. In *Becoming Adult, Becoming Christian*, Fowler uses the image of Protean Man ("fluid, flexible, and frequently ready to change fundamental convictions and outlooks") as illustrative of faith at this stage (13–15).

67. Not many young adult Catholics living in a university residential setting continue to go to Mass. Generally, the few who do attend see their understanding of why they go to Mass shift from conformity to external pressures to go to church to self-appropriation of their attendance at Mass. This is one of the conclusions of the *Young Adult Faith Study* conducted by the Jesuit Center for Faith Development and Values at St. Paul's College, University of Manitoba. A report on the findings of this four year (1988–92) investigation into the faith development of young adults as they move from high school through a university undergraduate program is found in David G. Creamer, "Faith Development in Young Adult Catholics," *Insight*, no. 4. Ottawa: Canadian Conference of Catholic Bishops (1991): 56–73.

68. The page references are to Viktor Frankl, *The Unconscious God* (New York: Washington Square Press, 1985).

69. The transition to Fowler's Stage 4 faith is, in my view, more or less equivalent to what Lonergan means by moral conversion — ". . . what are we to choose to be? What are we to choose to make of ourselves? In our lives there . . . comes the moment of existential crisis when we find out for ourselves that we have to decide for ourselves what we by our own choices and decisions are to make of ourselves . . ." (*Collection* 243). For a similar quotation see chapter 5, note 25.

70. Perhaps Allport's major contribution to the empirical study of religion is his distinction between two orientations to (or types of) religion; intrinsic [I] and extrinsic [E], which he views as the two ends of a continuum.

Intrinsic religion is a "religion that is lived." "Such religion does not exist to serve the person; rather the person is committed to serve it"(Will Herberg, *Protestant-Catholic-Jew* (Garden City, NY: Doubleday, 1960), 132). Extrinsic religion is "religion that is used." Those having this orientation find religion useful in a number of ways and emphasize its rewards over its demands (Robert W. Crapps, *An Introduction to Psychology of Religion* [Macon, GA: Mercer University Press, 1986], 156).

71. John Chirban, "Intrinsic and Extrinsic Religious Motivation and Stages of Faith" (Th.D. diss., Harvard Divinity School, 1980). This research is reported in *Stages* 300–301.

72. If the Roman Catholic church prior to the Second Vatican Council saw Stage 3 faith as the ideal, then to move beyond that put one on dangerous ground as Martin Luther found out on April 18, 1521, at the Diet of Worms. The remark "Here I stand, I can do no other," attributed to him, is a characteristically Stage 4 remark.

73. The term *transition* is used to refer to the process of growing *out of* one way of living faith preparatory to growing *into* the next.

74. The 1965 Vatican II document, *Gaudium et Spes* (Pastoral Constitution on the Church in the Modern World), points out that the modern world tends to privatize religion (Fowler's Stage 4), a tendency that it calls one of "the gravest errors of our time" (# 43).

75. Many of the descriptors of Stage 4 can be traced to Enlightenment ideals, in large measure the nucleus of our modern worldview.

76. Linda Lawrence, "Stages of Faith," *Psychology Today* 17, no. 11 (November, 1983): 58. The metaphor is attributed to Carlyle Marney.

77. *Conjunctive Faith* is a name Fowler traces to creation-centered medieval mystic Nicholas of Cusa (1401–1464) who put forward the notion of God as "the coincidence of opposites" (*coincidentia oppositorum*). This notion was altered by Carl Jung to "conjunction of opposites" (*Becoming* 64).

78. E. F. Schumacher, *A Guide for the Perplexed* (London: Sphere Books Ltd, 1977). Page numbers are given in brackets.

79. The reference in brackets (*Promise* 19) is to Parker Palmer, *The Promise of Paradox: A Celebration of Contradictions in the Christian Life* (Notre Dame, IN: Ave Maria Press, 1980), 19. Quotations from *The Promise of Paradox* will henceforth be indicated as here (*Promise* 19).

80. I think that my own Roman Catholic tradition needs a lot of Stage 5 people these days to make peace between the 4s and the 3s. Stage 5 adult Catholics understand that the magisterium of the Church is a very important cornerstone in the moral decision-making process but further understand that they can be loyal to the church without abdicating personal responsibility to church authorities, even the Pope. If people have been operating at the conventional level of moral decision-making for a long time, this faith transition can be difficult.

81. Abraham H. Maslow, *Religions, Values, and Peak-Experiences* (New York: Penguin Books, 1970), 13.

82. The notion of Stage 5 as existing in dynamic tension between the extremes of Stage 3 and Stage 4 reminds me of the position of the Earth (life giving water as solid, liquid, and gas) as in tension between the extremes of climate represented by Mars (lifeless rock) and Venus (veiled in poisonous gases). This is one of the reasons why I diagram Stage 5 as balanced between Stages 3 and 4.

83. Not long ago I met a 29 year old man who was embarking on a two year volunteer committment in a communal setting. He was a succcessful professional but unhappy with his lonely, individualistic lifestyle (Stage 4). It was a longing for the "team-work" that characterized his years in the scouting movement (Stage 3) that brought him to the volunteer program (Stage 5).

84. Ari L. Goldman, *The Search for God at Harvard* (New York: Times Books, 1991). In the discussion of Goldman's faith journey, the numbers in brackets refer to page numbers in his book.

85. Twenty-five years after his death (December 10, 1968), articles on Merton appeared in several journals. To name just two: Thomas P. Rausch, "Thomas Merton: Twenty-five Years After," *America* 170, no. 1 (January 1–8, 1994): 6–12; and Jim Forest, "A Very Public Hermit," *The Tablet* (December 25, 1993/January 1, 1994): 1685.

86. Thomas Merton, *The Seven Story Mountain* (New York: Harcourt, Brace and Company, 1948).

87. Thomas Merton, *The Sign of Jonas* (New York: Harcourt, Brace and Company, 1953), 11.

88. Thomas Merton, "Is the World a Problem?," *Commonweal* 84, no. 11 (June 3, 1966): 305.

89. Jim Forest, "A Very Public Hermit," *The Tablet* (December 25, 1993/January 1, 1994): 1685.

90. James W. Fowler, "Faith and the Structuring of Meaning" in *Toward Moral and Religious Maturity: The First International Conference on Moral and Religious Development* (Morristown, NJ: Silver Burdett, 1980), 73.

91. There are obvious parallels with John Macmurray's "mutuality of the personal" and Martin Buber's "I and Thou."

92. If Stage 3 faith interprets human action in the face of transcendental reality and Stage 4 faith interprets transcendental action in the face of human contingencies, then Stage 5 faith is concerned with interpreting the relational structure between the human and the transcendent. If Stage 3 faith can be characterized as tribal (dependent) and Stage 4 as individualistic (independent), then Stage 5 can be understood as communal (interdependent).

93. M. K. Gandhi, *My Autobiography* (Boston: Beacon Press, 1957), 504.

94. Coretta Scott King, ed., *The Words of Martin Luther King, Jr.* (New York: Newmarket Press, 1983), 73.

95. Fowler rationalizes this claim and discusses the objections to it in *Becoming* 71–75. See also the "character of the last stages" in developmental theories (*Becoming* 20).

96. James W. Fowler, "Stages of Faith: Reflections on a Decade of Dialogue," *Christian Education Journal* 13, no. 1 (Autumn 1992): 15.

Chapter 8

A Summing Up

There is, then, a road which all profoundly "serious," "ultimately concerned" people of good will can travel together for a very long distance. Only when they come almost to its end does the road fork so that they must part in disagreement. Practically everything that, for example, Rudolf Otto defines as characteristic of the religious experience — the holy; the sacred; creature feeling; humility; gratitude and oblation; thanksgiving; awe before the *mysterium tremendum*; the sense of the divine, the ineffable; the sense of littleness before mystery; the quality of exaltedness and sublimity; the awareness of limits and even powerlessness; the impulse to surrender and to kneel; a sense of the eternal and of fusion with the whole of the universe; even the experience of heaven and hell — all of these experiences can be accepted as real by clergymen and atheists alike. And so it is also possible for all of them to accept in principle the empirical spirit and empirical methods and to humbly admit that knowledge is not complete, that it must grow, that it is in time and space, in history and in culture, and that, though it is relative to man's powers and to his limits, it can yet come closer and closer to "The Truth" that is not dependent on man.

This road can be travelled together by all who are not afraid of truth. (Abraham Maslow)[1]

Introduction

John Macmurray, Bernard Lonergan and James Fowler represent different eras, places, and traditions. Yet, as I read Lonergan, I hear resonances with Macmurray and Fowler. As I teach Fowler's faith development theory I find myself using Lonergan and Macmurray to explain aspects of the faith stages. It is my position that the thought of Macmurray, Lonergan, and Fowler is congruent in ways which those of us journeying in these last years of the twentieth century need to take to heart. The very fact that they enter into the discussion of human meaning making and authentic living through different doors only to arrive at views which converge around a common normative endpoint (friendship, being in love, citizenship in a commonwealth of love and justice) is, in my view, most significant. It is this commonality that we will explore here. In turn we will consider Macmurray and Lonergan, Lonergan and Fowler, and conclude with a section on the three together.

Macmurray and Lonergan

Methodology

John Macmurray's philosophical summary, "All meaningful knowledge is for the sake of action, and all meaningful action for the sake of friendship" (*Self* 15) is, in my view, consistent with Bernard Lonergan's insight that as we move in consciousness from a judgment as to truth (meaningful knowledge), to a decision to act responsibly (meaningful action), to falling in love (friendship), we are engaged in progressively more human activity. Further, Macmurray's use of the adjective *meaningful*, in my view, expresses something of what Lonergan intends by *conversion*. *Meaningful* knowledge of truth (the result of intellectual conversion) brings us to the existential decision about what to do. A decision to do the good and to put others before ourselves, *meaningful* action in Macmurray's terminology, is only possible as a result of what Lonergan describes as moral conversion. And as meaningful action is "for the sake of friendship," so religious conversion takes us beyond intellectual and moral conversion to love (*Second Collection* 228). I chart this relationship between Macmurray and Lonergan as in Table 8.1.

Table 8.1

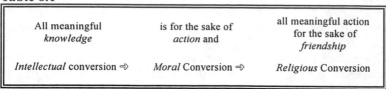

All meaningful *knowledge*	is for the sake of *action* and	all meaningful action for the sake of *friendship*
Intellectual conversion ⇨	*Moral* Conversion ⇨	*Religious* Conversion

John Macmurray's insistence on the primacy of action over think-ing parallels Lonergan's view that the end point of the transcendental method is not knowledge of truth but right *action* done in harmony with what I know to be true. The dynamics of human consciousness move us beyond questions of truth to questions of value; we need to know because we want to act responsibly. We pay attention to experi-ence and consciousness, we probe intelligently into the meaning of our experience, and we exercise critical judgment, so that we can act as befits our human dignity. To know the truth and not to do it is to acknowledge that we are living at less than our full human potential.[2]

According to Lonergan, when we begin the process of self-consti-tution from a reflective, critical stance on the responsible level of consciousness, we arrive at a crucial turning point in our lives — the point at which spiritual development really begins. Why does he say this? I think it is because spirituality implies a way of life and not just a system of ideas. Practical reflection moves us from the realm of fact into that of *value* where we deliberate about a possible course of action, and right action (done for the common good) moves us towards community, towards being-in-love, towards what Macmurray calls friendship. For both Macmurray and Lonergan the goal of knowing points far beyond cognition; the endpoint of the process is ethical and religious. Their central insight is that we are not mere *thinking things* but *moral agents*, capable of acting out of friendship or love. Our humanity, Macmurray and Lonergan would say, is more evident in our creations than in our ideas, and most evident in our loving relation-ships.

Community

In times past, both figuratively and concretely, the peoples of the earth built walls around themselves, the 6000 year old Great Wall of China being the most dramatic example. Whatever happened outside the wall had no bearing on life within. In fifth century B.C. Greece,

to be a civilized human being was to live in a Greek *polis* (city-state); all other peoples were barbarians (i.e., non-Greek and by implication not fully human) and their activity was of no consequence to Greek citizens. With the age of discovery and growth of world trade beginning in the sixteenth century, there was a need to regulate relationships among different peoples and nation states but this was more or less done along utilitarian lines, some notion of justice as fairness serving as the highest operative morality (I might need to *trade* with them but I don't have to *live* with them). Less than a century ago on our North American continent, within the confines of the extended family living on 'Walton's Mountain' or in the 'Little House on the Prairie' there was no need to be concerned about anybody or anything beyond perhaps the nearest town. Within my own religious tradition, the image I have of Roman Catholicism in the decades before the Second Vatican Council is of an institution with an ideological wall around itself.[3]

However, at this time in earth's story, in whatever sphere of life we may want to consider, retreating behind a wall or fortifying oneself on a mountain doesn't afford much protection or isolation. The world, to use Marshall McLuhan's (1911–1980) much overworked phrase, has shrunk to become a "global village."[4] After the Chernobyl nuclear disaster in the Ukraine, friends of mine in Paris were concerned about contamination in the milk their children were drinking and radiation levels had risen halfway around the globe in Manitoba. Like it or not, we all breathe the same air, drink the same water and live under the ultraviolet protection of the same shrinking ozone layer. Our need to achieve community today is on a global scale. Such was the vision of John Macmurray and Bernard Lonergan. What we are just coming to appreciate as we near the end of the millennium is that movement in this direction is not just an option, but a necessity. To continue to live in the old way is to condemn ourselves and the earth to extinction. What we *do* in the next decade or so will determine whether life as we know it on this planet continues or not:

> The changes presently taking place in human and earthly affairs are beyond any parallel with historical change or cultural modification as these have occurred in the past. This is not like the transition from the classical period to the medieval period or from the medieval period to the modern period. This change reaches far beyond the civilizational process itself, beyond even the human process into the biosystems and even the geological systems of the Earth itself.[5]

To save ourselves and the planet is a daunting task requiring cooperation on a scale heretofore never imagined. But the nagging question remains: 'If up until this moment we have not been too concerned about our children's children and the world they will inherit, why will we start now?' The answer, if we accept what Macmurray and Lonergan have to say, is because a new consciousness of what it is to be a fully authentic human person is forming; we human beings are discovering that we, as a species, are fashioned to live cooperatively and in friendship, that we exist because of and for love. As *human* creatures we are not designed to work together like the parts of a clock, nor are we genetically programmed to live like ants in an ant hill; we are imprinted with feelings and the ability to make commitments in order to live communally. Community, Macmurray has shown, is constituted by means of mutual personal relationships of friendship. Lonergan writes that we human beings have a "primordial sympathy" for one another (*Insight* 237).

Reminiscent of John Macmurray's "mutuality of the personal," Bernard Lonergan explains mutual love as an "intertwining of two lives" in such a way that an 'I' and 'thou' are transformed into a "'we' so intimate, so secure, so permanent, that each attends, imagines, thinks, plans, feels, speaks, acts in concern for both" (*Method* 33). Relationships of this kind (respectful, intimate, loving) which "bind a community together" (*Method* 51) are required to bring us into the Ecozoic Age:

> The Ecozoic Era can only be brought into being by the integral life community itself. If other periods have been designated by such names as the Reptilian or the Mammalian periods, this Ecozoic Period must be identified as the Era of the Integral Life Community. For this to emerge there are special conditions on the part of the human, for although this period cannot be an anthropocentric life period, it can come into being only under certain conditions that dominantly concern human understanding, choice, and action.[6]

In one of his last published essays, *The Philosophy of Jesus*, John Macmurray identifies the mission of Jesus Christ as most fundamentally that of a social reformer concerned about the salvation of *this* world: "A religion which despairs of this world, and takes for its task to prepare men in this life for a blessed future in another world is not the religion of Jesus."[7] Thus, he characterizes the early faith community which gathered around Jesus as "a way of life on earth" and "an

instrument for the salvation of a world gone wrong." The church of
Christ which succeeded it he understands to be a "brotherhood,"
existing "for the sake of the world outside it."[8] In the same vein,
Bernard Lonergan describes the Christian church as "the community
that results from the outer communication of Christ's message and
from the inner gift of God's love" (*Method* 361) and claims that it
ought to have as a primary function the promotion and renewal of
community; i.e., the promotion of intellectual, moral, and religious
conversion. At this point, allow me to add that we might even dare to
think of the emerging Ecozoic era as contiguous with the continual
inbreaking of the reign of God so central to Hebrew scriptures and the
life and mission of Jesus.[9]

> In days to come . . . they shall beat their swords into plowshares, and
> their spears into pruning hooks; nation shall not lift up sword against
> nation, neither shall they learn war anymore (Isaiah 2:2–4).

> The wolf shall live with the lamb, the leopard shall lie down with the
> kid: . . . The nursing child shall play over the hole of the asp, and the
> weaned child shall put its hand on the adder's den. They will not hurt
> or destroy on all my holy mountain for the earth will be full of the
> knowledge of the Lord . . . (Isaiah 11:6–9).

> All who believed were together and had all things in common; they
> would sell their possessions and goods and distribute the proceeds to
> all, as any had need. (Acts 2:44–45)

Lonergan and Fowler

Because Lonergan and Fowler are each concerned with the process of human meaning-making, it is reasonable to assume that they
may be describing different facets of the same human developmental
pattern. As near as I can tell, what Bernard Lonergan discovered
through self-appropriation of human consciousness, James Fowler
uncovered by means of empirical research. In a sentence, the point of
this discussion of Lonergan and Fowler is to argue that Lonergan's
way of tradition (from above downwards ↓), way of achievement (from
below upwards ↑), and the totality of development as an integration of
the two ways (↑↓) illuminate what Fowler describes as faith Stages 3,
4 and 5 respectively. Further, I will argue that the transitions between
faith Stages 3 through 6 parallel Lonergan's intellectual, moral, and

religious conversion.

Telling Us What We Already Knew

Both Lonergan and Fowler understand human beings to be natural meaning-makers and each puts forward a model for elucidating the dynamics of the meaning making process. Both would agree that they are not offering us something *new* but making explicit something that we already *knew* and can verify by critical reflection on our life experience. The introduction to a series of essays on Fowler's model proposes that:

> Fowler's theory is more than just one of any number of interesting and potentially useful academic analyses. It is an expression of a wider cultural and intellectual mood. It is a consolidation and crystallization of a whole way of seeing things that is already in some sense "out there." Fowler, we think, tells many of his readers, but in a way that they could not have put it themselves, what they in some sense already "knew" to be the case.[10]

Similarly, Lonergan's epistemological framework can be understood as something *out there* that in some sense we already *knew*. The generalized empirical method is not something that we learn or are taught but is a process of self-appropriation — it is ourselves maturing in experience, growing in understanding, and searching for what is true and good and lovable.

Roman Catholicism and Faith Development Theory

Fowler's Stage 3 faith, as we have seen, is characterized by conformity to the expectations of others and an uncritical regard for authority. At Stage 3 one is "embedded" in one's faith outlook; "I *am* my relationships; I *am* my roles" (*Pastoral* 66). Research has shown that this faith stage is the life stance of a large percentage of adults. In my view, it is coincidental with the classical understanding of religious faith and parallels what Lonergan calls the traditional way of knowing as from above downwards.

As we have seen, Stage 3 was *the* faith understanding of the majority of Roman Catholics until developments in our own century, culminating in the reforms of the Second Vatican Council. The Scholastic tradition in theology, best exemplified by Thomas Aquinas, was

the only acceptable expression of the basic doctrine of Catholicism for eight centuries. To question the authority of Thomism was to question one's very (Stage 3) faith. This was the church milieu in which Bernard Lonergan studied and did most of his teaching and writing. That he suffered as a teacher and author because of this limited understanding of faith is clear. In terms of Fowler's stage theory, Lonergan's life and career can be seen initially as an effort to extricate himself (remember that he studied Thomistic theology and began to teach and write in Latin!) and his religious tradition from embeddedness in the Stage 3 faith perspective.

Lonergan's elaboration of the way of achievement from below upwards as complementary to the way of tradition (from above downwards) provides an intellectual justification for the shift from Fowler's Stage 3 (*they say*) to Stage 4 (*I think*) faith. For Lonergan, part of the shift from a pre-modern to a modern worldview, from Stage 3 to Stage 4 faith, involves the "recovery of the subject," a focusing on the human subject searching for truth.[11] In terms of Lonergan's levels of consciousness, the way of development from below upwards is integral to faith growth and in mature *adult* faith it assumes priority.

Lonergan's notion that the way from above downwards (Fowler's Stage 3 faith) is not the only way that human beings come to knowledge but needs to be complemented by the way from below upwards (Fowler's Stage 4 faith) was not readily accepted within the church or the academy.[12] The insight of both Lonergan and Fowler is that full human maturity moves one beyond the either/or Stage 3/Stage 4 polarity to an awareness of the strengths and limitations of each way and the need to replace the old adversarial view with a *complementary* view of meaning-making.

If the ideal of the pre-modern Roman Catholic church was Fowler's Stage 3 faith (Lonergan's way of tradition), then the Second Vatican Council can be viewed as an attempt to move Catholicism through modern, historical, consciousness (Fowler Stage 4) to Conjunctive faith characterized by a promulgation of religious liberty and genuine dialogue with other Christian churches and religious traditions (Fowler Stage 5). Fowler's research has shown that the transition from Stage 3 to Stage 4 faith (if it happens at all) is often long and protracted. Speaking in 1970 about his own post-Vatican II faith community, Lonergan was aware of this difficulty as is clear in this astute observation:

Ours is a time that criticizes and debunks the past. . . .

It also is a time of confusion, for there are many voices, many of them shrill, most of them contradictory. . . .

To confusion there are easily added disorientation, disillusionment, crisis, surrender, unbelief. But . . . from the present situation Catholics are suffering more keenly than others, not indeed because their plight is worse, but because up to Vatican II they were sheltered against the modern world and since Vatican II they have been exposed more and more to the chill winds of modernity (*Second Collection* 93).

Cardinal G. Emmett Carter, retired Archbishop of Toronto, offers a perspective on the two extreme positions characteristic of the church in our time:

We must not fall into the trap of ultramontanism, a truly doubtful position which makes the Pope sort of the centre and fount of all wisdom and authority in the Church, or into the opposite excess, . . . namely that authority of the Church is almost uniquely from popular opinion.[13]

It seems to me that Cardinal Carter's view can be rephrased in terms of Fowler's stages of faith development. "Ultramontanism" is Stage 3 because of the certainty it offers; "popular opinion" is Stage 4. "True loyalty" (Stage 5), Cardinal Carter goes on to say, is not "blind obedience," nor is it intent on destroying everything handed down; it is "one thing to adjust and it is another thing to destroy."[14]

Bernard Lonergan and Faith Development Theory

Lonergan, I think, admirably represents the balance which characterizes "true loyalty." In his own life, he passed from the absoluteness of classical Catholicism, through a period characterized by the individuality of Stage 4 ("*I* can prove out of St. Thomas himself that the current interpretation is absolutely wrong"), and into the Conjunctive faith of Stage 5 ("I have no doubt, I never did doubt, that the old *answers* were defective"). It is not that we have traditionally been asking the wrong *questions* but our way of answering them failed to take into account modern scientific methodology and the dynamic of historical consciousness which characterize Stage 4 faith. The old questions were good (↓) but they need the best of current creativity (↑)

Table 8.2

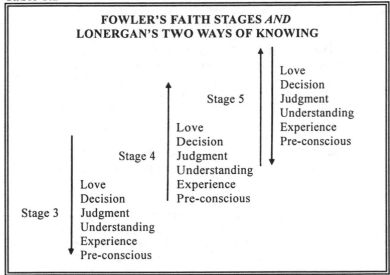

FOWLER'S FAITH STAGES *AND*
LONERGAN'S TWO WAYS OF KNOWING

to achieve the most accurate and helpful formulation of truth for our day (↑↓).

Lonergan was well aware of the limitations inherent in just passively receiving a tradition from the past (Stage 3) and also of the limitations rooted in ignoring the accumulated wisdom of the ages (Stage 4). He fought for the complementarity and integration of the two ways in adult development to produce creative agents of a new and improved tradition (Stage 5). His work is a philosophical foundation for the conjunctive meaning-making that Fowler calls Stage 5 faith. Cognizant of the power and grace of the conjunctive faith stance, Fowler says that the best thing that can happen to a person living Stage 4 faith is that they grow into Stage 5. Sadly, his research shows that only 7% of adults attain this level of faith consciousness.

There is an extraordinary *balance* between old and new, as I am sure is becoming apparent, in Lonergan's two ways of development (↑↓) and Fowler's conjunctive Stage 5 faith; a posture which is unacceptable to the majority of people who live their faith according to either the classicism of Stage 3 or the modernism of Stage 4. Remember that Bernard Lonergan's thought on Aquinas was attacked from both sides; as unorthodox by doctrinaire Thomists (Stage 3) and as holding onto a relic from the middle ages (scholastic thought) by

liberal thinkers (Stage 4). Lonerganian, Vernon Gregson, sums up the polarity in the critiques of Lonergan's position and their blindness to his "higher synthesis:"

> ... If one finds oneself firmly planted on one side or the other of the various dichotomies that Lonergan manages to transcend by a higher synthesis, if one belongs to one or other of the various groups that achieve ascendancy and then are supplanted in the shorter cycle, whether in the academy, the Church, or the wider society, will one not resent and reject a thought that would relativize one's own position by sublating it into a higher viewpoint, a viewpoint that brings forward what is to be brought forward and leaves behind what is to be left behind? Lonergan's thought meets with resistance from the advocates of both the old and the new, the right and the left, the reactionary, the liberal, and the Marxist. And the resistance is not due to the fact that, transcending these oppositions, he stands for nothing at all, but is rather the manifestation of an all too human tendency to oppose moving beyond the limitations of one's own position . . . (*Desires* 12).

It is precisely because of his lifelong effort to move "beyond the narrow confines of less inclusive viewpoints" and put forward the thinking consistent with Fowler's conjunctive and universalizing faith descriptions that Lonergan's work on methodology can be described as a remarkable achievement. Reaching up to the mind of Bernard Lonergan, just as Lonergan described his early work as reaching up to the mind of Thomas Aquinas, "will transform our own approach to every serious issue with which we attempt to come to terms; and precisely that transformation will be the most important ingredient that we can bring to the resolution of the issues with which we must be concerned today" (*Desires* 13).

That Bernard Lonergan was well aware of the tensions between what Fowler describes as Stage 3 and Stage 4 faith and also of the need to move to the integrated Stage 5 position is poignantly clear in a 1965 lecture at Marquette University, Milwaukee. At the time, the Second Vatican Council was preparing for its fourth (and last) session. In his concluding remarks, Lonergan offered this analysis of what would unfold within Roman Catholicism following the enthusiasm of the Council:

> Classical culture cannot be jettisoned without being replaced; and what replaces it cannot but run counter to classical expectations.

There is bound to be formed a solid right that is determined to live in a world that no longer exists. There is bound to be formed a scattered left, captivated by now this, now that new development, exploring now this and now that new possibility. But what will count is a perhaps not numerous center, big enough to be at home in both the old and the new, painstaking enough to work out one by one the transitions to be made, strong enough to refuse half-measures and insist on complete solutions even though it has to wait (*Collection* 245).

In a recent paper, Frederick Crowe characterized Lonergan's legacy as "a direction and momentum for others" to follow in working out the "transitions to be made."[15] For Lonergan the "center" was a position endowed with the best of the old tradition and the best of the new creativity. If I understand Fowler correctly, Lonergan's center is Conjunctive faith; a philosophical stance that includes an appreciation of both Stage 3 (traditional faith) and Stage 4 (autonomous faith).

Lonergan's "Conversions" and Fowler's Stage "Transitions"

I have argued that the parallel between Lonergan and Fowler is that Lonergan's way of tradition (from above downwards ↓), way of achievement (from below upwards ↑), and the totality of development as an integration of the two ways (↑↓) illuminate what Fowler describes as faith Stages 3, 4 and 5 respectively. At this point in our discussion I would like to go further in drawing a parallel between Lonergan and Fowler and suggest that the transitions between faith Stages 3 through 6 correspond to what Lonergan understands by intellectual, moral, and religious conversion.[16]

For Lonergan, intellectual conversion has to do with embracing and appropriating *for oneself* the dynamism that is foundational to the human search for meaning and truth. This *for oneself* is at the core of intellectual conversion (*meaningful* knowledge for Macmurray) — "one needs to know for oneself . . ." The move from Stage 3 faith to Stage 4 faith involves a similar *conversion*. Fowler states the case as follows:

> For a genuine move to Stage 4 to occur there must be an interruption of reliance on external sources of authority. The "tyranny of the they" — or the potential for it — must be undermined. In addition to . . . critical reflection on one's previous assumptive or tacit system of values . . . there must be, for Stage 4, a relocation of

Table 8.3

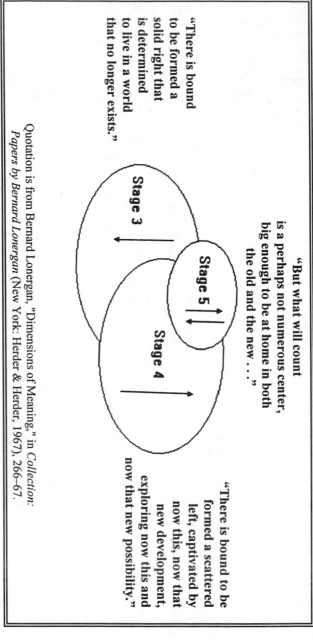

"There is bound
to be formed a
solid right that
is determined
to live in a world
that no longer exists."

"But what will count
is a perhaps not numerous center,
big enough to be at home in both
the old and the new . . . ."

Stage 3

Stage 5

Stage 4

"There is bound to be
formed a scattered
left, captivated by
now this, now that
new development,
exploring now this and
now that new possibility."

Quotation is from Bernard Lonergan, "Dimensions of Meaning," in *Collection: Papers by Bernard Lonergan* (New York: Herder & Herder, 1967), 266–67.

> authority within the self. While others and their judgments will
> remain important . . . their expectations, advice and counsel will be
> submitted to an internal panel of experts who reserve the right to
> choose and who are prepared to take responsibility for their choices
> (*Stages* 179).

Moral conversion, for Lonergan, requires a shift in the criterion
one uses for making decisions from personal satisfaction (what is good
for me) to communal values (what is good for others). Affirming and
appropriating for myself that my decisions about what to do are not
based on personal whim or satisfaction but on what is truly good or
worthwhile is key to a proper understanding of Lonergan's notion of
moral conversion.

Similarly, the movement from Fowler's Stage 4 to Stage 5 faith
involves a realization that autonomous individuality and freedom have
their limitations. I am part of a larger whole that needs to be taken
into account for my actions to be just (or "meaningful" in Macmurray's terminology). Fowler writes:

> . . . commitment to justice is freed from the confines of tribe,
> class, religious community or nation. And with the seriousness that
> can arise when life is more than half over, this stage [Stage 5] is ready
> to spend and be spent for the cause of conserving and cultivating the
> possibility of others' generating identity and meaning (*Stages* 198).

Lonergan's religious conversion arises out of intellectual and moral
conversion (*Method* 101) and, in the full critical sense is an ideal
which is rarely realized. Fowler, interestingly enough, has identified
only 0.5% of his inteviewees as at Stage 6 Universalizing faith.
Significant too is the fact that the movement from Conjunctive faith
to Universalizing faith, as many commentators on faith development
theory have noted, necessitates the introduction of "a particular 'content' — a particular image" having to do with God and religion:

> This image is Fowler's concept as a Christian theologian of the
> Jewish-Christian vision of the Kingdom of God as the fulfillment of
> faith. And this image determines a particular behavior — the capacity
> for "radical commitment to justice and love and . . . selfless passion
> for a transformed world."[17]

The connection between Fowler's understanding of the strengths
required for Stage 6 faith and Lonergan's understanding of religious

conversion seems obvious, especially when we recall that Fowler's rare examples of Universalizing faith are generally well known religious personages.

All of this leads me to diagram another connection between Lonergan and Fowler as in Table 8.4.

Table 8.4

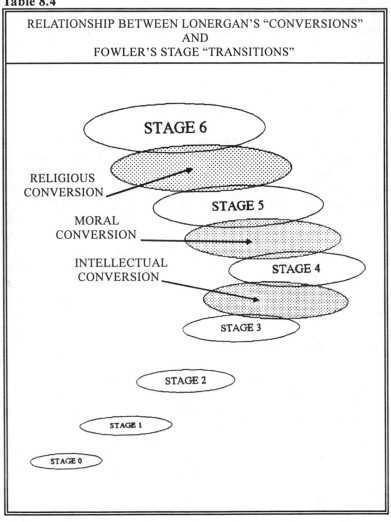

RELATIONSHIP BETWEEN LONERGAN'S "CONVERSIONS"
AND
FOWLER'S STAGE "TRANSITIONS"

STAGE 6

RELIGIOUS
CONVERSION

STAGE 5

MORAL
CONVERSION

STAGE 4

INTELLECTUAL
CONVERSION

STAGE 3

STAGE 2

STAGE 1

STAGE 0

Conclusion

This section in no way pretends to be a well worked out description of the similarities between Bernard Lonergan's epistemological model and James Fowler's faith development theory. What it does intend to propose, however, is that Lonergan's work provides a strong philosophical foundation for Fowler's empirical research and Fowler's research provides scientific verification of the dynamics of human consciousness which Lonergan has elucidated. If this proposal provokes reflection and dialogue about the dynamics of the ways human beings engage life, its purpose will have been achieved.

Macmurray, Lonergan, and Fowler

One of the things that excites me about all three thinkers under study is that their creative work is in continuity with what has gone before. They honor authentic tradition but at the same time don't accept it *uncritically*. What has been received must be investigated under both modernity's telescope and microscope and, in turn, subjected to a postmodern critique before it can be judged worthy. I am attracted by their concern to bring forward the best of our intellectual and faith traditions while at the same time not being blind to the searching questions generated in our present secular and scientific reality. With this thought in mind I want to use this final section to summarize my thoughts about Macmurray, Lonergan and Fowler under two headings; science and religion, and community.

Science and Religion

In Dayton, Tennessee, on July 21, 1925, John Scopes, a high school biology teacher, was found guilty of breaking state law by teaching Charles Darwins evolutionary *theory*. The so-called "monkey trial" featured celebrated criminal lawyer Clarence Darrow for the defense and three-time populist presidential candidate William Jennings Bryan as an assistant to the prosecution. The trial was later dramatized in *Inherit the Wind,* a Broadway play loosely based on the trial.[18] In a climactic scene from the stage play Darrow (Drummond) calls Bryan (Brady) to the stand as an expert in the bible and proceeds to use modern science to demolish his literal interpretation of scrip-

ture. In the minds of the liberal populus, allied with Freud's understanding of religion as "illusion," Darrow had demolished not just fundamentalist interpretations of the bible but *religion*. An excerpt from *Inherit the Wind* captures the animosity existing between the camps of science and religion in the early part of this century:

DRUMMOND Now tell me. Do you feel that every word that's written in this book should be taken literally?

BRADY Everything in the Bible should be accepted, exactly as it is given there.

DRUMMOND (*Leafing through the Bible*) Now take this place where the whale swallows Jonah. Do you figure that actually happened? . . .

BRADY I believe in a God who can make a whale and who can make a man and make both do what he pleases! . . .

DRUMMOND . . . I recollect a story about Joshua, making the sun stand still. Now as an expert, you tell me that's as true as the Jonah business. Right? (BRADY *nods, blandly*) That's a pretty neat trick. . . .

BRADY I have faith in the Bible!

DRUMMOND You don't have faith in the solar system.

BRADY (*Doggedly*) The sun stopped.

DRUMMOND Good (*Level and direct*) Now if what you say factually happened — if Joshua halted the sun in the sky — that means the earth stopped spinning on its axis; continents toppled over each other, mountains flew out into space. And the earth, arrested in its orbit, shriveled to a cinder and crashed into the sun (Turning) How come they missed *this* tidbit of news.

BRADY They missed it because it didn't happen.

DRUMMOND It must've happened. According to natural law. Or don't you believe in natural law, Colonel [Brady]? Would you like to ban Copernicus from the classroom along with Charles Darwin? Pass a law to wipe out all the scientific development since Joshua. Revelations — period!

BRADY (*Calmly, as if instructing a child*) Natural law was born in the mind of the Heavenly Father. He can change it, cancel it, use it as He pleases. . . .[19]

To show that the adverserial relationship between science and religion as dramatized in the "monkey trial" are not dead, I would like to offer two stories that shed light on this issue of the relationship between science and religion, one from the conservative right represented by fundamentalist religion and one from the liberal left of naive science.

A few years ago I had a student in my 'Psychology of Religion' class who was studying for the ministry in a conservative christian church. He found the first few months of the course quite difficult, particularly Freud's attack on religion and Skinner's behaviorist explanation of human living, but he persisted. Over time, he began to see that there were both strengths and weaknesses in the various theorists we encountered and even came to see elements of truth in Freud and Skinner. During a visit home for the winter vacation, his father saw the course text book[20] and told his son that it was 'written by the devil.' The son countered that he didn't agree with everything in the text but it did contain some significant truth and if that truth could not be integrated with his divinity studies then he would need to look for another church.

My second story recalls a brief exchange among participants in a seminar during my graduate studies in education. One of the members made reference to Bernard Lonergan during the discussion and another participant asked who Lonergan was. Having been informed that he was a "Canadian philosopher and theologian," he remarked, "I don't think I can learn anything from a theologian." Then, still another participant voiced my sentiments: "How sad."

I share these stories because one way to interpret the interest of Macmurray and Lonergan and Fowler in both science and religion as well as other fields is that they recognized the need for interdisciplinary work in attempting to resolve life's ultimate questions. Neither my student's father nor the new professor in graduate school could see beyond their own narrow horizons. All three of the thinkers we have been considering are aware that philosophy is just one brand of knowledge and philosophical answers must be integrated with those of the physical and biological scientists, social scientists, writers, poets and shamans.[21]

Macmurray, as we have seen, characterized himself as a Christian in that he stood "in the contemporary world for and with the movement that Jesus originated" but "outside all the Churches" because they "do not stand in and with that movement."[22] His boyhood attraction to science was reflected in his early articles and lifelong effort to conceive of science and religion as partners, not adversaries. Lonergan, a Catholic philosopher and theologian, offers a model of human knowing that shows how the so-called scientific method is really the way human beings know, period.[23] And Fowler, a theologian from the reform tradition, takes a seemingly religious concept, faith, and

gratefully draws on insights from developmental psychology to analyze its "human side." Their work echoes Abraham Maslow's thesis that "it is because both science and religion have been too narrowly conceived, and have been too exclusively dichotomized and separated from each other, that they have been seen to be two mutually exclusive worlds."[24] Spiritual values are not the exclusive possession of organized churches, but the general heritage of humankind.[25] Any important question worthy of consideration is a human question that can only be adequately answered cooperatively.

Community

To pick up on Fowler's understanding of faith as a verb and not a noun, we can characterize community as a verb; not as something that *is* but as something that people *do*. Let me illustrate this point with a story.

In July 1993 I was in Denver, Colorado, for a workshop on community building sponsored by the Foundation for Community Encouragement (FCE) begun by Dr. M. Scott Peck.[26] The focus of the five days was the building and maintaining of community according to the stage model Peck sets forth in *The Different Drum*.[27] On the last afternoon of the workshop one of the participants shared a dream that has stayed with me ever since and is relevant here. The central feature of the dream was a large workshop full of tiny little clay figures all busily working together at various tasks (a kind of Santa's workshop full of elves was the image that came to mind). The dreamer saw herself as above and apart from the scene looking down, conscious that the apparently disjointed activity in the workshop was being directed by some higher power. Her interpretation was that the scene represented the whole earth and that, just as Denver was a community building workshop for 175 participants from around the continent, the earth was the Creator's community building workshop. It had taken a great deal of work, pain and time before our Denver group blossomed forth in community, she shared, and it would take a little more time for the significantly larger and more complex earth community to achieve its glory.

In my opinion, the direction we must take in our search for a "personal" vision of community is expressed in the thought of John Macmurray, Bernard Lonergan, and James W. Fowler. Macmurray's ideal is a world of persons relating in "friendship." For Lonergan

"being in love" is the crowning level of human consciousness. And Fowler's highest stage is reserved for those willing to be "pioneers in the commonwealth of love and justice."

Today, of course, community includes our relationship not only with one another but with the fragile blue planet with which we live. First Galileo and Newton and more recently astronauts viewing the earth from space have forever changed the way we human beings conceive of our place in the universe. Dethroned from our exaggerated feeling of self-importance as the center of things, we now know ourselves to be inhabitants of a small, fragile planet circling an ordinary star at the edge of the Milky Way, one of more than one hundred billion galaxies. And the awareness is growing that our destiny is one with the destiny of that blue-green sphere thrown against the blackness of space. In the words of Scottish-American naturalist, John Muir (1838–1914), "when we try to pick out anything by itself, we find it hitched to everything else in the universe."[28]

Macmurray, Lonergan, and Fowler tell us that the most *real* world we live in is the world of relationship with our fellow human beings, with the Other and with Mother Earth. Without all of them, we experience a sense of enormous emptiness because our humanness is made in our relationships. We are gradually coming to full consciousness of the fact that we live in a participatory universe.

I often think of Bernard Lonergan's acknowledgement that while world community is still a "dream," dreams do in fact emerge from our unconscious "as an intimation of a reality to be achieved" (*Third Collection* 66).[29] I humbly suggest that the ecozoic "dream" of cultural historian and "geologian," Thomas Berry, and physicist and cosmologist, Brian Swimme, is such an intimation of a reality that *must* be achieved:

> As industrial humans multiplied into the billions to become the most numerous of all of Earth's complex organisms, as they decisively inserted themselves into the ecosystemic communities throughout the planet, drastically reducing earth's diversity and channeling the majority of the Gross Earth Product into human social systems, a momentous change in human consciousness was in process. Humans discovered that the universe itself is a developing community of beings. Humans discovered by empirical investigation that they were participants in this fifteen-billion-year sequence of transformations that had eventuated into the complex functioning Earth. A sustained and even violent assault by western intelligence upon the universe . . . had brought forth a radically new understanding of the universe,

not simply as a cosmos, but as a cosmogenesis, a developing community, one with an important role for the human in the midst of the
process. . . .
The future of earth's community rests in significant ways upon the
decisions to be made by the humans who have inserted themselves so
deeply into even the genetic codes of earth's process. This future will
be worked out in the tensions between those committed to the
technozoic, a future of increased exploitation of Earth as resource, all
for the benefit of humans, and those committed to the Ecozoic, a new
mode of human-earth relations, one where the well-being of the entire
Earth community is the primary concern.[30]

As a species, then, we are facing a problem of an order of magnitude never encountered by human beings on the planet before — the
issue now is survival, ours and the planet's. In these pages we have
grappled with three congruent philosophical models of *becoming*. The
world today Macmurray says "has reached the borders of Utopia,"[31]
yet Fowler's research shows that only 7% of adults (Lonergan's "not
numerous center") seemed to have crossed over. More of us need to
move into this new ecozoic consciousness to achieve a new humanity
living in harmony with Mother Earth.

In the Book of Deuteronomy, Moses sets forth the fundamental
option before the people: "I call heaven and earth to witness against
you today that I have set before you life and death, blessings and
curses. Choose life so that you and your descendants may live . . ."
(Deuteronomy 30:19). What we learn from Macmurray, Lonergan,
and Fowler is that we have before us a choice between a continuation
of old ways of being which are now shutting down the very life
systems of the planet and a new communal consciousness inviting us
to a new partnership in an Earth community. To engage you in a process of thought leading to action in this regard is why I have written
this book!

Notes

1. Abraham H. Maslow, *Religions, Values, and Peak-Experiences* (New
York: Penguin Books, 1970), 54–55.

2. I am reminded of an expression I heard somewhere: "impression
without expression leads to depression," which I take to mean that truth
(impression) which is not acted upon (expressed) makes us less than human
(depressed).

3. From 1870, when the Italian forces of unification marched into Rome, until 1929, when Mussolini and Pope Pius XI reached a settlement of the Roman Question, the Popes considered themselves prisoners in the Vatican, literally living behind a wall on 14.7 acres.

4. Marshall McLuhan, *The Gutenberg Galaxy* (Toronto: University of Toronto Press, 1962), 31.

5. Thomas Berry, "The Ecozoic Era," a paper presented as part of the E. F. Schumacher Society Lectures (October 19, 1991), 1.

6. Thomas Berry, "The Ecozoic Era," a paper presented as part of the E. F. Schumacher Society Lectures (October 19, 1991), 1.

7. John Macmurray, *The Philosophy of Jesus* (London: The Society of Friends, 1973), 3.

8. John Macmurray, *The Philosophy of Jesus* (London: The Society of Friends, 1973), 9.

9. The central image Fowler uses to describe people characterized by Stage 6 faith is that of "colonists in the Kingdom of God" or, as he phrases the same image today, "pioneers in the commonwealth of love and justice."

10. Craig Dykstra and Sharon Parks, eds., *Faith Development and Fowler* (Birmingham, AL: Religious Education Press, 1986), 2.

11. In Lonergan's model, the subject systematically searches for truth through empirical, intellectual, reasonable, and responsible levels of consciousness. It is this systematic aspect of the search by means of *two* ways of knowing which places Lonergan's work in the context of Fowler's Stage 5 faith, avoiding the dogmatism of Stage 3 and the relativism of Stage 4. It is my contention that all three of the thinkers discussed in this book write from a conjunctive (Fowler Stage 5) faith stance.

12. The great either/or debate which raged for centuries (and continues in some domains), can be characterized in the terminology of Fowler and Lonergan as a debate between Stage 3 faith and the traditional understanding of religion as from above downwards, on the one hand, and Stage 4 faith and the traditional understanding of science as from below upwards, on the other hand.

13. "Address by His Eminence Gerald Cardinal Carter, July 30, 1991," is printed in *Companions of Jesus, Pilgrims with Ignatius: Congress '91* (Toronto: Canadian Institute of Jesuit Studies, 1991), 32.

14. It seems to me that this is the rationale for the concept of the "loyal opposition" in the British parliamentary tradition — "loyal" is characteristic of Fowler's Stage 3 faith, "opposition" of Stage 4, wherreas the paradoxical phrase "loyal opposition" strikes me as compatible with Stage 5 faith.

15. Frederick E. Crowe, "An Expansion of Lonergan's Notion of Value," a paper presented at the twelfth annual Lonergan Workshop, Boston College, June 17–21, 1985. It is reprinted in Michael Vertin, ed., *Appropriating the Lonergan Idea* (Washington: The Catholic University of America Press, 1989), 344–59.

16. A similar suggestion is found in Brendan Carmody, S.J., "Faith Development: Fowler and Lonergan," *The Irish Theological Quarterly* 54, no. 2 (1988), 93–106.

17. Craig Dykstra and Sharon parks, eds., *Faith Development and Fowler* (Birmingham, AL: Religious Education Press, 1986), 144. The quotation within the quotation is from *Stages* 201.

18. Jerome Lawrence and Robert E. Lee, *Inherit the Wind* in Cy Groves *Plays on a Human Theme* (Toronto: McGraw-Hill Ryerson Limited, 1967). It opened at the National Theatre, New York, in 1955.

19. Jerome Lawrence and Robert E. Lee, Act 2 of *Inherit the Wind* in Cy Groves *Plays on a Human Theme* (Toronto: McGraw-Hill Ryerson Limited, 1967), 177–78.

20. David M. Wulff, *Psychology of Religion: Classic and Contemporary Views* (New York: John Wiley & Sons, 1991).

21. Macmurray, Lonergan and Fowler were positive in their evaluation of science and scientific methods. At the same time, all three recognized that, just as the seventeenth century world of René Descartes was sceptical about the revelations of religion, there is a great deal of scepticism in our twentieth century world but now it is with science!

22. John Macmurray, "Here I Stand," a somewhat autobiographical talk found in the John Macmurray Collection, Regis College, University of Toronto, Canada. It is undated.

23. The Vatican II document *Gaudium et Spes* states that there can be no conflict between the wisdom derived from honest research and the truth of the Christian faith because both come from God: "We cannot but deplore certain attitudes (not unknown among Christians) deriving from a shortsighted view of the rightful autonomy of science; they have occasioned conflict and controversy and have misled many into opposing faith and science" (# 36).

24. Abraham H. Maslow, *Religions, Values, and Peak-Experiences* (New York: Penguin Books, 1970), 11.

25. *Gaudium et Spes* (December 7, 1965), considered by many scholars to be the most advanced document of the Second Vatican Council, is a good example of expansive religion, a Stage 5 faith formulation influenced by Lonergan's work during the council. *Gaudium et Spes* speaks of the willingness of the Catholic church to work cooperatively with others (even non-Christians and atheists) to solve the many problems which threaten peaceful living and impede the progress that is God's will for the human family on this fragile planet: "The joy and hope, the grief and anguish of the men of our time, are the joy and hope, the grief and anguish of the followers of Christ as well. Nothing that is genuinely human fails to find an echo in their hearts . . ." (# 1). The document speaks of the "basic equality" of all people and reminds us of our responsibility to participate in the struggle for justice for our brothers and sisters everywhere as "moulders of a new humanity" (# 30). It is an extraordinary example of the dramatic and unprecedented changes in Roman Catholic practice and attitude mandated by Vatican II.

26. The FCE Mission Statement reads, in part: "FCE encourages people, in a fragmented world, to discover new and better ways of being together. Living, learning, and teaching the principles of community, we serve as a catalyst for individuals, groups and organizations . . ." The Foundation for Community Encouragement can be reached at 109 Danbury Road, Suite 8, Ridgefield, CT, 06877.

27. M. Scott Peck, *The Different Drum: Community-Making and Peace* (New York: Simon & Schuster, 1987).

28. Charlene Spretnak, *States of Grace: The Recovery of Meaning in the Postmodern Age* (San Francisco: HarperCollins, 1991), 30.

29. Bernard Lonergan, "Prolegomena to the Study of the Emerging Religious Consciousness of Our Time," in a paper on the *emerging* religious consciousness of our time presented at the Second International Symposium on Belief, Baden/Vienna, January, 1975. It is reprinted in *A Third Collection* 55–73.

30. Brian Swimme and Thomas Berry, *The Universe Story* (New York: Harper Collins Publishers, 1992), 14–15.

31. John Macmurray, *To Save From Fear*, a BBC Lenten talk (London: Friends Home Service Committee, 1964), 13.

GLOSSARY

Action: John Macmurray understands action as technically descriptive of human beings: "In the strict sense of the term only a person can 'act,' or in the proper sense 'do' anything" (*Self* 88-89). He adds that "action is activity in terms of the distinction between 'right' and 'wrong'." It is "knowledge-imbued activity" (*Self* 88–89).

Aquinas: In his *Summa Theologica*, Dominican friar Thomas Aquinas (1225–1274) provided the medieval, pre-modern world with a synthesis of Greek philosophy (Aristotle) and Christian thought (Augustine). This synthesis accepted the Aristotelian concept that science deals with *necessity*. With the birth of the modern world, an understanding that science is empirical and contingent replaced the Aristotelian notion of science as *necessary* and made the Thomistic synthesis obsolete. Within Roman Catholicism, Thomism was *the* theology until well into the twentieth century.

Aristotle: Aristotle (384–322 B.C.) studied in Athens under Plato who was his mentor and friend for twenty years (he eulogized Plato as "one who showed in his life and teachings how to be happy and good at the same time"). From 343–336 B.C., Aristotle served the king of Macedonia as tutor to his son Alexander (the Great). Later, in Athens, Aristotle founded a school (Lyceum) and came into his own as an empirical observer or scientist. He was the last and most influential of the classical Greek philosophers. Aristotelianism is not the opposite of Platonism but a development of that body of philosophic thought, correcting Plato's 'theory of forms' and his dualistic psychology. Aristotle begins his *Metaphysics* with the optimistic statement: "All men by nature desire to know." Elsewhere Aristotle defines the human being as a "rational animal." His understanding of what it is to be human has had a tremendous influence on subsequent thought in the Western World. For Aristotle, there are different degrees of knowledge; "mere experience," *techne* (technical knowledge), and *sophia* (wisdom). Wisdom is not utilitarian but aims to apprehend the first principles or first causes of reality; knowledge is for its own sake. Aristotle places the person who seeks for wisdom (knowledge for its own sake) higher than the person who seeks for technical knowledge with a view to bringing about some practical effect.

Baltimore Catechism: Catechisms are manuals of doctrine in a question and answer format; one of the first was Martin Luther's. The *Roman Catechism* of the Council of Trent (1566) served as the model for the *Catechism of the Third Plenary Council of Baltimore*, commonly called the *Baltimore Catechism*, first printed in 1885.

Behaviorism: Behaviorism is the philosophy (psychology) that strictly limits itself to the study of objective observable behavior. During his life, B.F. Skinner (1904–1990) was the standard-bearer of the behaviorist school of psychology. The following quotation from his autobiography makes his position clear: "I am sometimes asked, 'Do you think of yourself as you think of the organisms you study?' The answer is yes. So far as I know, my behavior at any given moment has been nothing more than the product of my genetic endowment, my personal history, and the current setting. . . . I have tried to *interpret* my life in the light of what I have learned from my research. . . . I do not believe that my life shows a type of personality à la Freud, an archetypal pattern à la Jung, or a schedule of development à la Erikson. There are a few abiding themes, but they can be traced to environmental sources rather than to traits of character. They became part of my life as I lived it; they were not there at the beginning to determine its course" (B. F. Skinner, *A Matter of Consequences*, Epilogue).

Buber: Martin Buber (1878–1965) was an influential Jewish philosopher whose central philosophical concept is "I-Thou" as descriptive of the relationship that ought to exist among human beings and between humanity and God. "Next to being the children of God," he wrote, "our greatest privilege is being the brothers [and sisters] of each other" (Martin Buber as quoted by Seymour Siegel in *Martin Buber: An Appreciation of His Life and Thought* [New York: American Friends of the Hebrew University, 1965], 6). Macmurray writes: "As a philosopher I could not see the Hegelian system as the summing up of all philosophy. . . . I found myself in these things much closer to the prophetic insight of one of the very greatest of modern thinkers, Martin Buber" (*Search* 24). For a comparison of the two, see Gerald A. Largo, "Two Prophetic Voices: Macmurray and Buber," *America* 129 (March 31, 1973): 283–86.

Cartesian: Adjective referring to the rationalist philosophy (and mathematics) of René Descartes [See **Descartes**].

Classicism: This term is more or less synonymous with the terms premodern, traditional, and feudal [See also **Scholasticism**].

Cognitional Theory: Cognitional (Latin *cogito*, I think) theory is about the process by which knowledge is acquired [See **Epistemology**].

Consciousness: Consciousness is inner awareness of myself and my activities.

Copernicus: Nicholas Copernicus (1473–1543), a polish Canon (a priest

with the right to vote for a new Bishop), proposed in *The Revolution of the Terrestrial Orbs* (published in 1543 and dedicated to the reigning Pope!) that the sun is at the center of our planetary system and the earth (which turns on itself) and the other planets revolve around it. The Inquisition condemned Copernicus and heliocentrism in 1616 and his work was put on the Index of Forbidden Books "until such time as it is corrected." The German atheistic philosopher, Ludwig Feuerbach, called Copernicus the "first revolutionary of modern times" (Hans Kung, *Freud and the Problem of God* [New Haven: Yale University Press, 1990], 3.

Critical Realist: Bernard Lonergan's position on knowing is that of a critical realist. He writes, "Only the critical realist can acknowledge the facts of human knowing and pronounce the world mediated by meaning to be the real world; and he can do so only inasmuch as he shows that the process of experiencing, understanding, and judging is a process of self-transcendence" (*Method* 239).

Crowe: Fr. Frederick Crowe, S.J. (b. 1915) has been a student, friend, co-worker, and interpreter of Lonergan for more than forty years. He is the co-founder (with Robert M. Doran, S.J.) of the Lonergan Research Institute of Regis College, Toronto and co-editor of the *Collected Works of Bernard Lonergan*, projected to be twenty-two volumes. A theologian in his own right, he is recognized as one of the leading experts in Lonergan's thought.

Darwin: Charles Darwin (1809–1882) is best known for his *Origin of Species* (1859) which proposed the theory of evolution and the idea that only the fittest living species survive. In 1871, Darwin published *The Descent of Man* which argued that human beings were not the product of an immediate creation as Genesis records but the result of a long evolutionary process. This was the origin of conflict in the early twentieth century between the *facts* of science and *revelation* of scripture. Teilhard de Chardin (1881–1955), a Jesuit priest-scientist, argued that the discoveries of science, far from threatening faith, show forth more deeply the glories of God's creation.

Descartes: René Descartes (1596–1650) was educated at the famous Jesuit College of La Fleche, France. Descartes soon rejected what he had been taught, passed through a period of scepticism and eventually sought certainty in his own rational powers. Impressed by the certainty and precision of mathematics, he invented co-ordinate geometry (Cartesian co-ordinate system). In philosophy, following the four rules of "doubt," he arrived at one indubitable principle, *cogito ergo sum* (I think, therefore, I am), upon which he built his philosophy. Considered the "father of modern philosophy," Descartes' two most important works are *Discourse on Method* (1637) and the *Meditations* (1642) [See also **Cartesian**].

Determinism: Determinists hold that all events, including human actions and choices, are fully determined by preceding events and states of affairs, making freedom of choice illusory.

Dialectic/al: Dialectic is the name Bernard Lonergan gives to the fourth functional specialty in his theological method. Dialectic, he acknowledges, is a term that is used with a variety of meanings but his use of the term "has to do with the concrete, the dynamic, and the contradictory . . . in the history of Christian movements. . . . The materials of dialectic, then, are primarily the conflicts centering in Christian movements" (*Method* 129). Dialectical, as used to describe Fowler's Stage 5 faith, refers to the characteristic of Conjunctive faith as seeking to resolve differences between opposing views as opposed to establishing one of the other as true.

Ecozoic: Ecozoic is a "biological term that can be used to indicate the integral *functioning* of life systems in their mutually enhancing relations." Ecozoic is a broader term than ecological (eco-logos "refers to an *understanding* of the interaction of things") (Thomas Berry, "The Ecozoic Era," a paper presented as part of the E. F. Schumacher Society Lectures (October 19, 1991), 9).

Empiricism: A philosophical viewpoint which holds that the 'real' is only what can be known through the senses [See **Hume**].

Epistemology: Epistemology [Greek *episteme*, knowledge] is more than just cognitional theory. Whereas cognitional theory is satisifed with a phenomenology of knowing, epistemology is concerned with the *validity* of our knowing [See **Cognitional Theory**].

Erikson: Erik H. Erikson (1902–1994) trained with Freud in Vienna before becoming Boston's first child psychoanalyst in 1933. He is recognized as one of the founders of the field of *life-span* development. His assertion (1963) that personality development does not end with the achievement of physical maturity but continues over the entire life span (eight ages in the life cycle) is one of his major contributions to psychology. More than a psychologist, Erikson is also an ethicist and supporter of religion, credited with having introduced the concept of the human spirit through the back door of psychoanalytic theory.

Ethics: In philosophy, ethics is the study of moral principles. The term comes from the Greek word *ethos* which in the plural means 'character'.

Existentialism: The existentialist maxim is "existence precedes essence"

(Jean-Paul Sartre). The point is that we are what we make of ourselves and we are also responsible for the self we create. Existentialism is in harmony with the approach to philosophy of both Macmurray and Lonergan. Existentialists can be divided roughly into theistic and atheist wings, understanding the critical problem of twentieth century philosophy in the alternatives *God* or *nothing*. The *nothing* alternative has been argued passionately by Karl Marx, Sigmund Freud, and others.

Form: The pre-Socratic philosophers in sixth century B.C. Greece were the first thinkers concerned to discover the basic 'stuff' or substance found in all things. According to the ancient Greek philosophers, things needed to be 'formed' to be 'real'. In Macmurray's terminology, their philosophical question was the 'form' of the material.

Fowler: James Fowler (b. 1940) and associates have done the ground breaking work on the application of developmental psychology to an understanding of faith (meaning-making) as developing.

Galileo: Galileo Galilei (1564–1642) was an Italian mathematician and physicist who discovered the laws of falling bodies. He used the newly invented telescope to prove the truth of Copernicus's theory that the earth and other planets revolve around the sun. His work brought him into conflict with the church. His influential Jesuit friend, Cardinal Robert Bellarmine (1542–1621), refused to look into his telescope because he said Galileo's proposition couldn't be so because it would contradict the Bible. In his defense, Galileo argued that in the Bible "the intention of the Holy Spirit is not to show us how the heavens move but how we get to heaven." Galileo was condemned by the Inquisition in 1633 and ended his days under house arrest. On October 31, 1992, Pope John Paul II accepted a report by the Pontifical Academy of Sciences which acknowledged that Galileo was correct!

Gifford Lectures: The Gifford Lectures on Natural Religion were inaugurated in 1888 with an endowment from Lord Adam Gifford, a Scottish jurist. They alternate between Glasgow and Edinburgh. *Varieties of Religious Experience* by William James represents his Gifford Lectures at the turn of the century. Physicist, A. S. Eddington presented the lectures for 1927 on the topic "The Nature of the Physical World." American philosopher of education, John Dewey, was a Gifford lecturer on the topic "The Quest for Certainty" (1929). Other lecturers include A. J. Ayer, Karl Barth, Henri Bergson, Rudolf Bultmann, and Alfred North Whitehead.

Hegel: Georg Friedrich Hegel (1770–1831) was a German Idealist philosopher whose thought had a major influence on nineteenth and twentieth century thought and history [See **Idealism/Idealist**].

Hooke: Robert Hooke (1653–1703), a physicist, invented the compound microscope which enabled us to see that the human body far from being a kind of complicated machine is a complex living *organism*.

Hume: David Hume (1711–1776) was the most important and influential of the British empiricists (knowledge is derived from sense experience). The sceptical approach of his most important philosophical work, *A Treatise of Human Nature*, established the limits of empiricism's claims to knowledge. On Hume, Lonergan writes: "Hume thought the human mind to be a matter of impressions linked together by custom. But Hume's own mind was quite original. Therefore, Hume's own mind was not what Hume considered the human mind to be" (*Method* 21) [See **Empiricism**].

Idealism/Idealist: This is the name applied to philosophies which in some way or other affirm that it is the mind (not the senses) which give us whatever knowledge we have of truth [See **Kant** and **Hegel**].

Intentionality: "Intentional," for Lonergan, does *not* mean deliberate. By intentionality he means that the operations of experiencing, understanding, judging, and deciding, in their very operation, *intend* objects; i.e., when I open my eyes, seeing is an *intentional* operation.

Jesuit: Jesuit is a shorthand designation for a member of the Society of Jesus, a religious order within the Roman Catholic church, founded in the mid-sixteenth century by Ignatius of Loyola. The initial two year formation period for Jesuits is the *Novitiate*. Those following the program are called Novices. In traditional Jesuit formation, the *Juniorate* refers to two years (following the Novitiate) devoted to the study of classics, literature, history, and modern languages. The term *Regency* is used to describe that period in Jesuit formation, which normally involves teaching in a Jesuit high school or college for two or three years, falling between the completion of philosophical studies and the beginning of theology. *Tertianship* is the final stage of Jesuit formation; a kind of second Novitiate following ordination to the priesthood.

Kant: In philosophical terms, Immanuel Kant (1724–1804) was a German idealist. Kant's three great critiques, *Critique of Pure Reason*, *Critique of Practical Reason*, and *Critique of Judgment*, provided a synthesis and new direction for philosophy. His major contribution was an attempt to synthesize empiricism and rationalism. The process of knowing was unified; without raw sense experience we would not become aware of any object but without understanding we would not be able to form an intelligible concept of it (See **Empiricism, Idealism**, and **Rationalism**).

Kierkegaard: Soren Kierkegaard (1813–1855) was a Danish religious philosopher. He is perhaps best known for his view that a "leap of faith" is required to take us from the ethical to the religious point of view. His thought is viewed as a precursor to existentialism [See **Existentialism**].

Kohlberg: Lawrence Kohlberg (1927–1987) was an American moral philosopher and educator. He is best known for his stage theory of cognitive moral development which was an addition to and elaboration of the work of Jean Piaget [See **Piaget**].

Lonergan: Bernard Lonergan (1904–1984) was critical of both traditional and modern ideas about knowing. Most of his life was devoted to developing an integrated and generalized method of inquiry which he saw as able to overcome modern divisions and fragmentation in knowledge.

Macmurray: Personalist philosopher John Macmurray (1891–1976) has been called "'the best-kept secret of British philosophy in the twentieth century.' He was frequently misunderstood; and when it seemed he was being understood, he was frequently rejected" (John Costello, in the Introduction to John Macmurray, *Reason and Emotion* [Atlantic Highlands, NJ: Humanities Press International, Inc., 1992], vii).

Metaphysics: Metaphysics (Greek *meta* means beyond and *physics* refers to the physical world) is the branch of philosophy which deals with the fundamental questions about existence, the nature of reality, cause and effect, being, and God.

Method: For Lonergan, "a method is a normative pattern of recurrent and related operations yielding cumulative and progressive results" (*Method* 4). In *Insight* Lonergan usually calls this structured process the "generalized empirical method" and in *Method* the "transcendental method." He also refers to it as the "rock" and "common ground" (*Insight* 19–20), "normative source of meaning" (*Third Collection*176), and often just as "method."

Modernism/Modernity: The intellectual foundations of the modern world were conceived in the Renaissance and born in the Enlightenment. In the late nineteenth and early twentieth centuries "modernism" was a term applied to the movement within Christian theology seeking to align itself with modernist trends in philosophy, literature, history, and science. As regards the interpretation of scripture, Modernists embraced liberal views. Using the work of liberal Protestant bible scholars, Catholic scholars, like Alfred Loisy (1857–1940) and George Tyrrell (1861–1909), hoped to close the growing gap between the Catholic Church and the modern world. Their working principle

was that the discoveries of modern science had made much of the traditional language of Catholic belief obsolete and even ridiculous at times. Critics argued that their use of the historical-critical method of interpretation emptied church doctrine of its traditional meaning and content. Modernism was condemned by Pope Pius X in his encyclical *Pascendi Dominici Gregis* (September, 8, 1907) which made it quite clear than any new idea in theology, church history or scripture study was suspect. Modernism was described as "the synthesis of all heresies" intent on "the destruction not of the Catholic religion alone but of all religion." The "remedies" Pius X proposed included the study of scholastic philosophy and theology, church censorship of publications, and "diocesan watch committees." Many respected Catholic scholars felt the Pope's fury; Loisy and Tyrrell were excommunicated when they refused to reconsider their "modernist" positions [See **Classicism**, its opposite].

Naive Realism: A philosophical viewpoint which identifies knowing with seeing.

Newton: British mathematician and thinker, Sir Isaac Newton (1642–1726), is best known for his theory of universal gravitation. His mathematical representation of nature became the paradigm for modern science.

Normative: To say that there is a normative pattern in the unfolding of the generalized empirical method is to say that the dynamic structure of human consciousness cannot change or be revised. Although revision of the structure is not possible, a more adequate account of the structure is always possible and Lonergan gave a progressively more adequate account of the structure over his career. Normativity does not mean that the structure cannot be violated; as free agents we can choose to be inattentive, imperceptive, unreasonable and irresponsible.

Pascal: Blaise Pascal (1623–1662) was a French mathematician, physicist, and religious thinker. Already at age nineteen he had invented a calculating machine that worked and his research into hydrodynamics and fluid mechanics is preserved in Pascal's Law which is the basis for hydraulics. His religious thought which emphasized the reasons of the heart over those of rationalism or empiricism is found in his *Pensées* (*Thoughts*) published posthumously by his friends. He felt that metaphysical proofs for God's existence had very little impact on people. "Pascal's wager" (*Pensées* 149–153) recommends that we bet on God because if we win we win everything and if we lose we really lose nothing because religious people are happier anyway. Elsewhere (*Pensées* 155–163), Pascal says that there are only two kinds of reasonable people; those who serve God with all their heart because they know God, and those who seek God with all their heart because they

don't know God.

Personal: John Macmurray writes: "The unit of personal existence is not the individual, but two persons in personal relation. . . . we are persons not by individual right, but in virtue of our relation to one another. The personal is constituted by personal relatedness. The unit of the personal is not the 'I', but the 'You and I'" (*Persons* 61).

Personalism/ist: Both John Macmurray and Bernard Lonergan are personalist philosophers in that their central understanding of humanness is not as "thinking thing" but as human subject, as moral "agent," even as capable of relating personally out of "friendship" (love). In philosophy, the term personalism generally refers to a movement originating in the nineteenth century (usually theistic and stressing the value of the free, responsible human person) as a reaction to the prevelant materialism (Hegel), evolutionaism (Darwin), and idealism (Kant).

Piaget: Jean Piaget (1896–1980) dedicated his life to the "biological explanation of knowledge" and the relationship between this knowledge and religion. He published more than sixty books and is ranked as one of the greatest geniuses of the twentieth century and this century's foremost theorist in human intellectual development. Before Piaget, most educators thought intelligence (fixed at birth) was measured according to the amount of knowledge acquired over time. Piaget demonstrated that growth in intelligence takes place in stages. It is not more knowledge that is added from stage to stage but transformations of mind. A good metaphor for the process Piaget uncovered is the metamorphosis of a caterpillar into a butterfly.

Plato: Plato (c. 427–347 B.C.) was a student of Socrates. One of his most notorious and often quoted remarks is: "I thank God that I have been born a Greek and not a barbarian, a free man and not a slave, a man and not a woman; but above all that I have been born in the age of Socrates." Plato's Academy in Athens can be thought of as the first European University. His distinction between soul (*psyche*) and body (or mind and matter) and his emphasis on rational thought has had a significant impact on the Western philosophical tradition. Neo-Platonism exercised a great influence on Christianity (Augustine was a neo-Platonist) and Plato has been called the most influential philosopher of the early Christian Church even though he died about 350 years before the birth of Jesus! In *Process and Reality*, Alfred North Whitehead wrote: "The safest general characterization of the European philosophical tradition is that it consists of a series of footnotes to Plato."

Positivism: Positivists admire the procedures of natural science and disdain intuitive or speculative approaches to knowledge.

Postmodern: This term first appeared in the 1930's as descriptive of new form of architecture. Broadly, it means that which takes us beyond the failed assumptions of modernity. As I am using the term it refers to a sense that the "modern" is in need of reconception; a revisioning along holistic lines. "Constructive," "deconstructive," or "ecological" postmodernism "recognizes not only that all beings are structurally related through our cosmological lineage, but also that all beings are internally constituted by relations with others, even at the molecular level" (Charlene Spretnak, *States of Grace* [San Francisco: HarperCollins, 1993], 20). As used in this book, "postmodern" is more or less synonomous with John Macmurray's understanding of the "personal" [See also **Ecozoic, Personal** and **Personalism/ist**].

Quaker: A Quaker is a member of the Society of Friends, a "church" founded in seventeenth century England by George Fox. Quakers reject the organization of traditional churches and dogmatic creeds. They are known for their pacifism and humanitarian works. With no formal creed or clergy they put their faith in the "inward light" of God's guidance. Persecuted in England, many Quakers emigrated to America where they have prospered and today have their largest concentration of members (c. 130,000).

Rationalism: Rationalism is the philosophical position that reality has a logical structure that can be known by means of deductive reasoning. Descartes is a rationalist. By the nineteenth century, rationalism, allied with liberalism, was understood as hostile to religion. In defense of Christianity, John Henry Newman wrote: "Rationalism is a certain abuse of Reason; that is, a use of it for purposes for which it was never intended, and is unfitted. To rationalize in matters of Revelation is to make our reason the standard and measure of the doctrine revealed. . . . The Rationalist makes himself his own center, not his Maker . . ." (John Henry Newman, *Essays Critical and Historical* [London: Longmans, Green, & Co., 1895], 31) [See **Descartes**].

Relativism: Relativists hold that all knowledge is relative to the historical and personal context in which it is formulated and interpreted.

Romanticism: The "Romantic" period in Western cultural history covers the eighteenth and nineteenth centuries. Romantic thinkers saw *reason* solely as that within us which enables us to produce science. *Faith*, which really mattered, was our capacity for aesthetic experience. The Romantics substituted the artist's standpoint for the scientist's as the basis of our knowledge of the real. Their concerns were ideas about the 'true,' the 'good,' the 'beautiful' (the Romantic poet Keats wrote, "Beauty is truth"). The productive spontaneity of the imagination (an artistic activity, consisting in combining the elements of experience in a way that is not given in experience) underlies all experience, and particularly all cognition (knowing). This is an

activity of synthesis. It is the source of knowledge. Therefore, all knowledge is synthetic [See **Rousseau**].

Rousseau: Jean-Jacques Rousseau (1712–1778) argued for *feeling* rather than *reason* as the basis for philosophy. He argued in *Discourse on the Arts and Sciences* that the arts and science had "degraded" human beings and that before the development of civilization human beings were perhaps "rude" but "natural." His political theory (Social Contract) played a major influence during the French Revolution and continued through the period of the German Enlightenment (*Self* 32) [See **Romanticism**].

Scholasticism: In the Collins English Dictionary (1986), scholasticism is defined as "the system of philosophy, theology, and teaching that dominated medieval western Europe and was based on the writings of the Church fathers and (from the twelfth century) Aristotle" [See **Classicism**].

Second Vatican Council: The twenty-first ecumenical council of the Catholic church, the second such council held in the Vatican, took place between 1962 and 1965. Vatican II has been called the most important event in the history of the Church since the Protestant Reformation. Karl Rahner said that "with the Second Vatican Council, the Church . . . has expressly and consciously become a world Church. . . . The Second Vatican Council is the first council of a World Church that really wants to be a World Church and not a Church with European exports to all parts of the world. . . . This Council also brought to an end . . . a neo-scholastic period of theology" (Karl Rahner, *I Remember: An Autobiographical Interview*, 88– 89). It is fair to say that most of the laity, clergy and religious were not prepared for the cultural and religious revolution that Vatican II unleased in the Catholic church.

Self-Appropriation: Self-appropriation, self-affirmation, self-knowledge is central to the thought of Bernard Lonergan. It is on the basis of our knowledge and appropriation of our own interior consciousness that we come to appreciate who we are as human beings and what is true and good.

Self-Transcendence: As John Macmurray and Bernard Lonergan use the term they mean it to refer to pointing beyond oneself.

Society of Friends: [See **Quaker**].

Transcendent/Transcendental: Transcendent refers to God. Transcendental (outside of oneself) is used by Lonergan to refer to a type of knowledge, a method for achieving knowledge. It is because the levels of consciousness are so foundational that Lonergan calls them "transcendental."

They transcend all other methods and are operative in all other methods. One first uses the method which one is (the transcendental method is no mere technique or procedure, it is ourselves, the dynamic structure of our creativity) to establish any other technique or procedure, or method, one will use. For example, to decide on the technique to be used in building a bridge or the procedure for filling out the income tax form, one first gathers data, seeks to understand the data, makes judgments about truth and takes decisions about what is the right way to proceed.

Transcendental Precepts: The transcendental precepts or "transcendental imperatives" are, for Lonergan, "native spontaneities and inevitabilities."

Ultramontanism: Literally the word means "on the other side of the mountains" (Alps). It refers to a movement within Roman Catholicism favoring strong centralized authority under the pope.

Vatican II: [See **Second Vatican Council**].

BIBLIOGRAPHY

Astley, Jeff, and Leslie Francis, eds. *Christian Perspectives on Faith Development: A Reader.* Grand Rapids, MI: William B. Eerdmans Publishing Company, 1992.

Bach, George R. and Ronald M. Deutsch. *Pairing: How to Achieve Genuine Intimacy.* New York: Avon Books, 1971.

Barnes, Kenneth C. *Energy Unbound: The Story of Wennington School.* York, England: Williams Sessions Ltd., 1980.

Barnes, Kenneth, Kathleen Lonsdale, and John Macmurray. *Quakers Talk to Sixth Formers: A Series of Broadcasts.* London: Friends Home Service Committee, 1970.

Baur, M. "A Conversation with Hans-Georg Gadamer," *Method: Journal of Lonergan Studies* 8, no. 1 (March 1990): 1–13.

Bellah, Robert N., et al. *Habits of the Heart.* Berkeley: University of California Press, 1985.

Berry, Thomas. *The Dream of the Earth.* San Francisco: Sierra Club Books, 1988.

———. "The Ecozoic Era," a paper presented as part of the E. F. Schumacher Society Lectures, October 19, 1991.

Bibby, Reginald W. *Fragmented Gods: The Poverty and Potential of Religion in Canada.* Toronto: Irwin Publishing, 1987.

———. *Unknown Gods: The Ongoing Story of Religion in Canada.* Toronto: Stoddart Publishing Co. Limited, 1993.

Buber, Martin. *I and Thou.* Translated by Ronald Gregor Smith. New York: Charles Scribner's Sons, 1958.

Burnham, Frederic B., ed. *Postmodern Theology: Christian Faith in a Pluralist World.* San Francisco: Harper & Row, Publishers, 1989.

Carey, John J. *Carlyle Marney: A Pilgrim's Progress.* Macon, GA: Mercer University Press, 1980.

Carson, Harry A. "Macmurray's Prophetic Voice," *America* 129, no. 7 (September 15, 1973): 172–74.

Carter, Gerald Emmett. "Address by His Eminence Gerald Emmett Cardinal Carter," July 30, 1991, in *Companions of Jesus: Pilgrims with Ignatius.* Toronto: Canadian Institute of Jesuit Studies, 1991: 26–34.

Catechism of the Catholic Church. Ottawa: Canadian Conference of Catholic Bishops, 1994.

Chiban, John. "Intrinsic and Extrinsic Religious Motivation and Stages of Faith." Th.D. dissertation, Harvard Divinity School, 1980.

Coles, Robert. *Walker Perry: An American Search.* Boston: Little, Brown & Company, 1978.

Conn, Walter. *Christian Conversion: A Developmental Interpretation of Autonomy and Surrender.* New York: Paulist Press, 1986.

Contemporary Authors 104. Edited by Frances C. Locher. Detroit: Gale

Research Company, 1982: 154.

Costello, John E., S.J., Introduction to *Reason and Emotion* by John Mac-murray. Atlantic Highlands, NJ: Humanities Press International, Inc., 1991.

Crapps, Robert W. *An Introduction to Psychology of Religion*. Macon, GA: Mercer University Press, 1986.

Creamer, David G. "Faith Development in Young Adult Catholics," *Insight*, no. 4. Ottawa: Canadian Conference of Catholic Bishops (1991): 56–73.

Crowe, Frederick E. *Lonergan*. Outstanding Christian Thinkers Series. Series Editor Brain Davies, OP. Collegeville, MN: The Liturgical Press, 1992.

————. *The Lonergan Enterprise*. Cambridge, MA: Cowley Publications, 1980.

————. *Old Things and New: A Strategy for Education*. Atlanta: Scholar's Press, 1985.

————. *Appropriating the Lonergan Idea*. Edited by Michael Vertin. Washington, DC: The Catholic University of America Press, 1989.

Crysdale, Cynthia S. W. *Lonergan and Feminism*. Toronto: University of Toronto Press, 1994.

Davies, Brian. *God and the New Physics*. New York: Simon and Schuster, 1983.

Dictionary of Jesuit Biography: Ministry to English Canada 1842–1987. Toronto: Canadian Institute of Jesuit Sources, 1991.

Doran, Robert M. *Theology and the Dialectics of History*. Toronto: University of Toronto Press, 1990.

————. "Collected Works of Bernard Lonergan, S.J.," *America* 165, no. 2 (July 27, 1991): 46–48.

Droege, Thomas A. *Faith Passages and Patterns*. Philadelphia: Fortress Press, 1983.

Duncan, A. R. C. "No Man is an Island . . .," *Listening: Journal of Religion and Culture* 10, no. 2 (Spring, 1975): 40–53.

Dunne, Tad. *Lonergan and Spirituality: Towards a Spiritual Integration*. Chicago: Loyola University Press, 1985.

Dykstra, Craig, and Sharon Parks, eds. *Faith Development and Fowler*. Birmingham, AL: Religious Education Press, 1986.

Eigo, Francis, ed. *From Alienation to At-Oneness*. Villanova University Press, 1977.

Erikson, Erik H. *Identity and the Life Cycle*. New York: W. W. Norton & Company, 1980.

————. *The Life Cycle Completed: A Review*. New York: W.W. Norton & Company, 1982.

————. *Young Man Luther: A Study in Psychoanalysis and History*. New York: W. W. Norton & Company, 1958.

Flannery, Austin, ed. *Vatican Council II: The Conciliar and Post Conciliar Documents*. Vol. I. Northport, NY: Costello Publishing Company, 1988.

Fleming, D. L. *The Spiritual Exercises of St. Ignatius: A Literal Translation and a Contemporary Reading.* St. Louis: The Institute of Jesuit Sources, 1978.

Ford-Grabowsky, Mary. "The Concept of Christian Faith in the Light of Hildegard of Bingen and C. G. Jung: A Critical Alternative to Fowler." Ph.D. dissertation, Princeton University, 1985.

———. "Flaws in Faith-Development Theory," *Religious Education* 82, no. 1 (1987): 80–93.

———. "The Fullness of the Christian Faith Experience: Dimensions Missing in Faith Development Theory," *Journal of Pastoral Care* 41, no. 1 (1987), 39–41

———. "The Journey of a Pilgrim: An Alternative to Fowler," *The Living Light* 24, no. 3 (1988): 242–254.

———. "What Developmental Phenomenon is Fowler Studying?", *Journal of Psychology & Christianity* 5, no. 3 (1986): 5–13.

Forest, Jim. "A Very Public Hermit," *The Tablet* (December 25, 1993/ January 1, 1994), 1685.

Fowler, James W. *Becoming Adult, Becoming Christian: Adult Development and Christian Faith.* San Francisco: Harper & Row, 1984.

———. *Faith Development and Pastoral Care.* Philadelphia: Fortress Press, 1987.

———. "Fowler on Faith," in *Christianity Today* (June 13, 1986): 7-I–8-1

———. "Keeping Faith With God and Our Children: A Practical Theological Perspective," *Religious Education* 89, no. 4 (Fall, 1994): 543–60.

———. "Stages of Faith: Reflections on a Decade of Dialogue," *Christian Education Journal* 13 , no. 1 (1992): 13–23.

———. *Stages of Faith: The Psychology of Human Development and the Quest for Meaning.* San Francisco: Harper & Row, 1981.

———. *To See the Kingdom: The Theological Vision of H. Richard Niebuhr.* Nashville: Abingdon Press, 1974.

———. *Weaving the New Creation: Stages of Faith and the Public Church.* San Francisco: Harper Collins, 1991.

Fowler, James W. and Sam Keen. *Life Maps: Conversations on the Journey of Faith.* Waco, TX: Word, Inc., 1978.

Fowler, James W., Robin W. Lovin, et al. *Trajectories in Faith: Five Life Stories.* Nashville: Abingdon, 1980.

Fowler, James W., Antoine Vergote, et al. *Toward Moral and Religious Maturity.* Morristown, NJ: Silver Burdett, 1979.

Fowler, James W., Karl Ernst Nipkow, and Friedrich Schweitzer, eds. *Stages of Faith and Religious Development: Implications for Church, Education, and Society.* New York: The Crossroad Publishing Company, 1991.

Frankl, Viktor. *The Unconscious God.* New York: Washington Square Press, 1985.

Freire, Paulo. *Pedagogy of the Oppressed.* New York: Seabury Press, 1970.

Freud, Sigmund. *The Future of an Illusion.* Edited and translated by James

Strachey. New York: W. W. Norton & Company, Inc., 1961.

Fromm, Erich. *Psychoanalysis and Religion.* New Haven, CT: Yale University Press, 1950.

Gandhi, M. K. *My Autobiography.* Boston: Beacon Press, 1957.

Gilligan, Carol. *In A Different Voice.* Cambridge, MA: Harvard University Press, 1982.

Goldman, Ari L. *The Search for God at Harvard.* New York: Times Books, 1991.

Goldman, Ronald. *Readiness for Religion: A Basis for Developmental Religious Education.* London: Routledge & Kegan Paul, 1965.

Gregson, Vernon, ed. *The Desires of the Human Heart: An Introduction to the Theology of Bernard Lonergan.* Mahwah, NJ: Paulist Press, 1988.

Griffin, David Ray, ed. *Spirituality and Society: Postmodern Visions.* New York: State University of New York Press, 1988.

Groome, Thomas H. *Christian Religious Education.* San Francisco: Harper & Row, 1980.

———. *Sharing Faith: A Comprehensive Approach to Religious Education and Pastoral Ministry.* New York: Harper Collins Publishers, 1991.

Haughton, Rosemary. *The Catholic Thing.* Springfield, IL: Templegate Publishers, 1979.

Helminiak, Daniel A. *Spiritual Developemnt: An Interdisciplinary Study.* Chicago: Loyola University Press, 1987.

Hennessey, Thomas, ed. *Values and Moral Education.* New York: Paulist Press, 1976.

Herberg, Will. *Protestant-Catholic-Jew.* Garden City, NY: Doubleday, 1960.

Hiebert, Dennis Wayne. "Schools of Faith: The Effect of Liberal Arts, Professional, and Religious Education on Faith Development." Ph.D. Dissertation, University of Manitoba, Winnipeg, MB, 1992.

How Faith Grows: Faith Development and Christian Education. London: National Society/Church House Publishing, 1991.

Kegan, Robert. *The Evolving Self: Problem and Process in Human Development.* Cambridge, MA: Harvard University Press, 1982.

King, Coretta Scott, ed. *The Words of Martin Luther King, Jr.* New York: Newmarket Press, 1983.

Kung, Hans. *Freud and the Problem of God.* New Haven: Yale University Press, 1990.

Largo, Gerald A. "Two Prophetic Voices: Macmurray and Buber," *America* 128, no. 12 (March 31, 1973): 283–86.

Lawrence, Jerome and Robert E. Lee. *Inherit the Wind.* In Cy Groves *Plays on a Human Theme.* Toronto: McGraw-Hill Ryerson Limited, 1967.

Lawrence, Linda. "Stages of Faith," *Psychology Today* 17, no. 11 (November, 1983): 56–62.

Leddy, Mary Jo and Mary Ann Hinsdale, eds. *Faith That Transforms.* New York: Paulist Press, 1987.

Leddy, Mary Jo, Bishop Remi de Roo and Douglas Roche. *In the Eye of the Catholic Storm.* Toronto: Harper Collins Publishers, Ltd., 1992.

Lewis, C. S. *Surprised by Joy.* London: Collins Fount, 1977.

Liddy, Richard M. *Transforming Light: Intellectual Conversion in the Early Lonergan.* Collegeville, MN: The Liturgical Press, 1993.

————. *Collection.* Vol. 4 of the *Collected Works of Bernard Lonergan.* Edited by Frederick E. Crowe and Robert M. Doran. Toronto: University of Toronto Press, 1988. *Collection* was first published in 1967.

————. *Insight: A Study of Human Understanding.* Vol. 3 of the *Collected Works of Bernard Lonergan.* Edited by Frederick E. Crowe and Robert M. Doran. Toronto: University of Toronto Press, 1992. *Insight* was first published in 1957.

————. *Method in Theology.* Toronto: University of Toronto Press for Lonergan Research Institute, 1990. *Method in Theology* was first published in 1972.

————. "Questionnaire on Philosophy," *Method: Journal of Lonergan Studies* 2, no. 2 (October 1984): 1–35.

————. *A Second Collection.* Edited by William F.J. Ryan and Bernard J. Tyrrell. Philadelphia: The Westminster Press, 1974.

————. *A Third Collection: Papers by Bernard J.F. Lonergan, S.J.* Edited by Frederick E. Crowe, S.J. New York: Paulist Press, 1985.

————. *Topics in Education.* Vol. 10 of the *Collected Works of Bernard Lonergan.* Edited by Frederick E. Crowe and Robert M. Doran, revising and augmenting the unpublished text prepared by James Quinn and John Quinn. Toronto: University of Toronto Press, 1993. These lectures were delivered at Xavier University, Cincinnati, in August, 1959.

————. *Understanding and Being.* Vol. 5 of the *Collected Works of Bernard Lonergan.* Edited by Elizabeth A. Morelli and Mark D. Morelli; revised and augmented by Frederick E. Crowe with the collaboration of Elizabeth A. Morelli, Mark D. Morelli, Robert M. Doran, and Thomas V. Daly. Toronto: University of Toronto Press, 1990. *Understanding and Being*, the Halifax Lectures on *Insight*, was first published in 1980.

————. *Verbum: Word and Idea in Aquinas.* Edited by David B. Burrell. Notre Dame: University of Notre Dame Press., 1967.

————. *The Way to Nicea: The Dialectical Development of Trinitarian Theology*, a translation by Conn O'Donovan from the first part of *De Deo trino.* London: Darton, Longman & Todd, 1976.

Lonergan Research Institute *Bulletin*, nos. 4–6, November 1989–91. Toronto: Lonergan Research Institute.

Lovelock, J. E. *Gaia: A New Look at Life on Earth.* Oxford: Oxford University Press, 1979.

Macmurray, John. "Address to Wennington Students," June 12, 1949, John Macmurray Collection, Regis College, University of Toronto, Canada.

————. "Beyond Knowledge," in *Adventure: The Faith of Science and the Science of Faith.* Edited by B. H. Streeter. New York: Macmillan, 1928,

21–45.

―――. *The Boundaries of Science*. London: Faber & Faber Limited, 1939.
―――. *Challenge to the Churches*. London: Faber & Faber Limited, 1941.
―――. "Christianity — Pagan or Scientific?," *The Hibbert Journal* 24, no. (1926): 421–33.
―――. *The Clue to History*. London: Student Christian Movement (SCM) Press, 1938.
―――. *Conditions of Freedom*. Atlantic Highlands, NJ: Humanities Press International, 1993. Based on the 1949 Chancellor Dunning Trust Lectures delivered at Queen's University in Kingston, ON and first published in Toronto: The Ryerson Press, 1949.
―――. *Constructive Democracy*. London: Faber & Faber Limited, 1943.
―――. *Creative Society*. London: Faber & Faber Limited, 1935.
―――. *Freedom in the Modern World*. Atlantic Highlands, NJ: Humanities Press International, 1992. *Freedom in the Modern World* was first published in 1932.
―――. "Here I Stand," John Macmurray Collection, Regis College, University of Toronto, Canada. It is not dated.
―――. *Interpreting the Universe*. London: Faber & Faber, 1933.
―――. "Is Art a Form of Apprehension or a Form of Expression?," *Proceedings of the Aristotelian Society* (Supplement 5, 1925): 173–89.
―――. "Logic and Psychology," an unpublished paper in the John Macmurray Collection, Regis College, University of Toronto, Canada.
―――. "The Nature of Reason," *Proceedings of the Aristotelian Society* 35 (1934–35): 137–48.
―――. "Objectivity in Religion," in *Adventure: The Faith of Science and the Science of Faith*. Edited by B. H. Streeter. New York: Macmillan, 1928, 177–215.
―――. *Persons in Relation*. Atlantic Highlands, NJ: Humanities Press International, 1991. *Persons in Relation* was first published in 1961 by Faber & Faber, London.
―――. *Philosophy of Communism*. London: Faber & Faber Limited, 1933.
―――. *The Philosophy of Jesus*. London: The Society of Friends, 1973.
―――. Postscript to *Green Pastures* by Mark Connelly. London: Delisle, 1963.
―――. *Reason and Emotion*. Atlantic Highlands, NJ: Humanities Press International, 1991. *Reason and Emotion* was first published in 1935.
―――. *Religion, Art, and Science*. Liverpool: Liverpool University Press, 1961.
―――. "Science and Objectivity," *Listening: Journal of Religion and Culture* 10, no. 2 (Spring, 1975): 7–23.
―――. *Search for Reality in Religion*. Swarthmore Lecture Pamphlet. London: Friends Home Service Committee, 1969. The Swarthmore Lecture was first published in 1965, the year of its presentation, by

George Allen and Unwin Limited.

————. *The Self as Agent*. Atlantic Highlands, NJ: Humanities Press International, 1991. *The Self as Agent* was first published in 1957 by Faber & Faber, London.

————. *Structure of Religious Experience* (Terry Lecture at Yale). London: Faber & Faber, 1936.

————. *To Save From Fear*, a BBC Lenten talk. London: Friends Home Service Committee, 1964.

————. "They Made A School," a handwritten manuscript, dated December 4, 1968. It is found in the Macmurray Collection, Regis College, University of Toronto.

————. "Ye Are My Friends," a 1943 address to the Student Christian Movement, issued as a pamphlet by the Friends Home Service Committee in 1943 and reprinted many times.

Marney, Carlyle Marney. *The Recovery of the Person*. Nashville: Abingdon, 1979.

Maslow, Abraham H. *Religions, Values, and Peak-Experiences*. New York: Penguin Books, 1970.

McBrien, Richard P. *Catholicism* (Study Edition). San Francisco: Harper & Row, Publishers, 1981.

McCarthy, Michael H. *The Crisis of Philosophy*. Albany, NY: State University of New York Press, 1990.

McLuhan, Marshall. *The Gutenberg Galaxy*. Toronto: University of Toronto Press, 1962.

McShane, P., ed. *Foundations of Theology* Dublin: Gill and Macmillan Ltd, 1971.

Merton, Thomas. "Is the World a Problem?," *Commonweal* 84, no. 11 (1966): 305–309.

————. *The Seven Story Mountain*. New York: Harcourt, Brace and Company, 1948.

————. *The Sign of Jonas*. New York: Harcourt, Brace and Company, 1953.

Meynell, Hugo A. *An Introduction to the Philosophy of Bernard Lonergan*. Toronto: University of Toronto Press, 1991.

Moltman, J. et al. *Hope for the Church*. Nashville: Abingdon, 1979.

Mooney, Philip. "Freedom Through Friendship, John Macmurray: In Memoriam (1891–1976)," *Friends Journal* (January 1, 1977): 4.

Moseley, Romney M., David Jarvis, and James W. Fowler. *Manual for Faith Development Research*. Atlanta, GA: Centre for Faith Development, Emory University, 1986.

Munsey, Brenda, ed. *Moral Development, Moral Education, and Kohlberg: Basic Issues in Philosophy, Psychology, Religion, and Education*. Birmingham, AL: Religious Education Press, 1980.

Nephew, Albert H. "The Personal Universe," *Listening: Journal of Religion and Culture* 10, no. 2 (Spring, 1975): 99–108.

Newsletter of the Center for Research in Faith and Moral Development, no.

7 (January 1989).

Occhiogrosso, Peter. *Once A Catholic*. New York: Ballantine Books, 1987.

O'Conner, D. "John Macmurray: Primacy of the Personal." *International Philosophical Quarterly* 4, 1964: 464–84.

Orr, David W. *Ecological Literacy: Education and the Transition to a Post-modern World*. Albany, NY: State University of New York Press, 1992.

Palmer, Parker. *The Promise of Paradox: A Celebration of Contradictions in the Christian Life*. Notre Dame, IN: Ave Maria Press, 1980.

———. *To Know as we are Known: A Spirituality of Education*. New York: Harper Collins, 1983.

Parks, Sharon. *The Critical Years: The Young Adult Search for a Faith to Live By*. San Francisco: Harper & Row, 1986.

Pascal, Blaise. *Pensées*. Translated by A. J. Krailsheimer. London: Penguin Books, 1966. *Pensées* was first published soon after Pascal's death in 1662.

Peck, M. Scott, M.D. *The Different Drum: Community-Making and Peace*. New York: Simon & Schuster, 1987.

———. *The Road Less Travelled: A New Psychology of Love, Traditional Values and Spiritual Growth*. New York: Simon & Schuster, 1978.

———. *In Search of Stones: A Pilgrimage of Faith, Reason, and Discovery*. New York: Hyperion, 1995

Postman, Neil. *Teaching as a Conserving Activity*. New York: Delacorte Press, 1979.

Postman, Neil and Charles Weingartner. *Teaching as a Subversive Activity*. New York: Dell Publishing Co., Inc., 1969.

Pregeant, Russell. *Mystery Without Magic*. Oak Park, IL: Meyer Stone Books, 1988.

Rahner, Karl. *Theological Investigations* 3, The Theology of the Spiritual Life. London: Darton, Longman & Todd, 1967.

Rausch, Thomas P. "Thomas Merton: Twenty-five Years After," *America* 170, no. 1 (January 1–8, 1994): 6–12.

Redfield, James. *The Celestine Prophecy: An Adventure*. New York: Warner Books, 1993.

Rolheiser, Ronald. "Chronicle," *Catholic Herald*. London: Herald House, (June 3, 1994): 10.

Ronda, Bruce A. *Intellect and Spirit: The Life and Work of Robert Coles*. New York: The Continuum Publishing Company, 1989.

Roof, Wade Clark. *A Generation of Seekers: The Spiritual Journey of the Baby Boom Generation*. San Francisco: Harper Collins, 1993.

Russell, Peter. *Global Brain*. London: Routledge & Kegan Paul, 1982.

Sala, Giovanni. "The *A Priori* in Human Knowledge: Kant's *Critique of Pure Reason* and Lonergan's *Insight*," *The Thomist* 40, no. 2 (April 1976): 179–221.

Sawicki, M. and B. Marthaler, eds. *Catechesis: Realities and Visions*. Washington, DC: U.S. Catholic Conference, 1977.

Schumacher, E. F. *A Guide for the Perplexed.* London: Sphere Books Ltd., 1977.

Siepmann, C. A. Foreword to *Freedom in the Modern World* by John Macmurray. Atlantic Highlands, NJ: Humanities Press International, 1992.

Spretnak, Charlene. *States of Grace: The Recovery of Meaning in the Postmodern Age.* San Francisco: HarperCollins, 1991.

Stokes, Kenneth. *Faith Development in the Adult Life Cycle.* New York: W. H. Sadlier, 1982.

Sullivan, Edmund V. *Critical Psychology and Pedagogy: Interpretation of the Personal World.* Toronto: OISE Press, 1990.

Swain, Bernard F. "Lonergan's Framework for the Future," *Commonweal* 112, no. 2 (January, 1985): 46–50.

Swimme, Brian and Thomas Berry. *The Universe Story.* New York: Harper Collins Publishers, 1992.

Tillich, Paul. *What is Religion?* New York: Harper Torchbooks, 1973.

Tracy, David. *The Achievement of Bernard Lonergan.* New York: Herder and Herder, 1970.

Veltri, John, S.J. *Orientations: A Collection of Helps for Prayer* (vol. 1, revised). Guelph, ON: Loyola House, 1993.

Vertin, Michael. "Lonergan on Consciousness: Is There a Fifth Level?," *Method: Journal of Lonergan Studies* 12, no. 2 (Spring, 1994): 1–36.

Wren, Thomas E. "John Macmurray's Search for Reality: Introduction," *Listening: Journal of Religion and Culture* 10, no. 2 (Spring, 1975): 1–6.

Wulff, David M. *Psychology of Religion: Classic and Contemporary Views.* New York: John Wiley & Sons, 1991.

Scriptural quotations are from The New Revised Standard Version, 1989.

Index

Note: Page numbers in
boldface type refer to Tables.